British America, 1500–1800

Creating Colonies, Imagining an Empire

STEVEN SARSON

Lecturer in History
University of Wales Swansea

Hodder Arnold

A MEMBER OF THE HODDER HEADLINE GROUP

First published in Great Britain in 2005 by
Hodder Education, a member of the Hodder Headline Group,
338 Euston Road, London NW1 3BH

http://www.hoddereducation.com

Distributed in the United States of America by
Oxford University Press Inc.
198 Madison Avenue, New York, NY10016

Hodder Headline's policy is to use papers that are natural, renewable and
recyclable products and made from wood grown in sustainable forests.
The logging and manufacturing processes are expected to conform to the
environmental regulations of the country of origin.

The advice and information in this book are believed to be true and
accurate at the date of going to press, but neither the author nor the publisher
can accept any legal responsibility or liability for any errors or omissions.

British Library Cataloguing in Publication Data
A catalogue record for this book is available from the British Library

Library of Congress Cataloging-in-Publication Data
A catalog record for this book is available from the Library of Congress

ISBN-10: 0-340-76009-5 (hb)
ISBN-13: 978-0-340-76009-3 (hb)
ISBN-10: 0-340-76010-9 (pb)
ISBN-13: 978-0-340-76010-9 (pb)

1 2 3 4 5 6 7 8 9 10

Typeset in 10/12 Sabon by Servis Filmsetting Ltd, Manchester
Printed and bound in Malta

What do you think about this book? Or any other Hodder Education title?
Please send your comments to the feedback section on www.hoddereducation.com

Contents

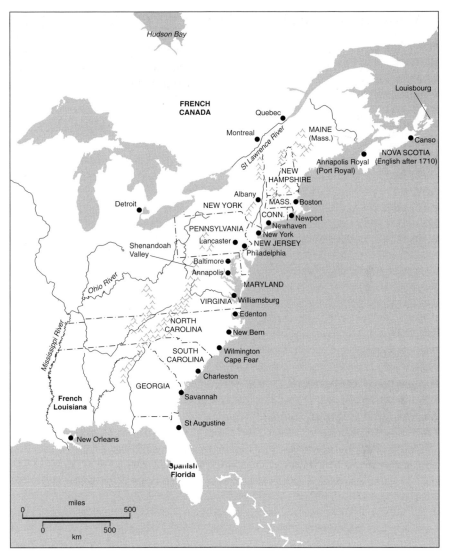

Map 1
Eastern North America, 1690–1748

From Richard R. Johnson, 'Growth and Mastery: British North America, 1690–1748', in P.J. Marshall, ed., *The Oxford History of the British Empire* Volume II *The Eighteenth Century* (Oxford, 1998), p. 278. By permission of Oxford University Press.

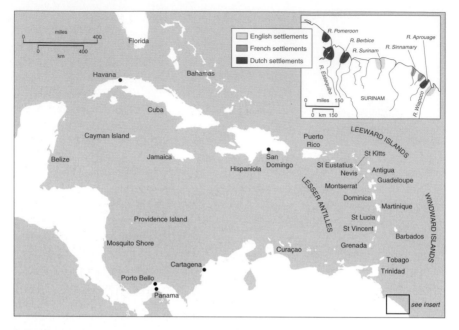

Map 2
The Caribbean

From Hilary McD. Beckles, 'The "Hub of Empire": the Caribbean and Britain in the Seventeenth Century', in Nicholas Canny, ed., *The Oxford History of the British Empire* Volume I *The Origins of Empire: British Overseas Enterprise to the Close of the Seventeenth Century* (Oxford, 1998), p. 220. By permission of Oxford University Press.

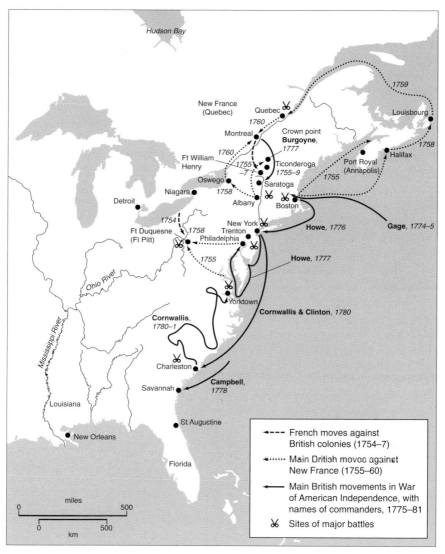

Map 3
War in North America, 1754–1783

From John Shy, 'The American Colonies in War and Revolution, 1748–1783', in P.J. Marshall, ed., *The Oxford History of the British Empire* Volume II *The Eighteenth Century* (Oxford, 1998), p. 315. By permission of Oxford University Press.

For my parents,
Joy and Roy Sarson

Introduction

The settlement of our colonies was never pursued upon any regular plan; but they were formed, grew, and flourished, as accidents, the nature of the climate, or the dispositions of private men happened to operate.

—Edmund Burke, 1757

The rulers of Great Britain have, for more than a century past, amused the people with the imagination that they possessed a great empire on the west side of the Atlantic. This empire, however, has hitherto existed in imagination only.

—Adam Smith, 1776[1]

Four centuries ago, on 14 May 1607, 105 English men and boys disembarked from the *Susan Constant*, *Godspeed* and *Discovery*, and began building a settlement they named Jamestown by the James River off the Chesapeake Bay. These and the early migrants who followed them to Virginia struggled against malnutrition, disease, each other and Amerindian resistance. Thousands died; several times the colony came close to collapse; and the company that organized the mission eventually went broke. Yet, despite everything, these settlers founded England's first permanent colony in America. Over the next century and a half, hundreds of thousands of other English, Scottish, Welsh, Irish and other European people migrated to Virginia and other colonies, some of them on the run from religious authorities, some deported by judicial authorities and some through economic desperation. But most went voluntarily, some to found religious utopias, but most to follow the promise of personal and political liberty that land ownership and self-government in America seemed to offer. Together with the even more numerous Africans who were kidnapped and enslaved in the New World, these men and women founded colonies and repeopled North America and numerous islands in the Atlantic Ocean and the Caribbean

Sea. By the 1760s, they and their descendants had created the wealthiest and most powerful empire on earth.

Until recently, however, the American colonies were somewhat neglected by historians of Britain and its empire. One reason for this amnesia may be that 13 colonies humiliated their imperial masters by winning their independence. Speaking to an audience in, significantly, Boston, Massachusetts, in 1900, the great imperial historian Sir John Seeley joked that the American Revolution was something 'which we have tacitly agreed to mention as seldom as we can'. Seeley was of course a historian of the 'second' British Empire. The later empire was much more wealthy and powerful than the 'first' one and, stretching across Africa, the Middle East, Asia and Australasia, was so immense that Seeley and his contemporaries might be forgiven for having lost sight of the earlier American empire. For whatever reason, though, the British American colonial experience for some time was designated as American, Canadian and Caribbean history, not really part of the history of Britain or even of the British Empire.[2]

In Seeley's day, histories of the (second) British Empire were plentiful and tended to be celebratory. In the 50 years after it collapsed, however, the number of imperial histories declined or turned more condemnatory, perhaps out of a combination of embarrassment, yet again, at the fall of the once mighty beast and shame at atrocities committed by the monster. But the passing of half a century allows more removed and hopefully clearer perspectives to develop. Furthermore, the reconfigurations of British national identity required by the devolution of political authority to Northern Ireland, Scotland and Wales, by European integration and by the growing multiculturalism that is itself a product of Britain's imperial history, positively encourage us to explore the nation's relationship with the world in the past as well as in the present and for the future. There is, therefore, a newly revived interest in the history of the Empire. And, perhaps because the United States is such a singularly great power in the world nowadays, this new scholarship is embracing the earlier empire in America as well as the later one in Asia and Africa. A number of British historians have recently written overviews of one or both of the empires and others have produced detailed studies of aspects of imperial history. Combinations of British and overseas scholars have produced books of essays on imperial history, including a *Cambridge Illustrated History of the British Empire* and a five-volume *Oxford History of the British Empire*. Our most eminent historians are in on the act as well. Simon Schama devoted an entire episode of his television series, *A History of Britain*, to the earlier empire and another to the later one, and the third volume of the accompanying book trilogy is subtitled *The Fate of Empire, 1776–2000*. Niall Ferguson did a whole television series and an accompanying book on the British Empire from its rise to its fall. And Linda Colley recently published *Captives: Britain, Empire and the World,*

1600–1850, using captivity narratives as a window on human relations in imperial history.[3]

These new British histories of empire owe a great deal to older and continuing traditions of scholarship emanating from the former colonies themselves, where, of course, the history of the empire has never been forgotten. American historians and foreign historians of America (like myself), for example, have together produced mountains of books and articles on New World colonies and empire. In fact, the evolution of increasingly sophisticated economic, social and cultural analyses from the 1950s saw the rise of such a multitude of specialized, detailed and often very localized studies that historians began complaining of the 'fragmentation' of early American history. Subsequent years saw attempts to 'synthesize' colonial history, identifying economic, social, cultural and political themes and developments that were common throughout British America. These syntheses gave rise to 'Atlantic' history, emphasizing themes and developments in Britain and throughout the empire, including Africa, the Caribbean and Canada, not just the 13 colonies that eventually became the United States. This 'Atlantic' history has perhaps contributed most to the growing perception in Britain that the history of New World colonies and empire is part of the British as well as the American past.

This book is, therefore, a work of both British and American history. It aims to add to the growing awareness of the importance and the role of the American colonies and first empire in early-modern British history, and it attempts to contribute to debates about the nature of early American colonial and British imperial history. It offers a broad textbook coverage that will introduce newcomers to these subjects (with a chronology and bibliography at the end), but it also presents an interpretation, a synthesis, of colonial and imperial history that I hope will interest old hands as well as newcomers. The enormity of the subject makes the task of interpretative synthesis difficult, and the aforementioned syntheses have usually concentrated on particular themes and developments, notwithstanding their attempts to cover those themes and developments across wide expanses of time and space. They have tended therefore to focus primarily and separately on such subjects as Atlantic economy, society, culture, geography, migration, politics, ideology, and so on. *British America* attempts to cover all these topics and to analyse the relationships between them.

Admittedly, however, this book does not give equal weight to everything and everyone. The tendency towards and the best reasons for equal inclusiveness are exemplified in Peter Charles Hoffer's excellent book, *The Brave New World: A History of Early America*. As Hoffer explains, groups such as Amerindians, African-Americans and women exercised agency in and thereby profoundly shaped 'everyday life' in early America. But *British America*, as its subtitle indicates, focuses on the processes of creating colonies and imagining an empire, and 'subaltern' groups exercised less influence in these areas than they did in everyday life. To be sure, Amerindians fought against and therefore slowed and shaped Euro-American colonization of their lands; African-Americans resisted and thereby helped to mould the institution of slavery; and women influenced various aspects of colonization and empire building too, especially when their small numbers gave them great power in the early stages of colonization. Yet, ultimately, Amerindians could not prevent their own displacement or in many cases extermination; African-Americans only escaped enslavement in exceptional circumstances; and women never attained the equal rights to property and political liberty that white men coveted and guarded jealously. The initiators and main players in the processes of creating colonies and imagining an empire were therefore European or Euro-American men, most especially those of the planter and merchant elites that came to dominate the polities, economies, societies and cultures of colonial British America.[4]

This book's most basic propositions are illustrated in the quotes from Edmund Burke and Adam Smith at the beginning of this introduction: that the American colonies were created by those who settled them and that the British-American 'empire' was largely an imaginary construct. Sixteenth-century English explorers and thinkers imagined what an empire might be like and urged their monarchs to implement their ideas. Yet those monarchs passed the buck, chartering joint stock companies and individual or groups of proprietors to colonize parts of the New World in their stead and in return for nominal fees, allowing them to run their colonies more or less as they pleased, provided they did not contradict English laws or interests. Only Jamaica was colonized through government-sponsored military conquest, and only Georgia and Nova Scotia with British government finance.

This first stage in the privatization of colonization was followed by another, for in the event it was not chartered companies or proprietors who created the colonies, but the migrants they encouraged to follow them. Private companies and individual proprietors imagined various models of colonization, ranging from get-rich-quick schemes to new Jerusalems, and from feudal palatinates to egalitarian utopias, but all of them were in some way corporate enterprises serving some sort of business interest or idealized commonwealth and none of them worked for very long. To make their colonies viable, companies and proprietors needed settlers, and to attract settlers they had to offer opportunities for individual material betterment, most especially for land ownership. In turn, migrants who suffered the hardships of the Atlantic crossing in search of self-improvement were little interested in serving companies or proprietors, and they were so numerous that, especially in the contingent, experimental and often chaotic environment of early colonization, their wishes could not be resisted. Corporate imaginings thus gave way to the individual ambitions of migrants and settlers. It was these migrants and settlers who wrested territory from Amerindians, cleared the forests, broke the soil, planted, built on and improved the land (or who made their servants and slaves do so), laid out the towns, parishes and counties and established religious and civic institutions at the local and provincial levels. It was, as Burke suggested, migrants and settlers who created the colonies.

Because English and British governments' approach to the early empire was so laissez-faire, and because it was migrants and settlers who created the colonies, the empire was, as Smith suggested, an imaginary construct. As the colonies became more and more prosperous and populous, however, they increasingly attracted the attention of their countrymen back home. Just as companies and colonial proprietors imagined colonies as corporate enterprises serving the corporate interests of the company or commonwealth, so administrative officials, monarchs and parliaments increasingly imagined a corporate empire in which colonies served the interests of the mother country. When imperial authorities attempted to assert their vision of empire, as they did only intermittently from the 1650s to the 1750s, they found the colonists no more willing to suborn their propertied interests and political rights to the mother country or empire than they had been to do so for colonial companies and proprietors. When parliament attempted systematically to assert a new British concept of empire, as it did after the end of the French and Indian War (or Seven Years War) in 1763, 13 colonies declared their independence and created a new nation instead. By 1776, the year of American Independence, the British were already reimagining empire. They had come to understand that the root of their problems in governing the American colonies lay with the private and autonomous origins of those colonies. It was because colonization came before and drove imperialism in the first British Empire that the reverse would be the case in the second.

Chapter 1 is a foreword to the book that outlines Portuguese, Spanish, French and Dutch imperial advances that eventually encouraged English imperial ambitions. It also explains how the English came comparatively late to New World colonization, as English leaders first prioritized domestic issues, including creating an 'empire of Great Britain' throughout England, Wales, Scotland and Ireland. The chapter finishes with the explorations and aborted colonizations that prefigured Jamestown. Chapter 2 details the various imaginings of colonies and empire in the minds of sixteenth-century thinkers, explorers and would-be colonizers, and introduces those of seventeenth- and eighteenth-century colonial charter groups and migrants.

The imaginings, actions and fates of colonial companies, proprietors, migrants and settlers in the Chesapeake, West Indies, New England, the Middle Colonies and the Lower South are detailed in chapters 3 to 6. These chapters challenge or at least argue for amending the 'charter group' theory of colonization, wherein the first colonists are perceived largely to determine the character of the colony that eventually emerges (although the difference may be one of definition rather than substance, for whereas some define 'charter group' so broadly as to encompass all white migrants, I define the term narrowly to include only those to whom a charter was given and their employees and close associates). As noted above, the waves of secondary migrants and settlers overturned the imaginings of the charter holders and created the colonies in their own ways. Of course, some benefited more than others from the opportunities offered by the undermining of charter groups and the appropriation of colonization. In almost all the colonies, a new elite emerged within two or three generations of original settlement, largely lawyer and planter elites in the islands and southern mainland, and lawyer and merchant elites in the Middle Colonies and New England. These elites, especially in the islands and on the southern mainland, amassed enormous wealth and economic power, and, dominating local magistracies, vestries and provincial assemblies, they exercised immense social, cultural and political authority too. Yet opportunity for landed and other propertied forms of independence was more widespread in the colonies than it was in Britain or anywhere else in Europe, so elites only exercised their authority with the consent of a large and therefore powerful population of 'middling' property owners.

Some historians have claimed that early American society was therefore predominantly 'middle class'. There was in fact much more economic and social inequality and conflict than that description would allow. The very existence of widespread landownership, for example, relied on the dispossession, removal and sometimes extermination of Amerindians. Many people's fortunes were built on the backs of unfortunate slaves, who were never likely to own themselves let alone own land. Though many women owned or otherwise controlled property and wielded political influence, at least indirectly, they did not possess the same property rights as men, could not vote, however wealthy they were, and were deemed 'dependant' by their very nature. Over time, increasing numbers of 'dependant' white men were unable to make it from servitude and, in turn, out of tenancy and wage labour and into landownership and other forms of property holding.

These chapters also challenge the still widespread perception that the puritans of New England were the archetypal Anglo-American settlers. As historian Jack P. Greene has shown, the puritan experiment in corporatist religious colonization was an exceptional event in Anglo-American history. No colonies outside New England were settled as exclusivist religious communities (Maryland's Catholic and Pennsylvania's Quaker proprietors practised toleration) and the social organization of early New England was profoundly different from that of all other colonies. All the puritans had in common with other Anglo- or British-American charter groups was that their corporate aims were undermined, albeit more slowly, by individual and materialistic interests and ambitions.[5]

Chapters 3 to 6 also show how the societies and cultures of the colonies and mother country gradually converged. Chapter 7, though, brings us to the politics of empire, in which metropolitans and provincials increasingly diverged, for the former began reimagining the empire and attempted to impose a new vision of it that was inimical to the presumptions and wishes of colonists. Most of the provinces eventually became royal rather than private colonies, though they retained their own systems of government. Even so, kings and parliaments created departments and offices of state to administer the colonies, tried to enforce trade laws, increase the powers of governors and rein in those of the colonial assemblies, and generally attempted to create a more coherent empire out of a disparate and disobedient collection of colonies. Time and time again, between the middle of the seventeenth and eighteenth centuries, they failed, and the empire remained the largely imaginary construct that Adam Smith described.

In the meantime, after the Glorious Revolution of 1688, a new notion entered the English and, in turn, British constitutional imagination: that of parliamentary sovereignty. The supremacy of parliament eventually stabilized English and British domestic politics, but threatened to destabilize imperial politics, for colonists believed that their own houses of assembly, and not Westminster, were sovereign within their own provincial domains. Chapter 8 shows how the American Revolution was triggered by disputes over taxes and property rights, but that it soon developed into an equally controversial contest between English parliamentary supremacy and American colonial self-government. The Glorious Revolution also helped bring about a more cooperative form of political culture in Britain, as the eighteenth-century constitutional device of the crown-in-parliament settled the seventeenth-century strife between Crown and Parliament. Yet the Glorious Revolution was experienced in America as just another phase in the battles between (colonial) legislatures and (imperial) executives. The Americans therefore remained essentially Cromwellian roundheads, and the American Revolution was in a sense a final phase of Britain's seventeenth-century civil wars.

Chapter 9 is an afterword to the book that explores the American Revolutionary settlement and British imperial reconfigurations that followed American Independence. Americans had to replace old colonial governments with new state governments and create a brand new central, national authority. Various states experimented with proto-democratic government, but experience at state and national levels seemed to demonstrate the need for new devices that made governments less responsive to the governed. In particular, and in a partial reversal of tradition, they increased the power of executive governors. Also, the United States Constitution of 1787 created a much more powerful presidency and indeed a much more powerful central or national government than Americans could have conceived of in 1776. To implement these changes, however, reformers had to resort to constitutional conventions and referenda. In other words, to make government more remote from the people, they had to accede to a new principle that came to define American republicanism: the sovereignty of the people.

Remaining determined to gain greater control over their overseas possessions, British imperial authorities nevertheless learned from the American Revolution to respect colonial autonomy when and where they had to, such as in the older West Indian colonies, where massive slave populations made independence impossible, but where traditions of self-government were just as entrenched as they were in the colonies that became the United States. Elsewhere, however, the British would see to it that imperial will would prevail. That meant ensuring that traditions of economic autonomy and self-government would either not be allowed to develop or that effective means of suppressing them would have to be developed. That meant reimagining the whole process of colonization and empire building. In fact, it meant reversing the order of these things. In the second British Empire, colonization would not happen independently, as it had in America, but would instead be the very basis of empire building.

A book of this nature emerges from a process of learning that takes place over a long period of time. During that time, the writer acquires many debts. I first became interested in colonial America as an undergraduate at the University of East Anglia through the inspirational teaching of Roger Thompson. My love of the subject grew even greater while I was a graduate student at Johns Hopkins University under the mentorship of the inestimable Jack P. Greene. His intellectual influence runs through the whole book, as does that of my other Hopkins mentor, Ron Walters. Fellow graduate students at Hopkins (c.1988–92) who made seminars so exciting and thought-provoking include Trevor Burnard, Joyce Chaplin, Christine Daniels, Lige Gould, Kurt Nagel, Rina Palumbo, Bob Olwell, Jim Sidbury, Steve Whitman and Karin Wulf. My specialty is Chesapeake history, and I have benefited immeasurably from many conversations at the Hall of Records in Annapolis and elsewhere with Lois Green Carr, Ron Hoffman, Woody Holton, Mary Jeske, Sally Mason, Peter Onuf, Ed Papenfuse, Jean Russo, Fredrika Teute and Lorena Walsh, among others. Britain has a lively community of early American historians (of various nationalities) – too many to mention them all, in fact – and I have had especially long and enlightening conversations at British Early Americanist conferences and other events with Tony Badger (an honorary early Americanist), Christopher Clark, Mary Geiter, Marjoleine Kars, Tim Lockley, Ben Marsh, Andrew McKillop, Simon Middleton, Gwenda Morgan, Sarah Pearsall, Jack Pole, Bill Speck, Rebecca Starr, Peter Thompson and Betty Wood. Special thanks to Julie Flavell for reading much and Mike McDonnell for reading all of the draft manuscript of this book. Both gave immensely helpful advice, leavened with their characteristic good humour and kindness. I am also very much indebted to current and former colleagues in the History Department at the University of Wales Swansea. Nathalie Morello is a Swansea academic to whom I owe a particularly enormous intellectual debt, but as she is also my partner I owe her so much more besides. I also thank the Arnold editors Christopher Wheeler for helping me formulate this book, Michael Strang for helping me finish it (finally), and Tiara Misquitta for invaluable assistance along the way. Of course, any errors of fact or interpretation are mine alone. The people who have influenced me the most and for the longest time are my parents, Roy and Joy Sarson, and the book is dedicated to them.

Notes

1 *An Account of the European Settlements in America* (2 vols, London, 1757) 2, p. 288 (written by William Burke, but, historians believe, with considerable input from Edmund Burke); *An Inquiry into the Nature and Causes of the Wealth of Nations* (1776), in R.H. Campbell, A.S. Skinner and W.B. Todd, eds, *The Glasgow Edition of the Works and Correspondence of Adam Smith* (2 vols, Indianapolis, 1976) 2, pp. 946–7.

2 Cited in Eliga H. Gould, *The Persistence of Empire: British Political Culture in the Age of the American Revolution* (Chapel Hill, 2000), p. xvi.

3 P.J. Marshall, ed., *The Cambridge Illustrated History of the British Empire* (Cambridge, 1996); Nicholas Canny, ed., *The Oxford History of the British Empire* Volume I: *The Origins of Empire: British Overseas Enterprise to the Close of the Seventeenth Century* (Oxford, 1998); P.J. Marshall, ed., *The Oxford History of the British Empire* Volume II: *The Eighteenth Century* (Oxford, 1998); Simon Schama, *A History of Britain* Volume I: *At the Edge of the World? 3500 BC–AD 1603*; Volume II: *The British Wars 1603–1776*; Volume III: *The Fate of Empire 1776–2000* (London, 2000–03); Niall Ferguson, *Empire: How Britain Made the Modern World* (London, 2003); Linda Colley, *Captives: Britain, Empire, and the World, 1600–1850* (London, 2002).

4 Peter Charles Hoffer, *The Brave New World: A History of Early America* (Boston, 2000), p. xiv.

5 Jack P. Greene, *Pursuits of Happiness: The Social Development of Early Modern British Colonies and the Formation of American Culture* (Chapel Hill, 1988).

1

Foreword: Before the British Empire

For a variety of reasons, the English came late to American colonization, and even later to empire building. The attentions of early modern English and British monarchs and parliamentarians focused primarily on domestic political and religious issues. What expansion schemes they had were internal, concerned with creating an 'empire of Great Britain' out of England, Scotland, Wales and Ireland. When they looked beyond the British Isles, it was usually to continental Europe rather than across the Atlantic. New World ventures were therefore passed on to private enterprise. English entrepreneurs, however, did not initially indulge in schemes of territorial settlement, preferring the cheaper and more lucrative options of trade and plunder. It was not until the late sixteenth century that Englishmen attempted to settle in the Americas, and not until the early seventeenth century that they managed to do so successfully.

Before examining how the English slowly and hesitatingly moved towards colonization and imperialism, though, it is worth briefly looking at other European New World ventures. First, Portuguese and Spanish colonization prefigured English settlement in various ways, not least in its origins in the search for a western passage to the east, the failed and disastrous attempts to find New World treasure, the subsequent realization that the establishment of civil societies was the way to make colonies work and, in turn, in the removal or extermination of Native Americans and the enslavement of Africans. Also, Iberian imperialism influenced the timing and character of English colonization and imperialism in critical ways. The Portuguese and the Spanish extracted enormous wealth from their New World possessions, and although that made some advocate an English empire, others judged it easier and more profitable to raid Spanish New World settlements and ships, or to trade with them, than to found their own colonies. Only when the French and the Dutch established settlements in

North America and the Caribbean, did Englishmen feel compelled to join in rather than get left behind by their rivals. At that point, though, the English invested much of the capital and the seafaring know-how, gained from trade and plunder, in their own colonial enterprises. Furthermore, the fact that trade and plunder were mostly undertaken by privateers inculcated a habit of thinking, which endured even after colonization began, that colonization was best carried out as a private business. That attitude established the conditions in which the 'first' British Empire was able to evolve into a loose federation of more or less self-governing colonies, rather than a centralized, unified entity under direct imperial rule. It thus helps explain why, as Edmund Burke suggested in 1757, the colonies were self-created, and why, as Adam Smith complained in 1776, the empire 'existed in imagination only'.

Portuguese and Spanish imperialism in the fifteenth and sixteenth centuries

Since the Crusades (1095–1291), Europeans had increasingly coveted spices and sugar, luxuries that had to be imported from the Middle East and Asia. By the fifteenth century, however, European traders were keen to bypass the middlemen in this commerce and trade directly at the source. It was the hope of finding a western passage to the riches of the east that first inspired European exploration of the African coast and Atlantic Ocean. It was the discovery that they could cultivate sugar on the lands they subsequently encountered that inspired European colonization. The Portuguese and the Spanish had been Europe's principal importers and distributors of sugar and spices, and it was they who initiated European exploration and colonization. They also had the advantage of extensive Atlantic and Mediterranean seaboards, ports with merchant communities that possessed the willingness and the capital to finance overseas ventures, and the seamen with the skills to carry them out.

Portugal, in the age of Prince Henry the Navigator (1394–1460), inaugurated the age of empire with its capture of Ceuta in Morocco in 1415 and subsequent colonization of the Azores, Canaries and Cape Verde Islands (collectively called the Fortunate Isles) between 1419 and 1460. Their colonization destroyed the native Guanches, a West African people, first by disease and then by warfare. The Portuguese also began incursions in the Muslim West and North African slave trade after discovering Capo Blanco in 1440, supplying their Atlantic island sugar plantations with bonded labour. Around 1470, the Portuguese began colonizing uninhabited equatorial islands off the Bight of Biafra, using them for sugar planting and slave trading too. In 1482, they established the El Mina fort on the Guinea coast, Europe's first gold- and slave-trading stronghold on the African mainland, although settlement in the region was stymied by Europeans' susceptibility to tropical diseases, especially yellow fever and malaria, which caused death rates as high as 80 per cent.

Spain captured the Canary Islands from Portugal in 1475 and, like the Portuguese, the Spanish quickly turned to slave-based plantation agriculture. Yet, for both powers, colonization of Atlantic islands presaged a much larger enterprise. In 1492, the year of the *reconquista* of the Iberian Peninsula from the Moors and the expulsion of the Jews, Christopher Columbus, a Genoese mariner in the service of King Ferdinand of Aragon and Queen Isabella of Castile, whose marriage united Spain, dropped anchor at an island he called San Salvador, in the Bahamas, while searching for a western route to the east. Even after 4 voyages over 11 years, and until the day he died in 1506, Columbus believed that he had been to Asia and refused to countenance the notion that he had encountered a New World. He would not be the last European to misunderstand the meaning and impact of his actions in America.

After Columbus's failed attempt to found a settlement (named Isabella, after the Castilian Queen), Spain established its first permanent colony in the Americas when Nicolas de Ovando founded Santo Domingo, with 30 ships carrying 2500 colonists in 1502. These first colonists hoped to strike gold, but instead founded successful colonization with tobacco, sugar and cattle worked by enslaved Indians. This economy formed the basis for a Spanish-style society, a Castilian town with churches and even a bishopric from 1512. This pattern of colonization, whereby get-rich-quick schemes failed and were replaced by the establishment of a slave plantation economy and European-style society, would replicate itself elsewhere in the Americas.

The 1494 Treaty of Tordesillas divided the New World along a notional north–south line that ran 370 leagues (1200 nautical miles) west of the Cape Verde Islands. Lands west of that line belonged to Spain and those to the east to Portugal, allowing the latter to claim Brazil. Amerindian resistance and a shortage of settlers initially limited settlement to the Pernambuco region, but there the colonists established the sugar-slave plantation agriculture that allowed them to join Spain (formally so with the unification of the Iberian nations from 1580 to 1640) in claiming all and conquering much of South and Central America and the islands of the Greater Antilles by the end of the sixteenth century.

Between 1509 and 1511, Spain colonized Puerto Rico, Jamaica and Cuba, and founded mainland trading posts in Venezuela and Colombia. In 1513, Vasco Núñez de Balboa explored the Isthmus of Panama and discovered the Pacific Ocean. The most awful incursions came with Hernán Cortés' expedition into Mexico and conquering of Montezuma's Aztec empire in 1519–21, and were followed by the conquest of Honduras and Guatemala in 1523–30 and Francisco Pizarro's defeat of the Inca and colonization of Peru in 1532–35. By the end of that decade, conquistadors, notably Francisco Pizarro and Pedro de Valdivia, ventured into Ecuador, Chile, northern Argentina and Bolivia. By the end of the sixteenth century, before the English had established permanent colonies in the Americas, the Spanish Empire covered 8000 miles, from the southern tip of South America to the south-west points of North America.

Spain claimed much of North America under the Treaty of Tordesillas. Alvar Núñez Cabeza de Vaca sailed the gulfs of Mexico and California in 1528–36. Juan Cabrillo travelled up the west coast as far as San Francisco Bay in 1542, and the following year Bartolomé Ferrelo went as far north as Oregon. Others travelled deep into the North American interior. Hernando de Soto explored much of the south-east in 1539–41, discovering the Mississippi River, and Francisco Vásquez de Coronado much of the south-west, as far north as Kansas and Colorado, in 1540–42, in a failed attempt to find the mythical golden city of El Dorado. These and subsequent travellers reported a land of little promise, peopled only by aggressive Indians, and these regions, though nominally part of the Spanish Empire, remained largely unsettled by Europeans or their descendants until the expansion of the United States in the nineteenth century.

Spanish settlement in North America amounted only to small and temporary trade and missionary posts and isolated settlements. The first attempted colonization of Florida by Juan Ponce de León in 1521 was repelled by Indians, as were some later settlements, though Spain eventually established a military base at St Augustine that ultimately failed in its aim to deter other Europeans from settling the continent. The Spanish also sent missionaries in 1570 to the James River region, the area settled nearly four decades later by the English, but the Powhatan Indians killed them. Portuguese penetration of North America was similarly limited. In 1521, João Fagundes obtained royal permission to establish a colony on the Grand Banks of Newfoundland, but, like others, the Portuguese only established temporary fishing bases at this time, and the region remained sparsely settled until after the American Revolution.[1]

French and Dutch imperialism in the sixteenth and early seventeenth centuries

There were various European presences in the northern fisheries in the sixteenth century, and the greatest was that of the French. In 1524, Giovanni de Verrazzano, a Florentine mariner sponsored by Francis I, explored North America's coast from South Carolina to Newfoundland and thereby established long-lasting French territorial claims. Carib Indians killed him in 1528, but the French, in particular Bretons and Normans, continued to explore extensively and even attempted to establish colonies. The most influential early French explorer was Jacques Cartier of St Malo, who, in 1534–35, sailed the St Lawrence River as far as modern-day Montreal, which was then a Micmac Amerindian settlement called Hochelaga. Like others before and after, he was searching for a north-west passage to Asia, but managed in the meantime to establish footholds in America, first by wintering near Quebec (after 'Kebec', Algonquin for 'where the river narrows'), then called Stadacona. In 1541, he established a base at Charlesbourg-Royal on the St Lawrence, near Quebec. His colonists abandoned camp, however, after suffering attacks by Indians and scurvy. Cartier subsequently established a mixed-sex colony of carpenters, masons and farmers, indicating his intention to create a civil society, under the protection of 300 soldiers and the governorship of Jean François de la Rocque, Sieur de Roberval. It folded after one freezing winter. Cartier's eventual return to France with iron pyrite and quartz, rather than the gold and diamonds he thought he had found, curbed the enthusiasm of Francis I for North America, though merchants remained interested in fish and beaver pelts.

French Huguenots were the first to advance the idea of the New World as a sanctuary for religious refugees. In 1555, Nicolas Durand, Chevalier de Villegagnon, established a Huguenot colony on an island off Rio de Janeiro with help from French Protestant Admiral Gaspard Coligny (later killed in the St Bartholomew's Day massacre of Protestants in 1572), who also saw military potential in a French settlement in South America. The Rio colony included 14 Genevans personally selected by John Calvin, a college associate of Villegagnon. However, Villegagnon's conversion to Catholicism undermined the struggling colony, even before the Portuguese killed the settlers in 1560. Two years later, Jean Ribault founded another Huguenot settlement, Charlesfort, in what would later be Port Royal Sound, South Carolina, once again under sponsorship from Coligny. Ribault's other aim was to found a base from which to trade with or plunder the Spanish. The settlers suffered disease, food shortage and Indian attacks, and when Ribault returned to France to fetch reinforcements he found Le Havre under siege and fled to England from the French Wars of Religion. In 1564, René de Laudonnière (formerly Ribault's deputy) attempted a settlement on the St John's River in Florida, but, once again, disease, Indian troubles, neglect of food cultivation in the search for gold and, finally, the dispersal of Ribault's resupply fleet of 1565, made the settlement extremely tenuous even before the Spanish destroyed it.

The Wars of Religion slowed but did not stop French expansion. Fishing and fur trading continued, with some 300 to 400 French vessels arriving and departing the fisheries region every year, though merchant monopolies granted and then rescinded by a capricious crown did little to encourage colonization. In any case, merchants generally preferred to set up employees at trading posts rather than to establish colonies where settlers might threaten their commercial monopolies. There were some attempts at colonization, though. In 1577, Marquis de la Roche, a Breton merchant, received a patent to found a base on Sable Island from which to penetrate Acadia and hunt seal and walrus. The crown finally authorized a colony of convicts in 1598, but it collapsed after a settler rebellion five years later. In 1604, another Huguenot, Pierre du Guast, Comte de Monts, obtained a patent as lieutenant-governor of Acadia, Canada and other unspecified territories. He settled with about 120 colonists at St Croix Island (now Dochet Island), and was obliged by his charter to recruit another 60 settlers annually thereafter. Half his original settlers died during the first winter, however, and the rest moved across the Bay of Fundy to Acadia, founding Port Royal, though the colony collapsed after de Monts lost his fur trade monopoly in 1607. In 1608–09, having persuaded de Monts to fund an expedition to establish an interior fur trading post, Samuel de Champlain and 28 men wintered in Quebec. Though no French families settled there until 1617, and though colonists still numbered only 60 in 1620, the settlement proved permanent and eventually prosperous. The crown offered little practical assistance, but the king recognized his fledgling empire by appointing lieutenant generals and viceroys of Canada. In 1610, Jean de Poutrincourt, who had worked under de Monts, attempted to resettle Port Royal. These efforts resulted in nothing more than a fur trading post that the English sacked in 1614. By this time, the English were beginning to make North America theirs.

The Dutch also developed interests in the Americas. After the 1580 unification of Spain and Portugal, the Portuguese became natural allies of a Dutch people similarly struggling against Spanish imperialism within Europe, and they welcomed Dutch trading ships in Brazil, Africa and Asia in the 1590s. The Dutch intruded significantly on Iberian interests in Africa, invading Guinea in 1598 and sacking São Tomé in 1599. After capturing Goree Island, near the Cape Verdes, in 1617, they moved in on hitherto Portuguese-dominated slave trading in Senegambia. In 1602 and 1621 respectively, the Dutch established their East and West India companies. The former employed English navigator Henry Hudson to search for a north-west passage in 1609, a mission that soon laid the basis of Dutch claims to New Netherland, although the English would later appropriate these territories.[2]

Internal colonialism: an empire of Great Britain

Rivalry with the French and Dutch in North America partly explains why the English colonized when they did. Until the middle of the sixteenth century, however, the English remained surprisingly uninterested in the New World, bearing in mind the vast fortunes that Portugal and Spain were extracting from America. Only when the wool trade with Antwerp collapsed in the 1550s did English merchants turn their attentions to the west. Even then, the English state paid little attention to America, leaving New

World exploration, trade, plunder and even colonization to licensed private companies and individuals. That early English laissez-faire is attributable to a variety of domestic travails, including the securing and toppling of monarchical dynasties and religious reformation and counter-reformation. Perhaps most distracting, however, was that before the English could imagine an empire overseas, they first had to conceive and create an empire at home.

Henry VII, England's king at the time of the Columbian encounter, was too concerned with securing the Tudor dynasty after the Wars of the Roses and with asserting monarchical authority over his nobles to pay much attention to New World imperialism. Henry VIII busied himself with domestic and European issues, especially from 1527 when he became embroiled in securing his divorce from Catherine of Aragon. The consequent break with Rome inaugurated the long and fraught process of religious reformation that, while it eventually contributed to New World emigration by religious dissenters, drew governmental attention away from empire building. The reign of Edward VI, Henry's physically fragile only son, from 1547 to 1553, was too short to establish a lasting Protestant settlement, notwithstanding Protector Somerset's strenuous efforts. Queen Mary's Catholic counter-reformation of 1553 to 1558 comprised a reign of terror that stultified the energies of the nation until religious peace was temporarily restored early in the reign of Elizabeth I. Even then, puritans who rejected or wished to reform the religious settlement of 1559 remained problematic for Elizabeth and her ministers. Mary, Queen of Scots and her French and Spanish supporters presented serious distractions for Elizabeth too, until Mary's execution in 1587 and the defeat of the Spanish Armada the following year. After that, there was war with Spain, harvest failures and famines to contend with.

Moreover, before the English began colonizing across the Atlantic, there was an empire to establish at home. Early modern English imperialism first entailed securing the independence of Henry VIII and his successors from papal authority. Indeed the word 'empire' at that time did not necessarily connote territorial expansion. The Act in Restraint of Appeals of 1533, which eliminated papal judicial authority in England, asserted that 'this realm of England is an empire, entire of itself'. That meant, according to William Blackstone's *Commentaries on the Laws of England* (1765–69), 'that our king is equally sovereign and independent within these his dominions, as any emperor is in his empire'.[3]

Yet 'empire' also had a more expansive meaning even before it referred to transatlantic conquest, one involving what historian Michael Hechter has called 'internal colonialism'. The pretensions of English kings to domination of the 'Three Kingdoms' of England, Scotland and Ireland, and to the Principality of Wales, were ancient. Anglo-Saxon King Athelstan (924–40) proclaimed himself 'Imperator' over the various Anglo-Saxon kingdoms, and Edgar I (959–75) adopted the titles 'King of the Angles' and 'Emperor and Lord' of the nations, seas and kings of all Britain. Geoffrey of Monmouth's *Historia Regum Brittaniae* (*c*.1136) recalled an even older British Isles named after and united under Brutus. With Brutus's younger sons, Albanact of Scotland and Camber of Wales, paying homage to his eldest son, Locrine, king of England, this was an English-dominated kind of Britain. Medieval English claims were made most ferociously during the reign of Edward I (1272–1307), and more symbolically when Henry V in the 1420s adopted a 'closed' crown, a circlet with two crossed bands, referred to explicitly as an 'imperial crown'.[4]

It was, however, the Tudors and Stuarts who finally put into effect this 'Galfridian' concept of empire. Violent Welsh resistance to English authority largely ceased after the conquest of 1382, and even residual resentment drastically diminished, though it did not entirely disappear, with the accession of the part-Welsh Henry VII to the throne in 1485. Wales was brought more thoroughly under English legal and political authority in the reign of Henry VIII with two Acts of Union in 1536 and 1543. Unification with Scotland, however, was a quite different matter. In 1469, the Scottish Parliament claimed the same 'ful Jurisdictione and fre Impire within his realm' of James III that English kings did not explicitly claim until the 1533 Act in Restraint of Appeals. Scottish kings also appeared with their own closed imperial crowns from around 1485. Yet the *Declaration, Conteyning the Just Causes and Consyderations of This Present Warre with the Scottis*, published for Henry VIII on the eve of the Anglo-Scottish war of 1543–46, insisted on a Scottish submission dating from Brutus, and on the right of the English to bring civility to Scotland. During the Anglo-Scottish war of 1547–50, propagandists made various claims for 'Englande the onely supreme seat of the empire of greate Briteigne' to justify the aggression of Edward VI and Protector Somerset. Another of Somerset's aims was to secure Protestantism in Scotland, and English intervention assisted the Scottish reformation of 1559–60, although the Presbyterian Church of Scotland remained distinct from the Episcopalian Church of England. In Elizabeth's reign, writers John Dee and Humphrey Llwyd would use the term 'British Empire', citing the precedent of unification within the isles under Brutus. In *The Faerie Queen* (1590–96) and *View of the Present State of Ireland* (*c*.1596), Edmund Spenser cited Merlin's prophecy of Arthur's Britain being reconstituted by 'a royall virgin'. Spenser's concept of British Empire, though, was a broad one that made a link between internal and overseas colonization. He dedicated *The Faerie Queen* to 'Empresse Elizabeth . . . Queene of England Fraunce and Ireland and of Virginia'.[5]

Tudor claims and arms failed to subdue Scotland entirely, however. After the death of the childless Elizabeth I in 1603, the accession of the Stuarts inaugurated a composite monarchy under James VI and I. It was James who initiated modern usage of the term 'Britain' to denote this union of kingdoms. Nevertheless, Scotland retained its own parliament, rose against the English during the civil wars and gave up its own legislature only with reluctance and, in some quarters, unquenchable bitterness in the Act of Union of 1707. Even then, Jacobites remained ready to undo the Union and indeed the Glorious Revolution of 1688 in which William of Orange dethroned James II. There were Jacobite landings and invasion scares in Scotland, Ireland and even England until as late as 1759. The most serious incidents occurred in 1715 and 1745. The former year saw an uprising in support of James Edward Stuart (James III or the Old Pretender) in parts of Scotland and northern England. In July 1745, Charles Edward Stuart (Bonnie Prince Charlie or the Young Pretender) landed in the Hebrides. By September, 25,000 Highlanders had joined his cause, captured Edinburgh and defeated a small British force at Prestonpans. By December, his 5000-strong army reached as far south as Derby, but thereafter retreated to Scotland and was massacred at Culloden in April 1746, while Charles fled back to France.

English imperial claims extended to Ireland too. While attempts to conquer Ireland again distracted governmental attention and, in this case, significant numbers of potential settlers from America, Ireland was to some extent a precursor to and a model for American colonization. In 1541, the Irish Parliament declared that Henry VIII was not just lord but 'King of Ireland', and the king attempted unsuccessfully to secure the allegiance of the native Irish through feudal impositions and by introducing English church and common law. But English intervention went further in Ireland than it did in Scotland and Wales. The Scottish reformation of 1559–60 united most of the British Isles in Protestantism, but the Irish remained stubbornly Catholic and ferociously rebellious. In response, the idea of the 'plantation' (in the earlier and fullest sense of the term – as a colony of settlement, and not just a large-scale, private agricultural enterprise) emerged as a means of achieving English domination, meaning that the Irish would not be absorbed into England's political ambit as were the Welsh and later the Scottish, but like Amerindians would be dispossessed, removed and, if necessary, killed. Irish land was thus to be cleared of all but loyal natives and divided among gentlemen who would cultivate it with English and Scottish tenants.

From the 1560s, these 'New English' settlers attempted to displace the Gaelic Irish and the 'Old English' descendants of settlers from the time of Edward I. A 1566 invasion established 'the pale', a region of New English domination, as distinct from the 'rude partes' where the 'wild Irish' lived. In 1571–72, Thomas Smith and the Earl of Essex made ill-starred efforts to establish military settlements in the Ards Peninsula and at Clandeboye in Ulster. Further attempts were made to establish plantations in Munster in 1585–98, where 35 English gentlemen received land grants ranging from 4000 to 12,000 acres that were confiscated from the Earl of Desmond and resettled with 12,000 English tenants. After the Nine Years War (1594–1603), King James awarded 1000- to 2000-acre tracts to 100 English and Scottish 'undertakers', 50 ex-army 'servitors' and 300 loyalist Irish. He also allocated land for churches, schools and Trinity College, Dublin, intended as civilizing institutions. Meanwhile, Scottish eminences Sir Hugh Montgomery, Laird of Braidstone, Ayrshire, James Hamilton and Sir Randall MacDonnell established unofficial, private, but crown-approved colonies peopled by Scottish Protestants in Down and Antrim. Though Irish colonization was styled as British, not least by James VI and I, it was English-dominated. English people, law, language, culture and agriculture predominated in the Irish plantations. When lands were divided among settlers, it was English ones who got the best of them. Segregated as they often were, Scottish settlers often established what historian Nicholas Canny has called a 'colony-within-a-colony' where their own culture predominated, anticipating the partly separate national, religious and ethnic enclaves that existed in British North America.[6]

After Tyrone's Rebellion (1595–1603) and the Confederate Wars (1641–52), Irish colonization accelerated. Oliver Cromwell famously conquered vast reaches of Ireland, as did William of Orange. In 1641, Catholics held 59 per cent of the land, but confiscations reduced that to 22 per cent in 1660 and a tiny 5 per cent in 1776. By 1641, 70,000 English and Welsh and 30,000 Scottish migrants had moved to Ireland, far outnumbering those crossing the Atlantic in the 1630s' Great Migration to New England. Britons migrated to Ireland at a rate of more than 8000 a year in the second half of the seventeenth century. People of English, Scottish and Welsh birth or descent made up just 2 per cent of the Irish population in 1600, but grew to 18 per cent by 1660 and 30 per cent in the mid-eighteenth century, forming a majority in Ulster. The total Irish population rose from 1,400,000 in 1600 to 2,100,000 in 1641, and then fell due to wars, plague and famine, only reaching 2,000,000 again in the 1680s.

Such were the similarities between Irish and American colonization that one historian described the former as a 'blueprint' for the latter. Given the number of unexpected contingencies and consequent adaptations that characterized the process of American colonization, though, that may be an exaggeration. Nevertheless, there were many broad similarities. The most fundamental was that, for all the occasional military mayhem wreaked and more routine oppression imposed by the English in other parts of the British Isles, the dispossession of lands and displacement of peoples was far more extensive and destructive in Ireland than it was in Wales and Scotland. Indeed, the establishment of the 'empire of Great Britain' in Wales and Scotland had more to do with *imperium* than with *dominium*. In other words, it was more about establishing the political hegemony of the English monarchy and parliament than about displacing people and stealing their land. Like Wales and Scotland, Ireland was eventually incorporated into the English polity through the 1800 Act of Union and, unlike Amerindians, the Irish survived, lived alongside and eventually even expelled many of their colonizers from most of their island. Nevertheless, like Amerindians, vast numbers of Irish people experienced dispossession and death at the hands of colonial invaders.[7]

Furthermore, like Amerindians, the Irish were routinely regarded as barbaric and Irish colonization was justified on these grounds. Scottish Highlanders and Islanders were often similarly regarded, not least by James VI and I, but such perceptions of the Irish were more deep-seated. Notions of Gaelic incivility dated to at least the twelfth century, when Giraldus Cambresis described the Irish as 'living themselves like beasts' who 'practice nothing but the barbarism in which they are born and bred, and which sticks to them like a second nature'. One commentator of 1615, three decades after Roanoke colonists were supposedly killed by Indians and just a few years after the first Anglo-Amerindian war with the Powhatan people of the Chesapeake, rated the Irish as 'more barbarous and more brutish in ther costomes and demeanures then in any other parte of the worlde that is knowne'. Two years later, Francis Bacon wrote of an Ireland 'reclaimed from desolation . . . and from savage and barbarous customs, to humanity and civility'. As we shall see, this language was similar to that used to justify appropriation of Amerindian lands and, when deemed necessary, the destruction of Amerindian lives.[8]

Irish colonization prefigured American in other ways too. English West Country gentlemen such as Humphrey Gilbert, his half-brother, Walter Raleigh and their cousin, Richard Grenville, among others, were involved both in colonizing Ireland and in attempts to colonize America in the late sixteenth and early seventeenth centuries. More importantly, the main impetus behind settlers' decisions to migrate there, whatever the crown or parliament had in mind, was individual economic self-improvement. For aristocratic and gentry recipients of Irish land grants, colonization represented opportunity for betterment or, for second sons, alternatives to the ministry and military. For the bulk of migrants, the 'undertenants', Irish colonization was an alternative to unemployment and poverty and an opportunity for self-improvement. Indeed, propagandists for Irish colonization employed the same inducements as writers of American colonial promotional literature. Typical was Thomas Blennerhasset, who wrote in *A Direction for the Plantation of Ulster* (1612) that farmer and artisan migrants there would expect to 'be in estimation and quickly enriched by [their] endeavours'.[9]

Accordingly, migrants to Ireland, like those to America, were predominantly single men, and they did not provide the kind of well-ordered settlement that planners of colonization envisioned. Seeking improvement for themselves rather than working towards the achievement of corporate ends, they preferred to scatter across the countryside rather than settling in

towns, and they competed economically with each other rather than coop-
erating in tightly knit communities. In other words, settlement socially
resembled colonization in all parts of the Americas except early New
England. The exceptions in Ireland were Scottish Presbyterians, who
arrived in large numbers in Ulster in the 1620s. Deeply religious, communitarian and family-orientated, they eschewed markets and mixing with the
native Irish, rather like the English puritans who were settling in New
England at roughly the same time.

English Atlantic exploration, trade and plunder in the sixteenth century

Despite domestic distractions, Englishmen – mainly private individuals
acting sometimes with state support (albeit invariably more moral and legal
than financial support) – increasingly involved themselves in American
exploration from the late fifteenth century. It is possible, though unproven,
that an English voyage of 1481 to 'Brasil' represented the first English and
indeed European contact with the Americas. John Cabot, a Venetian citizen
of Genoese extraction living in the seafaring city of Bristol in the mid-1490s
made the first verifiable English-sponsored contact with the North
American continent. Cabot convinced Henry VII, as Columbus had convinced Ferdinand and Isabella, that he could locate a western route to the
east, and Henry gave the mariner licence to conquer any people and colonize any lands not already claimed by Christians. Henry was less generous
than the Spanish monarchs, though, and Cabot and his small crew of 18
aboard the *Matthew* landed at what the mariner called 'new found land' in
1497. He hoped to bring back riches in a second voyage of 1498, but he
and his four ships and crews went missing. Henry VII chartered a joint
English-Portuguese merchant venture in 1501, but its two missions failed to
find a north-west passage and the king lost interest in New World exploration. Cabot's voyages did, however, provide a basis for later English claims
to North American territory.

Others remained keen to emulate the Iberians, however, and English voyagers, sometimes joining up with the Portuguese in the Azores, departed
from Bristol every year from 1501 to 1505, returning with American fauna,
artefacts and even people. The first Amerindians to visit England appeared
in London in 1501 or 1502. In 1508, Sebastian Cabot, son of John,
explored what is now Hudson Bay and may have navigated far down the
eastern seaboard of North America, though his missions of 1508–09 were,
like his father's, primarily attempts to find a north-west passage. With little
English governmental assistance following, the younger Cabot continued
his explorations under Spanish patronage. He did, though, find 'so great
multitudes of certeyne bigge fysshes . . . that they sumtymes stayed shippes',
and fishermen from western Europe continued to exploit the piscatorial

riches of the northern seas, landing on the coasts to dry their nets and catches but not yet settling there permanently. These men, though, were rather more keen to keep their fisheries a secret from competitors than they were to share their knowledge of the North American littoral.[10]

In 1519–20, Ferdinand Magellan rounded Cape Horn and proved that there was a south-west passage to Asia at the bottom of South America. The ancient Greek idea of a symmetrical world (an idea given new life during the European Renaissance) fuelled the belief that there must be an identical passage at the top of North America, reinvigorating the European search for it. John Rut made the first known full reconnaissance of North America's eastern seaboard in 1527, though English interest in exploration remained intermittent, not encouraged by the experience of London merchant Richard Hore and his crew who, in 1536, were reduced to cannibalism before they were able to raid a French vessel for the supplies they needed to get back home. Although William Hawkins of Plymouth in the 1530s briefly undertook trade between Europe, Africa and the Azores, including slave trading to Brazil, it was not until the generation of his son, John Hawkins, that English Atlantic activity became systematic and sustained.

In the early 1550s, economic problems revived English interest in exploring and possibly settling North America. Wool exports to Antwerp, England's principal overseas trade, fell by 35 per cent in 1551–52, forcing merchants to seek new commercial outlets elsewhere. In 1553, Hugh Willoughby and Richard Chancellor reopened trade with Russia and thereby helped revive interest in oceanic navigation. At this point, also, merchants began forming joint stock companies to share the expense and risks of long-distance commerce, forming the Muscovy Company (1553) to trade in Russia, the Guinea Company (1555) in Africa, the Eastland Company (1579) in the Baltic, the Venice and Turkey companies (1581) in the Mediterranean and Middle East (merged into the Levant Company in 1592) and the East India Company (1600) in India and China. All these corporations represented precursors to the Virginia Company and other corporations that organized and financed settlements in North America and the West Indies.

In 1558, England ceded Calais to France, losing the last remnant of its Angevin empire in continental Europe. Yet, that same year, the political and diplomatic condition of England changed in ways that eventually encouraged further American exploration and other enterprises, though that was far from clear at the time. Later in 1558, Queen Mary, Catholic wife of Philip II of Spain, died, and her Protestant sister Elizabeth ascended the throne, shifting England's enmity away from France and towards Spain, especially once the execution of Mary, Queen of Scots removed a focus for French intrigue. Rivalry with Spain encouraged the plundering of Spanish New World treasure ships and settlements and intrusions on Spanish trade, especially when the Revolt of the Netherlands and the beginning of the Eighty Years War against Dutch Protestants from 1566 weakened Spanish power to protect its New World interests.

In 1562, John Hawkins, England's first major slave trader, began carrying human cargo and other merchandise between Africa and the Spanish Caribbean, as well as plundering Spanish settlements. Six years later he was attacked by a fleet of the Viceroy of Mexico off Veracruz, heightening hostility between Spain and England and encouraging the kind of privateering, or licensed piracy, by English 'sea dogs' that was already being practised by French corsairs against the Spanish. Most famously, Francis Drake, 'El Diablo' to the Spanish, and a fleet of six ships led by the *Golden Hind*, attacked Spanish ships and settlements near the Isthmus of Panama and encouraged slaves to destabilize the Spanish empire in Central America and parts of South America from the 1570s. Drake combined plunder with exploration. In 1577, he rounded Cape Horn and proceeded north to claim Nova Albion, now California, raided Callao and Lima, and then sailed west across the Pacific, stopping at the Philippines and the Moluccas spice islands. After crossing the Indian Ocean and rounding the Cape of Good Hope, he finally completed his circumnavigation of the globe with his arrival in Plymouth in 1580. The 4600 per cent profits enjoyed by shareholders in the joint stock-sponsored enterprise added to people's interest in New World profiteering. After 1585, during the war with Spain, Drake resumed his western actions, attacking Cartagena de Indias, Santo Domingo and St Augustine, and numerous Spanish ships, until he was lost at sea in 1595.

Meanwhile, in 1570, Martin Frobisher set out on the first of a series of voyages to find a north-west passage, despite Elizabeth's continued reluctance to invest state revenue in exploration or colonization. Forming the Company of Cathay with Michael Lok and other London merchants, Frobisher undertook three more voyages in 1576–78. The gold mine he founded on Baffin Island, however, produced nothing but iron pyrite, and the company folded. John Davis, backed by investors who included Adrian Gilbert, brother of the more famous Humphrey, made three other unsuccessful searches for a north-west passage north of Labrador in 1585–87.

More than simply muscling in on Spanish markets, attacking Spanish ships and settlements and searching for a north-west passage, the English began to think seriously about establishing their own New World territories, though it took them some time to attempt it and even longer to do it successfully. In November 1565, Elizabeth's Privy Council considered arguments for colonization as well as for further attempts to find a north-west passage by Sir Humphrey Gilbert, the Devonshire landowner and half-brother of Sir Walter Raleigh. The next year Gilbert wrote *A Discourse of a Discoverie for a New Passage to Cataia* (published in 1576), although unsuccessful involvement in Ireland kept him out of Atlantic affairs for a decade. In 1577, however, he proposed capturing Santo Domingo and

Cuba as bases for conquering Mexico. The crown demurred but instead gave him permission, though no financial assistance, to establish colonies some way north of Spanish Florida, preferably 'Norumbega' (named after a mythical inland sea that would lead to Asia). Gilbert's 1578 settlement mission, however, quickly reverted to the relatively limited aims of attacking Spanish ships. By 1582, though, he was more convinced that North America was a place to colonize, and by the end of the next year had sub-patented some 8,000,000 acres of land to potential colonizers, including large grants to a group of Catholic gentry headed by Sir George Peckham and Sir Thomas Gerrard, anticipating, like the French Huguenots, the New World as a haven for religious dissenters. In 1583, he landed at St John's harbour and declared Newfoundland English, but that September he was lost at sea and nothing came of his colony.[11]

The lost colonies of Roanoke

Gilbert's death, unlike Cabot's almost a century before, did not dampen the growing English appetite for exploration and colonization. In 1584, Elizabeth I granted Sir Walter Raleigh the same grant Gilbert was given, again with no financial backing and this time without Newfoundland fishing rights. Nevertheless, in April 1584 Raleigh despatched captains Arthur Barlow and Philip Amadas to explore and claim the region and islands from Chesapeake Bay to the Carolinas. The expedition reached Roanoke Island off modern North Carolina in July, returning to England with two local Indians, Manteo and Wanchese. The captains' recommendation of the region for colonization encouraged Raleigh to name it 'Virginia', in honour of one of the virtues of his queen, and, as Lord and Governor of Virginia, to send Richard Grenville there to establish a settlement.

Grenville departed Plymouth in April 1585 with 5 ships and 800 men, arriving off the outer banks in early July. On the way he diverted to raid the Spanish West Indies and in the process depleted many of the supplies intended to assist colonization. That was just the first thing that went wrong. On arrival, only the smallest of the vessels could negotiate the sandbanks. Then, when a silver cup went missing, Grenville burned an Indian village in revenge. Grenville departed in late August, leaving Captain Ralph Lane and 108 men to establish a fort, search for treasure and trade with the Amerindians in craft products for which the local Roanoke had no use. Lane's reluctance to engage in agriculture proved disastrous. As supplies ran low, he requested food from the Indians. He took their offer of cleared fields and seed corn as an insult and launched another attack, murdering chief Wingina, whose experiences with the English had already prompted him to change his name to Pemisapan, meaning 'watchful' or 'wary'. The Indians then withdrew, leaving Lane and his men without supplies, and when Francis Drake unexpectedly arrived with new supplies in June 1586, all insisted on returning to England. When Grenville reappeared a few weeks later, therefore, he found his colony abandoned. He nevertheless left 15 men behind and returned to England for new settlers, but when the English returned the next year these men had vanished, probably victims of revenge for Lane's aggression. They would not be the last Roanoke colonists to disappear.

Despite these setbacks, interest in Roanoke remained high. Grenville's mission had included Thomas Hariot, a mathematician and botanist who learned Carolinian Algonquin from Manteo and Wanchese, and John White, a surveyor and artist charged with identifying and drawing local flora, fauna and other natural features of the New World. This trip thus produced Harriot's *A Briefe and True Report of the New Found Land of Virginia*, published in 1588 and republished in 1590 with Theodore de Bry's engravings of White's paintings. It was White who, in April 1587, obtained Raleigh's permission to lead another attempt at colonization, this time an agricultural settlement of freeholding family farmers who could form a permanent colony. White hoped to get 150 colonists, but in the event probably fewer than 100 men, women and children embarked for the putative City of Raleigh, on the mainland in the Chesapeake Bay region. White landed at Roanoke, however, forced there by a ship's crew keen on Caribbean plunder. Finding Grenville's 15 men missing and no buildings or crops, White returned to England for more supplies and new recruits. Among those he left behind were his daughter, son-in-law and their baby, Virginia Dare, the first English child born in North America. Then came another disaster, as the Spanish Armada trapped White in England. When he finally returned to Roanoke in August 1590, the colonists had disappeared, leaving behind them only the word 'CROATOAN' carved in a doorpost and 'CRO' carved in a nearby tree, suggesting attempts to reach the island birthplace of Manteo, about 50 miles south of Roanoke. No one knows for sure what happened to the Roanoke islanders. It seems likely they were lost at sea, though some historians have found impressive evidence that they joined with local Indians.[12]

After the Roanoke disasters, Grenville turned to his Irish estates and Raleigh to privateering against Spanish shipping and settlements. Raleigh did not lose interest in colonization permanently though, and in 1595 made his first visit to Guiana, on the north-east coast of South America, where he hoped to emulate the Spanish conquistadors by subjugating Amerindians, and then to outdo the Spanish plunderers in the treasure hunt for the lost golden city of El Dorado. He built forts to establish domination over local Indians from whom he would demand tributes while his soldiers would 'fight for gold'. In *The Discoverie of the large and bewtiful Empire of Guiana* (1596), he anticipated that his commanders would 'find here more rich and beautiful cities, more temples adorned with golden images, more sepulchres filled with treasure, than either Cortez found in Mexico, or Pizarro in Peru'. That did not happen, however, and Raleigh's final voyage of 1617, after several years' imprisonment, cost him his son, his fortune and the remnants of his reputation. He was executed on his return to England in 1618, a victim of King James's desire to restore good relations with Spain. In Raleigh's life, in his explorations, depredations and colonizations in Ireland and the Americas, we can see represented the entrepreneurship and aggression that characterized England's colonial adventures in America. Also, though, in his failures and his death, we can see symbolized the contingencies, adaptations, disasters and, ultimately, the suborning of everything he attempted that future colonial charter holders would face when attempting to create something much larger than they could ever control.[13]

In the later years of Elizabeth's reign, England was preoccupied with famines, Irish colonization and the continuing war with Spain. Campaigns in northern France and the Netherlands in support of the Dutch Revolt required attentions and resources that might otherwise have been expended on American adventures. The English nevertheless maintained a presence in the Atlantic Ocean, principally through the 100 to 200 privateering vessels that embarked from English ports annually with thousands of sailors who continued to gain the navigational knowledge and hone the seafaring skills that would be important in English colonization in the seventeenth century. After Elizabeth died, the 1604 Treaty of London established peace with Spain. Merchants who had hitherto profited mightily from shares in privateering, an enterprise that had been worth upwards of £200,000 a year, now needed new outlets for their ambitions and had plenty of capital to invest. Within two years, merchant adventurers formed two Virginia Companies that embarked on colonizing the east coast of North America in 1606 and 1607. Before these colonizing ventures could begin, however, they had to be justified and planned. Successful colonies and empire first required visions and ambitions.

Notes

1 Felipe Fernández-Armesto, *Before Columbus: Exploration and Colonisation from the Mediterranean to the Atlantic, 1229–1492* (London, 1987); Samuel Eliot Morison, *The European Discovery of America: The Southern Voyages, AD 1492–1600* (Oxford, 1974); Bailey W. Diffie and George D. Winius, *Foundations of the Portuguese Empire, 1415–1580* (Minneapolis, 1977); J.H. Elliott, *Imperial Spain, 1469–1716* (London, 1963).
2 Samuel Eliot Morison, *The European Discovery of America: The Northern Voyages, AD 500–1600* (Oxford, 1971); W.J. Eccles, *The French in North America, 1500–1783* (Ann Arbor, 1998); Oliver A. Rink, *Holland on the Hudson: An Economic and Social History of Dutch New York* (Ithaca, 1986).

3 David Armitage, *The Ideological Origins of the British Empire* (Cambridge, 2000), p. 11.

4 Michael Hechter, *Internal Colonialism: The Celtic Fringe in British National Development, 1536–1966* (London, 1975); Armitage, *Ideological Origins*, pp. 34–5.

5 Armitage, *Ideological Origins*, chapter 2, quotes on pp. 52, 53.

6 Nicholas Canny, 'The Origins of Empire: An Introduction', in Nicholas Canny, ed., *The Oxford History of the British Empire* Volume I: *The Origins of Empire: British Overseas Enterprise to the Close of the Seventeenth Century* (Oxford, 1998), p. 14.

7 A.L. Rowse, 'Tudor Expansion: The Transition from Medieval to Modern History', *William and Mary Quarterly*, 3rd ser., XIV (1957), p. 315; *The Expansion of Elizabethan England* (London, 1955), chapter 4; Nicholas Canny, *Kingdom and Colony: Ireland in the Atlantic World, 1560–1800* (Baltimore, 1988).

8 Giraldus Cambresis, *The Topography of Ireland* (1188–89) and Fynes Moryson, 'The Anatomy of Ireland' (1615), both cited in Jane H. Ohlmeyer, '"Civilizinge of those rude partes": Colonization within Britain and Ireland, 1580s–1640s', in Canny, *Origins of Empire*, p. 131; Bacon in H.C. Porter, *The Inconstant Savage: England and the North American Indian, 1500–1600* (London, 1979), p. 203.

9 Canny, 'Origins of Empire', p. 9.

10 Peter Martyr, *The Decades of the Newe Worlde or West India*, trans. Richard Eden (London, 1555), cited in Morison, *Northern Voyages*, p. 203.

11 David Beers Quinn, *England and the Discovery of America, 1481–1620* (London, 1974); Kenneth R. Andrews, *Trade, Plunder, and Settlement: Maritime Enterprise and the Genesis of the British Empire, 1480–1630* (Cambridge, 1984).

12 Karen Ordahl Kupperman, *Roanoke: The Abandoned Colony* (Totowa, 1984); David Beers Quinn, *Set Fair for Roanoke: Voyages and Colonies, 1584–1606* (Chapel Hill, 1985).

13 Norman Lloyd Williams, *Sir Walter Raleigh* (Harmondsworth, 1965), p. 149.

2

Visions and ambitions, 1516–1775

Those who envisioned English and, from 1707, British colonies and empire over the course of two and a half centuries of New World expansionism fall into several overlapping categories. First were the growing numbers of imperialist writers who, from the sixteenth century onwards, attempted to promote state-sponsored empire building. These people rarely travelled to the Americas, but they were often associated with and were champions of members of a second group of visionaries who did: explorers, traders and plunderers, some of whom were would-be colonizers. These two groups also sometimes connected with a third category: the charter groups – joint stock companies and individual proprietors or groups of proprietors who were given licence to colonize and who financed and organized colonization. A fourth category consists of promotional writers who encouraged others to migrate to and settle in America. Among their number were some of the charter holders themselves, and there were others who wrote at the behest of companies or proprietors. But promotional literature belongs in a different category of colonial and imperial thinking and writing because, while the visions and ambitions of charter groups tended to be corporate in nature, serving the interests of the company or colony, promotional literature was aimed at the more individualistic aspirations of potential migrants. The hundreds of thousands of migrants who settled in the colonies constitute yet another category. These people had little time for the corporate imaginings of imperial writers and colonial charter groups, and they created the colonies in accord with their own visions and ambitions.

The early sections of this chapter analyse, under various categories, the thinking of imperial writers, would-be colonizers and colonial charter groups (although charter groups' plans are explored in more detail in chapters 3 to 6). The later sections of this chapter examine the migrants: where they came from, who they were and why they moved to the New World (the details of what they did there are, again, related in chapters 3 to 6). It is worth noting briefly here, though, that there was yet another group who envisioned an empire in America, albeit belatedly: English and British imperial authorities. The visions and ambitions of kings, parliaments, boards and departments of state and royal governors, like those of imperial writers and charter groups, tended to be corporate in nature, this time privileging the national above provincial and individual interests. Chapters 7, 8 and 9 explore the evolution of English and British imperial authorities' visions and ambitions, how attempts to implement them after 1763 led to American Independence in 1776 and how the American nation and the second British Empire subsequently evolved.

Imagining an empire: imperial writers, would-be colonists and charter groups

Early modern English imagining of overseas colonies and empire began with Sir Thomas More. *The Best State of a Commonwealth and the New Island of Utopia* was published in Latin in 1515–16 and in English in 1551, just as interest and activities in Scotland, Ireland and America were on the rise. This was also the time that writers began using the modern language of imperialism. More reintroduced to English writing the Roman term *colonia*, referring to a community transplanted onto new territory. Robert Wedderburn was first to use the term in Scots in his *Complaynt of Scotland* (1550), justifying the Earl of Somerset's ventures there, and Richard Eden used it in English in his 1555 translation of Peter Martyr's *De Orbo Novo*, the Italian's 1530 chronicle of the findings of numerous explorers, including Christopher Columbus. John Dee was first to employ the term 'British Empire' in reference to North America as well as to the empire of Great Britain in his *General and Rare Memorials Pertayning to the Perfect Art of Navigation* (1577).

Richard Eden, however, was the first Englishman to write at length, in detail and repeatedly about the New World. In 1553 he translated Sebastian Münster's *Cosmographia* as *A Treatyse of the Newe India*. Most significant was his translation of Martyr as *The Decades of the Newe Worlde or West India* (1555). Eden added a preface to his translation, advocating English emulation of Spanish imperialism. Yet, even in Eden's time, much imperial writing was about or even by other Europeans rather than by Englishmen or other Britons. Jean Ribault, the French Huguenot, who, in between efforts to establish French settlements on the east coast of North America, appeared in England after escaping besieged Le Havre, attempted to interest Elizabeth I in an English Protestant settlement, publishing *The whole and true discovereye of Terra Florida* in 1563 for that purpose. Numerous English translations of foreign accounts of conquest and colonization appeared in subsequent years, including the works of

André Thevet, cosmographer to Henry IV of France, in 1568, Francisco López de Gómara's history of Spanish conquest in 1578, Jacques Cartier's journals in 1580 and Bartolemé las Casas' *Brief narration of the destruction of the Indies* in 1583, the first major critique of European destruction of Amerindian peoples and cultures.

The quantity of English writing about the New World nevertheless increased with the growth in English exploration and then colonization. The appearance of the most significant literature was partly a result of commissions by Sir Francis Walsingham, Queen Elizabeth's Secretary of State. As we have seen, though, the crown's interest in the New World was brief and passing, and most new imperial writers in the late sixteenth century wrote in direct support of and often with sponsorship from private adventurers, although they hoped the effect would be to encourage state-sponsored empire building. Eden wrote to laud the attempts by Hugh Willoughby and Richard Chancellor to find a north-east passage to the riches of the east. Poet Thomas Churchyard wrote eulogies for Martin Frobisher and Humphrey Gilbert, printed in 1578. Richard Hakluyt the elder wrote instructions for Frobisher on how to establish a colony, and in 1585 published *Inducements Toward the Liking of the Voyage Intended Towards Virginia* in support of efforts replicating those of Raleigh at Roanoke.

The most prolific and influential early English advocate of New World imperialism was Hakluyt's cousin, Richard the younger. Furthermore, in emphasizing opportunities for individual improvement offered by the New World, the younger Hakluyt was the most prescient of all the early imperial writers. His first publication was a preface to John Florio's translations of Jacques Cartier's travel accounts in which he advocated English settlement of the American north-east. He subsequently produced *Divers Voyages touching the discoverie of America* (1582), 'Discourse of Western Planting' (1584), a report presented at the behest of Walsingham to Elizabeth I as a policy proposal, and *Principal Navigations, Voyages, Traffiques and Discoveries of the English Nation . . . within the compasse of these 1600 yeres* (1589), expanded in 1598–1600 into three volumes. Hakluyt's influence and reputation were subsequently enhanced by his protégé Samuel Purchas, whose *Hakluytus Posthumus or Purchas His Pilgrimes* appeared in four volumes from 1625.

In the 1580s, some explorers, sea dogs and would-be colonizers wrote of their own New World experiences, among them Humphrey Gilbert, Thomas Hariot and Walter Raleigh, who respectively produced *A Discourse of a Discoverie for a New Passage to Cataia* (1576), *A Briefe and True Report of the New Found Land of Virginia* (1588) and *The Discoverie of the large and bewtiful Empire of Guiana* (1596). But even writers who never went to the New World often had significant interest or involvement in it. Hakluyt never fulfilled his plan to accompany Gilbert on his 1583

Norumbega mission, but did later become a shareholder in the Virginia Company of London. Some of the greatest literary and philosophical figures of the time had some New World interest or connection too. Thomas Hobbes attended Virginia Company meetings as secretary to William, Lord Cavendish, and held shares of his own in both the Virginia Company and the Somers Island Company that financed the colonization of Bermuda. Hobbes's State of Nature was partly based on his American knowledge, as was that of John Locke, later one of the writers of the Carolina constitution. John Donne, who went to the Azores with the Earl of Essex in 1596, applied to be secretary of the Virginia Company in 1609 and was appointed an honorary member in 1622. William Shakespeare never went to the New World, but *The Tempest* (1611) provided a dystopian view of America, inspired as it was by the story of the wrecking of the *Sea Adventurer* on Bermuda in 1609.

Despite the imprecations of colonial writers, colonization occurred not under direct government auspices (except in Jamaica in 1655), but through joint stock companies and colonial proprietors who were licensed by the crown to settle America or who, in some cases, sub-patented other charter groups to do the work for them. Raleigh's licence eventually devolved on the Virginia Company that in 1606 was divided into the London Company of Virginia that settled Jamestown and the Plymouth Company of Virginia that attempted unsuccessfully to settle Sagadahoc in what is now Maine (at that time 'Virginia' referred to most of North America). These Virginia companies were the first of many charter groups under whose direct auspices colonization actually took place. Within a few years of the Virginia Company sending settlers to Jamestown, the Somers Island Company settled Bermuda and the Providence Island Company had charge of Providence Island off the Nicaraguan coast. The Plymouth group, after failing in its quest to establish settlements in the cold and rocky north, was replaced with a Council of New England and the New England Company that respectively devolved their licences on the pilgrims who founded the Plymouth colony in 1619 and the puritans who formed the Massachusetts Bay Company 10 years later. There were also individual proprietors, as well as joint stock companies and religious organizations among the charter groups. The first of these was Cecil Calvert, the second Lord Baltimore, who was granted Maryland by Charles I in 1632 and whose descendants ran it until American Independence (except for a period of royal rule between the Glorious Revolution of 1688–89 and 1715). Another was Quaker William Penn, proprietor of Pennsylvania. The Carolinas were founded by a group of gentlemen known as the lords proprietors, and a similar arrangement was made in the case of Georgia. Almost all the colonies eventually came under royal rule, beginning with Virginia in 1625. The only two charters that remained in place until American Independence were those of Connecticut and Rhode Island. The only two colonies that remained proprietorships were Maryland and Pennsylvania, and their charter holders had long since abandoned their original plans.

A central and common motif in most imperial writers' and proprietors' thinking and writing was the idea of the 'commonwealth', whether that meant the English or British nation, or else the corporation or the colony. Their visions were corporate in a very modern sense: colonization was supposed to generate profits for themselves and their shareholders. But they were also corporate in the sense that they envisioned colonization or empire building as a collective mission carried out in the interests of a larger community: company, colony or country. As well as outlining their corporate visions, though, most imperial writers and colonial charter holders felt it necessary to justify their ambitions, to legitimate their claims over those of rival European powers and those of Amerindians.[1]

European rivalries, Amerindians and the legitimization of colonies and empire

Many of the claims for the legitimacy of colonization and empire by English imperial writers appear almost crassly utilitarian. Any educated, outward-looking, sixteenth-century Englishman could see the economic and military benefits gained by Spain and Portugal, and those being gained by France and the Netherlands, in the Americas. Hence Richard Hakluyt the younger wrote, in rather vivid language, that it was imperative to 'staye the spanische kinge from flowinge over all the face' of America, and to follow 'the late plaine examples of the Frenche'. As well the geopolitical imperative to 'cutt the combe of the frenche, of the spanishe, of the portingale, and of enemies, and of doubtfull frendes to the abatinge of their wealth and force', colonization would 'inlarge the Revenewes of the Crown very mightely and inriche all sortes of subjectes ingenerally'. Hakluyt revealingly subtitled his 'Discourse of Western Planting' as 'A perticuler discourse concerninge the greate necessitie and manifolde comodyties that are like to growe to this Realme of Englande by the Westerne discoveries lately attempted', claiming 'That this westerne voyadge will yelde unto us all the commodities of Europe, Affrica and Asia . . . and supplye the wantes of all our decayed trades.'[2]

Utilitarian these arguments for empire were, but crass they were not. Behind them lay elaborate justifications for usurping other people's claims, and behind those justifications lay an anxious ontology of colonization and imperialism. Some of that anxiety came from English historical experience and memory, in particular the problem the English had had with the concept of conquest since the Norman invasion of 1066. That traumatic event and its aftermath had been accommodated in the English psyche through a 'continuity theory' in which it was understood that William the Conqueror had assimilated English constitutional essentials. This interpretation of the

Norman invasion both reflected and reinforced a notion, when it came to colonizing America, that conquest alone could not confer legitimacy. Might was not right; there had to be more.

One way of legitimating English claims to New World territories over those of other European powers was to assert that English discoveries pre-dated Spanish ones. Richard Hakluyt the younger thus related the alleged travels of Welsh Prince Madoc in 1170 to present-day Alabama, so he was able to argue that 'the west Indies were discovered and inhabited 322. yeres before Columbus made his firste voyadge' in 1492. Hakluyt further developed this 'charter myth' by writing 'that a very greate and large parte as well as of the continent as of the Ilandes was firste discovered for the kinge of England by Sebastian Gabote an Englishe man borne in Bristolle'. In addition to creating a powerful case for English over Spanish claims, the cumulative effect of Hakluyt's tales of English voyages created a sense of growing momentum that provided an impression of the inevitability of imperialist expansion.[3]

Imperial writers and, in turn, colonial proprietors were well aware that other Europeans were not the only people with prior claims to American lands. On the eve of English colonization, approximately 1,000,000 Amerindians lived between the east coast of North America and the Mississippi River (of the perhaps 12,000,000 who lived in the Americas as a whole before the Columbian encounter). Two main groups lived in this large north-east region: the Algonquin language group along the coastal plain and the Iroquois of the lower Great Lakes region, though these language groups could include up to 300 dialects that were distinct enough to be incomprehensible to different Algonquin and Iroquois tribes. When the English encountered these people, they did not immediately dismiss them as an irreconcilably alien 'other' who must be removed or exterminated. The English were staggeringly condescending towards Amerindians, to be sure, but they were not at first violently hostile. Despite the actions of men like Ralph Lane, it was not until after the massacre of Virginia settlers in 1622 that English attitudes towards Amerindians became overwhelmingly hostile and aggressive. Before that, and even sometimes after, imperial writers and colonial charter groups had a wide range of opinions about Amerindians and their rights, took the trouble to justify their occupation of America and reflected on how English settlers and Native Americans might live together.

Englishmen did not unthinkingly assume the right to settle in America, but asked themselves, as in Robert Gray's *A Good Speed to Virginia* (1609): 'by what right or warrant we can enter into the land of these Savages, take away their rightful inheritance from them, and plant ourselves in their place, being unwronged or unprovoked by them?'[4] The colonizers found their answers, of course. Indeed, Gray's question contains a clue to one of them: the idea of Amerindians as 'savages'. The concept of Amerindian savagery was married to ideas about their paganism, although the former mattered most. Native Americans held various kinds of polytheistic, animist beliefs and had hierarchies of shamans who presided over many kinds of ceremonies. Had the English recognized the complexity of Amerindian religions, it would barely have mattered. Since the Crusades against the Muslims, Christians had declared wars on infidels, yet the English considered Amerindian paganism on its own insufficient grounds for depriving them of political rights and rights in property. John Locke, in his 1685 *Letter Concerning Toleration*, wrote that 'No man whatsoever . . . ought to be deprived of his Terrestrial Enjoyments, upon account of his religion.' He had previously noted in the Carolina Constitution of 1669, written with Lord Shaftesbury as a charter for the southern mainland colony, that Amerindians' 'Idollatry Ignorance or mistake gives us noe right to expell or use them ill.' On the other hand, nor were Amerindians immune from dispossession and forced removal even if they did convert to Christianity, for it was notions of English civility, contrasted with Amerindian savagery, in particular in the areas of government and property ownership, that provided the main grounds for expelling them and using them ill.[5]

In their earliest encounters with Amerindians, the English immediately asserted rights to imperium, the political subjugation of Indian peoples to the English crown. At Roanoke, the English relied on precedents established in Ireland whereby Gaelic lords' local authority was acknowledged in return for recognition of the ultimately supervening authority of English kings. According to one account, Roanoke chiefs 'formally acknowledged Her Majesty as servants and homagers to her and under her to Sir WR' (Walter Raleigh). This practice, subsequently followed on the North American mainland, not only conferred legitimacy (for the English) on acts of subjugation, but also aimed to win the cooperation of local leaders.[6] This method of establishing imperium required the English to conceptualize Amerindian political authority and nationhood not merely as inferior to their own (the same could be and was said about that of other Europeans), but also as inadequate in and of itself. Amerindians had villages (and in South, Central and south-west North America they had great cities), tribes, nations, alliances and empires, and engaged with each other in complex diplomacy. Amerindian nations did not, however, claim and govern what the English considered to be clearly demarcated political territories. This fact followed from an even more fundamental flaw, as the English saw it, in Amerindian political economy: their failure to hold property properly. For Englishmen, one of the principal purposes of government was the protection of private property, or of every man's right to 'life, liberty, and property' in the words of John Locke, so the absence of private property ownership necessarily implied at least the partial absence of or deficiency in government. Locke made this connection himself, arguing that because Indians 'exercise very little Dominion' they 'have but a very moderate sovereignty'. Indeed, for

Locke, Indians existed in a later stage of the State of Nature. Though they exercised individual self-government, they had not handed over their 'natural power' to a superordinate political authority.[7]

As well as using concepts of property to justify imperium over Indian peoples, the English used them to justify their claims to American *dominium*; that is, claims to property in American territory as well as over Amerindians politically. Some Native American tribes were primarily nomadic or semi-nomadic hunter-gatherers, others practised settled agriculture or horticulture, many mixed the two, but that made little difference to the English, who practised settled agriculture on private, fenced-off farms and estates. English contempt for Amerindian agriculture was compounded by the fact that when Indians did cultivate crops, it was women who planted, tended and harvested them, while men hunted. Moreover, Amerindian economies were communal: land, animals and crops belonged to whole villages. Individual private property ownership and the fencing-off of family farmsteads was unknown in pre-conquest America. The English thus regarded the land that Amerindians occupied as unused and therefore open to European appropriation, habitation and exploitation.

These European notions and assertions, known to historians as the 'agriculturalist argument', came in part from biblical injunction, in particular from God's command in Genesis that man should go forth, multiply and have dominion over every living thing. More frequently cited, though, was the Roman law of *res nullius*, indicating either vacancy (*vacuum domicilium*) or lack of ownership (*terra nullius*). The agriculturalist argument first appeared in English imperial literature among Thomas More's Utopians, occupants of an imaginary island in the middle of the Atlantic Ocean who colonized 'on the mainland nearest them, wherever the natives have much unoccupied and uncultivated land'. John Donne's *A Sermon Preached to the Honourable Company of the Virginia Plantation, 13 Nov. 1622*, just after the March 1622 Powhatan attack that killed 347 Anglo-Virginians, claimed that 'In the Law of Nature and of Nations, a land never inhabited by any, or utterly derelicted and immemorially abandoned by the former inhabitants, becomes theirs that will possess it.' John Locke later elaborated the agriculturalist argument, asserting that no man had a claim to property in anything until he 'mixed his Labour with [it]; and joyned to it something that is his own'. When Locke famously stated in his Second Treatise of Government that 'In the beginning all the world was America', he meant that Indians possessed no property and engaged in no commerce; that America was, to all (English) intents and purposes, unused and, in effect, therefore, unclaimed.[8] The argument was also used to nullify Spanish and Portuguese claims to North American territory, because although the Treaty of Tordesillas had given them the right to settle, they had forfeited that right by failing to exercise it.

The agriculturalist argument ultimately had profound if accidental effects on the process of colonization and the constitution of the empire that eventually emerged from English colonizing practice. It gave a kind of legitimacy, based on precepts of natural law, for the individual economic and political autonomy that characterized colonists' sense of identity and obligation as Anglo-Americans and, later, British Americans. It was settlers, after all, who colonized the land, who mixed their labour with it and who expelled the Amerindians from it. The material benefits of these actions were therefore the colonists' own and no one else's, by natural right. They owed no feudal or other economic or social obligation to anyone: not to the colonial proprietors whose political and economic powers the settlers soon overturned, nor to any British government that might eventually wish to tax them. As we shall see, the justifications used and sacrifices made during the displacement of Amerindians had profound resonance during the American Revolution.

If the agriculturalist argument justified appropriation of American lands, there were still questions over what to do about Amerindian peoples. Though, on the one hand, prior Native American claims to land represented a legal and moral problem for imperialists, albeit a resolvable one, on the other hand, the existence of a New World filled with 'savage' and 'pagan' people positively required Christian attention. Ideas for dealing with this issue came in part from the Gospel injunctions in Matthew and Mark that the word of Jesus should be preached throughout the world and published in all nations. Thus it occurred immediately to Columbus to advise Ferdinand and Isabella that 'Your Highnesses ought to resolve to make [the Indians] Christians: for I believe that if you begin, in a short time you will end up having converted to our Holy Faith a multitude of peoples and acquiring large dominions and great riches and all of their peoples for Spain.' The *inter cetera* papal bulls of Alexander VI (made on 3 and 4 May 1493 to justify Spanish claims to newly encountered lands) directed 'that the Catholic faith and Christian religion be particularly exalted in our day and everywhere spread and enlarged, so that souls be saved and barbaric peoples be humbled and brought to the faith'.[9]

If Spanish Catholic Christianity was spreading in the New World, then it was all the more important to reformed Englishmen to spread the Protestant version. The first chapter of Richard Hakluyt's 'Discourse of Western Planting' proposed that 'this westerne discoverie will be greately for thinlargement of the gospell of Christ, whereunto the Princes of the refourmed Relligion are chefely bounde', and for 'reducing the infinite multitudes of these simple people that are in errour into the right and perfecte waye of their salvacion'. He even claimed that 'the people of America crye unto us their nexte neighboures to come and helpe them, and bringe unto them the gladd tidinges of the gospell'. The legend 'Come over and Help Us', with the image of a praying Indian, appeared on the seal of the Massachusetts Bay Company in 1629. Even before the puritans, the Virginia Company made the Christian and Protestant conversions of

Amerindians its business. According to *A True and Sincere Declaration of the Purpose and Ends of the Plantation begun in Virginia* (London, 1610), the colony's 'principal and main ends . . . were first to preach and baptize into Christian Religion, and by propagation of that Gospel to recover out of the arms of the Devil, a number of poor and miserable souls, wrapped up unto death, in almost invincible ignorance'. The declaration that the Virginia Company's first end was Indian conversion was neither true nor sincere, as we shall see, but it was nonetheless important to make it.[10]

English writers disagreed on the extent to which Amerindians could be assimilated to European Christianity and civility, but most thought it worth trying and indeed considered it their duty to attempt it. Thomas More went so far as to suggest a degree of mutual cultural accommodation, arguing that colonists and natives could 'merge and together absorb the same way of life and the same customs' and 'may make the land sufficient for both, which previously seemed poor and barren to the natives'. Most imperial writers, charter groups and colonists, however, condescendingly presumed that accommodation meant more or less wholesale Amerindian assimilation to European ways (though, in fact, many Europeans adopted or adapted all kinds of Amerindian economic and cultural practices).

In 1586, Thomas Harriot's account of Roanoke depicted local Indians as primitives who were nevertheless capable of Christianity, although Ralph Lane's treatment of them did not live up to Harriot's standards. Harriot's accounts and White's paintings, especially when Europeanized in Theodore de Bry's engravings, made the Indians look as if they could be assimilated, especially as publication was complete with pictures of Picts, ancient Britons who, it was thought, had been civilized by the superior culture of imperial Rome. Harriot's text noted that 'the Inhabitants of the great Bretannie have bin in times past as sauvage as those of Virginia'.

With few other points of reference available to them, English writers frequently likened Amerindians to ancient Britons. William Strachey asked his readers: 'Were not we ourselves made and not born civil in our progenitors days? And were not Caesar's Britaines as brutish as Virginians?' Had it not been for the Romans, he added, Britons might 'yet have lived overgrown satyrs, rude and untutored in the woods, dwelling in caves, and hunting for our dinners . . . prostituting our daughters to strangers, sacrificing our children to our idols, nay eating our own children as did the Scots in these days as reciteth Thomas Cogan'. Strachey's was a low opinion of Indians, to be sure, but it was an equally low one of his own ancestors. Strachey even speculated that Amerindians might have been of British, or at least Celtic, origin, confiding that their language contained 'many words, both of places and names of many creatures, which have the accents and Welsh significations'. In 1608, a Welshman named Wynne was appointed interpreter for the Monacan people, 'their pronunciations being very like Welsh', although they were deemed to have 'a far different language from the subjects of

Powhatan'. Edward Winslow theorized that the 'poor Indians of America' were the lost tribes of Israel who had 'filled that vast and long unknown country of America'.[11]

Not all Englishmen were so sure about the prospects for Amerindian assimilation. The Virginia Company in part justified its activities by reference to the ruling of Lord Chief Justice Sir Edward Coke that all infidels were 'perpetual enemies' and that 'between them, as with devils, whose subjects they may be, and the Christians, there is perpetual hostility, and can be no peace'. In any case, even assimilationist attitudes by no means precluded the use of force against Amerindians. Strachey, continuing with his comparison of ancient Britons and sixteenth-century Amerindians, noted that 'Roman swords were best teachers of civility to this and other countries near us.' Indeed, assimilationists advocated immense brutality when faced with Amerindian resistance to Christianity, civility and colonists' claims of *dominium* and imperium. Thomas More wrote that if mainlanders resisted, Utopians 'could wage war against them', it being 'a most just cause for war when a people which does not use its soil but keeps it idle and waste nevertheless forbids the use and possession of it to others who by the rule of nature ought to be maintained by it'. John Donne's 1622 sermon to the Virginia Company argued that if Indians resisted, they could rightfully 'be destroyed as a *Lyon* or a *Tyger*, one of those wild Savage Beasts, with whom men can have no Society nor Security'.

Eight months before Donne's sermon, the Powhatan Indians had killed 347 English settlers in Virginia. That event precipitated a brutal backlash of appropriation, expulsion and extermination of Amerindians by Anglo-Virginians, and provoked a markedly more pessimistic turn of mind among the English about the future prospects of Anglo-Amerindian relations. The new pessimism was evident in Donne's and others' increasingly common and strident advocacy of violence. The underlying attitude was exemplified in a 1663 copy of John Eliot's *The Holy Bible . . . Translated into the Indian Language* that was presented to Charles II by the commissioners of the United Colonies of New England. The preface, specially written for the king, described Amerindians as

> a lost people, as remote from knowledge and civility, much more from Christianity, as they were from all knowing civil and Christian nations; a people without law, without letters, without riches, or means to produce any such thing; a people that are deep in darkness, and in the shadow of death, as (we think) any since the creation.

The purpose of the Bible, of course, was to convert, but to the civilized, Christian people of the seventeenth century, there could hardly be better grounds for the expulsion or extermination of Native Americans than if they proved unwilling to accept Christian conversion and civilization.[12]

Imagining Anglo-America

Just as Europeans conceived of Amerindians in Eurocentric ways, so they envisioned a resettled and remade New World in the image of the Old. As historian J.H. Elliott has pointed out, Europeans could only envision the New World within the confines of Old World intellectual frameworks with which they were familiar. Sometimes that meant that their visions and ambitions were informed by the biblical and classical literature in which they were invariably immersed. Imperial writers were especially enamoured, not surprisingly, by literature of and about the Roman Empire. Their thinking and writing was also influenced by a feudal world recently lost, albeit often imaginatively and idealistically recalled. Their ambitions for the New World were also shaped by ideals and perceived problems of their own time. These different influences were not necessarily mutually exclusive. Biblical, classical, feudal and contemporaneous influences are often evident in the writings and schemes of single individuals. Whatever the mixture of these influences, though, imperial writers and colonial proprietors were rarely radical visionaries who imagined a new kind of future, but more often were reactionaries who imagined a rejuvenated past or a purified present in the New World.[13]

What they imagined nevertheless varied enormously. Some pictured the Old World as a Garden of Eden, others as a religious refuge, and others still as a New Jerusalem. Some envisioned New World settlements as military garrisons, though most recognized that successful colonization required the transplantation of some sort of civil society. For some, that civil society would be hierarchical, for others it would be more egalitarian. Few (Richard Hakluyt the younger was the most notable exception) foresaw the New World as what it would actually become: a field of competition for the visions and ambitions of migrants and settlers.

Thomas More's *Utopia* presented the New World as a purified version of the Old. 'Utopia' meant literally 'nowhere', but indicated a place free from poverty and misery which was thus an 'example for correction' of European 'errors'. Historian Arthur Slavin argues that Thomas More's attack on private property was inspired by Amerigo Vespucci's account of the lack of it among Amerindians. More's imaginary New World was thus, as Jack P. Greene has said, 'the antithesis of the Old', but it nevertheless drew on concepts of an imagined golden age of the ancient world. Some went even further back than More in their attempts to mould the New World within their own historical, moral and intellectual frameworks, depicting America as a new Garden of Eden. Arthur Barlow's 1584 account of Roanoke, edited by Walter Raleigh, was one of many that portrayed the New World in prelapsarian terms, and Thomas Harriot wrote of the same place that 'The earth bringeth forth all things in abundance as in the first creation, without toil or labor.'

In more practical and concrete terms, some saw the New World as a possible haven for religious refugees. This notion originated with French Huguenots, for whom England itself was a religious refuge and of whom there were around 60 with seafaring knowledge and experience in the service of Edward VI in 1546. Under Elizabeth I, in 1562, Jean Ribault was licensed with Thomas Stukeley to found a Protestant colony on the Florida coast, though nothing came from the English side on that. Richard Hakluyt the younger thought America might 'provide a safe and sure place to receave people from all parts of the worlde that are forced to flee for the truthe of gods worde'. In 1582, Sir Humphrey Gilbert sub-patented some 8,000,000 acres of land to potential colonizers, including large grants to a group of Catholic gentry headed by Sir George Peckham and Sir Thomas Gerrard, anticipating the settling of Maryland as a refuge for Catholics. Later, settlers would found Plymouth and Massachusetts as godly commonwealths for puritans dissatisfied with or persecuted by the Church of England. Other New Englanders founded Rhode Island as a refuge from intolerant Massachusetts puritans, and William Penn would found Pennsylvania as a haven for Quakers and a bastion of toleration.[14]

Though it is widely believed that Atlantic migration was motivated in large part by flight from religious persecution, this was in fact uncommon. First, it was confined to puritan New Englanders, Quaker Pennsylvanians and Catholic Marylanders, and to some other smaller migrations to particular localities, such as German Moravians in Pennsylvania. Second, even those who migrated to these areas were rarely fleeing persecution. More often, they were simply seeking to create a better religious community. Furthermore, there were many among the migrants to these regions who were not co-religionists of the charter holders in any case. Although imperial writers took it for granted that settlers would be Christian and would found churches of one sort or another, usually Anglican, their most elaborate imaginings of New World society were, in fact, secular in nature.

Because the origins of colonization were closely connected to trade with and plunder of Spanish New World settlements and ships, the colonization schemes of sixteenth-century sea dogs tended to have military foundations. And though these men sometimes realized that permanent colonization would require the transplantation of some form of civil society, their ventures often put military priorities first. Sir Humphrey Gilbert's plan of 1577 involved establishing a New World military base and the mission of 1578 eventuated in nothing more than a series of depredations against the Spanish. By 1582, however, he was proposing the establishment of civil government, churches, schools and charities in the New World, and the state-subsidised emigration of the poor to these new societies. The particular kind of social order he wished to create in Norumbega, however, was an idealized agrarian England under his own inheritable lordship. In a distinctly feudal hypothetical arrangement, tenants would provide military equipment and manpower and pay seigneurial dues. Land would be given over to the Anglican Church to pay for a fully developed ecclesiastical establishment with parishes in which inhabitants would pay tithes. The colony would be a commercial enterprise, though, with licensed merchants monopolizing imports and exports in exchange for fees and shares of customs duties going to Gilbert. Gilbert's quasi-feudal plans came to nothing, but their importance perhaps lies in the example they provided to later colonial proprietors, especially the Calverts of Maryland and the lords proprietors of the Carolinas.

Like Gilbert with Norumbega, Raleigh envisioned the first Roanoke colony militarily. Ralph Lane's original colony was, therefore, a military outpost feeding off Indians with settlers searching for gold, rather than farming or forming a civil society. In Lane's view, 'nothing else can bring this country to be inhabited by our nation'. Yet, the second Roanoke plan, White's City of Raleigh in the Chesapeake, did envision a civil and political order, although it was finally built in Roanoke thanks to the military predilections of some of the seamen on the mission who wished to plunder the Spanish. Again it was hierarchical, though it lacked the elaborate feudal structure that Gilbert wished to create. Raleigh, as overlord, would choose a governor who would make almost any political arrangements that seemed expeditious, within the bounds of English law. In this instance, land was to be granted to families and merchants, creating a large freeholder population similar to those created (intentionally or not) by later colonial proprietors. After these efforts failed, though, Raleigh reverted to emulating the Spanish conquistadors in his Guiana misadventures.[15]

The Jamestown colony of 1607 began, like the first Roanoke venture, as a military enterprise not unlike those of the Spanish conquistadors. Only through trial and error did a settled, civil society emerge. As subsequent chapters show, all other charter groups envisioned some form of civil society for their colonies, varying from neo-feudal ventures in Maryland and the Carolinas and religious communities in New England, to the egalitarian experiment of Georgia. Military considerations remained part of the process of colonization, though, because of the enduring threats of the Spanish, French and Amerindians. Even in philanthropic Georgia, slavery and the agglomeration of large landholdings were forbidden, not only to engineer a white yeoman society, but also to provide a secure population against the threat of Spanish Florida to the south, the black majority of South Carolina to the north and the potential for these hostile forces to forge Amerindian alliances.

Of course, the creation of civil societies, or the recreation of England or Britain in whatever form in America, required the mass movement of English men and women across the Atlantic. Hakluyt perceived how that requirement was consonant with England's need to depopulate. England, Hakluyt said, echoing a common contemporary view, was

more populous than ever heretofore: So that nowe there are of every arte and science so many, that they can hardly lyve one by another, nay rather they are readie
to eat upp one another: yea many thousands are wthin this Realme, wch havinge
no way to be sett on worke be either mutinous and seeke alteration in the state,
or at leaste very burdensome to the common wealthe, and often fall to pilfering
and thevinge and other lewdnes, whereby all the prisons of the lande are daily
pestred and stuffed full of them, where either they pitifully pyne awaye, or els at
lengthe are miserably hanged.

Hakluyt's 'remedy to all these inconveniences' was that

these pety theves mighte be condemped for certen yeres in the westerne partes . . .
in sawinge and fellinge of timbers for masts of shippes and deale boordes; in bur-
ninge of the firres and pine trees to make pitche tarr rosen and sope asshes, in
beatinge and workinge of hempe for cordage: and in the more sowthern partes in
settinge them to worke in mynes of golde, silver, copper, leade, and yron, in drag-
ginge for perles and currall

and in cultivating wine, sugar and other goods that could not be grown or
produced at home. And America, if not England, had use for all 'kindes of
artificers, husbandmen, seamen, merchauntes, souldiers, capitaines, phisi-
tions, lawyers, devines, Cosmographers, hidrographers, Astronomers,
historiographers, yea old folkes, lame persons, women, and younge children'. Some early would-be colonizers had similar views. Humphrey
Gilbert's *A Discourse of a Discoverie for a New Passage to Cataia* (1576),
clearly an influence on Hakluyt, advocated shipment to America of 'such
needie people of our Countrie, which now trouble the common welthe, and
through want here at home, are inforced to commit outragious offences,
whereby they are dayly consumed with the Gallows'. His Norumbega plan
even offered free land to families who financed their own emigration.[16]
As Gilbert foresaw, colonial charter holders would have to offer land to
attract the settlers who would make their colonies work. The Virginia
Company initially attempted to run its colony using employees and servants, but after a decade it implemented a headright system that offered 50
acres of land to people who moved to the colony at their own expense, and
another 50 acres for every family member and servant they brought with
them. Other charter holders followed suit, some offering free land to indentured servants after they completed their terms of service. Once agricultural settlements were established, though, colonists needed more migrants to
satisfy their demand for labour. Charter holders, colonial governments and
even private members of elites thus began publishing promotional literature
that stressed, first and foremost, the economic opportunity that America
offered. William Penn, who established Pennsylvania in 1681, attempted to
attract settlers by writing that land in the colony was available for 'next to

nothing'. That land was fertile too. Gabriel Thomas wrote that farmers in
the Middle Colonies could get 'twice the encrease of Corn for every Bushel
they sow' than English farmers could 'from the richest land they have'. The
New World therefore offered the opportunity to escape what Thomas
Nairne called the 'Vexation of Dependance' that afflicted so many Britons.
John Norris assured his readers that migrants to America could *'thrive in
the World, and become Rich'*.

Promotional writers also highlighted the absence in the colonies of those
institutions that in England encumbered the middling sorts and impoverished the poor. Many emphasized the cheapness and simplicity of government and consequent low levels of taxation, the absence of an overbearing
aristocracy, of a landed class that could impose enclosure, and of established religious authority and therefore tithes. In short, they stressed the
security in property that resulted from freedom. The Earl of Warwick perceived the attractiveness of these conditions for migrants as early as 1640.
Seeking to recruit colonists from Bermuda and St Lucia to go to Tobago, he
offered free transportation, arms and 'great freedomes' to 'incourage them
to stay and perfect that plantacion'. A century later, Archibald Cummings,
using a frequently cited biblical image, wrote that, in the absence of oppres-
sive political and religious authorities, an American could dwell *'safely
under his own Vine, and securely enjoy the fruits of his labour'*.[17]

Colonial promotional literature exaggerated the level of opportunity for
individual betterment that the New World offered. It also played down the
risks of oceanic travel, the New World disease environment and the sheer
hard labour involved in carving out a new life in the colonies. It does not
therefore describe what the bulk of migrants actually experienced, but it
was calibrated as precisely as possible to appeal to potential migrants' aspirations and ambitions, and thus tells us much about why so many people
migrated to the New World. For a fuller explanation of these aspirations
and ambitions, though, we must look at the migrants themselves and the
society they were seeking to leave.

British population, economy, society and migration

Hakluyt and his contemporaries believed that England and Wales were
overpopulated and that this problem could be solved by migration. The
population of England and Wales grew steadily from around 3,000,000 in
the middle of the sixteenth century to 4,000,000 by 1600 and 5,000,000 by
1650. It then fell slightly in the later seventeenth century, but passed
5,000,000 once again by 1720 and then rose with unprecedented rapidity
to near 9,000,000 by 1800, when industrialization was taking effect in
some areas of the country. The growing need for labour in developing
extractive and manufacturing industries was by then making some commentators complain that England and Wales were underpopulated.[18]

In truth, then, there were times and places when there were mismatches between population, on the one hand, and resources, wealth distribution, labour supply and availability of work, on the other, and these mismatches prompted people to migrate. A lot of people migrated within Britain, many of them eventually making their way overseas. Historian Peter Laslett first identified the extent of early modern English migration in his detailed studies of local life. Among the 180 residents of Cogenhoe, Northamptonshire, in 1628, for example, far from all of them being long-term residents whose ancestors had lived there since time immemorial, 94 had arrived in the previous decade. In just a dozen years, between 1676 and 1688, some 40 per cent of the residents of Clayworth, Nottinghamshire, moved away from the parish. Typically, of 100 families living in a given parish in 1600, the descendents of only 16 would still be there a century later. Many of these migrations were local in character, as with the many who moved to neighbouring parishes to get married. One study of 5 eastern counties shows that few moved more than 10 miles and most simply moved to the parish next door. Nevertheless, many moved further and more often. Longer-distance migration was endemic, as boys and young men moved to serve apprenticeships, and long-distance migration increased dramatically during periods of population growth and economic hardship, such as the 1580s to 1650s in England and Wales and, with continued harvest failures, up to 1700 in lowland Scotland and after 1750 in the Highlands. Enough people lived and died in the villages and towns where they were born to provide some stability within English, Welsh and Scottish communities, but so many moved that, as historian Alison Games puts it, migration was 'an entirely normal activity, a regular part of the life cycle, a common response to personal ambition, economic hardship, or perceived opportunities elsewhere'.[19]

Sufficient numbers of people moved to cause rapid urbanization. In 1600, Bristol and Norwich had 12,000 to 13,000 residents each and were the only cities besides London with 5-figure populations. A century later, Bristol had 20,000 and Norwich 30,000, while 5 others had populations over 10,000, joined by 7 more after another 50 years. In 1500, just over 3 per cent of English and Welsh people lived in towns of 10,000 people or more. By 1800, just over 20 per cent did so. In Scotland, the urban proportion of the population rose from 1.6 per cent to over 17 per cent. In Ireland, no one lived in a town of 10,000 people in 1500, but 7 per cent did so in 1800. The growth of London was especially remarkable. London's population increased more than threefold from 60,000 in 1500 to 200,000 by 1600. In the next century it grew almost threefold again, reaching 575,000 by 1700, despite plague and fire. By the time of the first decennial census in 1801, London had 950,000 inhabitants. Population historians E.A. Wrigley and R.S. Schofield estimated that, amazingly, one-in-six of the populations of England and Wales in the early modern era spent at least part of their lives in London. Port cities like London, Bristol and, later,

Liverpool and Glasgow, were not only destinations for internal migrants but also points of departure to the New World.[20]

In the vast majority of cases it is impossible to identify what motivated individuals' particular decisions to migrate, internally or overseas, but the state of local and national economies provides a general contextual background. Throughout the seventeenth and eighteenth centuries, people moved because of poor local conditions, because they were drawn by opportunities elsewhere or because of a mixture of both reasons. The overall weight of push and pull factors, however, seems to have shifted towards the latter from the mid-seventeenth century. A series of poor harvests resulted in starvation and disease from the 1590s, including a plague epidemic in 1604, although thereafter the economy was dynamic enough to keep famine at bay most of the time, and the poor relief system was generally extensive enough to prevent local or family subsistence crises. Nevertheless, economic and associated hardships were a normal part of life for many early modern English, Welsh and Scottish people. Plague returned in 1665–67, and this outbreak only ended with the fire that killed tens of thousands of Londoners. Throughout this era, enclosures of common lands severely impoverished many of those whose subsistence was the most marginal. The decline of the cloth industry from the 1550s meant a century of high rates of unemployment in areas that had depended on this trade, East Anglia in particular. After Culloden, the Highland clearances prompted particularly high rates of Scottish emigration.

By the mid-seventeenth century, however, conditions in general improved, notwithstanding regional exceptions and variations. Historians debate whether there was any such thing as an 'agricultural revolution' at this time, but crop yields rose by 30 per cent between 1450 and 1650 and England became not only able to feed itself but also to export agricultural produce. From the middle of the seventeenth century, the economy grew, inflation declined and wages rose. Furthermore, the economy developed, as rising wealth allowed people to afford increasing varieties of consumer goods. The period 1660 to 1800 thus saw a large increase in the size of the 'middling sort', especially smaller traders and skilled craftsmen, and the beginnings of the rise of industrial capitalists and mass wage labour. Just as dramatic, if not more so, was the development of England's overseas trade. A backwater dependent on wool exports to Antwerp in 1550, by 1700 England was the hub of a global trade network, created in large part by colonization.

People's decisions about moving on or staying put also depended to some extent on their place in a changing socio-economic order (although, of course, people's circumstances also depended on other variables such as individual diligence and good luck and bad). It is difficult to categorize people in precise socio-economic terms because of the innate complexity of social systems, local and regional variation and changing times, and more difficult to link socio-economic status to individual decisions about migration. But, again, certain general facts about poverty and opportunity are knowable and salient to a general understanding of what motivated some to move. Early modern English society was highly complex and hierarchical, reflecting a belief in a Great Chain of Being descending from God and the angels, through kings, down to servants and slaves. In 1688 Gregory King compiled the first ever census of socio-economic status, based on a mixture of rank, occupation and income, and modern studies usually corroborate his general findings. He identified 31 'Ranks, Degrees, Titles and Qualifications', beginning with 200 temporal lords whose average annual family incomes were £6060, far outstripping the 800 baronets, bishops, knights, esquires, greater merchants, gentlemen and higher civil servants, whose incomes ranged from £1500 to £240. Those categories accounted for only 1 per cent of the population. The next 4 per cent included lesser merchants, lesser office holders, lawyers and greater artisans, whose incomes ranged from £200 to £91. Below what contemporaries called these 'better sorts' of people (an imprecise term that does not correspond precisely with King's categories) were the 'middling sorts' of lesser merchants, tradesmen, shopkeepers, freeholders, military officers and clergymen, who comprised about 15 per cent of the population and earned between £80 and £45 a year. The 'middling' to 'lower' or 'poorer sorts' included ordinary farmers, seamen, miners and lesser traders, who constituted 20 per cent of the population and had annual incomes ranging from £42 10 shillings to £15. Among the 'lower sorts' were 284,997 labouring people and outservants, who comprised 20 per cent of the population and had average incomes of £15. Individuals and families who subsisted on less than £15 a year, including 35,000 common soldiers, 313,183 cottagers and paupers and 23,489 vagrants, made up 40 per cent. Vagrants' average annual income was £2. In the period 1685 to 1701, up to half the population would at some time depend on poor laws, with about a fifth of families receiving alms on a regular basis. For many, things improved little over the eighteenth century. In a survey of 1801–03, Patrick Colquhoun found that the average annual family income was £8000 for 287 peers and £10 for 260,179 paupers and 175,218 vagrants. Gregory King did not mention slaves, but roughly 14,000 of them lived in England by 1770, working mostly in port cities as servants, seamen and general labourers. In 1772, however, in the case of *Somersett* v. *Stuart*, William Murray, Lord Mansfield and Chief Justice of the Court of King's Bench, ruled that slavery could not exist without positive law, paving the way for the institution to wither away within Britain.[21]

What did these inequalities mean? One important measure of fortune and status in early modern Britain was the line between 'independence' and 'dependence'. Independents were those with the economic wherewithal to be free from the will of anyone else, while dependants were subject to the interests and whims of others. Independence and dependence were therefore

consonant with one of the most prevalent contemporary definitions of freedom and unfreedom. And the possibility of dependence at home or independence in America seems to have played a key role in many people's decisions
to migrate. At the head of the different categories of independents was an
increasingly wealthy aristocracy. In 1700, peers of the realm held up to a
fifth of landed wealth, rising to almost a quarter by 1800, much of it
acquired from the declining gentry and yeomanry of substantial farmers. In
1800, the gentry still held 50 to 60 per cent of landed wealth and the yeomanry 15 to 20 per cent. If some categories of independents were declining
in relative size, others, ranging from artisans and traders to merchants and
industrialists, were growing. It is often difficult to identify the exact point at
which independence and dependence divided, but one crude measure is the
property qualification for voting. Only those with a stake in government (a
principal function of which, for many people, was to secure property) and
those whose votes could not be influenced by others were thought to be
qualified for the franchise. That measure of independence was set in 1430
at ownership of a freehold property worth 40 shillings a year according to
the land tax; and another measure was membership of the male sex (women
were considered dependent, however much property they owned). The size
of the electorate, a rough indication of the number of independents, reached
a peak of 300,000 in 1715 – 24 per cent of adult men (it declined to 17 per
cent by 1800).

The vast majority of the population were therefore dependants. Besides
all women and children, dependants included husbandmen and smaller
artisans and traders whose subsistence was modestly secure in good years
but vulnerable in bad ones. Next were agricultural and mechanical labourers and, in the eighteenth century, growing numbers of industrial labourers,
who worked long, hard hours for low wages. In the early seventeenth century, just over 13 per cent of the population of England and Wales were
agricultural servants and 60 per cent of people aged 15 to 24 were servants
and apprentices. Most servants worked on annual contracts and lived in the
households of their masters. Servitude was not necessarily permanent, as
many young people acquired enough capital to make independent lives for
themselves later, so a degree of mobility was built into the social system and
people's life cycles. Apprenticeship could result in nothing more than wage
labour, but could lead to master artisanship. Dependants also included paupers and vagrants, whose numbers increased even after the economy grew
and wages rose. Slaves were regarded as being at the end of a long chain of
dependent people, and their condition was not widely regarded as pecu-
liarly unfree until at least the late eighteenth century.

People from all across this social spectrum, from lords to slaves,
migrated, although the very wealthiest and the very poorest free people
moved in proportionally smaller numbers than others. Some migrants were
members of the gentry who wished to enhance their fortunes or sons of gen-

tlemen who wished to make theirs, and some of them were royalist refugees from the civil war and interregnum. The bulk of migrants, however, came from the 'middling sorts', ranging from smaller merchants and lawyers to sons and daughters of yeoman farmers, and, in roughly equal numbers, from the 'lower sorts', including husbandmen, labourers, servants, debtors, vagrants (migrants by definition) and criminals. A great many existed on the cusp of independence and dependence, either because of their own fluctuating fortunes or because they were offspring of parents who were independent but did not have the means to cede that condition to all their children. Many others were dependants who wanted more for themselves, who wished to break free from the Great Chain of Being.[22]

Atlantic migration

The scale of Atlantic migration was enormous. The most recent research finds that between 1600 and 1800, 1,042,100 Europeans migrated to British North America and the West Indies. In the first quarter-century of English colonization, migrants numbered only just over 6000. As the colonies established themselves, though, migration increased rapidly: almost a quarter of a million people crossed the Atlantic between 1626 and 1675. During the next half-century, the number of migrants fell to under 170,000. Then it rose increasingly rapidly to 137,500 between 1726 and 1750, 227,600 between 1751 and 1775, and 252,300 from 1776 to 1800, growing fastest after the end of the War of American Independence in 1783.

These overall figures hide some important patterns in the particular directions of transatlantic migration. Migration rates to the Caribbean, for example, were higher in the seventeenth century than in the eighteenth. Some 81,000 migrated to the islands between 1600 and 1650, almost all of them after 1625, well over twice the number who travelled to mainland North America. Numbers of Caribbean-bound migrants tailed off, however, as the sugar boom allowed small cadres of large planters to amass the bulk of limited island real estate. There were still 64,600 European migrants to the British Caribbean between 1651 and 1675, slightly fewer than went to North America. Between 1676 and 1700, there were just 32,900, and there were fewer than 30,000 in the next two quarter-centuries. Numbers rose to 33,300 between 1751 and 1775, and then fell to 22,300 from 1776 to 1800.

In all, between 1600 and 1800, 289,900 Europeans went to the British Caribbean, compared to 752,200 who went to mainland North America. Only about 6000 travelled to the mainland between 1607 and 1650, but numbers rose to 34,300 in 1626–50 and 69,800 in 1651–75. Migration then declined slightly to 67,000 in 1676–1700 and, more significantly, to 42,000 in 1701–25. After the end of the War of the Spanish Succession, migration to North America grew again, to 108,800 in 1726–50, and then hugely to 194,300 in 1751–75 and 230,000 in 1776–1800.[23]

British emigration to the New World far outstripped that from any other European country. The highest estimations claim that 437,000 Spaniards left their homeland for their enormous overseas territories, an average of 3000 a year from 1500–1650 (and triple the traditionally accepted estimate). About 500 Portuguese per year migrated across the Atlantic in the same era, and about 600 French (less than a third of them moving to French mainland North America). While the English rapidly settled the east coast of North America in the seventeenth century, the semi-feudal *seigneuries* of New France and especially the settlements of Spanish Florida grew only slowly. Even New Netherland was peopled by, at most, 10,000 Dutch migrants.

In the seventeenth century, about six out of seven migrants to Anglo-America were English and Welsh, the rest were mostly Irish, though there were some Scots too. Following the establishment of Pennsylvania in 1681, however, many more continental Europeans migrated to British New World territories. Irish and especially Scottish migrants outnumbered the English by more than three-to-one in the eighteenth century, and around 100,000 Rhineland Germans and smaller numbers of French migrants also moved to British America. The early domination of the English, however, ultimately gave British America an English cultural orientation, although different regions of North America reflected the different regions of the British Isles. As historian David Hackett Fischer has shown, migrants to the Chesapeake and Lower South regions tended to come from London and the Home Counties, those to the West Indies from the English south-west, those to New England from East Anglia and those to the Middle Colonies from the north Midlands and Wales, while eighteenth-century migrants to the colonial western backcountries often came from northern England, Scotland and northern Ireland. Hackett Fischer may have overstated the exactness of regional cultural transplantation, however, first by overestimating the cultural homogeneity of these broad regions of origin. Also, as Alison Games points out, every part of England and eventually Britain was represented in every part of colonial America, especially following what historian Virginia DeJohn Anderson has called 'the great reshuffling' that resulted from secondary internal migration within North America. Furthermore, as subsequent chapters show, colonial and regional geography and economies and other historical contingencies played a part in shaping the varying cultures that developed in Anglo- and British America.[24]

One of those contingencies was that migration was heavily male dominated, which partly accounts for the inchoate character of early colonial life. Alison Games found that 94 per cent of migrants from London in 1635 were men, although, as she says, there may have been more women in earlier and later years and from other ports of departure. Even so, 75 per cent of English indentured migrants in the seventeenth century were male, rising to 90 per cent in the eighteenth century. Another contingency was the social background of migrants. Of European migrants to America, over 75 per cent went there unfree – a statistic that cautions against regarding early America as 'middle class' (and that is before we even begin to consider enslaved migrants from Africa). Some of the unfree were redemptioners, as many as 54,000 were convicts, but most were indentured servants, that is, they were contracted to work for and live with a master for a time in exchange for the costs of their transportation and early subsistence in America. Voluntary migrants in the seventeenth century were usually contracted to 4 or 5 years of servitude, while convicts following the Transportation Act of 1718 usually served between 7 and 14 years, depending on the seriousness of their crime. The main information on seventeenth-century servant migration derives from the records of 3000 who moved to the Chesapeake from Bristol in 1654–61 and 750 more who travelled there from London in 1683–84. Roughly equal numbers of these migrants came from four English social groups: yeomen and husbandmen; tradesmen and craftsmen; apprentices and servants; and unskilled labourers. The social mixture of migrants varied somewhat from one colonial region to another and was most exceptional in the case of migrants to New England, who tended to be better off, older and travelled more often in family and even neighbourhood groups, helping to account for the distinct history of the puritan colonies.

The conditions and treatment of New World indentured servants varied, as did the availability of legal redress in cases of abuse. Generally, though, colonial indentured servitude commodified labourers to a far greater extent than did English agricultural and other forms of service. English agricultural labourers could negotiate year-long contracts with yeomen and husbandmen at annual agricultural fairs, but indentured servants typically found themselves sold by ships' captains to American planters, at whose hands they often fared ill. The new, loose communities of the New World did not, at least at first, offer the social and cultural restraints that long-established community customs exercised on English masters, especially if masters were tempted in the early years of colonization by the enormous profits to be made from staple commodities such as sugar and tobacco. Even so, those who reported back home on the ill-treatment of servants in the colonies helped to moderate the institution. Too much bad publicity, after all, would have discouraged other potential servant migrants. For migrants, servitude offered a means to finance their travel across the Atlantic and a way to secure food, clothing and lodgings for their early years in their new homes. At the end of their terms, servants sometimes received 'freedom dues'. These usually included clothes and some agricultural produce or seeds, but they occasionally included money and even land. In the early years of settlement, when labour was scarce and land was abundant and cheap, many former servants took up tenancies and gradually acquired the capital to buy land. With a lot of hard work and a little bit of luck, therefore, even quite poor white migrants might achieve the kind of landed independence that colonial promotional literature promised, although the growth of slavery and rise in land prices diminished opportunity in most colonies as time went by.[25]

Migrants soon discovered that promotional literature and especially immigration agents, who made even more attractive promises, played down the risks and hardships involved in migration and carving out a new life in the New World. Early travel across the Atlantic rarely took less than five weeks. More often it took two months; deaths aboard ships were common and hardship was inevitable. If migrants survived the journey, up to half of early seventeenth-century arrivals to the semi-tropical colonies from Maryland southwards would die during 'seasoning' within a year of their arrival. As Alison Games has said, there was a 'tone of macabre lunacy to colonial undertakings'. Yet these risks and hardships only made migrants more determined to reap the benefits of their endeavours for themselves, to achieve their own visions and ambitions, whatever imperial writers and colonial proprietors might have had in mind.[26]

The slave trade, slaves and slavery

Whether European travellers to America were subsistence migrants or betterment migrants, and whether or not they were fleeing religious or political dangers, most went there by choice, quite unlike those who went there in chains. Of the 3,375,250 people who crossed the Atlantic to settle in Anglo- and British America, some 2,333,150 (69 per cent of the total) were African captives of the slave trade. Of these, 2,045,550 went to the Caribbean as a first destination, though some later moved to mainland North America, while 287,600 went directly to the mainland.

Because Anglo-Americans relied heavily on indentured servants to begin with, only about 3400 slaves arrived in the colonies by 1650, 1400 in the mainland, 2000 in the Caribbean. Rapid economic growth in the colonies and the falling numbers of English servant migrants in the second half of the seventeenth century, however, led to a spectacular growth in the African slave trade, especially after 1675. In the second half of the century, some 10,700 slaves were imported to the mainland and 235,700 to the Caribbean. Between 1701 and 1750, another 134,200 went to North America and 609,000 to the Caribbean. The third quarter of the eighteenth century saw the peak of the slave trade to British America, with some 116,900 going to the mainland and 634,950 to the Caribbean. Between 1776 and 1800, numbers fell to 24,400 going to the United States and 563,900 to the British Caribbean, as opposition to the slave trade developed in Britain and America. Britain abolished the trade in 1807, the United States in 1808, although most American states had banned it earlier.

Like almost everything else in early America, the institution of slavery evolved slowly, shaped by trial and error and the unanticipated contingencies of colonial settlement and development. It therefore changed over time and varied in character from place to place. Although Anglo-American colonists could have followed the example of large-scale Iberian-American plantation slavery, they did not do so at first. Early planters in the Chesapeake depended most heavily on the labour of indentured servants, which was cheaper and more readily available. Slavery only arrived in North America by accident, when a Dutch man-of-war unexpectedly arrived in Jamestown in 1619 with 20 slaves raided from the Spanish West Indies. Even then, it was not until the 1660s that Anglo-Americans began importing slaves in great numbers, something that was only desirable as the supply of servants declined, and only possible because of growing capital accumulation in the colonies.

Large-scale plantation slavery eventually turned most Anglo- and British-American colonies into what historians call 'slave societies', in which economy, society, culture and politics were definitively shaped by the institution of slavery, as distinct from 'societies with slaves', where enslavement did not substantially affect any other social or cultural arrangements or civil or political institutions. The plantation regions of Anglo-America were societies with slaves before they became slave societies. As societies with slaves, the institution of slavery was relatively flexible and race relations were quite fluid. Racism and oppression existed in these early years, but they had no force of law and little force of custom. Slaves were therefore sometimes freed, on occasion becoming land- and even slave-owners, and blacks and whites worked together, socialized together and even married each other. But as dependence on slave labour grew, Anglo-Americans made what historian Winthrop D. Jordan called an 'unthinking decision', which, pragmatically and with little consideration about justification, prompted them to batten down the hatches of enslavement. At that point, they defined slaves as chattels for life, defined slavery as a condition inherited through the female line, limited opportunities for slaves to attain freedom, dictated almost all areas of their lives, prescribed torturous and often deadly punishments for infractions of the law (paradoxically ascribing legal responsibility to people who were defined as legal non-persons) and established laws to police slave quarters and search the countryside for bondspeople who were off their plantations without permission.

As well as slavery itself, race prejudice took time to develop. When the English first enslaved Africans, they, like the Spanish and the Portuguese, drew on negative connotations of blackness that already existed in European culture. These included, for example, the biblical curse by which Noah condemned to perpetual servitude Canaan's 'dark-skinned' son Ham and all his descendants after Canaan mocked his father's nakedness. Yet in the early years of American colonization, there was a good deal of uncertainty about whether the right to enslave rested on race, religion or the ancient tradition of sparing the lives of prisoners of war in exchange for their enslavement. Some masters freed their slaves as soon as those slaves were baptized as Christians (a means of escape from slavery that many slaves were quick to seize). But the new slave laws (including ones that explicitly asserted the right to enslave black Christians) and developing customs increasingly associated slavery with blackness.

Even within the plantation slave societies thereby created, there were variations in the characteristics of the institution. Massive slave populations and increasing levels of absentee ownership in the Carolinas and especially the Caribbean meant that plantations there often resembled factories, with slaves brutally reduced to the status of expendable commodities. Chesapeake planters were by no means incapable of brutality, but, with fewer slaves and less absenteeism, they were more inclined towards a paternalistic approach to relations with their bondspeople. New England and the Middle Colonies, on the other hand, never became plantation economies and remained societies with slaves.

Given the vast power differential that slavery created, African-Americans were less able than free people actively to shape the course of colonial and imperial history. That did not mean, however, that they did not influence these histories, at some points and in some ways quite profoundly. A great deal of the wealth that free Americans coveted and jealously guarded consisted of slaves (enslaved people were, after all, capital assets). Slave labourers cleared and worked the land and slave hands planted and picked the crops that American prosperity was largely built upon. The personal dependence enforced upon slaves provided a counterpoint to the personal independence that other colonists enjoyed or aspired to, and thus American slavery helped to define American freedom. Furthermore, slaves aspired to freedom by resisting and rebelling against the institution, including making bids for the same rights and liberties that white colonists claimed during the American Revolution. The pressures that slaves thereby put on masters altered the way the institution worked in the plantation colonies, and the pressures they put on American consciences led to the institution's abolition in the non-plantation mainland after American Independence.[27]

Initially, the populations of Anglo-America grew only slowly, reaching just 9500 by 1630, on the eve of the Great Migration, and 145,000 by 1660. By 1710, though, the British-American population reached just over half a million, and in the longer settled regions most of the population was by that time Creole or American born. By the time the rebellions against British tax measures began in 1764, the colonial population topped 2,000,000.[28] The first permanent Anglo-American settlement was founded at Jamestown, Virginia, in May 1607. The establishment of St Mary's City, Maryland, in 1634, gave Virginians a colonial neighbour in the Chesapeake region. Within two years of the founding of Jamestown, English men and women began settling islands in the Atlantic Ocean and the Caribbean Sea. Twelve years after Jamestown, the Pilgrim Fathers landed at Plymouth, and in 1630 the Great Migration began, carrying thousands to the other New England colonies of Massachusetts (which absorbed Plymouth Colony 62 years later), New Hampshire, Connecticut and Rhode Island. Later in the seventeenth century, the English founded the Middle Colonies of New York, New Jersey, Pennsylvania and Delaware, and the Lower South mainland colonies of the Carolinas and, in 1732, Georgia. After the 1713 Treaty of Utrecht, Britons established domination in the northern colonies of Nova Scotia and Newfoundland. A half-century later, after the Peace of Paris settled the Seven Years War, Britain took over Quebec, Florida and some of the French Caribbean as well. Most of these colonies were founded with some kind of vision in mind, but, as the following chapters show, in every case those visions gave way to the ambitions of the hundreds of thousands of migrants who settled them and the millions of their descendants who inhabited them.

Notes

1 Jack P. Greene, *The Intellectual Construction of America: Exceptionalism and Identity from 1492 to 1800* (Chapel Hill, 1993), chapter 2; David Armitage, 'The New World and British Historical Thought: From Richard Hakluyt to William Robertson', in Karen Ordahl Kupperman, ed., *America in European Consciousness, 1493–1750* (Chapel Hill, 1995), pp. 52–75 and *The Ideological Origins of the British Empire* (Cambridge, 2000), chapter 3.

2 'Discourse of Western Planting', in E.G.R. Taylor, ed., *The Writings and Correspondence of the Two Richard Hakluyts* (2 vols, London, 1935), 2, pp. 314, 280, 317, 270, 211, 222.

3 'Western Planting', Taylor, *Writings of the Two Hakluyts*, 2, pp. 290–1, 293; J.G.A. Pocock, *The Ancient Constitution and the Feudal Law* (Cambridge, 1987), pp. 237–8.

4 Anthony Pagden, 'The Struggle for Legitimacy and the Image of Empire in the Atlantic to c.1700', in Nicholas Canny, ed., *The Oxford History of the British Empire* Volume I: *The Origins of Empire: British Overseas Enterprise to the Close of the Seventeenth Century* (Oxford, 1998), p. 37.

5 Armitage, *Ideological Origins*, p. 98; Pagden, 'Struggle for Legitimacy', p. 41.

6 'Virginias Verger', in Samuel Purchas, *Hakluyt Posthumus or Purchas His Pilgrimes* (20 vols, Glasgow, 1905), cited in Nicholas Canny, 'England's New World and the Old, 1480s–1630s', in Canny, ed., *Origins of Empire*, p. 157.

7 John Locke, *Second Treatise*, 108, in Peter Laslett, ed., *Locke's Two Treatises of Government* (2nd edn, Cambridge, 1967), p. 358; Pagden,

'Struggle for Legitimacy', pp. 40–7; Barbara Arneil, *John Locke and America: The Defence of English Colonialism* (Oxford, 1996).

8 Edward Surtz and J.H. Hexter, eds, *The Complete Works of St Thomas More* (4 vols, New Haven, 1965), 4, p. 137; Donne cited in Pagden, 'Struggle for Legitimacy', pp. 42–3; Locke, *Second Treatise*, 49, p. 319.

9 Karen Ordahl Kupperman, 'The Changing Definition of America', in Kupperman, ed., *America in European Consciousness,* p. 5; Luca Condignola, 'The Holy See and the Conversion of the Indians in French and British North America, 1486–1760', in ibid., p. 195.

10 Taylor, *Writings of the Two Hakluyts*, 2, pp. 214, 216; Pagden, 'Struggle for Legitimacy', p. 35.

11 David Beers Quinn, Alison M. Quinn and Susan Hillier, eds, *New American World: A Documentary History of North America to 1612* (5 vols, London, 1979), 3, p. 151; Paul Hulton, *America, 1585: The Complete Drawings of John White* (Chapel Hill, 1984), p. 130; Strachey, *The Historie of Travell into Virginian Brittania* (1612) and Winslow, 'Good News from New England', cited in Canny, 'England's New World', pp. 160, 168.

12 Robert A. Williams, *The American Indian in Western Legal Thought: The Discourses of Conquest* (New York, 1990), p. 200; Surtz and Hexter, *Complete Works of More*, 4, p. 137; Pagden, 'Struggle for Legitimacy', pp. 42–3; Canny, 'England's New World', p. 168.

13 J.H. Elliott, *The Old World and the New, 1492–1650* (Cambridge, 1970); Edmundo O'Gorman, *The Invention of America: An Inquiry into the Historical Nature of the New World and the Meaning of Its History* (Westport, CT, 1972); Kupperman, ed., *America in European Consciousness*; Greene, *Intellectual Construction of America*.

14 Greene, *Intellectual Construction of America*, pp. 31, 29, 43; D.W. Meinig, *The Shaping of America: A Geographical Perspective on 500 Years of History* Volume I: *Atlantic America, 1492–1800* (New Haven, 1986), p. 33.

15 David Beers Quinn, ed., *The Roanoke Voyages, 1584–1590: Documents to Illustrate the English Voyages to North America under the Patent Granted to Sir Walter Raleigh in 1584* (2 vols, London, 1955), I, p. 273.

16 'Western Planting', Taylor, *Writings of the Two Hakluyts*, pp. 234, 235; Gilbert cited in Samuel Eliot Morison, *The European Discovery of America: The Northern Voyages, AD 500–1600* (Oxford, 1971), p. 498.

17 'Some Account of Pennsylvania' (1681), 'An Historical and Geographical Account of Pensilvania and of West-New-Jersey' (1698), *Letter from South Carolina* (1710), *Profitable Advice for Rich and Poor* (1712), *The Character of a Righteous Ruler* (1736), cited in Greene, *Intellectual Construction of America*, pp. 69, 69–70, 75, 73, 114; Warwick's letter to Captain Henry Ashton and the Commissioners

of Barbados (1640) is cited in Alison Games, *Migration and the Origins of the English Atlantic World* (Cambridge, MA, 1999), p. 37.

18 E.A. Wrigley and R.S. Schofield, *Population History of England, 1541–1871* (Cambridge, MA, 1981), pp. 208–9.

19 Peter Laslett, *The World We Have Lost: England Before the Industrial Age* (New York, 1965), especially chapter 2; Ian D. Whyte, *Migration and Society in Britain, 1550–1830* (London, 2000); Alison Games, 'Migration', in David Armitage and Michael J. Braddick, eds, *The British Atlantic World, 1500–1800* (Basingstoke, 2002), p. 31.

20 Whyte, *Migration and Society*, pp. 23–5; E.A. Wrigley and R.S. Schofield, 'A Simple Model of London's Importance in Changing English Economy and Society', *Past and Present*, 37 (1967), pp. 44–70.

21 Douglas Hay and Nicholas Rogers reproduce King's and Colquhoun's data (and that of Joseph Massie in 1759) in *Eighteenth-Century English Society: Shuttles and Swords* (Oxford, 1997), pp. 19–21; M. Dorothy George, *London Life in the Eighteenth Century* (London, 1965), p. 140. My thanks to Catherine Molyneux for sharing information from her forthcoming Ph.D. thesis, 'The Peripheries Within: Race, Slavery and Empire in Early Modern England' (Johns Hopkins University).

22 Whyte, *Migration and Society*; Games, *Migration and the Origins of the English Atlantic*; B.A. Holderness, *Pre-Industrial England: Economy and Society from 1500 to 1750* (London, 1976); Keith Wrightson, *English Society, 1580–1680* (London, 1982); J.A. Sharpe, *Early Modern England: A Social History, 1550–1760* (London, 1987); Hay and Rogers, *English Society*, chapters 2, 5, 8, 12.

23 James Horn and Philip D. Morgan, 'Settlers and Slaves: European and African Migrations to Early Modern British America', in Carole Shammas and Elizabeth Mancke, eds., *The Creation of the British Atlantic World* (Baltimore, forthcoming); Games, 'Migration', p. 41.

24 Bernard Bailyn, *Voyagers to the West: Emigration from Britain to America on the Eve of the Revolution* (London, 1986), pp. 7–28; David Hackett Fischer, *Albion's Seed: Four British Folkways in America* (Oxford, 1989); Games, *Migration and the Origins of the English Atlantic*, chapter 6; Virginia DeJohn Anderson, *New England's Generation: The Great Migration and the Formation of Society and Culture in the Seventeenth Century* (Cambridge, 1991).

25 Games, *Migration and the Origins of the English Atlantic*, pp. 24–31, 46–52; Ann Kussmaul, *Servants in Husbandry in Early Modern England* (Cambridge, 1981); Mildred Campbell, 'Social Origins of Some Early Americans', in James Morton Smith, ed., *Seventeenth-Century America: Essays in Colonial History* (Chapel Hill, 1959), pp. 63–89; David W. Galenson, '"Middling People" or "Common Sort"?: The Social Origins of Early Americans Reexamined' and 'Rebuttal by Mildred Campbell', *William and Mary Quarterly*, 3rd ser., XXXV

(1978), pp. 499–540; David Souden, '"Rogues, Whores, and Vagabonds"?: Indentured Servants to North America, and the Case of Mid-Seventeenth Century Bristol', *Social History*, 3 (1978), pp. 23–38; David W. Galenson, *White Servitude in Colonial America: An Economic Analysis* (London, 1981).

26 Games, *Migration and the Origins of the English Atlantic*, p. 101.
27 Horn and Morgan, 'Settlers and Slaves'; David Eltis, 'Volume and Structure of the Transatlantic Slave Trade: A Reassessment, *William and Mary Quarterly*, 3rd ser., LVIII (2001), p. 45; Winthrop D. Jordan, *White Over Black: American Attitudes Toward the Negro, 1550–1812* (Chapel Hill, 1968), chapter II; Ira Berlin, *Many Thousands Gone: The First Two Centuries of Slavery in North America* (Cambridge, MA, 1998); Richard B. Sheridan, *Sugar and Slavery: An Economic History of the British West Indies* (Barbados, 1974).
28 Jack P. Greene, *Pursuits of Happiness: The Social Development of Early Modern British Colonies and the Formation of American Culture* (Chapel Hill, 1988), pp. 178–9.

3

The Chesapeake

England's first permanent New World colony was founded in the Chesapeake Bay region at Jamestown, Virginia, in 1607. A second Chesapeake colony was founded at St Mary's City, Maryland, in 1634. The origins and development of these colonies are not attributable to the imposition of the imperial visions of kings or parliaments or to the implementation of the corporate aims of the colonies' charter holders, the Virginia Company and the Lords Baltimore. Their evolution, after periods of trial, error and instability, rested on the appropriation of political, economic, social and cultural power and authority by settler populations headed by emergent local planter elites. The Virginia Company, a private corporation licensed by the crown, initially intended to recreate England in America, but its first agents acted like Spanish conquistadors, attempting to subjugate local Indians and collect gold, silver and sassafras, the medicinal panegyric. Only when these efforts failed did they hesitantly attempt to build a settled, civil society. By the time that society began to emerge, the company was near bankrupt and after an Indian massacre in 1622 the colony devolved on the crown. The Lords Baltimore kept their proprietary until American Independence, except for a brief interlude of royal rule between 1689 and 1714, but their attempts to create a haven for Catholics and a feudal palatinate in Maryland similarly failed in the face of a settler population who had their own notions of an ideal colonial society and polity.

The Virginia companies

In 1589, disillusioned by the failures of Roanoke, Sir Walter Raleigh gave his Virginia patent to a group of wealthy London merchants led by Sir Thomas Smith. The Spanish war and the dire state of the domestic economy prevented any immediate attempts at American settlement, and it was

not until after the accession of James I and the 1604 Treaty of London
between Britain and Spain that explorers and merchants began once again
to consider colonization, as opposed to trade and plunder, as an outlet for
their enterprising and entrepreneurial energies. Late in 1605, though, a
group of merchant 'adventurers', including Smith, Richard Hakluyt the
younger, and West Country merchants and political magnates such as Sir
John Popham, Lord Chief Justice of Somerset, and Sir Fernando Gorges,
governor of Plymouth, petitioned the king to incorporate two rival joint
stock companies, the London Company and the Plymouth Company, to
establish separate colonies in North America.

The crown issued a charter on 10 April 1606 for the London Company
or the South Virginia group to colonize the region 34–41 degrees north
(Cape Fear to New York City) and for the Plymouth Company or North
Virginia group to settle 38–43 degrees north (the Potomac River to Bangor,
Maine). These territories overlapped, but the charter directed that settlements undertaken by the companies be at least 100 miles apart. Both companies were under the supervision of a royal council in London of 14 men,
with one representative from each colony. The charter granted both companies the same rights and responsibilities for their respective jurisdictions.
Each held, according to their charters if not according to Amerindian inhabitants, 'all the Lands, Woods, Soil, Grounds, Havens, Ports, Rivers, Mines,
Minerals, Marshes, Waters, Fishings, Commodities, and Hereditaments',
and the right to mine for precious metals, with one-third of any such treasures going to the crown. Land was to be held not in fee simple or freehold
but in common socage; that is, leased with payment of an annual quitrent
to the crown. Settlers were, however, guaranteed all the 'liberties, franchises,
and immunities' of Englishmen. As to Indians, colonists could 'tend to the
Glory of his Divine Majesty' by spreading 'the christian Religion to such
People, as yet live in Darkness and miserable Ignorance' and 'in time bring
the Infidels and Savages, living in those parts, to human Civility, and to a
settled and quiet government'.[1]

The Plymouth group attempted to settle the region of Nantucket to
Maine explored by Sir George Weymouth with sponsorship from the Earl
of Southampton in 1605, but the area was not colonized successfully for
another 15 years. The London group's promotion of settlement in the
Chesapeake Bay area, previously reconnoitred by John White in 1585, succeeded in creating the first permanent English colony in the Americas,
though it was some time before anyone could be sure of that.

Early disasters in Virginia

On 20 December 1606, the *Susan Constant*, *Godspeed* and *Discovery*
departed England and on 26 April the following year the advance guard
arrived at Cape Henry, the southern tip of Chesapeake Bay. The next

month, 105 men and boys alighted 50 miles up the James River, setting by a causeway that was both defensible should the Spanish attack and accessible to ocean-going vessels bringing new supplies, and named the spot Jamestown in honour of their king. Over half the company consisted of gentlemen, the rest was composed of 40 soldiers, a doctor, an Anglican minister and artisans and labourers. There were no farmers or women who might form the basis of a self-sufficient agricultural settlement. They constructed a fort within which they built one- and two-room thatched cottages with timber frames and brushwood and clay-plastered walls, and from this base began scouting for the goods that were supposed to secure their own and their company's fortunes, while relying on local Indians for food.

Things started going horribly wrong almost immediately. By September 1607 about half the company had died, some had run off to the Indians and only 35 survived the following winter. New settlers subsequently arrived, 120 in January 1608 and another 70 in September, but when a fleet carrying another 600 appeared in August 1609, that many people in the disorganized settlement caused chaos. Food supplies rapidly diminished and, once again, about half the population died. The company persevered nevertheless. All told, it shipped 7500 people to Virginia between 1607 and 1624, yet by the time of the company's dissolution the colony's population was just 1200. Disease, starvation, overwork, mosquitoes and Indians killed four out of five early Virginia migrants, and more than one historian has likened life in the colony's early years to that in a Hobbesian State of Nature: 'hard, nasty, brutish, and short'.[2]

One reason for this demographic disaster was a failure by the company and by settlers to understand the local environment. The company directed colonists to settle 'the strongest, most wholesome and fertile place', but Jamestown was on a tidewater location where saltwater and the settlers' own excrement flowed back and forth, causing saline poisoning, typhoid and dysentery. They had also settled on a swamp and many succumbed to malaria. In those these afflictions did not kill, they created a general torpor that attracted the opprobrium of observers who interpreted colonists' behaviour as fecklessness. There was, furthermore, an even longer-lasting problem of 'seasoning', the period of adjustment required to accustom English bodies to the locality, not helped by the fact that the company persisted in sending new colonists to Virginia in the spring, rather than the cooler season of autumn. Mortality remained high in Virginia for many years. As commentator George Gardyner noted in 1650, colonists suffered 'much sickness or death. For the air is exceeding unwholesome, insomuch as one of three scarcely liveth the first year at this time.'[3]

Early Virginia colonists did not help themselves by searching for gold and other treasures rather than cultivating crops and husbanding animals, depending for food on Indians and relief ships. The Potomac Indians decided in 1609 that the English had outstayed their welcome, cut off their food supplies and began attacking outlying plantations, leaving the English dependent on relief from home. When a fleet of nine relief ships was scattered and some of them wrecked by a storm off Bermuda in October 1609 (the wreck that inspired Shakespeare's *The Tempest*), there followed the winter 'starving time' during which, yet again, more than half the settlers died (one man survived by cannibalizing his wife, and was subsequently executed).

Local Indians first saved then almost wiped out the English settlement in Virginia. Altogether there were about 13,000 to 22,000 Algonquin Indians in the Virginia tidewater at the time the English arrived. The Powhatan Empire of some 30 tribes stretched from the Potomac River to the Great Dismal Swamp, and the English settled near its strongest point. Fortunately for the colonists, the Indians initially assumed that the arrivals were temporary visitors and provided them with food. They also honoured Captain John Smith, once he had assumed charge of the settlement, by adopting him as a member of the Powhatan tribe. The English crowned Wahunsonacock (also known as Powhatan) a king, though a subject of the English king, in 1608. Yet the settlers quickly insulted their hosts by refusing to give gifts, negotiate for land and intermarry. And they increasingly perturbed them with their persisting presence. By 1609, Wahunsonacock, concerned about a 30-year-old prophecy of a nation arising from Chesapeake Bay to destroy his empire, was asking Smith when the English would be leaving. Receiving no satisfactory answer, his people began attacking settlers, burning crops and killing livestock in a war that lasted to 1614.

Relations improved following a 1613 raid that resulted in the English capture of Wahunsonacock's daughter, Pocahontas. John Rolfe, an illustrious earlier settler who first cultivated tobacco in Virginia and who recorded the arrival of the colony's first slaves, successfully petitioned Governor Sir Thomas Dale to marry the captive. The couple travelled to England, where James I had enough respect for Amerindian kingly authority to snub the commoner Rolfe for marrying a monarch's daughter, an indication that English settlement need not have eventuated in the near annihilation of Amerindian peoples and removal of the survivors. At the beginning of their return journey, however, Pocahontas died and Anglo-Indian relations returned to a state of uneasy coexistence, interspersed with attacks by both sides until events took a dramatic and deadly turn in the spring of 1622.

By the early 1620s local Amerindians were more perturbed than ever by English settlement, which by then stretched 100 miles into their territory, with consequent destruction of the forests and game on which native people depended. Also, Wahunsonacock died in 1618 and was succeeded by his half-brother, Opechancanough, a man with a more aggressive attitude towards the English. After the murder of a Werowance brought no redress from settlers, the Powhatan attacked on 22 March 1622, killing 347 colonists, almost a third of the settler population, and it would have been worse had not one of the Christian converts among the Indians tipped off the colonists on the morning of the raid.

The Anglo-Virginian response to the 1622 attack was ferocious. The colonists immediately destroyed all Amerindian settlements within the vicinity of Jamestown and the lower peninsula. Indeed, the 1622 attack precipitated a change in English attitude in favour of total intolerance of Indians rather than the pragmatic accommodations that previously prevailed. Governor Sir Francis Wyatt wrote afterwards that

> Our first worke is explusion of the Salvages to gaine the free range of the countrey for encrease of Cattle, swine, etc which will more then restore us, for it is infinitely better to have no heathen among us, who at best were but thornes in our sides, then to be at peace and league with them.

Over the next decade, three murderous missions per year systematically plundered Indian villages, until a 1630s' treaty drew a line across the Jamestown peninsula that Indians and colonists only crossed occasionally to trade. Outright war erupted again in 1644–46 after Opechancanough pulled off another surprise attack, on this occasion killing 500 settlers. By then, however, the settler population was easily able to absorb the losses. Opechancanough was later captured and killed and the ensuing treaty fatally weakened the confederacy. From 1646, the Powhatan were forced to acknowledge Charles I as their sovereign, banned on pain of death from the Jamestown peninsula and removed to lands reserved for them in return for military service and an annual tribute of beaver skins. Subsequently, they saw their lands north of the York River subjected to ever more rapid colonization by Englishmen. Eventually, local Indians moved to northern Pennsylvania and made peace with the Iroquois, but not before harassing settlers on the Henrico County frontier during Metacom's War (formerly known as King Philip's War) and thereby precipitating a major rebellion by western settlers under Nathaniel Bacon.[4]

The 1622 massacre seemed to confirm the inability of the Virginia Company to run the colony successfully and paved the way for the company's dissolution and the arrival of royal rule in 1625. Yet at critical moments company agents had brought the enterprise back from the brink of collapse and, by the late 1610s (though it was not necessarily apparent at the time) had laid the political, economic and social foundations for successful colonization.

Foundations of permanent colonization

In 1606–07 a sealed box had carried across the Atlantic the names of 12 councillors appointed to run the colony. Yet jealousies between council members, resentment among those not appointed councillors and weak leadership from the first president, Edward Wingfield, resulted in highly ineffective government. Some councillors plotted to escape the colony aboard the *Discovery* (the one vessel left behind while the others returned to England for supplies), including George Kendall, a Catholic who was executed as a Spanish spy. The colony survived because of the efforts of one man, Captain John Smith, at least according to his own account. Smith forced the colonists to resettle, cultivate food crops, ship timber for profits and trade or, when necessary, extort corn from local Indians. His authoritarianism made him unpopular, however, and he left the colony in October 1609 after a suspicious mishap involving gunpowder, just before the starving time.[5]

In February 1609 colonists requested a new charter allowing more local governance and setting the colony on a more secure financial footing. The 1609 charter, set for seven years though it lasted only three, created a joint stock company (with 50 company and over 600 individual subscribers), the Treasurer and Company of Adventurers and Planters of the City of London for the first Colony of Virginia. The royal council was abolished and replaced by a board of governors, annually elected by stockholders, which had much greater capacity for making its own rules and regulations, provided that they were 'agreeable to the laws, statutes, government, and policy of this our realm'. Stock was sold in lots of £12.10s, £25 and £50, with the promise of a dividend after seven years. The new charter also enlarged the patented territory to 200 miles north and south of Point Comfort, and westwards all the way to the Pacific coast (no one then knew how far away it was). The charter was further revised in 1612 to include Bermuda and to allow the company to raise money through a lottery. This third charter also increased the number of annual council meetings to four, though from 1609 the council only had power to advise, not to control, the governor.[6]

The new provisions almost came to nothing. On 7 June 1610, survivors of the starving time abandoned Jamestown, heading for home. Their four ships, however, were met by the arriving governor, Thomas West, Lord De La Warr, at the mouth of the James River. De La Warr himself had an unhappy time in Virginia. In his own words, he was 'welcomed by a hote and violent Ague' followed by 'the Flux . . . then the Cramps assaulted my weak body with strong paines and afterwards the Gout' that 'drew upon me the disease called the Scurvy; which though in others it be a sicknesse of slothfulnesse, yet was in me an effect of weaknesse, which never left me, till I was upon the point to leave the world'. He left the colony before he left the world, but not before forcing the settlers back to agricultural work, this time in gangs of 15, large enough to deter Indian attack. Even so, when deputy governor Sir Thomas Dale arrived in May 1611 he discovered settlers at 'their daily and usuall workes, bowling in the streets'. But he forced the Indians into a truce and established a settlement at Henrico, a healthier location 50 miles further upriver. When new governor Sir Thomas Gates arrived later that year, with 200 more settlers, he found the colony in much improved circumstances.[7]

Governors De La Warr (1610–11), Gates (1611–13) and Dale (1614–16) took a firm hand with Virginia during their tenures. The 1609 charter allowed 'the able and absolute governor' to declare 'martial law in cases of rebellion or mutiny', and Dale made more than full use of this power by implementing his 'Lawes Divine, Morall and Martiall'. These notorious codes, instituted until April 1619, imposed the death penalty for desertion (some settlers had absconded to the Indians), mutiny and disrespect to the company or its officials, corporeal punishment for adultery, sodomy (early migrants were mostly male), blasphemy and robbing the chapel, and withdrawal of a day's food for non-attendance at church. As important, though, they established a work routine in which colonists laboured from 6 to 10 a.m. and 2 to 4 p.m. for the company, with the rest of the time given over to building and repairing dwellings and cultivating garden plots.

'Dale's Laws' probably helped see the colony through a vulnerable stage of its infancy and set it on the path to productivity. In 1618, however, Sir Edwyn Sandys replaced Sir Thomas Smith as company treasurer and chief executive and charged new governor Sir George Yeardley with removing the 'cruell' laws and implementing 'those free lawes which his Majesty's subjects live under in England'. The new regime provided that Virginians 'might have a hande in the governinge of themselves', and to that effect

> a generall assemblie should be helde yearly once whereat were to be present the Governor and Counsell with two Burgesses [from each hundred or parish] freely to be elected by the inhabitants thereof: this assembly to have power to make and ordaine whatsoever lawes and orders should by them be thought good and proffittable for our subsistence.[8]

The first meeting of the Virginia Assembly, with 22 burgesses as well as the governor and council, took place in the Jamestown church, beginning 30 July 1619. The assembly's laws were subject to gubernatorial veto and laws passed during its first meeting merely confirmed company practice. Yet it also ruled that it was to be elected and to meet annually, asserting the right to at least a limited form of representative government in Virginia. The devolution of political power to Jamestown reflected a shift in the thinking of English authorities as to what sort of colony Virginia was supposed to be. Gradually, settlers and company men alike realized that if Virginia were to be a colony at all it would have to be a colony of settlement and as such would require a good measure of self-government.

As well as local political institutions, the colony needed an economic foundation. Virginians found it in the form of tobacco agriculture, accompanied by the gradual freeing up of company land rights in favour of individuals. Indigenous *nicotiana rustica* was bitter and unpalatable, but in 1611 John Rolfe introduced to Virginia the West Indian *nicotiana tabaccum*. The first four hogsheads exported in 1614 contained just 2600 pounds of tobacco, but four years later Virginians shipped almost 50,000 pounds and four years after that 200,000 pounds. Tobacco eventually ensured Virginia's survival and prosperity, but not before it caused yet more death and destruction. The problem was that prices peaked at three shillings per pound, tempting plant-ers to ignore the necessity of planting food crops and raising animals and to exploit labourers with deadly ruthlessness in pursuit of profit. This problem was only alleviated (despite the efforts of successive treasurers and governors to encourage food production and diversification) in the mid-1620s, when Virginian tobacco supply began to catch up with English demand and prices fell significantly, diminishing the imperative to exploit labourers so extremely.

As important as growing tobacco was the manner in which it was culti-vated. The first settlers were due to be freed from service to the company in 1614 and needed incentives to stay. That year, therefore, Governor Dale allotted three acres of land to all those who had settled before 1612 in return for a month's service to the colony and 12 bushels of corn in rent. Problems of underinvestment and under-recruitment remained, exacerbated in 1616 when the company found itself unable to honour its stockholders with their 100 acres of land. Instead it offered 50 acres of land, and only if stockholders stumped up another £12.10s.

Clearly the company needed more settlers to make profits. In 1617 the Virginia Company shipped more servants, with the intention of offering them tenancies at the end of their terms for which they would pay the com-pany half their produce in rent. Gradually, then, the company found itself giving away more and more of its own resources to make Virginia viable. The greatest innovation in that direction came with the appointment of Edwin Sandys as company treasurer in 1618. He began the practice of granting sub-patents with administrative and judicial privileges (to be called 'private plantations' or 'hundreds'), almost like manors, in return for a small quitrent. They were each to be spaced at least 10 miles apart to encourage more extensive settlement. In every case the sub-patentees were 'to erect and build a town and settle and plant dyvers inhabitants there for the advancement of the general plantation of that country'. The first was Martin's Hundred, named after its principal investor, John Martin, a huge operation, owned by London merchants, of 21,500 acres, 10 miles east of Jamestown and originally settled with 200 colonists. By 1622, the Martin's Hundred population was reduced to 50 by hunger and disease, and then it was obliterated by the Indian attack of 1622. But these private plantations helped Virginia develop. By 1663 there were 70 of them. Even more signif-icant in the long run, under treasurer Edwyn Sandys the company inaugurated the headright system, granting 50 acres to migrants who paid their own passage and 50 more for every family member or servant they took with them.[9]

By 1619, then, three key elements of Virginia's future success as a colony were established: self-government, tobacco agriculture and private property. Another mainstay of the future of colonial Virginia appeared that same year when a Dutch privateer arrived in Jamestown with 20 slaves plundered from the West Indies. It would take some years for slavery to become fully embedded in Virginia economy, law, society and politics, but it is a notable irony that slavery as well as representative government made their first appearances in North America in the very same year.

Yet it was far from clear even then that the colony would survive, and the venture was soon plunged into financial and political crises once more. First, King James threatened the colony's economy by revoking the company's right to hold a lottery. The king, who denounced smoking as a 'vile barbarous custome . . . lothsome to the eye, hatefull to the Nose, harmefull to the braine, dangerous to the Lungs, and in the blacke stinking fume thereof, nearest resembling the horrible Stigian smoke of the pit that is bottomelesse', also proposed a shilling per pound import duty on tobacco with marketing in the hands of tax farmers. Sandys, however, persuaded the king to allow Virginians to market their own produce, but with one-third of the crop due to the crown. The Earl of Warwick and Sir Thomas Smith thought this scheme too costly, however, and forced a Privy Council inquiry into company business. While that was proceeding, news reached London of the Indian attack of March 1622.

On 23 April, the Privy Council appointed a seven-man commission under Sir William Jones to reorganize the colony. When the bankrupt company refused to send aid to Virginia and to submit to reimposition of the 1606 charter, the commission successfully sought the company's dissolution in the courts in May 1624. Virginia was put under the temporary governorship of Lord Mandeville and two investigators who went to the colony. In May 1625, two months after the death of King James, Charles I placed Virginia under a governor and council answerable to the king. Virginia thus became England's first royal colony. After this upheaval, the culmination of 18 years of chaos and experimentation, the colony finally began to evolve at a steadier pace.[10]

A royal colony

Royal rule was a pragmatic response to seemingly intractable problems of management, not an example of Stuart authoritarianism. Indeed, dissolution of the company meant better conditions for settlers, including abolition of its monopoly on importation and sale of goods and of restrictions on the spread of settlement. The crown controlled tobacco exports, but

Virginia planters gained a monopoly in the English market thanks to Charles's exclusion of foreign imports and his suppression of domestic cultivation. Crucially, Charles's proclamation of royal rule was expressly 'not intended to take away or impeach the particular interest of any private planter or adventurer'. Charles even explicitly acknowledged assembly authority in 1629, the first of the 11 years in which he failed to call an English parliament. The king probably saw the provincial assembly as too insignificant to worry about, though leaving it alone proved highly significant in years to come. The assembly continued to meet, thanks to the utilitarianism of the next governor, Sir Francis Wyatt, and the express orders of his successor, Sir William Berkeley.[11]

Even the English Civil War from 1642 did little to dent Virginia's political autonomy, despite the colony remaining royalist. A 1651 London commission demanded and the Virginia assembly gave recognition of parliamentary authority, but in sending a delegation and making that demand parliament tacitly accepted the assembly's authority. The Anglican Church also retained its lands and other benefits, and though the commission insisted on toleration of dissenting Protestants it nevertheless pragmatically tolerated Virginia's offer of haven to royalist refugees.

Before Virginia society and politics settled down though, there were still local rivalries to negotiate, inevitably perhaps in a new colony filling up with ambitious immigrants. One domestic insurgence occurred in 1635, when the burgesses rebelled against governor Sir John Harvey's limits on territorial expansion, sending him back to England with the implicit message that governors could not rule without local legislative assent. There was also a servants' revolt in 1663. The most critical moment, though, came in 1676 in the form of Bacon's Rebellion, an uprising against Governor Sir William Berkeley by politically excluded western Virginians.

Berkeley had been governor since 1641 – his service interrupted only briefly during the interregnum – and had in his time been an agent of steady development and stability. After his own gubernatorial restoration in 1662 he built around him a set of political acolytes who became known as the Green Spring faction (named after his private mansion), which dominated the assembly. Yet political opposition to Berkeley developed and his political position grew progressively weaker. One reason for Virginians' fractiousness was falling tobacco prices, for which Berkeley found himself scapegoated despite his attempts to promote agricultural diversification. Furthermore, in 1670 the Green Spring faction forced through the assembly a curtailment of the franchise to freeholders only. Those consequently deprived of their vote were joined in their vexation by poorer freeholders whom a poll tax burdened disproportionately. Berkeley's position in the imperial order weakened too. His chief ally at court, the Earl of Clarendon, fell from favour in 1667. Berkeley had subsequently failed to endear himself to imperial authorities. He opposed granting royal quitrents to Lords

Arlington and Culpeper, and his opposition to the navigation laws naturally displeased Lord Treasurer the Earl of Danby. Indeed, Danby's Plantation Duties Act of 1673 had taken control of the navigation system away from governors, in favour of new customs officers. One of the Virginia customs officers was Giles Bland, who became a partisan of Nathaniel Bacon.

Nathaniel Bacon arrived in Virginia in 1674 and, notwithstanding kinship and early friendship with Governor Berkeley, soon became chagrined at his exclusion from Virginia's political elite. Quitting Jamestown for the frontier, he experienced western attacks by Doeg and Susquehanna Indians acting on the fringes of Susquehanna-Algonquin conflict in the north-west and Metacom's War against settlers in New England. The westerners' situation was not aided by Berkeley's withdrawal of local militias, an attempt to prevent Anglo-Amerindian relations deteriorating further still. When Bacon and his allies, a mixture of young, ambitious, but excluded men, former Cavaliers, poorer yeomen, tenants and servants, took it upon themselves to attack the Indians, Berkeley denounced him as a traitor. The new assembly of 1676, elected after the king refused Berkeley's request to be replaced with a younger man, was led by Bacon, who had confessed and insincerely renounced his previous misdeeds and been elected a burgess for Henrico County. The assembly commissioned Bacon to lead a force against the Indians and it then gave the vote back to all freemen. Berkeley approved but then withdrew the order to attack the Indians and attempted to have Bacon arrested. In response, Bacon and his 500 men forced Berkeley to flee to the colony's eastern shore on 18 September and then burned Jamestown.

On 30 July, Bacon issued a 'Manifesto concerning the Troubles in Virginia' with a 'Declaration of the People' to 'represent our sad and heavy grievances to his most sacred Majesty'. The sad and heavy grievances included Berkeley's having 'raised great unjust taxes upon the commonality for the advancement of private favourites and other sinister ends', 'not having, during this long term of his government . . . advanced this hopeful colony either by fortifications, towns, or trade, . . . abused and rendered contemptible the magistrates of justice by advancing to places of judicature scandalous and ignorant favourites, . . . protected, favoured, and emboldened the Indians against his Majesty's loyal subjects,' and doing nothing to prevent 'their many invasions, robberies, and murders committed upon us'. The Declaration also called on the Governor and his acolytes to surrender or be tried as traitors and freed their servants and slaves.

In October 1676, however, Bacon died of dysentery and his rebellion fizzled out. Berkeley had 23 rebels hanged anyway. Charles II, noting ruefully that this was more than he had executed for his father's regicide, nevertheless sent 14 ships and 1300 troops to suppress the rebellion, which at its height had Bacon calling for Virginian independence from England. But he also despatched a commission to investigate its causes. The commission found that the principal cause was indeed the unpopularity of the persons and policies of Berkeley and the Green Spring faction. Berkeley returned to England where he died in 1677. He was replaced by one of his former nemeses, Lord Culpeper.[12]

Subsequently, compared to many colonies, Virginia was relatively untouched during the tumultuous reign of James II and the Glorious Revolution that ended it. The assembly had requested the recall of arbitrary governor and crown henchman, Lord Francis Howard of Effingham, but William of Orange arrived in England before James made up his mind. William kept Howard in England and sent first as deputy then as governor Francis Nicholson, whose leadership would contribute significantly to the growing economic, social, cultural and political stability and prosperity of both Virginia and Maryland.

Lord Baltimore and the founding of Maryland

Maryland's early history was quite distinct in its details from Virginia's, not least in the Catholicism of its founders and in its origins as a noble palatinate rather than a company and then royal colony. Yet both colonies went through essentially the same transitions, with proprietorial plans soon foiled by New World exigencies and settlers' demands. Maryland's success also ultimately rested on tobacco planting, and the needs of the staple profoundly shaped the development of both colonies.

Maryland was a family proprietary of the house of Baltimore. The first Lord Baltimore was George Calvert, a scion of Yorkshire landowners who became a courtier of James I, but who withdrew from public life when his Catholicism rendered him unable to take the Oath of Supremacy in 1625. The king rewarded Calvert's loyal service with the title Baron Baltimore, after his lands in Ireland where he gained experience of and enthusiasm for colonization. Already an East India Company shareholder and member of the Virginia Company of London Board of Governors, Calvert was granted 'Avalon' (in Newfoundland) in 1620. A disappointing 1627 visit there convinced him to petition Charles I for a grant in northern Virginia, land upon which, the crown feared, Dutch settlers in what later became Delaware might encroach. Two months after George Calvert's death in April 1632, his 26-year-old son, Cecil, received a royal charter for all lands from the Potomac River (which then became the northern and eastern border of Virginia) northwards to present-day Philadelphia, and all lands west to Appalachia and the sources of Potomac River. Baltimore's tribute to the king was to be two Indian arrows per year and one-fifth of any precious metals found. In 1632, the Calverts began recruiting settlers. The *Ark* and *Dove*, with around 140 migrants, including Cecil's brother, Leonard, as governor, reached Maryland (named after Queen Henrietta Maria) in May 1634. They settled first at an old Amerindian village that they named St Mary's City.

Early Marylanders learned well the lessons of Virginia's chaotic early years. It helped that the new arrivals could pick up cattle, hogs and poultry in Jamestown. The proprietor further directed that his colonists not cultivate 'any other commodity whatsoever' until a 'sufficient quantity of corn and other provision of victuall' was in hand. It also helped that Maryland's 40 tribes of 8000 to 10,000 mostly Algonquin Indians were in no position to resist European settlers when they arrived in the 1630s. The Piscataway federation of the Chesapeake's lower western shore had been largely subjugated following Opechancanough's uprising of 1622, and northern Susquehannocks had attacked and weakened them and the eastern shore Nanticoke. Seeing Calvert's colonists in 1634 as potential allies, the local Yaocomico sold them land and advised them on hunting, fishing, planting and food preparation. Maryland's promoters were more pragmatic than idealistic about converting Amerindians to Christianity, a wise choice given their Catholicism. It seemed to them a better option from 'Prudence and Charity, to Civilize, and make them Christians, then to kill, robbe, and hunt them down from place to place as you would doe a wolfe'. In practice, Marylanders failed to integrate them in any significant way into Anglo-American life, and unwelcome and outnumbered Amerindian survivors moved northwards out of Maryland from the 1740s.[13]

Maryland's 'troubles'

A greater threat than Indians to the infant Maryland proprietary came from roughly 100 Protestant Virginians already living on Kent and Popely's islands in Chesapeake Bay. They had settled there in 1631 at the instigation of William Claiborne, a former surveyor and member of the Virginia Council, in an act of resistance to the proposed Calvert grant. After an April 1635 naval encounter in the bay, the fur-trading William Clobbery and Company replaced Claiborne with George Evelin and sued for peace. The Kent Island controversy was the first of many, often violent, political conflicts in early Maryland.

Maryland's political strife was interwoven with religious conflict. Though founded by Catholics and envisioned as a refuge for them, Maryland was never a Catholic colony. Baltimore was excruciatingly assiduous in his attempts to avoid offending non-Catholics, requiring 'all Acts of Romane Catholique Religion to be done as privately as may be and . . . Romane Catholiques to be silent upon al occasions of discourse concerning matters of Religion'. The majority of migrants to Maryland were Protestants, and unlike Baltimore's co-religionists they were allowed to worship freely and openly.

Yet many Marylanders saw Calvert Catholicism as the source of their alleged political despotism. In actuality, the political provisions of Maryland's charter were more vague and ambiguous than tyrannous, and even given the most authoritarian interpretation were little different from other colonial charters, all of which proffered extensive proprietorial powers. In any case, the proprietor and his representatives proved quite accommodating of more liberty-minded interpretations of his charter, albeit grudgingly. The Maryland charter gave Lord Baltimore 'as ample rights, jurisdictions, privileges, prerogatives, royalties, liberties, immunities and royal rights, and temporal franchises . . . as any Bishop of Durham', including 'absolute power . . . to ordain, make LAWS, with the advice, assent, & approbation of the free men' as 'delegates . . . called together for the framing of LAWS'. Governor Leonard Calvert assumed that this meant that initiating legislation was an executive prerogative, and he vetoed all legislative initiatives by the first assemblies. In turn, the assembly voted down proprietorial legislation. In 1638, however, the governor signed all 40 bills that emanated from the assembly. These acts included a loyalty oath to the king, in response to growing troubles within England, and the establishment of an annually elected legislature based on the English parliamentary model: a governor, council and one or two freeholder representatives from each hundred, similar to that in Virginia.[14]

These fundamentals established, conflict over the details of the structure of government and power of assemblies commenced, and these issues became entwined with English political and religious convulsions during Maryland's mid-century 'time of troubles'. Identified with Catholicism, Maryland was hardly likely to escape as easily as Virginia did from the effects of England's puritan revolution. That revolution reached Maryland with Richard Ingle's 1644 arrival in St Mary's City, where he proclaimed that 'the king was no king' and impounded all armed ships in the name of parliament. Ingle fled to England after his arrest, but returned to Maryland with parliamentary letters of marque to raid royalist homes there in 1645 and 1646. During this 'plundering time', the opportunistic Claiborne attempted to regain his trading post.

After Leonard Calvert's death in 1647, Cecil Calvert appointed Protestant William Stone as governor. Stone granted refuge to 300 Virginia puritans led by Richard Bennett in Ann Arundel County (which they temporarily renamed Providence), where puritan settlers from England joined them. Stone also confirmed acceptance of all Christian denominations with the 1649 Toleration Act. With news of the execution of Charles I, however, acting governor Thomas Greene and the assembly declared Charles II king. Despite Stone's retraction, enemies persuaded Oliver Cromwell of Maryland's rebelliousness and the protector appointed a commission, headed by Bennett and the irrepressible Claiborne, to govern the colony. The 1654 assembly, after excluding Catholics from voting but extending the franchise to all Protestant men, forbade public mass and abolished oaths of allegiance to Lord Baltimore. Baltimore ordered Stone to re-establish proprietorial authority, inaugurating Maryland's Civil War. The commission's forces routed Stone's 130 men at the Battle of the Severn on 25 March 1655, but by 1657 Baltimore's rule and religious toleration were restored, with amnesty to rebels, reflecting Cromwell's wish to restore colonial stability. New governor Josias Kendall, however, resigned his commission in 1660, accepting one instead from assembly delegates who proclaimed themselves 'a lawfull Assembly without dependence on any other power'. This 'Pygmie rebellion', so-called by Baltimore because of its short duration, ended after two months when the Restoration of Charles II put the Calverts back in favour.

Even so, Calvert authority was tested during the Restoration era. Baltimore reimposed property qualifications for voting and reduced the number of representatives in the assembly. He also insisted that 'What Privileges and Powers I have by my Charter are from the King, & that of Calling of Assemblies in any such manner & way as I think fitt being an undeniable one among the rest, I cannot Deem it Honorable Nor safe to Lodge it in the Freemen.' In 1669, though, Reverend Charles Nicholette, the chaplain of the lower house, urged the assembly to claim 'a Liberty equal to the people of England'. The Council extracted a fine and apology from Nicholette, and delegates subsequently complained that 'our laws, whereby our Liberty and Property subsists, are subject to Arbitrary Disposition'.

Concurrent with Bacon's Rebellion in Virginia in 1676, rebels in Charles County, led by Josias Fendall and John Coode, bemoaned Calvert vainglory, despotism, nepotism, corrupting of assembly members and the lack of an established Anglican church in *Complaint from Heaven with Huy and Crye & a petition out of Maryland and Virginia*. Two planters, William Davyes and John Pate, were hanged. In 1681, the Provincial Court found Coode guilty of plotting to kidnap Baltimore, fined him 40,000 pounds of tobacco and banished him from Maryland. Proprietorial attempts to stifle discontent by limiting votes to men with a 50-acre freehold or £40 estate in 1670, and by reducing the number of delegates from four to two per county in 1681, added to the sense of grievance. After learning of James II's overthrow in the Glorious Revolution of 1688, Coode and others formed the Protestant Association that once again listed antiproprietary grievances, declared William and Mary king and queen, and captured St Mary's City without resistance. Though Baltimore kept his land and quitrents, Maryland became a royal colony, only returning to proprietary hands in 1715, following the death of Charles Calvert, the third Lord Baltimore, and the – at least nominal – conversion of his son, Benedict Leonard Calvert, to Anglicanism. It would be the only colony besides Pennsylvania that remained a proprietary until the Declaration of Independence, but the Calverts' days as the colony's leaders were over.[15]

Given the insuperable difficulties of imposing political dominance, it is not surprising that the Calverts also failed in their plans to create a neo-feudal society in Maryland. The colony's charter gave Baltimore palatine powers, including the right to grant lordships, parcel out land, collect quitrents and hold manorial courts over tenants. The Calverts attempted to create a seign-eurial class in Maryland. Any investor purchasing 1000 acres from the pro-prietor was to have manorial rights, and some 60 manors were thereby created.

Yet Baltimore's plans for a manorial society of great landowners proved untenable. To attract settlers he had to offer small farms, as the leaders of Virginia had realized. Baltimore therefore had to establish a headright system under which free settlers received 100 acres for themselves plus 2000 acres per five family members or servants brought with them in 1634–35, and 100 acres per person, or 50 acres for children under 16, from 1635 to 1683, after which settlers purchased land with 'caution money'. Landowners had to pay annual quitrents, and if they died intestate then title reverted to the proprietor. Yet the availability of land undermined the Calverts' vision of a manorial society of proprietor, lesser landowners and tenants, creating instead the powerful planter elite and a large population of smaller independent farmers, similar to the kind of society emerging in Virginia.

The spread of settlement and population growth also forced the Provincial Council and manor courts to relinquish governmental burdens to local independent institutions. From the 1660s, county courts gained jurisdiction in criminal cases not involving life or limb, civil litigation, tax-raising powers and responsibility for building and maintaining roads and public buildings, licensing taverns, policing weights and measures, oversee-ing orphans, poor relief, appointing county officials and supervising elec-tions. In 1692 the legislature established that county courts superseded manorial and hundred courts, further diminishing manorial power. Indeed, and perhaps paradoxically, the period of royal rule from 1689 to 1715 wit-nessed a governmental revolution that further instituted the principles and practice of local self-government. As well as reforming the courts, the assembly established standing committees to expedite business, gained con-trol over money bills and began holding executive officials to account. In other words, it emulated the English parliament.

Maryland also became more emphatically Protestant after the Glorious Revolution. The Maryland Assembly established the Anglican Church in 1692 and endowed ministers with 40 pounds of tobacco a year from every taxable person. It also forbade Catholics from public office and worship and banned Quakers from sitting in the Assembly. Though Catholics kept their property, suppression of public worship, political disfranchisement and the constant threat of dispossession made Maryland much less attrac-tive to Catholics than it had been originally. By the 1750s, 5000 to 7000 Catholics represented only about a tenth of Maryland's population. In the colonies as a whole, by the time of American Independence, there were

20,000–25,000 Catholics, one per cent of the colonial population, about the same as in Britain. Outside of puritan New England and Quaker Pennsylvania, the vision of America as a religious refuge was a short-lived one.[16]

Tobacco and the development of the Chesapeake colonies

Though tobacco caused problems during the company period, it soon proved to be the basis of Virginia's prosperity and then Maryland's. After 1625, supply began to catch up with demand and prices fell from the high of three shillings per pound in the early 1620s to three pence per pound by the 1630s. The fall in prices ensured that the boom of the early years levelled off into steady growth, notwithstanding significant peaks and troughs in the tobacco economy caused by price fluctuations. Within four years of settlement, Marylanders exported 100,000 pounds of tobacco and in 1640 the two Chesapeake colonies exported 1,000,000 pounds. By 1690, the figure reached 25,000,000 pounds and then dipped during King William's War (1689–97) and Queen Anne's War (1702–13), but by 1728 Chesapeake exports reached 50,000,000 pounds and by the time of American Independence 100,000,000 pounds.

Mass consumption – 25 per cent of adults smoking a pipe a day – appeared in England by the 1670s and throughout Europe by 1750. Demand was greatest among the French, and by the 1770s four-fifths of Chesapeake tobacco was re-exported from Britain to France. The Navigation Acts of the 1660s and 1696 required Chesapeake tobacco to be exported directly to England. The 1707 Act of Union removed restrictions on Scottish firms' engagement in American commerce and, thereafter, Glaswegian merchants dominated tobacco trading. Glasgow firms established resident factors in the Chesapeake itself, distinct from the English practice of London or Bristol merchants trading with Chesapeake planters through ships' captains. The tobacco economy was structured in some ways against the interests of larger planters. Through the eighteenth century, smaller planters increasingly sold their tobacco to and purchased their imports from British and especially Glaswegian factors, lessening their dependence on large planters. Large planters, meanwhile, sent their tobacco on their own account to be sold through agents in Britain. Those agents, in turn, would send goods to Chesapeake planters. These arrangements led to a systematic indebtedness on the part of Chesapeake planters to whom agents provided credit on future crops. Nevertheless, credit helped the volume of trade increase, as did the exemption of tobacco from re-export fees under the Navigation Acts in 1723.

While tobacco remained the mainstay of the Chesapeake economy, planters and colonial authorities were aware that overproduction drove down prices and that excessive dependence on a single staple made the region's economy vulnerable to price fluctuations and wartime trade disruption. As early as the 1630s, planters agreed in principle to tackle the problem of falling prices by limiting production, but failed in practice to agree a means of doing so, abandoning the effort in 1642. During price depressions in the 1660s and 1680s, assemblymen from both colonies agreed a 'stint' method of stopping production for short periods to raise prices, and both legislatures enacted town-loading laws to cut transport costs, although on Maryland's side the Calverts vetoed both measures.

Concerns about the quality of Chesapeake tobacco inspired lawmakers in Virginia in 1730 and Maryland in 1747 to pass tobacco inspection acts wherein county inspectors burned poor-quality produce. Up to a third of produce was thereby destroyed. This policy hurt smaller yeoman farmers and tenants most especially, and they retaliated by cutting and burning gentlemen's plants in the fields. After the Revolution, states amended these laws so that while poorer farmers could still not export poor tobacco they could sell it locally instead. Nevertheless, tobacco inspection finally cut exports, raised prices and assured consumers of quality.

Colonial leaders also promoted diversification into all kinds of exotic crops that Europeans were increasingly demanding. The Virginia Company hoped planters would cultivate 'great plentie of Sugar Canes . . . also linseed and Rapeseed. . . . Orenges, Limons, Almonds, Anniseeds, Rice, Cummin, Cottonwool, Carowey seeds, Ginger; Madder, Olives, Oris, Sumacke', figs, peppers, pineapples, pomegranates, wine, hemp and flax, as well as tobacco. Yet despite laws requiring and bounties encouraging such diversification, few were interested in anything but tobacco in these early years. During the 1640s, though, many planters finally became self-sufficient in food cultivation, in particular by growing corn and husbanding livestock. Some even began exporting cattle to Barbados, where planters were even more single-minded about sugar than Chesapeake planters were about tobacco. From the early eighteenth century, large parts of the eastern shore of Chesapeake Bay and northern Maryland and Virginia switched to grain production as a local staple. Grain production grew with expansion westwards, most especially from the 1740s. By the 1760s, Virginia alone was exporting over 400,000 bushels of wheat and over half a million bushels of corn, and 3000 tons of flour and bread worth over £130,000 per year, and four times as much was consumed domestically. Cities like Fredericksburg, Petersburg, Richmond and Alexandria, Virginia, and Baltimore, Maryland, developed as wheat entrepôts, the transport, milling and marketing needs of that crop encouraging urbanization in ways that tobacco did not. Overseas and coastwise grain, livestock and timber trading also stimulated shipbuilding. Ironworks appeared in Cecil County in 1715 and in Baltimore in 1731, and annual Chesapeake exports of pig iron topped 2500 tons by the 1750s. Indeed, even in the tobacco-staple regions, some 15 per cent of Marylanders and Virginians worked in the service economy, in occupations ranging from merchants, factors, lawyers, tavern keepers and artisans of all kinds.[17]

Despite diversification, the tobacco staple remained the mainstay of Chesapeake wealth and even identity. Tobacco was so ubiquitous that it was used as currency in the Chesapeake throughout and beyond the colonial period. Above all, though, tobacco profoundly shaped the Chesapeake landscape and the nature of the region's economic and social relations. The region's planters settled first on the banks of the great tidewater rivers that gave access to ocean-going ships for cheap and easy export. Hogsheads, the barrels in which tobacco was stored, weighed between 200 and 1000 pounds and were not easy to transport on land. Only after the riverbanks were full did settlers move inland. Even then, the land-intensive nature of the crop closely shaped the human geography of the Chesapeake, as did the sheer abundance of land. To avoid soil exhaustion, Virginians and Marylanders engaged in extensive agriculture rather than the intensive form familiar in England. Manure was thought to taint tobacco, and although planters experimented with various other forms of fertilizer, planters tended to cultivate land in tobacco for a few years and then move the crop to a different patch, leaving the original ground to fallow for up to 30 years. Tobacco cultivation thus usually required about 40 acres of land per worker: three acres planted in tobacco, the rest in food crops or fallow. Even the smaller tobacco farms were therefore 40 acres in size, and the largest plantations ran to thousands of acres.

The soil-exhausting potential of tobacco thus required that settlement spread rapidly throughout the region. Virginia planters had already settled in northern North Carolina before the Carolinas officially became colonies in 1663. After the Indian settlement of 1646, Virginians staked claims on the York, Potomac and Rappahannock rivers. In Maryland, most of the lower western shore was settled by the mid seventeenth century, and the north and the lower eastern shores were settled after the Susquehanna treaty of 1652. Virginians moved up the tidewater rivers, beyond their falls and towards the Piedmont after 1713, and into the 'southside' region (south-west of the James River) in the late 1720s. By the 1740s they had crossed the Blue Ridge and moved into the Shenandoah Valley, meeting migrants moving south from Pennsylvania.[18]

But the land-intensive quality of tobacco also led to a thinly though contiguously spread population and, in English eyes, a ragged-looking landscape of forests and swamps interspersed with a few fields planted in grain and tobacco. Only a tenth of the land in the settled regions was under cultivation, the rest was either bare and in fallow or left in wood, soil unbroken and used for hunting and free-range livestock. Houses, especially in the seventeenth century, were typically one-roomed wooden shacks in poor states of repair. There was also a much lamented absence of towns, and even Jamestown never became more than a small village. Three critics complained in 1697 that Virginia was settled 'without any Rule or Order'. Robert Beverley, whose 1705 *History and Present State of Virginia* was written to answer the colony's detractors, referred to its 'unhappy Form of Settlement'. Another commentator, though, noted settlers' tendency to suit themselves, whatever the wishes of commentators and politicians, when he complained in the 1650s of 'every man having Liberty . . . to take up Land (untaken before) and there seat, build, clear, and plant without any manner of restraint from the Government'.[19]

There were many attempts to order the Chesapeake landscape, create more towns and generally counter a prevailing image of rusticity. When it created hundreds, the Virginia Company hoped that they would be settled as towns. When that failed, the Company divided the region into four 'incorporations' that again were supposed to have towns, but in 1634 the crown organized those and more recently settled areas into eight counties, which were again intended to be centred by towns. The most spectacular attempts to induce Virginians and Marylanders to live in towns were Governor Francis Nicholson's abandonment of Jamestown and St Mary's City in the early 1690s in favour of new, purpose-built capitals at Williamsburg and Annapolis. Both cities were designed to reflect the growing wealth and increasing refinement of the colonies they served. Both had wide avenues, squares and circles, prominent capitol buildings, governors' mansions and colleges. Both became important centres of power, at least during the legislative season, though neither grew very large in terms of private residency.

Even after the creation of Williamsburg and Annapolis, though, colonists generally found it most convenient to meet at crossroads near the centres of counties. When counties were established in the provinces local officials were required to 'take care that a court house, prison, pillory and stocks' be built at a central location accessible by a network of roads through the countryside. These often unnamed county seats were not only sites for the administration of justice, however. Forms of punishment were designed that created interpersonal obligations. In particular, those guilty of antisocial behaviour (slander, swearing, fighting, drunkenness, blasphemy and absence from church were the most common offences) were bound over to two others who posted bond with the court that the offence would not be repeated. Furthermore, twice-annual court days were important social occasions, witness to festivals of favoured Chesapeake pastimes such as wrestling, cockfighting and horse racing. Throughout the year, churches, stores and taverns served the religious, retailing and social needs of their communities, as the Chesapeake took on an increasingly settled aspect.[20]

Population, economy and society in the later colonial Chesapeake

Between the 1660s and 1690s the Chesapeake finally lost much of what historian Jack P. Greene called its 'improvisational' and 'contingent character'. The creation of a viable, stable society in the Chesapeake, made possible by political stability and a tobacco commodity combined with widespread landownership, meant that population rose steadily after the demographic disasters of the early years. From just 1200 souls in 1624, the population rose to 35,446 in 1660, 121,022 in 1710 and over half a million in 1760. For much of the seventeenth century, the populations of Maryland and Virginia remained predominantly immigrant. By the 1630s, 800 to 900 people a year migrated to the Chesapeake, but that figure doubled in the period 1650 to 1680, and then fell slightly due to depressed tobacco prices from about 1680 to 1713 and also the growing popularity of the newer colonies of Jamaica, the Carolinas, New York, New Jersey and Pennsylvania, all founded between 1655 and 1681.[21]

As important as the decline of immigration, though, were demographic developments within the Chesapeake. Until the late seventeenth century, malaria and severe epidemics meant death rates remained extraordinarily high. Half of marriages were broken by death within seven years, a quarter of children lost one or both parents by the age of five, and three-quarters by the age of their majority. These facts did not necessarily spell social disaster. High parental death rates even encouraged formation of stronger community bonds in some respects, as step-parents, guardians and orphans formed quasi-kinship connections and the community protected the interests and promoted the welfare of parentless children through the creation of orphans' courts. Nevertheless, parental death rates declined significantly and by the 1690s inhabitants of the Chesapeake were living as long as their contemporaries in England, creating a more stable form of family life.

Equally important was the gradual equalization of sex ratios in the late seventeenth and early eighteenth centuries. There were no women aboard the *Susan Constant*, *Godspeed* or *Discovery*, and only two on a resupply ship of September 1608. By 1609, company shareholders began to see the need for a more settled population in Virginia and that year sent 'a large supply of five hundred men, with some number of families, of wife, children and servants, to take faste holde and roote in that land'. The paucity of women and relatively high death rates among men made the early Chesapeake a place of considerable economic opportunity for women. It was so common for women to marry numerous times and inherit all or part of several husbands' estates that historians Lois Green Carr and Lorena Walsh have styled the early Chesapeake a 'widowarchy'. By the end of the century, though, with more women and with men living longer, Virginians and Marylanders established more traditional patterns of patriarchy in household and property relations. The growing number of women also ensured less anarchic social behaviour among men than had existed in earlier times.[22]

As the Chesapeake population grew and developed ever stronger ties of kin and community, a new socio-economic order emerged out of the relative chaos of the colonies' earliest years. Although there were gentlemen among the first Virginia migrants, and although Maryland was founded by a noble who attempted to create an instant New World aristocracy, early Chesapeake society remained fluid and susceptible to instabilities that were manifest in Maryland's many troubles and as late as Bacon's Rebellion in Virginia. Only in the late seventeenth century did indigenous elites establish themselves as a self-conscious gentry class. When they did, however, they amassed enormous wealth and power. The power possessed by these 'better sort' of people was, however, tempered by a 'middling sort' of yeoman farmers and a 'lower sort' of unpropertied people who expected one day to acquire the economic and usually landed independence possessed by the better and middling sorts. Economic independence and the fractiousness it engendered made the less wealthy and even the poor distinctly undeferential towards the elite, and if that elite had power it was thus contingent upon a social and political authority that could not be assumed but had to be earned.

The first signs of an emergent landed elite appeared in the form of the Green Spring faction around Governor William Berkeley. The royalist presence of Berkeley and the continued existence of the established Anglican Church in Virginia also attracted a large number of cavalier refugees after the civil war. Many of these men, mostly men of capital, would help found the dynasties that would eventually form Virginia's gentry. After that, the gradual settling down of the economy and society encouraged the arrival of some younger sons of gentry families seeking to establish themselves as tobacco planters.

The formation of an established indigenous elite in the late seventeenth century, however, was in part an outcome of demographic change. Before the late seventeenth century, low life expectancy meant that most wealthy men were immigrants with few long-term local social or political affiliations. By the 1690s, though, many were Creoles who had a local sense of identity and lifelong relationships with other Virginians, and were therefore able to make political, economic, social and even dynastic alliances, and to pass their status, position and identity on to their offspring. By the early eighteenth century, the gentry were distinguishing their sons with classical educations, often obtained in Britain.

William Byrd II of Westover, whose choice to append his plantation's name to personal name says much about planters' developing aristocratic identity, made a classic statement of that sense of self in a letter to an English correspondent in 1726. 'Like one of the Patriarchs', he wrote, 'I have my Flocks and my Herds, my Bond-men and Bond-women, and every Soart of trade amongst my own Servants, so that I live in a kind of Independence on everyone but Providence'. But their patriarchy was built on the most brutal form of capitalist exploitation, for their fortunes were often founded and were certainly enhanced by property in slaves. The labour of these slaves in turn enhanced tobacco production and helps account for a doubling of land values between 1680 and 1700, further enhancing the wealth of the emerging slave-holding planter elite. By 1700, the wealthiest 10 per cent of landowners, around 5 per cent of whole population, owned half to two-thirds of the land. As their fortunes increased, these wealthy planters displayed a developing class-consciousness through a cult of gentility, emulating that first adopted by Berkeley, and in keeping with the developing fashions of the landed classes of England. In the early eighteenth century especially, men of means built brick Georgian mansions, filled them with genteel accoutrements that were increasingly available following a consumer boom after the Treaty of Utrecht, and began appearing in public in increasingly refined clothing and carriages and pursuing ever more exclusive leisure activities.[23]

The large measure of political autonomy the colonies possessed also helps account for the rise of the Chesapeake gentry. Local gentlemen mostly filled the assembly seats. The upper chambers in each province allowed colonists to maintain some control over governors, while the lower houses of the assembly increasingly asserted influence over councillors and ordinary voters alike. Colonists soon came to regard their local assemblies as equivalent to parliament in England, which gave their members immense authority and which had awesome consequences in the 1760s and 1770s.

When the county court systems were established in Virginia in 1634 and in Maryland in 1643, the reach of wealthy planters extended further still, dealing as these institutions did with elections, taxes, maintaining land and probate records, orphans' estates, poor relief, licensing taverns and local infrastructural matters such as road and bridge building, as well as litigation and moral and criminal cases. Wealthy planters also gained control of the proliferating parish vestries throughout Virginia and Maryland, giving them further influence over both civil and ecclesiastical affairs. Most especially, vestrymen were responsible for collecting tithes (often the highest local tax) and appointing church ministers. The establishment of church authority and religious uniformity was important enough to be one of the first orders of business at Virginia's first assembly meeting, which insisted ministers act in accord with the rules of the Church of England. The Virginia assembly established over 60 Anglican churches by 1690 and the Maryland assembly established Anglicanism as the colony's official religion in 1692. Wealthy planters were also the principal source of the credit that small farmers depended on to purchase land, servants, slaves and other capital and consumer goods.

Colonial assemblies, county courts and churches were therefore places where planters exercised power. These locations were scenes of social display where the wealth and sophistication of members of the elite was paraded before more humble neighbours. As they became increasingly genteel and polite, so they became increasingly patriarchal in their family lives, paternalistic towards their slaves and condescending towards poorer white neighbours. Yet these institutions were the means of exercising contingent authority rather than naked power. Humbler settlers acceded to the leadership of wealthier neighbours consensually rather than deferentially. A condition of consent was that local leaders were indeed neighbours. Though they carried the king's imprimatur if they were high office holders, they nevertheless knew their communities and their communities knew them, and those communities could hold them accountable for their actions. One area in which they were held accountable was in their devotion to public service. That included promoting civic 'improvements' to make the colonies more economically viable, more socially and culturally sophisticated and indeed more demonstrably English. It also included acting in defence of local law, codes of morality, property rights and, ultimately, local political autonomy.

The ostentation and extravagance of planters came under attack during the Great Awakening, an intermittent religious revival of the 1740s and 1750s that drew discomfiting attention to the disjuncture between planter indebtedness and immorality and their proclaimed beliefs in the virtues of thrift, sobriety, religiosity and general moral rectitude. The Awakening certainly sundered the religious uniformity of Virginia. Maryland always had its sectarian divide, but both Chesapeake colonies saw significant increases in religious diversity, with growing congregations of Quakers and other Protestant dissenters as well as Catholics. Even so, there was little open religious or political conflict. Notwithstanding public discrimination against non-Anglicans, religion was increasingly regarded as a private matter and tolerated as such. Moreover, there were soon more important matters afoot. When parliament began taxing colonists' property and threatening their autonomy in the 1760s, the Chesapeake gentry acted in accord with a popular will that demanded their defence.

As well as being land-intensive, tobacco was also labour-intensive, and it thus powerfully shaped the nature of Chesapeake economic and social relationships. Early colonial planters relied mainly on indentured servants as labourers: men and women who received free passage across the Atlantic in return for, typically, four to five years of service to the planter, who paid their fare and housed, clothed and fed them during their terms. Some 100,000 servants migrated to the Chesapeake in the seventeenth century, constituting over 80 per cent of all migrants. In the peak period of the 1630s to the 1650s, up to 1900 servants arrived there annually. Roughly half came from poorer labouring backgrounds in England, though up to half were children of middling sorts of artisans and yeomen. Most were young, averaging about 20 to 21 years old, most were single and 5 out of 6 were male.

In the new, loose communities and intensive economy of the Chesapeake, servants were often treated as commodities. Nevertheless, servitude was often a way up in the world. Servants received 'freedom dues' at the end of their terms, assuming they survived, usually including a set of clothes, tools and a small amount of food and money, and sometimes land. These freedom dues allowed former servants to make a new start for themselves, usually by leasing land as a means of acquiring the capital to purchase a farm. Until the 1660s at least, some 70 per cent of Chesapeake householders owned land, although, thereafter, economic opportunity gradually declined as land filled up and became more expensive. Part of the reason for the decline in availability and rise of the price of land was the switch to slaves as the main source of plantation labour in the Chesapeake.

From servitude to slavery

In April 1619, John Rolfe recorded the arrival of '20 negars' aboard a Dutch man-of-war that had been raiding the West Indies and that, having failed to sell them elsewhere, had brought them to Jamestown. In other words, slavery arrived in North America by accident rather than by design. Even so, New World slavery was over a century old by this time and was by no means unfamiliar or alien, and Governor George Yeardley readily accepted the slaves in exchange for food. With a ready supply of cheap servants from England, though, slavery remained a minor institution in Virginia for some 40 years. Slaves first appeared in St Mary's City in 1642 and, again, slavery did not establish itself as a major institution until the second half of the seventeenth century. From the 1660s, however, the founding of new colonies drained the supply of indentured servants from Virginia and Maryland. Furthermore, the English economy improved, with real wages rising for the first time in living memory. In a reversal of the wisdom of Hakluyt's time, the idea that England was overpopulated was challenged by the view that the country's labour supply was too small because, according to Roger Coke's *A Discourse on Trade* (1670), 'a ruinous number of men daily flock to the plantations'. One response was for parliament to sponsor the establishment in 1663 of the Company of Royal Adventurers Trading into Africa. The company's bankruptcy failed to deter parliament from sponsoring the founding of the Royal African Company in 1672 and granting it a monopoly of the slave trade from Africa to Anglo-America. It sought out new markets for slaves in the southern plantation colonies.[24]

By that time, furthermore, Chesapeake planters had acquired the capital necessary to purchase significant numbers of slaves, who were costly to transport, whose service was lifelong, whose children could be enslaved and who were therefore more expensive. By 1720, slaves had overtaken servants as the region's primary source of labour and indentured servitude all but disappeared by the early nineteenth century. Meanwhile, the slave population of the Chesapeake rose from only 950 in 1660, to 8000 in 1710 and 49,000 in 1760. From the early eighteenth century, slaves represented over a third of the region's inhabitants.

As long as slave numbers stayed small and the Chesapeake remained 'a society with slaves' rather than 'a slave society', slavery remained a relatively moderate institution and race relations were more fluid than they would be later. Indentured servants and slaves worked together in the same fields, socialized together and sometimes even married each other. Punishment was not necessarily discriminatory and sometimes slaves negotiated for their freedom in the manner of indentured servants. Some former slaves even became substantial property owners. Anthony Johnson arrived enslaved in Virginia in 1621. After obtaining his own and his family's freedom, he bought a farm and slaves of his own. Evidence on how extensive this fluidity in race relations was, however, is inconclusive. Certainly there is evidence of invidious treatment of slaves and free black people from early on. Johnson, for example, lived in Northampton County, a relatively poor area with few plantations in the early seventeenth century, but once slavery and more difficult race relations arrived in this part of Virginia he felt compelled to move to Maryland. Also, slaves were frequently recorded alongside livestock in plantation inventories, with first names only – often either diminutive or ironically grandiose names; there were no formal contracts and most slaves served for life rather than four or five years.[25]

Even if early slavery was relatively moderate, the institution grew measurably worse once planters became more reliant on slave labour. Virginia and Maryland enacted the first slave laws in the 1660s. Most fundamentally, these laws defined slaves as chattel property (in contrast to Iberian American slave codes which defined slaves as people). In North America, Africans and their descendants were deprived of most of the rights that Englishmen coveted so keenly for themselves (the right to life was an exception, as the killing of slaves was defined as murder). The new slave codes closed down opportunities slaves had taken to obtain freedom, such as time of service and conversion to Christianity, by making slavery a life condition and by defining slaves as slaves on account of race rather than religion. As the slave population increased and consequently the security problem they represented grew, so slave laws became progressively more elaborate, especially when codified in Virginia in 1705, eventually encompassing almost all aspects of slaves' lives and behaviour. Laws also assured a strict separation of black and white. Legislation differentiated the provisions, work regimes and punishments of servants and slaves, and free people who married slaves were banished from the colony. Like so much else in colonial

America, slavery and racism had to be invented, experimented with and refined according to the dictates of experience and contingency.

Tobacco shaped the lives of black as well as white people in the Chesapeake. Because English settlers learned to cultivate tobacco from Amerindians, planters were able to impose the harsh sunup to sundown gang labour regime on Chesapeake slaves (in contrast to the Carolinas where African expertise in rice cultivation allowed them to craft a less time-consuming task system). Also, Chesapeake planters adopted a 'paternalistic' attitude towards their slaves. There was little that was benign about paternalism. It was based on the racist notion that black people were child-like and its system of mutual obligations required hard labour and obedience by slaves for very little in return, and yet entailed cruel physical punishment if slaves did not live up to the standards imposed on them. As unequal as this bargain was, it was the best slaves could manage in the circumstances. Slaves' acts of resistance, ranging from violent outbursts and running away to stealing and working slowly, helped craft a paternalistic system that acknowledged their humanity (whatever the law said) and mitigated the worst potential abuses of an essentially dehumanizing institution.

Slaves also managed to maintain some social and cultural space for themselves, a semi-autonomy made more pronounced by the relatively high rate of importation of new slaves from Africa. Slave importations to the Chesapeake averaged about 2000 per year in the 1730s and 1740s, but tailed off to an average of a few hundred per year in the two subsequent decades. By then the Chesapeake slave population had attained natural increase and even a Creole majority. These facts led to an important shift in Chesapeake life. Notwithstanding the relatively high levels of interference in slave life by masters, Chesapeake slaves had some measure of autonomy and they laid the foundations of a new and profoundly rich African-American culture in the New World.

Slavery introduced a new form of exploitation, brutality and potential instability into colonial Chesapeake society. It also increased economic inequality in white society. At first only larger planters with significant quantities of capital could afford to invest in slaves and, therefore, only they benefited from the economies that slavery allowed. Slavery also meant more land could come under cultivation. Land prices consequently increased, doubling between 1680 and 1700. It thus became more difficult for former servants to purchase land, and the proportion of heads of households who owned land diminished from 70 per cent in the 1660s to 50 per cent a century later. It remained the case that more than half could expect to become landowners at some point in their lives, but many were spending longer and longer, and some were spending lifetimes, as leaseholders and wage labourers.

Yet, while slavery increased the economic distance between rich and poor whites, it diminished the social and cultural distance. However wealthy gentlemen were, however ostentatiously refined they were, whiteness signalled a certain kind of equality with their poorer neighbours. However poor a white man was, he was not black, could not be enslaved and therefore felt a certain kind of equality with his wealthier neighbours (a kind of equality that became seemingly more pronounced as indentured servitude gradually declined to virtual non-existence by the 1820s). The equality before the law that was the birthright of all Englishmen appeared all the more stark and meaningful in a society where a large and highly visible proportion of the population was emphatically denied that equality and almost all the rights and liberties that accompanied it. Slavery also allowed the exclusion of most of the labouring poor – slaves – from any role in politics, paradoxically allowing planters to become egalitarian as far as white society was concerned. And herein lies the answer to the biting question that Samuel Johnson famously posed during the American rebellions against British taxation: 'How is it that we hear the loudest *yelps* for liberty among the drivers of negroes?'[26] The reason was that colonists knew the value of their freedom because they were daily witnesses of its opposite. As the historian Edmund S. Morgan has pointed out, the coexistence of slavery and freedom may have been contradictory and paradoxical, but in some ways they were actually interdependent and complementary.

Caste undermined the potential for class conflict in another way too. As slave numbers grew, so did the threat of slave rebellion, and so therefore did a security and disciplinary imperative that created a degree of social cohesion among whites. Although there were tobacco-cutting riots in both Virginia and Maryland in response to the tobacco inspection laws of the early eighteenth century, there was nothing on the scale of the Virginia servant revolt of 1663 or Bacon's Rebellion of 1676, in which servants participated, or the rebellion against the Calverts in 1689.

Also, even if economic opportunity declined and the economic gap between rich and poor whites grew in relative terms, in absolute terms the living standards of all classes of free people rose from the early eighteenth century. After the Treaty of Utrecht, the total value of imports from Britain increased from an average of £200,000 per year in the 1720s to near £885,000 in the 1770s, and the value of annual imports per capita rose from £1 in the 1730s to £1.53 in the 1770s. The sparse lifestyle of the seventeenth century thus gave way to a growing number of household items and farm improvements among all except the very poorest of free people. Also, British merchants in the Chesapeake from the 1730s enhanced access to credit and to slaves. Indeed, half of Chesapeake householders were slaveholders by the 1760s.

Virginia, England's first American colony, was not conquered by the king or his armies, but by a private corporation. The early phases of colonization were not guided by some grand plan, but by colonists' adaptations to numerous unexpected exigencies. The Virginia Company, the original charter group, tanked spectacularly in 1624, and yet it had created a local population with property and powers of self-government. What emerged by the late seventeenth century was a society with a local elite of tobacco planters, a 'middling' population of yeoman farmers and artisans, a 'lower sort' comprising indentured servants, tenants and wage labourers, and a mixture of African and African-American slaves. Over time, the wealth and status of the great planters grew, the middling sorts retained considerable economic, social and political power, and the relative wealth of and economic opportunity for the lower sorts declined, though their wealth and living standards increased in absolute terms. Potential conflict in this increasingly unequal white society was kept in check by the growth of a subculture of African-American slaves who accounted for 40 per cent of the province's population by the middle of the eighteenth century.

The details of the settlement of Maryland differed in various ways, but the pattern of development was essentially the same. A private proprietorial charter group, the Calvert family, initiated colonization and hoped to create a feudal palatinate and a haven for Catholics. The Calverts were soon overwhelmed by the migrants they encouraged to settle there, and the colony became much like Virginia: a tobacco-slave-plantation society led by a planter elite, but with widespread (though gradually diminishing) opportunity for landownership and other forms of property ownership for whites. Variations on these themes would characterize the settlement of all of British America.

Notes

1 'Letters patent to Sir Thomas Gates and others' (1606), in Philip L. Barbour, ed., *The Jamestown Voyages under the First Charter, 1606–1609* (2 vols, Cambridge, 1969), I, pp. 24–34.

2 Jack P. Greene, *Pursuits of Happiness: The Social Development of Early Modern British Colonies and the Formation of American Culture* (Chapel Hill, 1988), p. 12; James Horn, 'Tobacco Colonies: The Shaping of English Society in the Seventeenth-Century Chesapeake', Nicholas Canny, ed., *The Oxford History of the British Empire* Volume I: *The Origins of Empire: British Overseas Enterprise to the Close of the Seventeenth Century* (Oxford, 1998), p. 186; Edmund S. Morgan, *American Slavery, American Freedom: The Ordeal of Colonial Virginia* (New York, 1975), pp. 71–130.

3 Carville V. Earle, 'Environment, Disease and Mortality in Early Virginia', in Thad W. Tate and David L. Ammerman, eds, *The Chesapeake in the Seventeenth Century: Essays on Anglo-American Society* (New York, 1979), pp. 96–125; Darrett B. Rutman and Anita H. Rutman, '"Of Agues and Fevers": Malaria in the Early Chesapeake',

William and Mary Quarterly XXXIII (1976), pp. 31–60; Karen Ordahl Kupperman, 'Apathy and Death in Early Jamestown', *Journal of American History* LXVI (1979–80), pp. 24–40; George Gardyner, *A Description of the New World* (1650) cited in James Horn, *Adapting to a New World: English Society in the Seventeenth-Century Chesapeake* (Chapel Hill, 1994), p. 137.

4 Horn, *Adapting to a New World*, p. 134; Bernard Sheehan, *Savagism and Civility: Indians and Englishmen in Colonial Virginia* (Cambridge, 1980).

5 'A Map of Virginia. With a Description of the Countrey, the Commodities, People, Government and Religion' (1612), in Philip L. Barbour ed., *The Complete Works of Captain John Smith (1580–1631) in Three Volumes* (Chapel Hill, 1986), I, pp. 121–77.

6 W. Keith Kavenagh, *Foundations of Colonial America: A Documentary History* (3 vols., New York, 1973), III, pp. 1704–14.

7 Ralph Hamor, *A True Discourse of the Present Estate of Virginia* (1615), cited in Morgan, *American Slavery, American Freedom*, p. 73.

8 Yeardley cited in R.C. Simmons, *The American Colonies: From Settlement to Independence* (Harlow, 1976), p. 15; Third Virginia Charter (1612) and Ordinance of 1621 (the Great Charter of 1618 went missing but is supposedly similar to the 1621 document), in Jack P. Greene, ed., *Great Britain and the American Colonies, 1606–1763* (Columbia, SC, 1970), pp. 11–20, 27–9; 'Articles, Lawes, and Orders Divine, Politique, and Martiall for the Colony in Virginea' (1611), in Jack P. Greene, ed., *A Documentary History of American Life* Volume I: *Settlements to Society: 1584–1763* (New York, 1966), pp. 39–42.

9 Instructions to George Yeardley (1618), in Greene, *Settlements to Society*, pp. 43–4; Morgan, *American Slavery, American Freedom*, pp. 93–7.

10 *A Counterblaste to Tobacco* (1604), in James Craigie, ed., *Minor Prose Works of James VI and I* (Edinburgh, 1981), pp. 88, 99.

11 'Royal Proclamation of 13 May 1625' and 'Instructions to William Berkeley' (1642), in Greene, *Britain and the American Colonies*, pp. 35–43.

12 'Manifesto concerning the Troubles in Virginia' (1676), Greene, *Settlements to Society*, pp. 179–83; Bernard Bailyn, 'Politics and Social Structure in Virginia', in James Morton Smith, ed., *Seventeenth-Century America: Essays in Colonial History* (Chapel Hill, 1959), pp. 90–115; Morgan, *American Slavery, American Freedom*, pp. 250–79; Horn, *Adapting to a New World*, pp. 372–80.

13 'Instructions to the Colonists by Lord Baltimore' (1633), Andrew White, 'A Briefe Relation of the Voyage unto Maryland' (1634), and [John Lewger and Jerome Hawley], *A Relation of Maryland; Together with a Map of the Countrey, The Conditions of Plantation, His*

Majesties Charter to the Lord Baltemore (1635), in Clayton Colman Hall, ed., *Narratives of Early Maryland, 1633–1684* (New York, 1910), pp. 23, 37.

14 Cited in Aubrey C. Land, *Colonial Maryland: A History* (New York, 1981), p. 9; John D. Krugler, '"With promise of Liberty in Religion": The Catholic Lords Baltimore and Toleration in Seventeenth-Century Maryland', *Maryland Historical Magazine* LXXIX (1984), pp. 21–43; David W. Jordan, '"The Miracle of this Age": Maryland's Experiment in Religious Toleration, 1649–1689', *Historian* XLVII (1985), pp. 338–59; Maryland Charter of 1632, Greene, *Britain and the American Colonies*, pp. 20–5.

15 Cited in Land, *Colonial Maryland*, pp. 55, 56, 62.

16 Lois Green Carr and David W. Jordan, *Maryland's Revolution of Government, 1689–1692* (Ithaca, 1974); Luca Codignola, 'The Holy See and the Conversion of the Indians in French and British North America, 1486–1760', in Karen Ordahl Kupperman, ed., *America in European Consciousness, 1493–1750* (Chapel Hill, 1995), pp. 212–13.

17 D.W. Meinig, *The Shaping of America: A Geographical Perspective on 500 Years of History* Volume I: *Atlantic America, 1492–1800* (New Haven, 1986), p. 145; Lois Green Carr, 'Diversification in the Colonial Chesapeake: Somerset County, Maryland, in Comparative Perspective', in Lois Green Carr, Philip D. Morgan and Jean B. Russo, eds, *Colonial Chesapeake Society* (Chapel Hill, 1988), pp. 342–88.

18 Horn, *Adapting to a New World*, pp. 141–60; Lois Green Carr, Russell R. Menard and Lorena S. Walsh, *Robert Cole's World: Agriculture and Society in Early Maryland* (Chapel Hill, 1991); Allan Kulikoff, *Tobacco and Slaves: The Development of Southern Cultures in the Chesapeake* (Chapel Hill, 1986).

19 Henry Hartwell, James Blair and Edward Chilton, *The Present State of Virginia, and the College* (1697), ed. Hunter Dickinson Farish (Williamsburg, 1940), p. 4; Robert Beverley, *The History and Present State of Virginia* (1705), ed. Louis B. Wright (Chapel Hill, 1947), p. 57; 'Anthony Langston on Towns and Corporations; and on the Manufacture of Iron' (1650s), cited in Horn, *Adapting to a New World*, p. 140.

20 John W. Reps, *Tidewater Towns: City Planning in Colonial Virginia and Maryland* (Charlottesville, 1972), p. 315; Horn, *Adapting to a New World*, pp. 187–250.

21 Greene, *Pursuits of Happiness*, pp. 81, 82.

22 Cited in Simmons, *The American Colonies*, p. 13; Lois Green Carr and Lorena Walsh, 'The Planter's Wife: The Experience of White Women in Seventeenth-Century Maryland', *William and Mary Quarterly*, 3rd Ser., XXXIV (1977), pp. 542–71.

23 Letter to Charles Boyle, Earl of Orrery, July 5, 1726, cited in Rhys

Isaac, *The Transformation of Virginia, 1740–1790* (Chapel Hill, 1982), pp. 39–40.

24 Roger Coke, *A Discourse on Trade* (London, 1670), in Hilary McD. Beckles, '"The Hub of Empire": The Caribbean and Britain in the Seventeenth Century', in Canny, *Origins of Empire*, p. 232.

25 T.H. Breen and Stephen Innes, *'Myne Owne Ground': Race and Freedom on Virginia's Eastern Shore, 1640–1676* (Oxford, 1980); and for a different view see J. Douglas Deal, *Race and Class in Colonial Virginia* (New York, 1993).

26 Johnson cited in David Brion Davis, *The Problem of Slavery in Western Culture* (Ithaca, 1966), p. 3. On development of slavery see Morgan, *American Slavery, American Freedom*, pp. 293–387; Ira Berlin, *Many Thousands Gone: The First Two Centuries of Slavery in North America* (Cambridge, MA, 1998), pp. 29–46, 109–41, 256–89; Philip D. Morgan, *Slave Counterpoint: Black Culture in the Eighteenth-Century Chesapeake and Lowcountry* (Chapel Hill, 1998); Anthony S. Parent, Jr., *Foul Means: The Formation of a Slave Society in Virginia, 1660–1740* (Chapel Hill, 2003).

4

The West Indies

The West Indies comprises a long string of islands dividing the Atlantic Ocean and Caribbean Sea between Florida and Venezuela. They break into three groups: the Bahamas, comprising about 30 inhabitable islands and many more tiny islets; the Greater Antilles, including the large islands (west to east) of Cuba, Jamaica, Hispaniola and Puerto Rico, and the Lesser Antilles, which consist principally of the northern Leeward Islands and the Windward Islands south of Guadeloupe.

The Spanish settled or partly settled the Greater Antillean islands and Trinidad in the sixteenth century, but generally treated them as adjuncts of Mexico and Peru and left the other islands to the Carib Indians. In the early seventeenth century, other European powers began settling the islands off the Spanish periphery, after failing to gain permanent footholds on the mainland between the Orinoco and Amazon rivers. In the 1630s, the Dutch took co-possession with the French of St Martin, and of St Croix and the Virgin Isles with the English, and full possession of St Eustasius, Saba and Curaçao. St Martin was mostly useful for its salt flats; the other islands remained trading bases. The French took co-possession with the English of St Kitts (also called St Christopher) in 1624, but their main Lesser Antillean colonies were Guadeloupe and Martinique, secured in 1635. In the 1650s, the French captured the western third of Hispaniola, creating St Domingue (now Haiti). Spain formally ceded it to France at the Peace of Ryswick in 1697.

The first island that the English settled was Bermuda in 1612, 600 miles west of the Carolinas, 800 miles north of the Caribbean, and not part of the West Indies. In the West Indies, the English initially colonized a quadrangle of Leeward Islands: St Kitts in 1624, Nevis in 1628 and Montserrat and Antigua in 1632. The most significant early English colony in the Lesser Antilles, though, was Barbados, settled in 1627, about 100 miles east of the Windward archipelago. At the 1713 Treaty of Utrecht, the French ceded their half of St Kitts, leaving the island exclusively British. The English also captured Jamaica in 1655, the last island they successfully settled for over a century. It was not until after the French and Indian War (1754–63) that Britain secured possession of the Windward Islands of Dominica, Grenada, St Vincent and Tobago, also called the Ceded Islands.

In addition, the English and the Dutch shared St Croix and the Virgin Islands from 1626, and in the second half of the seventeenth century settlement spread to Anguilla, Barbuda and Tortola in the Lesser Antilles, and to Eleuthera and New Providence in the Bahamas. But these islands were small, lacked water and remained peripheral and insignificant in imperial terms. The English also temporarily settled islands closer to the Spanish American mainland, including Providence Island, Henrietta (San Andreas) and Tortuga in 1631, though the Spanish soon recaptured them. The English made several failed attempts to establish colonies in Guiana on the South American coast, and from about 1650 built an embryonic colony in Surinam, which was then ceded back to the Dutch in the Treaty of Breda of 1667. Ultimately, then, early English colonization focused on the Lesser Antillean islands of St Kitts, Nevis, Antigua, Montserrat and Barbados, and, a little later on, Jamaica in the Greater Antilles.

In contrast to most of the mainland Anglo-American colonies, few of the islands were established with any kind of idealistic scheme in mind. Puritans attempted to take over Bermuda and establish Providence Island as a 'godly commonwealth' resembling Plymouth and Massachusetts. The former effort was overwhelmed by an Anglican ascendancy, the latter by internal rivalries, pirates and then by Spaniards. But what shaped Anglo-Caribbean colonization more than anything else was some of the most complex and vicious geopolitics the world has ever witnessed.

'No peace beyond the line': war and the West Indies

For over a century, the Spanish insisted on their exclusive right to New World territory under the Treaty of Tordesillas of 1494. Over the next hundred years, the French, the English and, finally, the Dutch increasingly asserted what they saw as their right to a piece of the New World pie, first by raiding, then by trading and, finally, at the beginning of the seventeenth century, by making territorial claims. In the 1559 Treaty of Câteau-Cambrésis, Spain and France agreed to differ on the issue of what land belonged to whom, drawing a 'line of amity' along the prime meridian and the Tropic of Cancer, beyond which European peace treaties did not apply. In 1604 and again in 1630 the English explicitly agreed to the principle that, whatever laws or treaties governed diplomacy in Europe, there was 'no peace beyond the line'.

During the Anglo-Spanish war of 1585 to 1604, English privateers repeatedly attacked Spanish vessels and ports in Iberia and America. Wartime trade and plunder raised £100,000 to £200,000 a year, encouraging English adventurers to attempt to muscle in on South as well as North America. Following Spanish suppression of English involvement in illegal tobacco trading in South America and the Caribbean that began in the 1590s, some adventurers attempted to establish tobacco colonies. Charles Leigh attempted one in 1604 on the Wiapoco (Oyapok) River in the Lower Amazon region, but when he died in 1606 it died with him. The French tried and failed to settle the same area the following year, and in 1609 Robert Harcourt claimed the region between the Orinoco and Amazon rivers for the king. Though he received a patent for Guiana, he received little financial or other practical assistance and the venture folded after four years.

Others attempted to create trading posts, tobacco colonies and gold-searching bases in the Lower Amazon region during the next decade, though most were hounded out sooner or later by the Portuguese. The most promising was that of Roger North, who had accompanied Raleigh's last El Dorado mission in 1616, but who, with a group of gentlemen merchants, formed the Amazon Company in 1619 to settle and plant in South America. The venture endangered Anglo-Spanish attempts to negotiate the dynastic marriage of the future Charles I and Henrietta Maria and was dissolved in 1620. All the same, many English, Irish and other settlers remained in the region, even after the Spanish attempt to expel them in 1623. In 1627, after the deterioration of Anglo-Spanish relations following the death of James I, North and Robert Harcourt obtained a patent for the Company for the Plantation of Guiana. Despite governorship by no less a figure than the Duke of Buckingham, merchant disinterest left the company underfunded, and the Portuguese ejected the foreign colonists in 1632. Though the Amazon settlements eventually came to nothing, they provided opportunities to explore those Caribbean islands that the Spanish had not inhabited. It was merchants travelling between Europe, Africa and Guiana who initiated the settlement of England's Lesser Antillean colonies.

Even after English adventurers settled these islands, colonization was profoundly shaped by war with Amerindians and with European rivals. After the English and French massacred the Caribs of St Kitts, Amerindians did little to impede English expansion in this island. Barbados was unoccupied at the time of English colonization and the Arawak population of Jamaica had already been cut down by disease, slavery and warfare inflicted by the Spanish. But one reason for English delay in settling the Windward Islands was powerful resistance from Kalinago Indians. In the mid-seventeenth century, Anglo-West Indians resolved that these 'were a barbarous and cruel set of savages beyond reason or persuasion and must therefore be eliminated'. Yet the Kalinago held on to their lands with the help of the French, who did not want the English to possess Dominica, situated between the French possessions of Guadeloupe and Martinique, although the English remained preoccupied with colonizing and ensuring the security of their other islands.[1]

The Second Anglo-Dutch War (1664–67), the War of the League of Augsburg (1689–97) and the War of the Spanish Succession (1702–13) were particularly destructive times in the West Indies. Between 1666 and 1713, St Kitts was attacked seven times, Antigua and Montserrat twice each and Jamaica and Nevis once each. The British attacked Guadeloupe twice, and Martinique and St Domingue once apiece. Seventeenth-century privateers of all nations wreaked occasional havoc and imposed constant fear and vigilance on the colonists of other and sometimes their own nations. The main business of Jamaica for some time after its settlement was buccaneering. From the 1680s the English preferred trade to plunder, and privateering was finally outlawed with the Treaty of Ryswick in 1697. Many privateers, now classified as pirates, continued to operate out of the Bahamas and to attack European and colonial shipping indiscriminately. At their early eighteenth-century peak there were perhaps 5000 pirates in action, though they were largely suppressed by English actions by the mid-1720s. Even after that, though, the War of the Austrian Succession (1739–48), the French and Indian War (1754–63), the American War of Independence (1775–83), the French Revolutionary Wars (1793–1802) and the Napoleonic Wars (1803–15) brought chaos to the Caribbean colonies.

Despite this instability, in the seventeenth century more migrants moved to the Caribbean and other islands than to anywhere else in Anglo-America. Of the 378,000 English who migrated to the New World between 1630 and 1700, some 223,000, or 60 per cent, went to the West Indies. Some sought adventure and excitement in an environment where laws and social conventions were famously lax. Others sought land, as did migrants to the mainland. Fewer, however, succeeded in that aim. The sugar revolution, which began in Barbados in the 1640s and spread to the rest of the English Caribbean by the end of the century, created a plantation system that left less room for the middling sorts and less opportunity for the lower sorts than did the more partially developed plantation systems and, especially, the non-plantation economies and societies of mainland North America.[2]

Bermuda

Fifteen years before English colonists created a permanent settlement in the Caribbean, they accidentally established one on Bermuda. In July 1609, a fleet of supply ships bound for Virginia was caught up in a storm. The flag-ship, the *Sea Adventurer*, captained by Sir George Somers, was wrecked on the little island's shores. The Spanish had considered the storm-lashed atoll the Isle of Devils, but the English took a different view. Those stranded there were charmed by Bermuda's beauty, but also noted its suitability for tobacco cultivation, among them John Rolfe, who took tobacco to Virginia. Subsequently, 150 members of the Virginia Company formed the Somers Island or Bermuda Company, first a subsidiary of the Virginia Company and later an independent enterprise. In 1612, the company sent 50 settlers to begin populating the island. If an act of nature led to the English settlement of Bermuda then another one almost ended it when a 1620 hurricane destroyed crops and buildings. The absence of Amerindians gave Bermudan colonists an advantage over their Virginian counterparts, though in other ways early settlement suffered similar setbacks.

At first Bermuda was governed from afar, by a governor and assistants in London with a deputy governor nominally in charge on the island, until Governor Nathaniel Butler arrived in 1619 with a charter granting the kind of local autonomy obtained at the same time by Virginians. Bermuda was, however, made a royal colony in 1684. In the meantime puritans attempted but never managed to create the kind of society that they later would in New England. They established a school and tried unsuccessfully to impose social and religious discipline. It became less a puritan and more an Anglican colony, and by the early eighteenth century 88 per cent of its inhabitants belonged to the Church of England. Even so, it remained rather secular. A plan by Bishop Berkeley to establish an Anglican college to serve English planters and Indian converts was another Bermudan idea that came to nothing.

Making Bermuda economically viable proved as halting a process as it did in Virginia. Despite the known potential of tobacco, the Bermuda Company initially relied on ambergris, a whale product used in medicines and perfumes. Bermudans exported their first tobacco crop in 1617, but the small size of the island meant that it could never become the kind of economic staple that it was on the mainland. Within a decade, settlers had staked out claims throughout the island, leaving no room for further expansion at a time when Virginians were beginning to clear great swathes of mainland territory. By the 1680s, Bermudans had more or less abandoned tobacco, focusing instead on garden crops, although islanders had to continue importing food. Mostly, they exploited their advantageous geographical position, engaging increasingly in trade. The island's cedar trees were ideal for exporting lumber and for shipbuilding. At any one time in the eighteenth century, 20 to 30 per cent of Bermudan men were at sea. Another peculiarity of the Bermudan population was the high preponderance of women due to high death rates from seafaring.

Despite these difficulties the population of Bermuda grew steadily, reaching 2000 by 1630, near 4000 by 1660, over 7000 in 1710 and more than 11,000 in 1760. In 1616, Bermuda became the first English colony to import slaves, three years ahead of Virginia. Like Virginia, Bermuda relied heavily on indentured servants, though the slave population rose from 200 in 1660 to near 3000 in 1710 and over 5000 in 1760, and in the eighteenth century slaves constituted the same kind of large minority in Bermuda that they did in the Chesapeake. Slave-holding was generally small-scale and widely diffused, however, with 85 per cent ownership rates in some parts of the island. Slaves worked as farmhands, domestics and, in many cases, in shipbuilding and seafaring, rather than as plantation workers. Even so, Bermuda slaves harboured many of the same grievances as their fellows elsewhere, and in 1761 the island narrowly averted a large-scale slave rebellion. One reason for the high and rising ratio of enslaved to free people in the island population, despite the absence of large-scale plantation-staple agriculture, was that indentured servants were required to leave the island at the end of their terms, as were freed slaves. Though this law was not always enforced, many poorer whites and some free blacks moved to the mainland or to the Caribbean islands.

Providence Island

Puritans attempted to create Calvinist utopias on other islands besides Bermuda. In 1629, John Pym, the Earl of Warwick and proprietor of Bermuda, together with other puritan eminencies such as Lord Brooke and Viscount Saye and Sele, conspired to move in on the western Caribbean. In 1630, the king chartered the Providence Island Company that took the eponymous outcrop (Santa Catalina to the Spanish) off the Nicaraguan coast. They failed, however, to create the 'godly commonwealth' they envisioned. Company member Sir Benjamin Rudyerd wrote to island governor Philip Bell in 1633 that

> Wee well hoped (according to our Intentions) That wee had planted a Relligious Collonye in the Isle of Providence, instead whearof wee fynd the roote of bitterness plentifullye planted amongst you, and industrious supplanting one of another, and not a Man theare of Place (a straunge thing to consider) but hee doth both accuse, and is accused; these are uncomfortable fruits of Religion.

One reason for the lack of harmony was the absence of local political representation. While the puritan settlers of New England knew that settlement and local autonomy were essential to successful colonization, their Providence Island Company counterparts apparently did not. Members of the Company, believing that divided management had undone other colonial enterprises, excluded the merchants from the Company and attempted to run the enterprise themselves and from a distance. Furthermore, authorities in London insisted that land not be distributed among settlers and that settlers act as tenants, sharing half their profits with the company. While other proprietors attracted settlers and gave them a stake in colonization, the Providence Island Company did not. The irony is that the Company was peopled largely by leading members of the Long Parliament's 'Middle

Group', men in the thick of defending parliament against the tyranny of Charles I. Among them were Nathaniel Rich, who in March 1628 had enunciated in the House of Commons the principle and the practicalities of individual rights: 'No propriety, no industry; no industry, all beggars; no propriety, no valor; no valor, all in confusion'. Similarly, a few weeks later, Francis Pym asked 'For who will contend, who will endanger himself for that which is not his own'? They should not have been surprised, then, at the failure of their colonial venture. The island became nothing more than a base for attacking the Spanish, who duly took it back in 1643 and expelled the survivors of their attack, most of whom moved to Barbados.

The Bahamas

The puritans' failures in Bermuda and Providence Island did not deter them from trying again. In 1648, the Company of Eleutherian Adventurers founded the colony of New Providence on the main island in the Bahamas. The island chain was strategically important to both England and Spain, and the Spanish destroyed the English settlements in 1684. Seven years later the governor of Bermuda organized resettlement and established Nassau as a fortified town, but the Spanish descended again and, subsequently, the islands' main settlements were temporary lairs from which pirates raided passing ships.

In 1718, the British government, working through authorities in Bermuda, regained Nassau and established the Bahamas as a separate colony. Settlers initially made a bare living exporting timber, dyewoods, salt, fruit, turtles and turtle shells, though they eventually developed cotton, tobacco and sugar plantations. By 1760 the number of colonists reached 4000, with about two-thirds of the population living on New Providence, concentrated near Nassau. The growing proportion of slaves in the population reached the 50 per cent mark around 1760. Again, because the plantation economy was not highly developed, the large proportion of slaves is partly attributable to frequent out-migration by temporary white settlers. The islands offered fewer economic opportunities and were less attractive to migrants than other colonies. By far the most successful and significant ventures, therefore, were those of the Leeward Islands, Barbados and Jamaica.[3]

The Leeward Islands

Sir Thomas Warner was a Suffolk gentleman and a friend and neighbour of John Winthrop, the principal founder of Massachusetts. As Winthrop would, Warner went to the New World, but their American experiences and the colonies they respectively founded could hardly have been more different. Warner initially became involved with Roger North's adventure in

Guiana. In 1622, leaving the Lower Amazon, he stopped at St Kitts and noted its suitability for tobacco planting. After gaining mercantile backing in England, he returned with a small group of colonists in 1624 and planted a settlement on the island. Four years later, colonists would cross a three-mile channel on St Kitts's south-west coast to settle Nevis. Another four years on, others would colonize nearby Monstserrat and Antigua.

These islands are tiny. St Kitts covers just 68 square miles, Nevis 50, Montserrat 33 and Antigua 108. Yet it took almost 80 years for these islands to be fully settled. Some impediments to colonization were natural. The first three islands are mountainous, with peaks of over 3000 feet. The hillsides were difficult to clear and plant, and were prone to erosion. The mountains are also volcanic, and though there were no eruptions in the seventeenth century, there were nevertheless earthquakes and tremors. These events were usually more frightening than damaging, although an earthquake destroyed and caused the inundation of Jamestown, Nevis, in 1680. (Montserrat was rendered uninhabitable after a series of earthquakes from 1992 culminated in a volcanic eruption in 1997.) Antigua is lower lying, more like Barbados further to the south, and has a cooler climate, but no springs or rivers and therefore too little water. Hurricanes, most common in August, were a worse problem. A hurricane destroyed St Kitts's first tobacco crop in 1624 and others thereafter. A 1638 hurricane killed 75 people and destroyed 5 ships, and the damage might have been worse had not Carib Indians on neighbouring islands given the English advance warning (the English subsequently suspected them of witchcraft and blamed them for the hurricanes in the first place).

Yet earthquakes and hurricanes did not heap anywhere near as much havoc on the early colonists of the Leeward Islands as those colonists heaped on each other. The greatest impediment to successful colonization was frequent warfare between rival European powers, in particular between the English and the French. The damage done to each island might have been less had their respective residents engaged consistently in concerted resistance, but sometimes instead they preferred to sit on the sidelines and anticipate the commercial benefits they would gain from the misfortunes of their Anglo-Caribbean rivals. English settlers also fought among themselves, occasionally with deadly and always with disruptive consequences, over religion, politics, property and status. And they fought with Irish Catholic settlers and with imperial authorities. Early Leeward Island colonists therefore lived in what historian Richard Dunn called 'a state of perpetual crisis'. Their unstable pioneer period lasted much longer than that of the Chesapeake colonies, and yet, as in the Chesapeake, these colonies finally began to settle down. By the end of Queen Anne's War in 1713 a sugar plantation system was reaching the point of full development throughout the islands, one that in the eighteenth century created a much wealthier and more powerful plantocracy, and a society with far more slaves and far fewer middling and poorer whites than was the case in Virginia and Maryland.[4]

The Leeward Islands and European wars

A year after the arrival of Sir Thomas Warner in St Kitts, a party of French settlers arrived there too. Unequipped to resist them, Warner agreed to share the island with them; the French at either end, the English in the middle. In 1627, the governors of the two settlements agreed the first of at least 10 *ententes cordiales* drawn up during the period of co-occupancy. Occasionally the two nation's colonists acted in concert, as when they massacred the local Amerindians at night and by surprise. In 1629 they joined forces to resist a Spanish invasion, albeit unsuccessfully. The Spanish destroyed the colonists' property and expelled as many as they could find. French colonists who escaped to neighbouring islands and English colonists who took to the mountains subsequently returned and rebuilt, replanted and restored their settlements. But it would not be the last time that the colonists of St Kitts, French and English alike, abandoned their island. In future, they would chase each other out.

The worst international crisis of the seventeenth century in the English Leeward Islands came during the Anglo-French conflict of 1666–67. As war approached, Deputy Governor William Watts decided to expel the French from St Kitts, whom the English by then outnumbered two-to-one. He delayed until, in March 1666, the French commander persuaded him to reaffirm the island's Anglo-French accord. When news of the declaration of war in Europe arrived a month later, however, Watts decided to attack and gathered a gang of buccaneers and a force of 400 militiamen from Nevis. But it was too late, for the French swept through the island before Watts was ready, forcing an English surrender. The French expelled 5000 English colonists, destroying buildings and plantations, and stole 400 slaves. A hurricane subsequently wrecked a relief fleet from Barbados, leaving the French free to invade Montserrat and Antigua, again destroying buildings and crops and making off with 1000 slaves. An English counter-attack the following year failed to recapture St Kitts. Montserrat, Antigua and their part of St Kitts were restored to the English in the Treaty of Breda (1667) in exchange for England returning Acadia to France, though the French refused the English access to St Kitts for four years and never returned their stolen slaves.

Ten years later Christopher Jeaffreson, a St Kitts planter, noted glumly that 'wars here are more destructive then in any other partes of the world, as appears by this island, where the sad workes of the last unhappy difference, in the yeare sixty-six, are not half worne out; nor is the island a quarter so well peopled as it was then'. And there was more to come. The French invaded the English sector of St Kitts again in July 1689, at the outbreak of

King William's War, and captured it by August. Decisive leadership by Leeward governor Christopher Codrington, a Barbadian planter who part-financed the subsequent counter-attack from his own resources, as well as military support from his home island and from England, helped redeem the situation. In 1690, Codrington retook St Kitts with a force of 2500 men, though his attempts to invade French Guadeloupe and Martinique failed due to an absence of naval support and the ill will of English Leeward plant-ers who did not fancy market competition from any new English colony. In fact, English soldiers from the other Leeward Islands suggested plundering properties abandoned by the English on St Kitts after the French invasion. Instead, Codrington divided French lands into 10-acre plots to create a crit-ical mass of population for the formation of a militia (and took a sizeable chunk of land for himself), though these gains were returned to France in the Treaty of Ryswick of 1797.

After five years of peace, Queen Anne's War broke out. This time Christopher Codrington the younger drove the French out of St Kitts in 1702, and the next year spent two months with 3500 troops thoroughly sacking and plundering Guadeloupe. In response, the French sacked and plundered St Kitts and Nevis in 1706, and Antigua and Montserrat in 1712. The object of both sides by then was not to take territory but to wreck the economic competition and steal slaves. As well as destroying crops and buildings, the French took away 600 slaves from St Kitts, around 1000 from Nevis and 1500 from Antigua and Montserrat. The colonists of St Kitts sub-sequently attempted to claim £145,000 damages from parliament, though they only received £28,000. Parliament gave a larger sum of £75,000 to the islanders of Nevis. The French handed over their part of St Kitts to the English in the Treaty of Utrecht in 1713. Occasional raids during the War of Austrian Succession (1739–48), the Seven Years War (1756–63), the French Revolutionary Wars (1793–1802) and the Napoleonic Wars (1803–15) kept St Kitts and Leeward islanders on their toes, though the end of co-occu-pancy left them much freer to develop their plantations than they had been hitherto.

Political conflict in the early Leeward Islands

The domestic politics of the Leeward Islands were even more chaotic than those of Virginia and even Maryland, and were so for longer. Settlement was initially fraught because in July 1625 Charles I granted the right to col-onize the Caribbean to James Hay, Earl of Carlisle, and then in February 1628 he gave the same grant to the Earl of Pembroke, without rescinding that of Carlisle. Sir Thomas Warner survived these years and was confirmed as governor when disputed ownership was settled in Carlisle's favour in 1629. Not that Warner then had an easy time of it. In 1642 he faced a year-long rebellion led by a 'most arrogant and nowe sawcye proude fellowe' named Phance Beecher, also known as 'lyinge Beecher' and 'bragging Beecher'. Beecher had arrived at the island three years earlier, built a fortune 'by his Cutthroat dealings', mostly gambling, and then began challenging the governor as a member of the island council, a position he owed to kinship to the clerk of the Privy Council. Furthermore, St Kitts deputy governor Edward Warner survived an assassination attempt by Anthony Hilton, governor of Nevis, who himself survived an attempted murder by his servant. Henry Ashton, governor of Antigua in the 1630s, cut off a woman's hair after she rebuffed his sexual advances. Not surprisingly, perhaps, political authority was not much respected. In Montserrat in 1654, a wealthy Dutch planter named Samuel Waad was executed for calling the governor an 'Irish Murderer' and an 'Irish Barbarian'. Subsequently, the island council fixed fines of 500 pounds and 5000 pounds of sugar, respectively, for cursing assemblymen and councillors.

Leeward Island colonists eventually threw off the proprietorship of Carlisle, but royal government turned out to be not much more to their liking. At the Restoration of Charles II, the Leeward Islanders struck a deal with the king. In exchange for acknowledgement of their land titles and free trade with the Dutch, they would pay a 4.5 per cent duty on commodities exported from the islands. The Tariff Act of 1661 also placed a duty of 1s 5d per hundredweight on West Indian sugar imports, though a 35s 10d tax on sugar from elsewhere gave island planters a virtual monopoly in the home market.

Charles appointed Francis, Lord Willoughby as governor of all the Leewards and of Barbados, the rival colony to the south that was far outstripping the Leewards in sugar production and wealth generation. After the military catastrophes of 1666–67, though, Charles gave the Leewards their own governor once again. Charles Wheler, however, appointed in 1670, gave up his troubled office within a year. Subsequently, Governor William Stapleton (1672–86) managed to rule with some semblance of order, partly due to planters' need to focus on rebuilding their wrecked plantations. Even so, Stapleton could not get the colonies to abide by the Navigation Acts, build or rebuild fortifications or act in concert in any way. He called representatives from each island legislature for several general assemblies, but they refused to standardize their laws, coordinate their defences or vote joint revenue measures. He finally secured some revenue from Nevis, but only after threatening to relocate his administration to a rival island.

Stapleton, who died in 1686, was a local planter, and still he found the islanders almost ungovernable. His successor was even less likely to command their assent. Sir Nathaniel Johnson was an outsider, a former manager of the hearth tax, and was appointed by James II to rule by force if need be. He raised taxes, challenged land titles and invited smaller farmers to challenge larger ones for their political and judicial offices. Though an

Anglican, he also attempted to enforce James's pro-French and pro-Catholic policies by establishing good relations with Martinique and announcing religious toleration for Catholics. These were not popular moves among English planters who had so much trouble with the French and who also feared the many Irish colonists in their midst. In May 1689, Johnson informed the new king William that he would not accept the Glorious Revolution. In June, 130 Irish servants rebelled in support of James II, attacking English plantations on the leeward side of St Kitts. The unpaid and underfed garrison stayed in their barracks. The next month the French invaded. Then planters intercepted a letter that appeared to show Johnson ready to betray the islands to the enemy. Even so, the islanders, in contrast to their fellows in Maryland, Massachusetts and New York, did not rebel against the governor. The deputy governor of St Kitts expressed their sense of demoralization when he wrote to an unknown correspondent that 'We are Screwed and Taxed up to the Height and no manner of care is taken either of our persons or Estates'. But they did persuade Johnson to resign. He appointed Christopher Codrington in his place and then left for South Carolina, just before the French captured St Kitts.

Even Codrington, for all his military success, suffered at the hands of his fractious Leeward subjects. He had to persuade the militiamen of Nevis, Montserrat and Antigua not to complete the destruction of rival English plantations on St Kitts started by the French. It was not easy. He told the Lords of Trade that 'The trouble my Lords of Governing a volontary Army is Inexpressible.' By the time of Codrington's death in 1698, authorities in London were hearing from planters that he was a tyrant and a crook who had traded illegally with the Dutch and French during the war. These kinds of triangulated conflicts between colonists, governors and imperial authorities would continue to characterize Caribbean and other colonies' politics during the eighteenth century.

Anglo-Caribbean politics reached their lowest point at the rather abrupt end of the governorship of Daniel Parke on 7 December 1710. Parke was a Virginian, a former assemblyman and councillor in that colony, and a failed parliamentary candidate in England, who made his name when, as aide-de-camp to the Duke of Marlborough, he carried news of victory at the Battle of Blenheim to Queen Anne. The queen rewarded the messenger with 1000 guineas and a miniature portrait of herself. Parke was then appointed Governor-General of the Leeward Islands. He arrived in the Caribbean in July 1706, just after the French attacks on St Kitts and Nevis. Soon after his arrival, St Kitts councillor John Pogson killed lieutenant-governor John Johnson, who was blamed for the rout. Pogson, found not guilty, was removed from the council by the queen, but then elected to the assembly by the people. Parke made this already febrile atmosphere much worse. He ignored the four islands' assemblies, dealing only with a general assembly. He tried to forge alliances with smaller planters by ending forced debtor sales, thereby preventing large planters from consolidating their holdings. He persecuted the Codringtons, confiscating their 763-acre St Kitts planta- tion, sponsoring privateers to attack their island of Barbuda and suing to recover the gains they made during the French wars. He complained of the islanders' moral shortcomings, especially their 'unnaturall and monstrous lusts' for slaves, yet seduced several planters' wives and daughters.

In 1708 and 1709, Parke was shot at several times and on one occasion wounded in the arm. At the same time, Leeward planters bombarded the Board of Trade with denunciations of Parke and pleas for his recall, while Parke wrote numerous accusatory letters against them. In February 1710, the queen recalled him, but he held on. By winter he grew desperate to assert his authority and, taking control of the Leeward regiment from its colonel, led the soldiers to disperse a meeting of the Antigua Assembly. Parke then garrisoned his residence in St John with 70 soldiers and 5 cannon. Meanwhile, the furious assemblymen gathered a crowd of 300 armed men who surrounded the house on 7 December and demanded Parke's departure for Nevis. Parke fired a cannon at the rebels, and in turn they charged the house. One of the governor's last acts was personally to shoot and kill one of the rebel leaders. The other shot him in the leg, where- upon the crowd dragged him naked around his house, beat his head and broke his back. When he asked for water, they spat in the dying man's face. Forty-four of his guards were killed with him or wounded. Finally, the rebels stole all his effects, including the miniature of Queen Anne from around his neck.

Parke was so despised that, despite his pitiful and shocking death (even by the standards of the time and place), no one cooperated with the conse- quent investigation and no one was prosecuted for the murder. Nor was Parke's successor given much quarter. Ordered to restore order and pardon all bar the ringleaders, Walter Douglas was soon subjected to the barrage of condemnation for corruption to which many governors in future years would become accustomed. After the attacks on Antigua and Montserrat, Douglas was recalled and spent five years in prison. After 1713 and the Treaty of Utrecht, political relations between people and governors would rarely be in such a state of crisis again, though they would rarely be harmo- nious either.[5]

Economy, society and population in the early Leeward Islands

For almost 80 years, the Leeward Islands were characterized by the kind of fluid and inchoate social arrangements that had been a feature of life in Virginia for around 20 years and in Maryland for less than that. Like those colonies, though, a period of experimentation eventuated in a prosperous sugar economy and settled society. St Kitts's early planters grew tobacco, as Sir Thomas Warner initially envisioned. Tobacco was not, however, as lucrative a business for the island as its promoter originally hoped. St Kitts tobacco was better than that of Barbados but not as good as Virginia's. In 1639, Warner banned tobacco production, hoping to force prices up, but two years later John Jeaffreson complained that planters were at the 'pointe of undoeing, haveing spent their whole Tyme in peddling and chaffering to the multiplying of debt, the infecting them with the love of a long accustomed idleness'. Some planters diversified into cotton and indigo, and others raised cattle and fished. Few made fortunes, though, and none did so on the scale of Barbadians. Nor were things much different on the other islands. As late as 1655 a London guide entitled *America: An exact Description of the West-Indies* dismissed Nevis and Montserrat as 'of so little consideration, especially to our Nation, that it would seem but tedious to mention them further'. And, for all his exactitude, the anonymous author was unsure whether Antigua was even settled.

In the absence of a wealthy and well-articulated planter class, and with large numbers of white indentured servants, the Leeward Islands remained socially inchoate for some time. In 1678, Nevis, by far the wealthiest of the four islands at that time, had only 8 large planters with 60 or more slaves and 45 middling planters with 20 to 59 slaves, and in a white population of 3521 they were very much outnumbered by about 1000 small farmers with fewer than 20 slaves, and around 500 servants (there were also 3849 slaves). For reasons outlined above, their authority did not make up for their lack of numbers. These figures compare with 19 large planters and 14 middling planters in a white population of about 1500 in 1680 in St Thomas Parish, a wealthy sugar planting district in Barbados where small farmers and servants numbered respectively 160 and 226 (slaves numbered 3396) and where the formation of an elite was very much advanced.

Many servant migrants were Irish, especially after 1637 when Anthony Brisket, the Wexford-born governor of Montserrat, began inviting his countrymen to settle the island. In 1678, when Governor Stapleton made a census, 69 per cent of whites in Montserrat were Irish. Smaller but substantial proportions of the white populations of the other islands were Irish too: 26 per cent and 23 per cent in Antigua and Nevis respectively, and 10 per cent in St Kitts. Eleven years later, at the Glorious Revolution, an Irish servant uprising preceded the French takeover of St Kitts, and the Irish of Antigua and Montserrat threatened to rebel as well.

English servants could be trouble too. During the Spanish attack on St Kitts in 1629, English and French colonists cooperated with each other in self-defence, but when the Spanish fleet attacked Nevis some of the servants swam out to the Spanish ships to inform the enemy where they could plunder the planters' possessions, while others threw down their arms with cries of 'Liberty, joyfull Liberty'. Another group of servants liberated themselves in a different way. Planter-merchant Christopher Jeaffreson transported 28 English convicts to St Kitts as indentured servants in 1684. On reaching their destination, they 'threw off their cloathes overboard, and came as bare to the island, as if they had no cloathes'. Six months later he sent 38 more. As they were being marched to their ship, though manacled and guarded by 30 men, 'they committed several thefts, snatching away hats, perrewigs, etc., from several persons, whose curiosity led them into the crowd'. Sometimes merchants like Jeaffreson knew they were storing up trouble. Some of his convicts were experienced seamen, but he kept this fact quiet 'for nobody, I suppose, will be desirous to buy a servant that has convenience of freeing himself, by the first boat he can steal'.

The populations of the Leeward Islands remained small due to wartime disruptions and out-migrations, especially after the capture of Jamaica in 1655 gave Caribbean-bound migrants an alternative destination. In 1660, when the Barbados population was 53,300, St Kitts' was 2222, Antigua's 2987, Montserrat's 2449 and Nevis's 4913, a total of 12,571. By 1678, their respective populations rose to 2335, 4480, 3674 and 7370, or 18,857 in total. In both years, not quite half the Leeward Islands' populations were slaves, though slaves slightly outnumbered whites in Nevis, and whites outnumbered slaves nearly three-to-one in Montserrat. In the latter year, a half-century after settlement, white men still outnumbered white women by almost two-to-one (though the more stable slave population was near sexual parity). A visitor from New England to Antigua in the 1660s called the islanders 'a company of sodomites'. The lack of women and the attenuated nature of family life contributed further to social instability.

Yet the islands were beginning to take shape, slowly, though in the uncertain international circumstances not especially surely. Just as wealthy prospective planters had previously eschewed the Leewards for the better prospect of Barbados, some such as Governor Luke Stokes of Nevis resettled in Jamaica after 1655. After seeing his sugar plantations levelled twice by hurricanes in 1681, Christopher Jeaffreson moved back to England. Within four years of his departure, 13 of his 45 slaves were dead, as were all his livestock; his fields were bare, his mill was broken down and his steward had made off with his household goods, leaving the Jeaffreson estate with large debts. But for all these movements and misfortunes, some were beginning to build hefty fortunes. The wealthiest planters began abandoning tobacco and indigo and investing in sugar in the 1650s and, especially, the 1660s. Governor William Watts's St Kitts sugar plantation made £1500 per year before the French invasion of 1666. In 1678, the Leeward Islands exported about 3600 tons of sugar. Nevis led the way and at this point prospered most. Its estates, according to the Stapleton census of 1678, were worth £384,000 that year, compared to £196,500 for the other islands combined.

During the next three decades, despite a fall in sugar prices and the battering the islands took during the wars of King William and Queen Anne, the islands underwent an economic revolution. By 1713, the Leewards' annual sugar exports had risen to 10,000 tons. The capital investment in slaves and in refining equipment required by the switch to sugar meant that larger planters were at a great advantage and they gradually bought out smaller farmers and pushed out tenants. The impact on the islands' populations between 1678 and 1708 was enormous, as the white population halved and the black population tripled. Optimal production required 1 slave to work every 2 acres planted in sugar, compared to 1 slave per 40 acres in tobacco, and Leeward Islanders imported about 1000 slaves a year between 1678 and 1708. The number of whites in St Kitts fell from 1897 to 1670, while the number of blacks rose from 1436 to 3294. Antigua's white population rose, but only slightly, from 2308 to 2892, while its black population rose massively from 2172 to 12,290. Montserrat's white population fell from 2682 to 1545, and its black population rose from 992 to 3570. The number of whites in Nevis fell from 3521 to 1104 (probably 1600 including children, who were excluded from Governor Parke's 1708 census on that island), and its black population also fell slightly from 3849 to 3676 in the wake of the French raid that carried off almost half the island's slaves. Nevis was devastated during these wars, going from the richest to the poorest of the islands, but the pattern was the same. The islands were fast being taken over by hugely wealthy sugar planters and brutally exploited slaves. By 1760, the islands' white populations added up to 8700 while their black populations were near 74,000.[6]

Barbados

In 1625, Captain John Powell, in the employ of the Anglo-Dutch merchant Sir William Courteen, left Guiana and on his way home annexed Barbados for James I. Courteen was experienced in Caribbean trade and invested £10,000 in the subsequent settlement of Barbados. In 1627, two shiploads of colonists returned there on a mission backed by Courteen and the Earl of Pembroke, who that year received his patent as 'Lord Proprietor of the Caribbees'. After some years of political conflict and agricultural experimentation, Barbados began to prosper. During the seventeenth century it would be the jewel in England's imperial crown, as Jamaica would be later.

Barbados enjoys a number of geographical advantages that allowed it to surpass its Anglo-Caribbean rival islands in the early years. A hundred miles east of the Lesser Antillean chain, it was less susceptible to attack by England's imperial rivals. It also happened to be unoccupied by Carib Indians when the English arrived. With 166 square miles, and 21 miles long by 14 miles wide, it was a much larger island than the individual Leeward Islands, and although it was smaller than the four Leewards combined it was not a steep volcanic outcrop as were St Kitts, Nevis and Montserrat. Like Antigua, it had a rolling landscape, sloping to the sea on the Caribbean side and descending more steeply on the Atlantic side, but unlike

Antigua it had springs and rivers. The topography of Barbados was pleasing to English eyes and settlers soon nicknamed it 'little England'. It was also blessed with large natural harbours that made it an easy port of call for ships from Europe and Africa. The climate was generally moderate, though it was prone to hurricanes. The worst one of the century hit the island in 1675, killing 200 people and destroying 3000 houses, 3 churches and many sugar mills on the leeward side. As elsewhere in the Caribbean, though, most of its early tribulations were man-made.

Political conflict in early Barbados

Soon after Courteen's colonists settled Barbados, the Earl of Carlisle, the other chartered proprietor of the Caribbean, sent a mission of his own, so Barbados had two governors and two sets of settlers. The rivals fought, seized each other's supplies and banished each other's men from the island. At one point, Carlisle's agent gained control, but then betrayed his master by assassinating his successor and was finally removed when Carlisle sent another replacement a year later. The disputed proprietorship was settled in Carlisle's favour in 1629, but even after that there was plenty of political strife. Carlisle took little personal interest in Barbados, except for the quit-rents that colonists were obliged to pay him, and he left management in the hands of his governor, Henry Hawley. Hawley charged all freemen a poll tax by executive authority and ruled without an assembly for much of his tenure, though he finally called one in 1639.

The civil war saw the end of the proprietary regime and the ascendance of representative self-government. In 1643, the assembly simply stopped paying rents to the proprietor's estate (Carlisle died in 1636). They also began bypassing proprietorial authority. The same year, sugar planter James Holdip petitioned the king for 'a grant that noe other Sugars may bee imported into his Majesties Dominions but such as are made upon the Barbadas'. Soon, though, they found that the best way to nurture their nascent sugar industry was by free trade, in particular by trading with the Dutch, who had taught them how to cultivate and refine the cane, and who helped them market the crop.

During the civil wars, Barbadians declared themselves neutral, acting with remarkable calm and consensus. In 1645, Governor Philip Bell and the assembly asked for the freemen's approval of their favoured neutrality, and subsequently Bell reported that

> It pleased god so to unite their minds and harts together that every parish declared themselves resolutely for the maintenance of their peace and present government; and to admitt of noe alterations or new commissions from eyther side . . . against the kinge we are resolved never to be, and without the freindeshipe of the perliament and free trade of London ships we are not able to subsist.

After the execution of Charles I in January 1649, however, royalists began openly opposing parliamentary rule, even advocating independence from the Commonwealth. On 7 May 1650, royalists asserted and further enhanced their political ascendancy by accepting Francis, Lord Willoughby as their governor. Willoughby expelled numerous Roundheads from the island and confiscated their property, forcing parliament to despatch Sir George Ayscue and a fleet with 860 men to subdue the island. The Barbadian militia held out for three months, until 11 January 1652, when they accepted terms. By the Charter of Barbados the colony accepted the authority of parliament and the governorship of Daniel Searle, but parliament acknowledged the right to continued colonial self-government and allowed free trade with the Dutch, though it subsequently failed to honour that part of the bargain.

At the Restoration, Barbadians once again had to negotiate their relationship with the mother country. Governor Thomas Modyford, like so many former Roundheads, proclaimed Charles II king. Charles abolished free trade with the Dutch and brought Barbadians back into the mercantilist navigation system. Barbadians also had to buy slaves from the monopolistic African companies. In turn, Charles abolished the proprietorship, acknowledged Barbadian land purchases made in the 1650s and appointed Willoughby as his first royal governor.

The king also tacitly accepted the legitimacy of the local assembly and accidentally enhanced its powers. In 1663, Willoughby persuaded the assembly to approve the same 4.5 per cent tax on exports from the island that Leeward Islanders had accepted for the support of the governor and his government. Charles kept the money, however, thereby cheating Barbadians out of the revenue they raised. Yet that left the governor still financially dependent on the assembly. The purse strings are some of the toughest fibres in politics, as anyone who tried to govern anyone else in the seventeenth century quickly learned, and as Governor Sir Jonathan Atkins found in the 1670s. Sent by the Lords of Trade with specific instructions to make Barbados more accountable to the crown, and being an outsider with no local property of his own, the only way Atkins could raise revenue and thereby govern effectively was to go native. The Lords of Trade were not pleased to find Atkins becoming the mouthpiece of Barbadian objections to the Navigation Acts, the 4.5 per cent tax, the Royal African Company monopoly and private merchants' shipping charges, or that he signed legislation that the crown disliked. The home government persuaded Atkins to govern more and represent less, and to that effect in 1680 he produced a census and other statistical information, a significant achievement considering that Barbadians and other Anglo-Caribbeans were notoriously secretive lest they be taxed (indeed Richard Dunn estimates that Atkins's figures for property holdings are 10 to 15 per cent too low). As it turned out, this information is more use to historians than it was to imperial authorities, for they filed Atkins's survey and replaced him as governor with Sir Richard Dutton.[7]

The Restoration Stuarts interfered in colonial affairs more assiduously than any monarchs, parliaments or other imperial authorities before 1764, and they intervened in Barbados, the richest colony at the time, more extensively than they did anywhere else except in the short-lived Dominion of New England. Charles II personally created eight profitable offices in Barbados for English placemen. Governor Dutton was aggressive too, ultimately too aggressive. He used his own placemen in military and judicial offices, browbeat his councillors and extorted some £18,000 from the assembly in the form of 'presents' and bribes as well as salary. To avoid paying the salary of lieutenant-governor John Witham, he fined his deputy £5000 for 'misconduct'. This last act in 1685 led to his recall.

However beleaguered Barbadians were by Charles II, though, they gave back as good as they got. In 1668 and 1670 the assembly petitioned the king for a charter of self-government similar to that of Massachusetts. They did not get one because the agent carrying the request felt it was worded so incautiously that he was too afraid to deliver it. When Charles asked parliament to increase the sugar duty, the assembly told the king that the fact that the hike would ruin them ought to be 'Obvious to the most Vulgar Capacity'. The Assembly sent sugar worth £643 to assist 12 Barbadian planters living in London who formed a committee against the tax, and even Charles's own governor, Willoughby, opposed it in person in both Houses of Parliament. When the bill failed, the king was reportedly 'not over well pleased'. Lobbying against the new Navigation Act in 1673, Barbadians told MPs 'how unpracticable it was for them to lay a tax on those that had noe members in theire house' – exactly the point that colonists throughout British America would make against direct parliamentary taxation 90 years later.

James II was even more aggressive than his brother. Governor Dutton's replacement was Edwin Stede, a former agent of the monopolistic Royal African Company in Barbados and therefore already suspect in Barbadian eyes when appointed in 1685. Their suspicions were justified, for Stede used his office to persecute rogue slave traders. At the same time, King James created and sold 19 new island council seats, sometimes to smaller planters and others in an attempt to diminish the domination of the large sugar planters. When one post went to an overseer named Richard Harwood, other councillors complained of his 'servile condition, personall inabillities, and other Scandalous Circumstances'. James II also doubled the sugar tax. Barbadians were therefore as happy as any other colonists to see James gone in 1688–89. Even more so when the Royal African Company lost its monopoly and parliament restored the sugar tax to its pre-1685 level. Subsequent governors were more pliant too, although planters resisted attempts by Governor Francis Russell in the 1690s to extend the franchise to holders of 2 acres rather than 10. Russell hoped planters might treat poor whites better 'to gett their votes for 'em att the next Election', but planters insisted that 'men of interest only may share in soe great trusts'. Even so, freeholders with 10 acres or more constituted 25 per cent of adult white men, a smaller proportion of voters than in most of the Americas, but a substantial proportion nonetheless. The smaller freeholders evidently jealously guarded their privilege, for in 1680 there were some 250 with exactly the 10 acres required for the franchise.[8]

Economy, society and population in early Barbados

Barbados suffered some social instability before its society, economy and politics settled down, though not as much as the Leeward Islands or later Jamaica. All the earliest migrants were men, mostly young men. By the 1680s, though, about a quarter of migrants were women. Most were indentured servants, some of them kidnapped or 'barbadosed', though probably not as many as popular legend claims. Many seventeenth-century migrants were sons and daughters of small yeomen who were looking for land for themselves, and quite a few were skilled artisans. During the seventeenth century, many servant migrants were Irish, adding an ethnic and religious dimension to social conflict. One Irishman received 21 lashes for asserting over dinner that 'if there was so much English Blood in the tray as there was Meat, he would eat it'. Barbadians suspected Irish involvement in a slave insurrection conspiracy in 1692, and in subsequent years petitioned for Scots to migrate instead. When offered more Irish servants in 1697, the assembly responded that 'We desire no Irish rebels may be sent to us: for we want not labourers of that colour to work for us, but men in whom we may confide, to strengthen us'. Barbadians later imposed oaths of loyalty on Irish voters and office holders.

Barbados was particularly badly reputed for the treatment of indentured servants. The writer Richard Ligon, though a propagandist for the island, nevertheless noted 'much cruelty there done to servants, as I do not think one Christian could do to another', and reported that 'some cruel Masters will provoke their servants so, by extreme ill usage, and often and cruel beating them, as they grow desperate and so join together to avenge themselves'. Some did attempt to avenge themselves. Servile conspiracies were detected and rebellions averted in 1634 and 1647, the latter eventuating in the execution of 18 conspirators. Planters built their houses like forts, complete with bastions from which they could pour scalding water on servants or slaves who might charge their homes.[9]

The treatment of servants was such that the term 'white slaves' was a commonplace in the Caribbean. The reputation for ill-treatment of servants, however, produced a backlash that eventually contributed to the transformation of Barbadian and ultimately all Anglo-Caribbean societies.

Among 12,000 political prisoners who were transported between 1649 and 1655 were 73 who were sent there for participating in a riot in Salisbury in March 1654. Five years later they petitioned the House of Commons Grand Committee of Grievances regarding the injustice of their 'being sold into slavery in Barbados'. The two petitions, one by M. Rivers, O. Foyle and 70 others, the other by Rowland Thomas, were published as a pamphlet entitled *England's Slavery or Barbados Merchandize, Represented in a Petition to the High Court of Parliament* that attracted the attention of MPs and a wide public. The petitioners questioned 'by what authority so great a breach is made upon the free people of England . . . by merchants that deal in slaves and souls of men?' Even Martin Noell, the West Indian merchant who had sold the 73 under the authority of Cromwell, admitted in the House of Commons that 'I abhor the thought of setting £100 upon any man's person' as 'false and scandalous', though he also pleaded that servants were used 'not so hard as is represented to you'. Sir Henry Vane, among others, called 'white slavery' a violation of 'human rights', then a newly developing concept in English politics. After that, in 1661, the Barbadian Assembly enacted a servant code that consolidated customs and legislative and council acts. The Act for the Good Governing of Servants and Ordaining the Rights between Masters and Servants explicitly stated its intention to protect masters' investments in labour against runaways, rebels and those who questioned or attempted to terminate their indentures. That same year, though, Barbados passed a slave code that clearly distinguished the status of white servants and black bondspeople.

In the second half of the seventeenth century, planters were worrying about the growing influence of two other groups: Quakers and slaves. George Fox visited Barbados for three months in 1671, and four years later Irish Quaker William Edmundson claimed to speak to a crowd of 3000. Anglican clerics demanded political action against these 'Base Sort of Phanatick People'. The political authorities responded, in part because they were concerned about the influence of Quakers on slaves. Though most of the 58 Quakers on the island owned slaves, and 9 indeed were large planters with over 60 slaves, there was cause for concern, from a slave-holder's viewpoint. Fox had urged Barbadians to Christianize their slaves. Edmundson told Governor Atkins that if slaves rebelled, masters should blame themselves for 'keeping them in Ignorance, and under Oppression'. In 1675, Atkins encouraged the assembly to discourage Quakers from converting slaves to Christianity, 'of which they can make them understand nothing'. Clearly, Atkins regarded blacks as unintelligent, but not too unintelligent to understand their oppression and act against it, urging the assembly 'to consider whether, Liberty be a fit Doctrine for Slaves'. The assembly then imposed heavy fines on Quakers who took slaves to meetings (and who failed to muster for the militia). These punishments did not entirely repress Quakers. Governors Atkins and Dutton took some £7000 in fines from 'numerous, insolent and rich' Friends. Dutton even had the Tudor Street, Bridgetown, Meeting House vandalized and closed, and one Quaker executed for blasphemy. The other major religious minority were Sephardic Jews, who probably came from Brazil in the 1650s. In 1680 they constituted just 54 households and lived mostly on or around Jew Street in Bridgetown. Posing no obvious threat, they were subjected to heavy taxes but little persecution otherwise.[10]

As in the Leeward Islands, the social behaviour of early Barbadians was less circumscribed than it was in England. Henry Whistler, a participant in Cromwell's 1654–55 expedition that captured Jamaica, said of Barbados that

This island is the dunghill whereon England doth cast forth its rubbish. Rogues and whores and such like people are those which are generally brought here. A Rogue in England will hardly make a cheater here. A bawd brought over puts on a demure comportment, a whore if handsome makes a wife for some rich planter.

Nor was lewd behaviour the exclusive province of the poor. In the 1630s, an assemblyman named James Futter asked a councillor, 'If all whoremasters were taken off the Bench, what would the Governor do for a Council?' Governor Thomas Hawley had Futter put in the pillory. Irreligion was rife too. Even in the 1680s Governor Dutton complained that 'God's house and worship . . . was but too much neglected.' He was right too, for there were only 11 Anglican clerics for a population of 20,000 white Barbadians, and they failed to rouse colonists from their 'wretched Laodician tepidity'. In 1683–84, 7 out of Dutton's 10 councillors did not attend church. Governors did not help those who helped themselves. The Irish Catholics were allowed no priests, and a shoemaker named Joseph Salmon was chastised before the governor and council in 1682 for promoting Anabaptism. Quakers and Sephardic Jews were better tolerated than Catholics and Anabaptists and it appears that only they were especially devout.[11]

As in Guiana, Virginia, Bermuda and the Leeward Islands, Barbadians' first agricultural staple was tobacco. Enjoying less success than Virginians, though, they soon switched to cotton. But that turned out badly too. Then, from about 1643, Barbadians began experimenting in sugar. For the rest of the century, Barbados was the richest place in the Anglo-Atlantic world, though with vast numbers of slaves it was also the most exploitative. The earliest settlers produced little because Sir William Courteen granted no land, expecting migrants to work for wages instead. That was not why people moved to the New World, however, and of 74 migrants aboard Captain John Powell's *Peter*, one of the two original ships dispatched by Courteen in 1627, 68 had either died or moved on by 1638. When Carlisle gained control of the colony, he distributed land generously, allotting some 40,000 acres to just 250 colonists between 1628 and 1630. Governor

Henry Hawley had to be more circumspect with the island's limited territorial resources, however, granting 10-acre headrights to anyone who paid their own way to the island and another 10 acres for each family member and servant they brought with them. Indentured servants were also offered 10 acres at the end of their contracts, but in many cases the promise was unfulfilled, for all the island's land was patented within a decade of settlement. By 1638, Hawley had distributed some 85,000 acres to 764 claimants, mostly in 30- to 50-acre parcels, though some claimed hundreds of acres and had begun the process of creating a landed elite.

Barbadian tobacco was of a lower quality than Virginian and was taxed more heavily. Merchant Archibald Hay told his Barbadian kinsman Peter Hay in 1637 that 'Your tobaco of Barbados of all the tobaco that cometh to England is accompted the worst.' Three years later, after cotton prices fell, Peter Hay, like many fellow planters, had switched to cotton, but as he told Archibald Hay: 'This yeare hath beene so baise a cotton yeare that the inhabitantes hath not maide so much cotton as will buye necessaries for there servants.' By the early 1640s, therefore, Barbadian planters were seeking new ways to make their livings, and they came across one, rather by accident, just in time. The English had known about the value of sugar since it was grown in the Canary Islands and Madeira, before the discovery of the New World. During the Elizabethan days of plunder, English privateers targeted sugar as well as gold and silver. Thirty-four sugar ships captured in just three years after the Armada fetched a very sweet £100,000. The first Barbadian settlers had 32 Indians from Surinam teach them how to grow cane and turn it into a sweet drink, but not how to refine it into a marketable product. It was the Dutch who helped the English go commercial with the crop. From the 1630s the Dutch had exported Barbadian tobacco and other products and in the 1640s sought to expand their intermediary role and their profits by providing know-how, credit and equipment for planters to switch to sugar. The Dutch were also leading slave traders, and knew that if Barbadians cultivated sugar, they would need thousands of slaves.

Three unforeseeable events accelerated the process. Roundhead successes in the civil wars meant royalists sought refuge in Barbados, bringing with them capital to invest. In 1645, Portuguese Pernambuco planters revolted against the Dutch, ousting them by 1654 and forcing Dutch slave traders to sell their Brazilian-bound human wares cheaply in Barbados. Finally, a yellow fever epidemic killed off thousands of Barbadians in 1647, clearing the way for land purchases and the replacement of indentured servitude with slavery.

As early as September 1643, Barbados had become 'the most flourishing Island in all those American parts, and I verily believe in all the world for the producing of sugar', which 'for the space of eight moneths in the yeare can and doeth yeild 1500 lb. of sugar each 24 houres'. The first yields were

Muscovado sugar; unrefined, full of molasses, and brown and moist. The land was fresh, though, and producing two tons per acre, twice as much as they could cultivate later, Barbadians made plenty of money in the 1640s. By 1650, with more and more Dutch tutelage and their own trial and error, they were making less per acre but finer sugar, and still more profits. By the early 1650s, Barbados sugar exports were worth over £3,000,000 annually. In good years between the 1650s and the 1680s Barbadians produced some 15,000 tons of sugar, though production subsequently declined a little due to soil exhaustion, and eventually the Leeward Islands, and especially Jamaica, would surpass Barbados as the English Caribbean's principal source of sugar. In the meantime, they stopped growing food. William Hay wrote to Archibald Hay that planters suddenly became 'so intent upon planting sugar that they had rather buy foode at very dear rates than produce it by labour, soe infinite is the profitt of sugar workes after once accomplished'. The West Indies were already on the way therefore to becoming a lucrative market for the farmers and planters of the North American mainland.[12]

Almost as soon as the sugar revolution began, Barbadian land prices rose dizzyingly fast. Land that cost 10 shillings an acre in 1640 went for £2 in 1643 and £5 in 1646. In the latter year, one 500-acre fully equipped sugar plantation sold for £16,000, more than the whole proprietary had been worth five years before. Planters often coped with the high costs of investing in sugar – not only in land but also in the expensive buildings and equipment required to boil the cane and refine the grain – by forming partnerships with one or more others. Thomas Modyford was one such example. He arrived in Barbados in 1647, a royalist on the run, though a well-connected son of the Lord Mayor of Exeter. Not without money, he nevertheless wished to establish his own independent fortune, telling Richard Ligon, the writer who worked for him, that he aimed to make £100,000. He immediately bought a half share in a fully operating 500-acre plantation for £1000 down plus £6000 to be paid over the next two years. His partner was London merchant Thomas Kendall, who sent 'all the supplies to me at the best hand, and I returning him the sugars, and we both thrived on it'. He made his fortune quickly enough to be a councillor by 1651, speaker of the assembly in 1652 and governor in 1660. The Restoration terminated his Barbadian governorship, but he bounced back as royal governor of Jamaica by 1664. He also became one of five Barbadian Restoration knights and, along with the other dozen Anglo-Caribbeans knighted later in the seventeenth century, showed that the West Indies was developing an aristocracy. By the time Modyford died in 1679 he owned 600 slaves and servants and he and his family had staked out some 20,000 acres of Jamaica.

Modyford was a member of a plantocratic elite that was clearly forming in the Caribbean by the 1680s, certainly in Barbados. That year, according to Governor Atkins's survey, Barbados had 175 large planters with 60 slaves or more, 190 middling planters with 20 to 59 slaves, 1041 small planters with over 10 acres and up to 19 slaves, plus another 1186 freemen with fewer than 10 acres. Large planters headed a white population of around 20,000 and owned over half the black population of 38,782. Those 175 large planters formed just 7 per cent of property holders but held 54 per cent of declared wealth in land, slaves and servants (probably more, bearing in mind that planters hid as much of their property as they could from officials). They were beginning to live luxuriously too. The anonymous author of a pamphlet entitled *Great Newes from the Barbadoes* wrote in 1676 of the 'many Costly and Stately Houses' in Bridgetown, and the 'Hospitality, or Number of the splendid Planters, who for Sumptuous Houses, Cloaths and Liberal Entertainment cannot be Exceeded by this their Mother Kingdome it self'.[13]

Of these 175 families, 40 per cent had arrived in Barbados in the 1630s and another 20 per cent in the 1640s and 1650s. They were therefore an established elite by 1680. In 1680, 77 held one or more military or civil offices and at least 22 more did so at some point between 1675 and 1685 (25 of those who did not were women, minors or Quakers). Elites reserved the most prestigious and remunerative offices for themselves. In 1680, 10 out of 12 councillors, 20 out of 22 assemblymen, 19 out of 23 judges, 48 out of 64 justices of the peace and 20 out of 34 vestrymen were planters with 60 slaves or more. By island custom, no one with 100 acres or more would serve as anything less than a field officer in the militia, and by law only those with 100 acres could serve as field officers. Average property ownership among councillors was 420 acres of land and 190 slaves, and among assemblymen, 340 acres and 153 slaves. They were developing dynastic interconnections too. Governor Atkins's daughters married John Pears and Thomas Walrond, two of the island's wealthiest planters. As Richard Dunn has said, the late seventeenth-century Barbadian elite was 'the most perfectly articulated colonial aristocracy in English America'.[14]

Yet, as Dunn also says, the making of this elite was in some ways the island's undoing. The most basic problem Barbados faced was that it had fewer than 100,000 arable acres of land and all these were taken up by 1638. Governor Atkins noted in 1676 that 'There is not a foot of land in Barbados that is not employed even to the very seaside.' To move up, the ambitious had to move out. In 1679, according to Atkins's survey, some 593 obtained tickets to leave the island, many of them permanently. (The reason for requiring leavers to obtain tickets was to prevent servants and debtors from absconding.) These were among some 10,000 who emigrated from the island during the seventeenth century.

Many of the out-migrants were servants whose time was served but for whom there was no land to buy. Others were smaller farmers with 20 or 30 acres, who could not compete in sugar planting, and although many stayed on and made a bare existence, others sold up. Increasingly, though, the wealthy were moving too. Barbadians were a major source of migrants to the new colony of Carolina after it was chartered in 1663. Sir John Colleton, one of the Carolina lords proprietors, had been a civil war emigrant to Barbados. Three boatloads of people left Barbados to attempt settling Cape Fear between 1665 and 1667, and 20 Barbadians were among the party that settled on the Ashley River in 1670, South Carolina's first permanent Euro-American settlement. At least 175 free Barbadians went there in the 1670s, taking 150 servants and slaves with them. In the 1680s, significant numbers began taking up the option of absenteeism in England, pushed by the political strife of the 1680s, lower sugar prices, rising taxes and the onset of soil exhaustion. Some of the grandest planters, including Sir Peter Colleton, Henry Drax and Edward Littleton, moved back to England in these years, the latter authoring an extensive moan about taxation, the navigation system and generally overbearing imperial authority entitled *The Groans of the Plantations* in 1689. The wars of King William and Queen Anne, and a terrible yellow fever epidemic in the 1690s, made so many more move that absenteeism became quite normal by 1713. Indeed, while other colonies' environments grew healthier, those in the West Indies did not. In 1680, there were 506 more deaths than there were births among the white population of Barbados.

Figures are hard to come by, but there seem to have been 1227 taxpayers in 1635, rising to 3948 in 1637, and then increasing even more rapidly to 8707 in 1639. After the sugar revolution began, the population rose rapidly to about 26,000 whites and 27,000 slaves by 1660. Thereafter, as wealthy planters bought up more and more land for sugar, the white population steadily declined while the black population rapidly rose. In 1680, there were about 20,000 whites and 40,000 blacks. By 1710, the white population was down to 13,000 and the black population was up to 52,300. In the eighteenth century, the white population rose again, to 17,800 by 1760, but the black population rose more quickly, to 86,000. There were just about as many whites as blacks in 1660, but ratios of black to white were two-to-one by 1680, four-to-one by 1710 and five-to-one by 1760.

The most significant population shift, then, came with the switch to slave labour following the sugar revolution. The settlers of 1627 brought with them 10 black and 32 Indian slaves, and in 1636 Barbados established slavery for life, almost a quarter-century before Virginia did. But colonists imported few slaves during the early years compared to later. Unlike the Spanish and Portuguese, at the beginning of the seventeenth century the English were unaccustomed to slavery and it seemed natural to them to prefer white indentured servant labour. In any case, at £25 each, slaves were expensive for planters struggling to make profits in poor Barbadian tobacco and cotton. But sugar changed everything. The English knew well enough that Portuguese and Spanish American planters used slaves in vast numbers and that the Dutch, who assisted the transition to sugar planting, traded in them. It would be difficult to procure the numbers of labourers from Europe required to make sugar; they had hitherto used 1 servant per 10 acres, but would require 1 labourer per 2 acres for sugar.

Barbadians attempted intermittently to enslave Amerindians. The Caribs were too aggressive and their familiarity with the islands made it relatively easy for them to escape. Indians from Surinam, Carolina and New England were no good as slaves either. In many Amerindian cultures, women did agricultural work while men hunted and fished. Lord John Vaughan, governor of Jamaica in 1676, noted that Amerindian men 'if forced to any labor, eyther hang themselves or Runne away'. So Barbadians made that 'unthinking decision' to switch to African labour power. The institution of slavery became a chief feature of island societies thereafter, and large planters and slaves rather than middling and poorer whites would define the social character of Barbados as well as the Leeward Islands and Jamaica.[15]

Jamaica

Jamaica is 145 miles long and 50 miles wide, and therefore 26 times bigger than Barbados and 17 times the size of the 4 Leeward Islands combined. With so much land, it might have become the best poor man's country in the Caribbean, but like the other islands it eventually became a colony of huge sugar plantations, worked by armies of slaves. Before that, though, it went through a long era as the wildest colony in Anglo-America.

Jamaica was the only New World province in the seventeenth century that was sponsored and colonized directly by an English government. Oliver Cromwell wished to undermine Spain, dividing the world between the Dutch in Asia and the English in the Americas (minus Portuguese Brazil). But the first Anglo-Dutch war intervened and, in any case, the Dutch had little to gain from this scheme. The second phase of Cromwellian thinking was more modest and simply involved establishing English colonies in the Greater Antilles. Cromwell's 'Western Design' was a religious as well as a geopolitical plan, aiming at weakening Catholic and strengthening Protestant imperialism. General Robert Venables and Admiral William Penn (father of the Quaker of the same name who would later found Pennsylvania) recruited 8200 men, 3500 within England, the same number from Barbados and 1200 from the Leeward Islands, for that purpose.

In April 1655, this large force invaded Hispaniola and for three weeks thrashed about in the forests to no good effect. Venables despaired of his Leeward soldiers as 'the most profane debauch'd persons that we ever saw, scorners of Religion, and indeed men kept so loose as not to be kept under discipline, and so cowardly as not to be made to fight'. In fact, 1000 men were lost on this wretched mission, many to dysentery, yellow fever and malaria, and many may have been saved had Venables and Penn supplied their men adequately. The commanders eventually abandoned Hispaniola and turned their attention to Jamaica, a much easier objective. Only around 1500 Spanish, Portuguese, African (some enslaved, some runaway maroons) and Arawak Indians lived on the island, and they were mostly spread about on cattle ranches. There were no defences, and when the English stepped into Villa de la Vega (renamed St Jago de la Vega and Spanish Town by the English) on 10 May, the town was empty. The governor, suffering from smallpox, surrendered straightaway. Some Spanish settlers hid out in the mountains of Ocho Rios, occasionally attacking the English until they were finally expelled in 1660. Ten years later Spain formally ceded Jamaica to the English in the Treaty of Madrid. By these means the English captured a seriously large island for Caribbean expansion, but for some time that remained a mixed blessing.

The first English settlers in Jamaica were soldiers, and their leaders failed to prevent them from vandalizing the resources around them. They destroyed Villa de la Vega and then had to rebuild it again. They killed all the cattle in and around the town and failed to plant sufficient food, and had to eat snakes and dogs. This diet probably did little to protect them against disease. By November, the 7000 troops were reduced to 3700, and by 1660 to 2200. In 1656, 1400 migrants from Nevis colonized Morant Bay and, though already acclimatized to the Caribbean, almost 1000 of them died within a few months. Some 12,000 people moved to Jamaica during the first 6 years of settlement, yet in 1661 the population was just 3470. Like early Virginia, Jamaica was a death trap. It remained so for a long time. Tropical epidemics killed great swathes of the population between 1655 and 1661, and again in 1692 and 1713. Disease was one problem that slowed the development of the island. As elsewhere, French raids and political and social instability did so too. Eventually, however, Jamaica, like the other islands, settled down to become a sugar plantation society dominated by large planters and vast numbers of slaves.[16]

Political conflict in early Jamaica

To repopulate Jamaica and protect it from Spanish and maroon insurgents, in 1657 Governor Edward D'Oyley invited English buccaneers to move from Tortuga. By the mid-1660s some 1500 of them resided in Port Royal. The buccaneers proved useful but troublesome. After ousting the Spanish from Jamaica in 1660, they began a series of depredations against Spanish shipping and ports that reached a high point with the activities of Sir Henry Morgan in 1665 to 1671. Morgan assaulted Granada (Nicaragua), Puerto Principe (Cuba), Porto Bello (Panama) and Maracaibo (Venezuela). His most spectacular raid, though, was when he and 1400 buccaneers marched across the Central American isthmus and burned Panama City, carrying off £70,000 worth of booty.

The buccaneers, rich and fearsome as they were, became a powerful force in Jamaica, but the contingency of inviting them to settle complicated Jamaica's colonization. The aforementioned and other, smaller escapades made the Spanish reluctant to trade with Jamaica, to the detriment of the island's planters. Buccaneers and planters therefore rivalled each other for political and social domination of the colony, while simultaneously forming mutual enmities and alliances with each other, as events directed, to achieve autonomy from imperial authority. In most royal colonies, governors had to balance the authority of their imperial masters with local interests, a complicated enough task by itself. In Jamaica, they had two distinct local power groups to contend with.

At the Restoration, just five years after the capture of Jamaica, London merchants persuaded the king to keep the island as a royal colony. Subsequently, Governor Thomas Modyford, a Barbadian who knew Jamaica's potential for land-hungry sugar planters, successfully encouraged the king to promote sugar planting, but otherwise governed imperiously. In his seven-year term he called an assembly only once, controlling revenue and ruling by proclamation with the advice of a council (on which he placed his brother and two sons) that met three or four times annually. Though he envisioned a Barbadian-style plantocracy in Jamaica, he could only rule this way by allying himself with the buccaneers. He personally pocketed at least £1000 of Morgan's loot (or that is how much he admitted to), and some of the rest provided his government's revenue. After the excesses of the Panama raid, however, Modyford lost his job.

Modyford's successor for four years was his lieutenant-governor, Sir Thomas Lynch, who allied himself firmly with the planters and alienated the buccaneers. In 1675, though, Lynch was replaced by John, Lord Vaughan as governor, with Henry Morgan, first disgraced and then knighted for his exploits, as lieutenant-governor. Lynch was outraged, telling Secretary of State Arlington that 'Here's non ever thought it possible his Majesty should send the Admirall of the Pryvateers to governe this Island'. Vaughan soon became disenchanted with Morgan's public gambling, drinking and generally uncouth behaviour. Vaughan disdained Jamaicans in general as Roundheads, convicts and smugglers, who did illegal business with unlicensed slave traders rather than with the Royal African Company. He was also an outsider whose presence irritated the planters as well as the buccaneers. Under his governorship, the assembly finally began to assert its authority over taxation and other laws, ignoring the king's commands, sending laws to England for approval only after they had expired, authorizing unlicensed slave trading and impeaching imperial officials the assemblymen found objectionable.

In 1678, the new Lords of Trade appointed the Earl of Carlisle, another outsider, to the governorship. With a mind to asserting imperial authority, they equipped him with 40 new bills, including a revenue act that would render the governor financially independent of the assembly. The assembly rejected every single bill, and so Carlisle allied himself with the buccaneers in an attempt to salvage some authority, until he gave up and went home in 1681. The Lords realized they needed a governor with a local constituency and reappointed Lynch. Even he found that 'Arguing with Assemblys is like philosophising with a Mule.' He eventually obtained a 21-year revenue act, in alliance with planters against 'that little drunken silly party of Sir H. Morgan's'. When Lynch died in 1684, he was replaced by Hender Molesworth, a local planter who nevertheless irritated most with his attempts to enforce the Royal African Company's monopoly. Molesworth was a company agent, and there was no recourse to James II as he was the company's president and principal stockholder.

The rule of James II was not friendly to Jamaican planters. Two years after parliament doubled the sugar duty, the king replaced Molesworth with Christopher Monck. The second Duke of Albemarle had blown much of his own fortune and aimed to make a new one in the Caribbean. He therefore allied himself with the buccaneers, from whom he would person-ally make money, replaced large planter officials with smaller planters, including Irish Catholics, and employed armed men to ensure the election of his allies to the assembly. Jamaican planters began going home, forming a powerful lobby and complaining that their offices had been occupied by 'needy and mechanick men such as tapsters, barbers and the like'. Albemarle also made a friend of Henry Morgan and appointed Father Thomas Churchill, a priest, as the island's agent in England. He openly cel-ebrated King James's defeat of Monmouth and the pregnancy of the queen, although, while celebrating the birth of James's son and heir, Monck killed himself in a drinking binge. His erstwhile allies held on to power during the crisis of 1688–89, declaring martial law in the spring. But their days were numbered. James had already ordered the restoration of the large planter office holders and William III affirmed this directive.

William appointed Lord Inchiquin as governor, but when he found this not to Jamaicans' liking he appointed Sir William Beeston in his stead. Beeston was a leading advocate of colonial autonomy in the time of Charles II and then Jamaica's agent in London. His appointment signalled approval of the rule of the great Caribbean plantocrats. Subsequently, the small planters went back home and many of the buccaneers moved to St Domingue and the Bahamas. Other buccaneers disappeared after what seemed like Old Testament disasters destroyed the town they built. On 7 June 1692, an earthquake sent much of Port Royal crashing to the bottom of the sea. What was rebuilt was burned down in a fire on 9 January 1703. After the earthquake, Jamaicans built a new capital at Kingston.

The political ascendancy of the planters did not ensure stability for some time, however, for during the wars of 1689 to 1713 the French caused con-siderable havoc. From the beginning of King William's War, the French raided the Jamaican coastline, and then, in 1694, a French force of 3000 invaded. They attacked 2 eastern parishes, destroyed 50 sugar works and made away with 1600 slaves. The Jamaican militia repelled the French advance on the wealthy south-central coast, however, and afterwards 1000 regulars arrived from home to defend the island. The following year the English retaliated with a joint Anglo-Spanish sacking of Cap François and Port de Paix in St Domingue. During Queen Anne's War, Jamaica was garrisoned and governed by military officers Thomas Handasyd and Lord Archibald Hamilton. Vast numbers of soldiers succumbed to malaria, so it was fortunate that the French did not invade. The French instead assaulted the Leeward Islands, while their privateers attacked Jamaican ships in the western Caribbean. They lost numerous cargoes and saw freight and insurance rates rise. Like the other islands, Jamaica suffered during England's eighteenth-century wars, but by 1713 the worst was over, and the island was already becoming a major sugar plantation economy and society.[17]

Economy, society and population in early Jamaica

Early Jamaica was highly socially unstable, even by the standards of the seventeenth-century Caribbean. Many small farmers and especially indentured servants, for example, ran off to join the buccaneers. Buccaneering may have seemed an easier and more lucrative life than farming and servitude, and a more exciting if more dangerous one, although moving to the tropics to farm was risky anyway. Furthermore, the buccaneers shared their loot more fairly with each other than planters shared the profits of agriculture with their labourers, and they offered bounties for bravery and stored some of their resources as insurance for injured sailors. Joining the buccaneers was not therefore a reckless move.

Many indentured servants were Irish Catholics who were pro-French and resentful of the English. In response to the French invasion, Jamaica could only muster 2000 militia, though they did remarkably well against an experienced French force of 3000. Other groups included a small population of Sephardic Jews who migrated from Brazil and Surinam, mostly living in the centre of Port Royal where, as in Barbados, they enjoyed toleration but paid for it with a special Jew tax. Quakers congregated in Port Royal too, though they were less controversial in Jamaica than they were in Barbados. The most rebellious people in Jamaica were slaves. There were three large-scale slave revolts between 1675 and 1686. This period also saw the formation of a runaway community of maroons, who incited other slaves to join them and who regularly attacked white settlers in the island's interior.

As in other colonies, most white migrants were middling and poorer people whose ambitions were to make an independent living for themselves after a period of indentured servitude, but commentators found the most notable Jamaicans to be those with criminal or otherwise disreputable backgrounds and intentions. Governor Vaughan characterized many Jamaicans as people who 'chose transporting rather than hanging and Jamaica rather than Tyborn'. The taverns of Port Royal 'may be fittly called Brothel Houses', according to John Taylor, a 1688 visitor. The buccaneer town was reputed as the Sodom of the Indies. John Esquemeling, in one of the popular accounts of life among the buccaneers, wrote that a buccaneering bon viveur might spend up to £750 in one night in Port Royal. He also told of a favourite buccaneer do-or-dare pastime of placing a pipe of wine or a barrel of beer in the street and forcing passers-by, at gunpoint, either to drink it or to 'throw these liquors about the streets, and wet the cloathes of such as walked by'. As aforementioned, Henry Whistler called Barbados a dunghill on which England cast forth its rubbish, but a visitor to Jamaica named Ned Ward went a step further and called Jamaica 'the Dunghill of the Universe'. These dung-related similes are perhaps not surprising, considering that planters spread their fields with huge quantities of natural animal (and reputedly sometimes human) fertilizer. But it is nonetheless telling that what most struck some visitors to the Caribbean was the stench of dung, not the sweetness of sugar.

The greatest destruction seen in Port Royal was not man-made, though there were those who thought it was. Around noon on 7 June 1692, Jamaica suffered an earthquake that destroyed buildings all over the island but which hit Port Royal the hardest. King, Queen and High Streets, all their buildings, two forts and the bodies buried in the Palisadoes cemetery were plunged 30 feet under water. Skeletons from the graveyard rose to the surface, joining the rotting corpses of the earthquake victims. Hundreds were buried or drowned, though contemporary witnesses put the death toll at 2000. Jeremiads portrayed the natural disaster as God's judgement on the avarice, conceit and debauchery of Port Royal's residents. One Quaker survivor wrote,

> Oh brother! If thou didst see those great persons that are now dead upon the water thou couldst never forget it. Great men who were so swallowed up with pride, that a man could not be admitted to speak with them, and women whose top-knots seemed to reach the clouds, now lie stinking upon the water, and are made meat for fish and fowls of the air.

As we have seen, though, the destruction of Port Royal represented, above all, the decline of the buccaneers.[18]

Jamaican large planters' attainment of political supremacy over the buccaneers and the small planters was a measure of their developing economic power. The chaos of the early years meant that by 1662 only 2917 acres of Jamaica were under cultivation, but that situation soon began to change. Although Thomas Modyford allied himself to buccaneers for pragmatic political (as well as his own financial) reasons, he was at heart and by occupation a planter, and he did all he could to nurture a Jamaican plantocracy. He lobbied successfully for liberal distributions of land, Jamaica's exemption from the 4.5 per cent duty that other Caribbean colonies paid on their exports and from import duties in England. He arrived in the island in 1664 accompanied by 1000 Barbadian migrants, and during his time in office patented out some 300,000 acres to 1800 claimants, giving 30-acre head-rights to anyone who paid their way there and 30 acres more for any dependants they brought with them. Much land initially went to smaller planters, though some accrued large plantations over the years. Others bought huge tracts right away. Modyford himself claimed 12,000 acres and his 3 sons over 20,000 acres between them. By 1670, 14 planters had over 2000 acres and 44 had over 1000.

Modyford's claimants staked out and planted most of the south-central coast. His successor, Sir Thomas Lynch, who originally patented 6000 acres for himself, encouraged settlement of the north coast, the south-west, where he helped settle the 'Surranam Quarter' of large planters from the South American mainland, and some interior regions where buccaneers were squatting on unpatented land. Modyford and, especially, Lynch, however, patented out such large tracts to some wealthy planters that much of it remained uncultivated, slowing down the settlement process but making it easier for larger planters to secure their hegemony later on. By 1683, 3000 patentees had claimed just over 1,000,000 acres, an average holding of 360 acres each, though by then 88 claimed over 2000 acres. By that time Lynch himself claimed some 21,438 acres.

Some early planters and some later smaller farmers planted provision crops or ranched cattle as the Spanish had done; others cultivated cash crops such as tobacco, cotton, indigo, ginger, pimento and cocoa (another Spanish specialty), and quite a few mixed these activities. But, by the time Jamaica was settled, the potential for sugar was known and planters knew how to grow it. Between 1671 and 1684, sugar production rose from 1000 to 10,000 hogsheads. After that, the unfavourable political climate created by Monck, war, disease, the earthquake and maroons pegged production at between 5000 and 7000 tons a year until the end of the War of the Spanish Succession in 1713. Already, though, large planters had just about secured their economic and social as well as political domination. The evidence is sparser than in Barbados, but what there is indicates that before Monck, and certainly after, large planters had the same kind of lock on political, judicial and military offices and parish vestries as did their Barbadian counterparts. They were also already living in comparable style. The 1688 visitor, John Taylor, though unimpressed by some residents of Port Royal, commented that 'The Merchants and Gentry live here to the Hight of Splendor, in full ease and plenty, being sumptuously arrayed, and attended on, and served by their Negroe slaves, which all ways waite on 'em in Livery, or other wise as they pleas to cloath 'em.' Like Barbadians, some were absenting themselves from the island. Quite a few left in disgust at Monck rather than to live the high life in the metropolis, but it is telling that they could afford to do so.

As elsewhere in the Caribbean, population figures reflect the evolution of a sugar plantation society. There remained room for continuing white population growth in the larger island of Jamaica, but the rise of slavery meant that blacks increasingly outnumbered whites. In 1661, the white population totalled 2956 and the black population 514. Twelve years later, there were 7768 whites, but 9504 blacks. In the 1670s, on average 700 whites and 1500 blacks arrived in the colony each year. The next decade, 2000 slaves a year arrived, a figure that rose to 4500 after the ending of the Royal African Company monopoly in 1698. In 1710, the white population was 7250 and the black population was a massive 58,000. By 1760, Jamaica had 15,000 whites and 146,464 blacks – 9 out of 10 Jamaicans were black.[19]

Sugar, planters and slaves in the eighteenth-century West Indies

Annual British consumption of sugar rose from 4 to 20 pounds per head during the eighteenth century, accounting for the great and growing importance of the West Indies. Sugar imports rose from just over 20,000 tons in 1700, to over 40,000 by 1750 and 100,000 by 1780. Trade in sugar by-products was extensive too. By 1775, the islands exported 2,000,000 gallons of rum. In the second half of the eighteenth century, the islands annually exported over £3,000,000-worth of sugar and almost £700,000-worth of molasses and rum. Wealth gave the islands political clout back home. In 1733, for example, parliament passed the Molasses Act, raising a sixpence per gallon duty on French molasses, which was cheaper than English, to encourage New England importers to trade with their island countrymen. The balance of prosperity between the islands was shifting too. The Leeward Islands, especially Antigua, rivalled Barbadian production by the 1720s, and after the 1739 maroon treaty Jamaica became the wealthiest island. By 1780, Jamaica was producing 50,000 tons of sugar per year, half of Caribbean sugar production. Its economy remained diverse, and livestock, cacao and other products amounted to 25 per cent of the value of island exports. Total Jamaican exports were worth £2,400,000 in 1774.

Jamaica still had room for expansion. In the 1770s, only a third of its land was devoted to sugar; the rest was in other crops, pasture, woodland and provision grounds for slaves to feed themselves. Jamaica thus remained an attractive destination for British migrants. The white population of 18,000 in 1774 was much higher than in other islands. In the 1720s and 1730s, 40 per cent of British indentured servant migrants were Jamaica-bound, and Jamaican land was distributed as a reward to discharged British soldiers. Also, all the island economies were wealthy and sophisticated enough to support lawyers, merchants, artisans and shopkeepers, and planters made room for plantation managers.

Even so, eighteenth-century West Indian planters ruled their societies more completely than was the case elsewhere in the British New World. Charles Price, scion of a family that dominated Jamaican politics for three generations, had the assembly moved from the Kingston to Spanish Town, near his own home. When a governor moved it back again in the 1750s, he had the governor recalled. He also got the assembly to give him a monopoly of the tolls on the road between Spanish Town and the coast. Some were spectacularly wealthy by the standards of the time. By the end of the eighteenth century, Simon Taylor of Jamaica was a millionaire with an annual income of £47,000. Planters emulated English lifestyles and gentility as much as they could. Islanders adapted their houses to the local climate, but not their clothes, food or drink. It was impossible to grow certain English foodstuffs in the tropical environment, so rather than adapt, whites imported wheat and beef from England and North America. The rich drank locally produced rum but also imported French and Madeira wines and brandy, and they and the poor retained a taste for English beer and cider. Despite parvenu reputations, island elites achieved some level of gentility. As well as the aforementioned hospitality, in the eighteenth century West Indians invested in civic improvements. The Codrington family, for example, endowed a college for Barbados in 1710, and its fine Georgian buildings were erected between 1721 and 1738. Even so, levels of absenteeism were so high that Creole culture was never as fully articulated as it was on the mainland.

The fortunes of Anglo-Caribbeans rested more wholly on slavery than did those of other British-American colonists. As we have seen, sugar created enormous demand for slave labour and, although Chesapeake tobacco and Carolina rice created slave-plantation societies, the large and growing slave majorities of the West Indies made the social character of the Caribbean quite distinctive. Those majorities also made the system of slavery in many ways more complete and therefore more barbaric than was the case on the mainland.

During the 1659 House of Commons debate over 'white slavery' in Barbados, one MP excoriated the beating of white servants because it made their lives 'as cheap as those of negroes'. And the implementation of servants' 'human rights' was closely connected to the denial of those rights for slaves. Some parliamentary support for the founding of the Company of Royal Adventurers Trading into Africa and in turn the Royal African Company was grounded on diminishing the need for white labour by increasing the supply of slave labour. With their monopolies over the slave trade to the English colonies, these companies were able to expand their markets by ensuring that the lives of 'negroes' became cheaper and cheaper. In 1664, the former supplied slaves to the West Indies at £14 to £22 per head. Over the next decade, the price fell by between a quarter and a third, and supply quadrupled. White servant numbers declined from 13,000 in the early 1650s to fewer than 3000 in 1680. The slave trade to the West Indies maintained itself because Caribbean slavery was harsh – sugar refining made the economy industrial as well as agricultural – and prevented natural population increase. New arrivals often lasted little longer than a year, and West Indians were still importing 2000 to 16,000 slaves annually between 1720 and 1775. Also, the Treaty of Utrecht gave the *asiento*, permission to sell slaves in Spanish America, to British merchants. The slave trade became as big a business in the Caribbean economy as sugar.[20]

As in the Chesapeake there was less customary and legal distinction between slavery and indentured servitude when Caribbean islands were societies with slaves rather than slave societies. In 1661, however, the year of the servant code, the Barbadian legislature passed An Act for the Better Ordering and Government of Negroes (modified in 1676, 1682 and 1688, and later adopted more or less in whole by other West Indian assemblies) that defined blacks as 'an heathenish, brutish, and an uncertain and dangerous kind of people' created 'without the knowledge of God in the world'. The law defined slaves not merely as chattel or personal property, as contemporaneous laws in the Chesapeake did, but as real estate.

This fundamental harshness was reflected in the law's particular provisions. If a starving slave stole food, he or she would be executed, while the neglectful master would only be refused public compensation for the loss of property. Slaves could be killed not only for major offences such as arson, rape and murder, but also for petty misdemeanours such as theft (although that was a capital offence in Britain too), assault and for being absent from plantations for 30 days. Plots and rebellions incurred torture as well as death. All whites had the right to punish any slave, and every free white man aged 16 to 60 had to enlist in parish militias, first to fend off attacks from European rivals, then to guard against slave insurrection. Slavery turned the West Indies into police societies.

Furthermore, Caribbean slaves were placed outside the reach of God. There were no legal provisions for their Christianization, and Anglo-Caribbean Anglican churchmen regarded Africans as incapable of understanding the Christian faith. Masters generally refused to convert their slaves. A more enlightened age might see this neglect as more beneficent than oppression of African religious and cultural beliefs and practices, but in the context of the contemporary belief that the unconverted would go to hell, it reflects an outrageous indifference to humanity.

Despite the enormities of Caribbean slavery, slaves retained a good deal of autonomy and developed a powerful culture. In fact, the absence of planter paternalism, manifest in absenteeism, the constant importations of

Africans and the overwhelming majorities of slaves in the islands' populations created conditions in which a near-autonomous culture could flourish. Food, housing, family and community structure and function, religion,
song and dance – indeed all elements of the social and cultural – had some
degree of African inflection, even if generalized by the demographic and
cultural mixing caused by the slave trade, and even if somewhat attenuated
by the conditions of enslavement.

Slaves fought back, often ferociously, against the system. In 1675, a
group of Gold Coast slaves plotted to kill all the whites in Barbados, before
being betrayed by a house slave. To deter others, 36 conspirators were executed. But in the desperate environment of the West Indies, others would
not be deterred. In 1692, Barbadians uncovered a conspiracy that may have
involved up to 4000 slaves and some Irish indentured servants. The rebels
planned to kill their masters, organize into two regiments of cavalry and
four of infantry, kidnap the governor and seize the armoury and any warships in the harbour, but again the conspiracy was uncovered. Ringleaders
were hung in chains until they starved or confessed and gave away their
plans and co-conspirators, and 400 were executed. There was a further,
smaller conspiracy in 1701, and a larger one of 1736 in which blacks
intended to take over Barbados after bombing a ball attended by leading
citizens. There were small insurrections in Nevis in 1761 and in Montserrat
in 1768, both suppressed by alert militias. In Jamaica, Tacky's rebellion of
1760 resulted in the deaths of 400 slaves and 90 whites. The St Mary's
Revolt of 1765 and the Hanover Revolt of 1776 reminded Jamaicans and
other islanders why joining the other colonies in independence was impossible, and slaves thus helped shape the course of empire.

Jamaica's size and geographic features gave slaves other opportunities to
claim freedom by running away and hiding in 'cockpits' between the mountains in the middle of the island. African Caribbeans created numerous
maroon communities in the interior, though as fugitives they frequently had
to relocate. Even so, maroon settlements provided a place for other slaves
to run to and a base for raids on Jamaican plantations. Between 1700 and
1722, and again from 1729 to 1739, British Jamaicans and maroons fought
outright wars against each other. In the latter year, though, Cudjo and other
maroon leaders made peace. In exchange for freedom and land rights, they
ceased their attacks on whites and agreed to return runaways. As so often
in the British New World, freedom came at a price.[21]

The Caribbean colonies were not founded upon any idealistic plans. All
began as entrepreneurial or military adventures. Yet, for all their varying origins and experiences, there was a common pattern of historical development
throughout the West Indies, and it matched that of most of the mainland colonies. Each went through a period of social and political flux and social
instability that lasted until a profitable agricultural staple was discovered.

After that, local elites emerged, displaced the original charter holders, established their social and political pre-eminence over middling and poorer inhabitants and strove for political autonomy from the mother country. The significant distinction in the Caribbean, though more a difference of degree than kind, was that the sugar system created a richer and more dominant planter class, a much larger slave population and a less influential population of middling and poorer colonists than did tobacco in the Chesapeake and even rice in the Lower South.

Notes

1 Cited in Hilary McD. Beckles, '"The Hub of Empire": The Caribbean and Britain in the Seventeenth Century', in Nicholas Canny, ed., *The Oxford History of the British Empire* Volume I: *The Origins of Empire: British Overseas Enterprise to the Close of the Seventeenth Century* (Oxford, 1998), p. 234, and Philip B. Boucher, *Cannibal Encounters: Europeans and Island Caribs, 1492–1763* (Baltimore, 1992).

2 David Beers Quinn, *England and the Discovery of America, 1481–1620* (London, 1974); Kenneth R. Andrews, *Trade, Plunder, and Settlement: Maritime Enterprise and the Genesis of the British Empire, 1480–1630* (Cambridge, 1984); Carl Bridenbaugh and Roberta Bridenbaugh, *No Peace beyond the Line: The English in the Caribbean, 1634–1690* (Oxford, 1972); Clinton V. Black, *Pirates of the West Indies* (Cambridge, 1989); James Horn and Philip D. Morgan, 'Settlers and Slaves: European and African Migrations to Early Modern British America', in Carole Shammas and Elizabeth Mancke, eds, *The Creation of the British Atlantic World* (Baltimore, forthcoming).

3 Quotes from Karen Ordahl Kupperman, 'The Beehive as a Model for Colonial Design', in Karen Ordahl Kupperman, ed., *America in European Consciousness, 1493–1750* (Chapel Hill, 1995), pp. 283, 296; Richard S. Dunn, 'The Downfall of the Bermuda Company: A Restoration Farce', *William and Mary Quarterly*, 3rd Ser., XX (1963), pp. 487–512; Michael Craton, *A History of the Bahamas* (London, 1962); Karen Ordahl Kupperman, *Providence Island, 1630–1641: The Other Puritan Colony* (Cambridge, 1993).

4 Richard S. Dunn, *Sugar and Slaves: The Rise of the Planter Class in the English West Indies, 1624–1713* (Chapel Hill, 1972), p. 118; Richard B. Sheridan, *Sugar and Slavery: An Economic History of the British West Indies, 1623–1775* (Barbados, 1974), pp. 148–51, 161–2, 170–2, 184–5.

5 Dunn, *Sugar and Slaves*, pp. 134, 135, 143–6.

6 Quotes from Dunn, *Sugar and Slaves*, pp. 120, 122, 132, 126; population figures from Dunn, *Sugar and Slaves*, pp. 127, 141 and Jack P. Greene, *Pursuits of Happiness: The Social Development of Early*

Modern British Colonies and the Formation of American Culture (Chapel Hill, 1988), pp. 178–9. See also Sheridan, *Sugar and Slavery*, pp. 80–1, 84–8, 97–206.

7 Dunn, *Sugar and Slaves*, pp. 79, 84–93.

8 Dunn, *Sugar and Slaves*, pp. 82, 101, 93.

9 Hilary McD. Beckles, *White Servitude and Black Slavery in Barbados, 1627–1715* (Knoxville, 1989), pp. 44–6; Beckles, '"Hub of Empire"', p. 230; *A True and Exact History of the Island of Barbadoes* (1657, 1673), in Dunn, *Sugar and Slaves*, p. 69.

10 Beckles, '"Hub of Empire"', p. 231; Dunn, *Sugar and Slaves*, pp. 104–8.

11 Dunn, *Sugar and Slaves*, pp. 77, 59; Beckles, *White Servitude and Black Slavery*, pp. 36–68, 48.

12 Dunn, *Sugar and Slaves*, pp. 53, 54, 61, 59.

13 Dunn, *Sugar and Slaves*, pp. 81–2, 87, 88, 91, 85, 96–7.

14 Dunn, *Sugar and Slaves*, pp. 48, 97–100.

15 Dunn, *Sugar and Slaves*, pp. 85, 55; Sheridan, *Sugar and Slavery*, pp. 18–74, 80–3, 97–147; Hilary McD. Beckles, *A History of Barbados: From Amerindian Settlement to Nation State* (Cambridge, 1990).

16 Dunn, *Sugar and Slaves*, pp. 152, 149–53; Sheridan, *Sugar and Slavery*, pp. 92–5.

17 Dunn, *Sugar and Slaves*, pp. 157, 159, 162, 186–7.

18 Dunn, *Sugar and Slaves*, pp. 157, 186, 149, 187.

19 Dunn, *Sugar and Slaves*, pp. 183, 166–77, 155; Grcene, *Pursuits of Happiness*, pp. 178–9; Sheridan, *Sugar and Slavery*, pp. 208–33.

20 Beckles, '"Hub of Empire"', p. 231; *White Servitude and Black Slavery*, pp. 115–25; Sheridan, *Sugar and Slavery*, pp. 54–74, 261–475; David Watts, *The West Indies: Patterns of Development, Culture and Environmental Change since 1492* (Cambridge, 1987), p. 311.

21 Dunn, *Sugar and Slaves*, pp. 224–62; Sheridan, *Sugar and Slavery*, pp. 234–60, 479–86; Michael Craton and James Walvin, *A Jamaican Plantation: The History of Worthy Park, 1670–1970* (London, 1970).

5

New England

The colonies of New England had enough in common with each other for us to consider them as a single cultural region, but they differed from each other quite profoundly in some respects. The 'Pilgrim Fathers', puritan separatists, founded Plymouth Colony in 1621, though 70 years later it was absorbed into Massachusetts. Reformist puritans, who remained within the Church of England but who wished to create a purified and more Calvinist version of it in America, founded Massachusetts in 1630. Connecticut and short-lived New Haven resembled Massachusetts, except that their colonists' religious zeal was tempered by a more commercialist attitude. New Hampshire was originally a fishing colony, and although puritans moved there during the Great Migration of the 1630s, large numbers of its inhabitants were Anglicans. New Hampshire acted as a haven for those who were hounded out of Massachusetts for heresy. Rhode Island was also a religious refuge from a religious refuge, offering toleration to those who suffered intolerance in puritan Massachusetts. What the New England colonies had in common, though, was a preoccupation with religion that was unmatched in other regions and that tempered the rampant individualism and materialism that characterized other regions in their early years. Over time, though, New Englanders' religious zeal diminished, replaced by a worldliness that made the region increasingly resemble the rest of British America.

Britons and Americans alike often think of the puritans, at least those of Plymouth and Massachusetts, as the original and archetypal American colonists. The strong religiosity and the powerful sense of national mission among Americans today encourage the view that the puritan legacy still shapes American life. Both impulses are reflected in the enduring rhetoric of America as a 'city on a hill', a biblical reference first applied to New England by John Winthrop aboard the *Arbella* in a sermon to migrants to Massachusetts. Yet the most powerful strand of modern American religious sensibility emanates not from seventeenth-century New England Congregationalism but from eighteenth- and nineteenth-century southern and western Baptist, Methodist and even Episcopalian evangelicalism. And Americans' sense of mission derives as much from the nineteenth-century notion of 'manifest destiny' to win the West as it does from establishing a 'city upon a hill' and a 'beacon to the world' in seventeenth-century Boston. Moreover, the notion of America's puritan origins dates not so much to the actualities of colonial history as to 'the new birth of freedom' that Abraham Lincoln saw emerging from the American Civil War of 1861 to 1865. After that conflict, and the emancipation of the slaves that was its greatest achievement, it seemed more fitting to associate America's origins not with the ancestors of the rebel slave-holders of Virginia but with the pious refugees of Massachusetts. The idea of America's puritan origins is thus a founding myth, or a refounding myth: a historical memory fashioned in a later time for later purposes that distorts what actually happened in an earlier time. As the historian Jack P. Greene has said, the histories of Virginia and Maryland were much more characteristic of early America generally than were the quite eccentric histories of Massachusetts and the other New England colonies.

The religious motivations for the settlement of New England were unusual but not unique. Maryland was meant to be a haven for Catholics and Pennsylvania for Quakers, but the difference was that the charter holders of both colonies practised toleration of others, while Massachusetts was supposed to be a puritan commonwealth and as such was violently intolerant of dissent. Also, neither Marylanders nor Pennsylvanians saw anything wrong with the individualistic pursuit of wealth. Early puritan leaders did. Furthermore, many migrants and settlers shared the religious communitarianism of New England's founders, and it took a lot longer for the charter group's dream to die than was the case in other colonies. On the other hand, the colonization of New England was similar to that of other colonies in some respects. Even if their first priorities were religious, most migrants nevertheless sought the kind of individual economic and social independence that came with landownership. Furthermore, over time, the religious ardour of the puritans diminished and their material aspirations became more pronounced. In the late seventeenth century, especially after Massachusetts lost its charter in 1684, the power of the puritans began to fall while that of the lawyers, landowners and merchants began to rise. In time, then, New England became more like the other colonies: entrepreneurial, market orientated, materialistic and individualistic: less puritan, more Yankee.[1]

The Plymouth Company and Sagadahoc

For over a century before the puritans arrived, Basque, French and English fishermen cut and dried their catches on the coasts of what we now know as New England. The activities of fishermen and fur traders kept English entrepreneurs interested in the region, and, in 1605, with sponsorship from the Earl of Southampton, George Waymouth explored the area around Penobscot Bay and between Maine and Nantucket. On returning to Plymouth, he convinced his gentry-mercantile West Country contacts of the region's suitability for settlement, and these men formed the Virginia Company of Plymouth, with the intention of promoting settlement in what was then known to the English as North Virginia.

The same April 1606 charter that authorized the London Company to colonize South Virginia also licensed the Plymouth Company to settle the region from 38 to 43 degrees north, between the Potomac River and what is now Bangor, Maine. The Plymouth Company sent a ship to reconnoitre the region in August 1606, though it was blown off course and captured by the Spanish. The next May, the company sent 2 ships and 120 settlers to establish a settlement on the Sagadahoc (now Kennebec) River in Maine. They built a fort, a church, a store and 15 dwellings, but they also suffered political infighting and food shortages. After enduring the extremities of the northern winter, half the survivors left in the spring of 1608, and when their leader, Raleigh Gilbert, son of Humphrey, left for England to claim an inheritance the following year, the remainder returned with him.

Following the failure of the Sagadahoc settlement, the Plymouth Company continued to encourage exploration, licensing Captain John Smith to travel to what he renamed 'New England'. Smith's reports impressed Sir Fernando Gorges, another West Country gentleman, who proposed forming the Council of New England to sub-patent a portion of the region from the Plymouth Company. It was not until 1620, however, that significant numbers of people proposed to migrate permanently to these cold, northern climes, and those who eventually did so were not the entrepreneurial types that the original licensees envisioned employing. Having already passed from the Plymouth Company to the Council of New England, license to settle then devolved on a third group: the Pilgrim Fathers, the puritan religious separatists who founded Plymouth Plantation.[2]

Plymouth Plantation

The 39 Articles of 1563 brought a measure of religious stability to England following the uncertainties and strife that accompanied the Reformation in the reigns of Henry VIII and Edward VI and the fiery Counter-Reformation in the reign of Mary. Nevertheless, 'puritans' increasingly objected to the retention of what they considered Popish elements in the Elizabethan religious settlement, as they expressed in their Admonition to Parliament of 1572. They objected in particular to the tie between Church and state, the Episcopal Church hierarchy, the wearing of vestments by clergy, among other forms of perceived idolatry, and the fact that church membership was open to all, rather than just to visible saints, in keeping with the puritans' Calvinist belief in predestination. They favoured Congregationalism: a 'gathered' or 'called' church in which membership was confined to the elect, and in which congregations chose their own members and ministers. Many remained ready to 'tarry for the magistrate', to push for reform from inside the Church of England, but from the 1570s more extreme dissenters, following Robert Brown, began forming conventicles, their own separate congregations. In 1593, parliament directed that Brownites or separatists leave England or stand trial for their lives. Many went to the Netherlands, in particular to Leyden, though one group anticipated the pilgrims of Plymouth by a whole generation when, in 1593, they requested the queen's consent to settle in a 'foreign and far country which lieth in the West from hence in the Province of Canada'. In 1597, they sent a delegation that included a cleric to study the feasibility of colonization, but the ferocious weather and the rival claims of English, Breton and Basque fishermen discouraged settlement at this stage.3

Among the residents of Leyden was a group of puritans from Scrooby, Nottinghamshire, who withdrew from the established Church in 1607 to form their own illegal congregation and who then went overseas in 1609. The Dutch Republic offered religious freedom, but these puritans feared their children acculturating to the worldly environment of the urban Netherlands, and in any case that environment offered these rural Midlanders few means to make a decent living. Furthermore, the 12-year Dutch–Spanish truce was coming to an end, auguring an uncertain future. In 1617, then, some of their number petitioned the Council of New England for the right to settle in America, though they only received a patent in 1620, after merchant Thomas Weston agreed to underwrite their expenses. In return, the Plymouth settlers agreed to pay Weston their first seven years of profits.

On 20 July 1620, 35 of the 238 members of the Leyden congregation departed the Netherlands aboard the *Speedwell* to join with other would-be settlers aboard the *Mayflower* in Southampton. The *Speedwell* was discovered to be unseaworthy before leaving England, however, and so all crammed aboard the *Mayflower*: 101 people in total, including 87 separatist dissenters and some labourers hired by Weston's merchant group because they possessed the requisite skills to ensure successful settlement. They finally left on 16 September 1620 and landed at the northern end of Cape Cod on 11 November. Finding no suitable spot to settle there, they crossed the bay and founded the colony of Plymouth.

Knowing the troubles that Virginia and Bermuda had endured, William Bradford, 30-year-old leader of the group, and William Brewster, soon-to-be leader of the Plymouth Church, plus the other 39 men aboard ship (including the labourers and sailors) attempted to ensure successful colonization by signing a contract (they had been given no charter that might serve as a model for their enterprise). Under the Mayflower Compact of November 1620, the colonists agreed to

> covenant, and combine ourselves together into a civil Body Politick, for our better Ordering, and Preservation . . . And by Virtue hereof do enact, constitute, and frame, such just and equal Laws, Ordinances, Acts, Constitutions, and Officers, from time to time, as shall be thought most meet and convenient for the general Good of the Colony: unto which we promise all due Submission and Obedience.[4]

This compact – as we shall see, covenants were at the centre of puritan life – acted as the basis of Plymouth's politics and set a precedent for representative government under a written constitution. Because Plymouth was settled primarily by its own organizers, and because of the religious unity and purposefulness of the group, affirmed by the compact, Plymouth was one of the more lastingly successful colonizing ventures undertaken by English people at this time. Yet the process of colonization was not without its setbacks, and eventually the aims of even the Pilgrim Fathers succumbed to the more worldly ambitions of others.

During the *Mayflower*'s 11-week voyage, one person died and two were born, so the original Plymouth colonists numbered 102. According to William Bradford's history *Of Plimoth Plantation*, the new arrivals 'fell upon their knees and blessed the God of Heaven who had brought them over the vast and furious ocean and delivered them from all the perils and miseries thereof, again to set their feet upon the firm and stable earth, their proper element'. Yet the hardships of oceanic travel made many susceptible to the rigours of even one of New England's milder winters (though average winters were colder then than they are now). Bradford recorded the 'most sad and lamentable' fact 'that in two or three months' time half of their company died, especially in January and February, being the depth of winter and wanting houses and other comforts; being infected with scurvy and other diseases in which this long voyage and their inaccomode condition had brought on them'. Among the dead was the colony's first governor, John Carver, who was succeeded by Bradford.

The half of the Pilgrims who survived did so by scavenging food buried by local Amerindians who afterwards had died of European diseases. The settlers also used the fields left behind by these previous inhabitants. Their first main Amerindian contact was an English-speaking Abenaki named Samoset. In the spring, another English-speaking Indian named Squanto, who had been kidnapped by an English sea captain and thereby survived the annihilation of his fellow Patuxet people by disease, interpreted and helped teach the settlers how to grow and prepare native food crops such as squash and maize (Indian corn). The Pilgrims shared the first harvest in a feast with their native saviours: an event Americans still celebrate as Thanksgiving. Early Pilgrim-Amerindian relations were peaceful in part because European diseases drastically reduced local populations. For Bradford, though, this had nothing to do with one people crossing an epidemiological boundary and infecting another people who had no immunity to their diseases, and everything to do with the will of God. Writing in 1634 of a group of Connecticut River Indians who had recently developed trade relations with the Dutch to the exclusion of the English, Bradford wrote that 'it pleased God to visit these Indians with a great sickness and such a mortality that of a thousand, above nine and a half hundred of them died'. In the same year, while numerous Indians at Windsor were dying of smallpox, 'by the marvelous goodness and providence of God, not one of the English was so much as sick or in the least measure tainted with this disease'. Also, the colonists negotiated safe settlement and trade with the Wampanoag sachem, Massasoit, nominally subjecting him to the English king in exchange for an alliance against the rival Narragansett and Massachusett tribes.[5]

The stable relationship established with Amerindians allowed for political peace among the colonists, at least during the crucial settlement era. All freemen had the vote and they elected William Bradford as their governor for 30 years in a row. This very simple form of governance was all that the colonists initially required, although it later left them ill-equipped to resist their incorporation with Massachusetts. In the meantime, the colony grew steadily but only slowly. After a decade, the settlement still consisted of fewer than 400 people, despite a more benign environment and a lower death rate than in Virginia. By the end of William Bradford's longish life, in 1657, Plymouth's population had reached only 1300, and was still less than 7500 in 1691. Even so, the colony by then had expanded from just 1 settlement to 11 towns.

Financial problems afflicted Plymouth. The absence of an exportable commodity equivalent to tobacco meant meagre profits, and most of the venture's shareholders sold up rather than keep financing the commercially near-worthless enterprise. In 1621, the Council of New England took over legal responsibility for the colony and the Virginia Company of Plymouth finally went bankrupt in 1626, following the London Company into oblivion. The colonists nevertheless made Plymouth a going concern. They initially practised a kind of communism by holding all property in common and sharing all profits, although in 1627 the colony's land and other assets were divided into individual allotments. The settlers ensured their economic survival by semi-subsistence farming and local exchange, and by exporting furs, fish, lumber, maize and wampum. The colonists eventually paid their debt to the Weston group in 1642. Another key to survival was selling land to encroaching colonists from the Massachusetts Bay Colony, founded to the north in 1630. Interconnections with Massachusetts grew over time.

Without commodities it could export directly to Europe, Plymouth's trade grew increasingly dependent on the rapidly growing port of Boston.

Massachusetts and Plymouth thus converged demographically and economically. Crucially, they also converged theologically, as the Massachusetts puritans became increasingly attracted to separation from the Church of England. Plymouth recognized this development in 1667 by inviting the leading Massachusetts cleric, John Cotton, to become minister of Plymouth Church. In 1686, Plymouth was incorporated into the Dominion of New England, and after the Glorious Revolution it was incorporated into Massachusetts. There was some unhappiness in Plymouth at these turns of events, but the third-generation inhabitants of the small pilgrim colony had little inclination or ability to resist.[6]

The founding of Massachusetts: 'A Modell of Christian Charity'

John Winthrop's puritans were not the first Europeans to settle in the Massachusetts Bay region. As early as 1623, puritans from Dorset colonized Cape Ann, though theirs was a fish and fur enterprise organized by the Dorchester Company. Their settlements failed to thrive and the only one that survived was Naumkeag, renamed Salem by John Endecott, who arrived with a group of puritan migrants in 1628. That year, the Dorchester Company sold out to the New England Company, a group of about 90 puritans that the following year licensed the Massachusetts Bay Company to establish the puritan commonwealths that made New England so distinctive.

The puritans who settled Massachusetts were distinct from those who settled Plymouth in that they remained within the Church of England. They were nevertheless becoming increasingly embittered by the state of the Anglican Church. In 1618, James I accepted the Synod of Dort's condemnation of Arminius, the Leyden University professor who preached the anti-Calvinist doctrine that men could choose whether or not to accept God's grace. Charles I and William Laud (Bishop of Wells from 1626 and Archbishop of Canterbury from 1633), nevertheless promoted Arminian-leaning bishops and, in what was taken as a nod to Catholicism, moved the communion table (or altar, as they preferred to call it) to the east of churches from the middle. Though Laud rejected a cardinalship, the Pope's offer nevertheless alarmed puritans. As Richard Saltonstall, Jr., put it to John Winthrop, Jr.: 'Bishop Laud . . . doth daly more and more, both plott and practis to bring into the Church, downe right popery.' Furthermore, Laud's religious regime was becoming increasingly repressive. While few of the puritans who went to New England were personally persecuted, the Anglican Church certainly seemed to be moving in the wrong direction, and, though they did not split from the Church of England, those who moved to New England ceased to work within it and resolved instead to reform it by precept from afar.

Early 1629 saw military losses for continental European Protestant powers and the closing of parliament by Charles I. These events eliminated opportunities for religious and political reform that puritans had hitherto hoped to effect. Also, the economy of eastern England, a strongly puritan region, was in depression. In August 1629, then, 12 puritan leaders, including John Winthrop, a justice of the peace and lord of the manor at Groton, Suffolk, who rose as high as attorney to the Court of Wards and Liveries before the Laudian purges, met secretly at Cambridge and resolved that they and as many of their co-religionists as they could persuade to go with them should make their way to Massachusetts. The following March, 7 ships, led by the *Arbella*, departed England, beginning the Great Migration of 1630–43 in which over 13,000 people moved to Massachusetts. Archbishop Laud himself noted 'men running to New England, and God knows whither', who 'think nothing is their advantage, but to run from government'. Winthrop arrived at Salem in June 1630. Finding that half of Endecott's settlers had died, he quickly moved south and founded Boston on a peninsula by the Charles River.[7]

Winthrop and the other Cambridge conferencees persuaded the New England Company to relinquish its charter to them, transforming the company charter into Massachusetts' own constitution and ensuring that they could govern themselves and thereby independently create their own kind of polity and society. These men were determined to draw lessons from previous colonizations to ensure the success of their own. Winthrop reckoned that 'the ill successe of other Plantations' was attributable to three 'great and fundamentall errors': 'thir mayne end was Carnall and not Religious'; 'they used unfitt instrumentes, a multitude of rude and misgovernd persons the very scumme of the Land'; and 'they did not establish a right forme of government'. Winthrop aimed to create instead a religious commonwealth of mostly modestly wealthy and respectable families.

Aboard the *Arbella*, John Winthrop, as William Bradford had done aboard the *Mayflower*, described the kind of colony he and other puritan leaders intended to create. In his famous sermon, 'A Modell of Christian Charity', he propounded the kind of religious corporatism that would characterize Massachusetts:

> . . . wee must be knitt together in this worke as one man. Wee must entertaine each other in brotherly affection. Wee must be willing to abridge ourselves of our superfluities, for the supply of others necessities. Wee must uphold a familiar commerce together in all meekeness, gentlenes, patience and liberality. Wee must delight in eache other; make others' conditions our oune; rejoyce together, mourne together, labour and suffer together, allwayes haueing before our eyes our Commission and Community in the worke, as members of the same body.

Soe shall wee *keepe the unitie of the spirit in the bond of peace.* The Lord will be our God, and delight to dwell among us, as his oune people, and will command a blessing upon us in all our wayes.[8]

As in Plymouth, puritan religious corporatism ensured a much more harmonious society than that which existed in contemporary Virginia. But it was not just ideas and words that ensured that early colonization conformed to the charter holders' aims. The puritans arranged that most migrants to Massachusetts fitted Winthrop's notion of 'fit instruments'. Emigrants to the Chesapeake and West Indies were more often young, single men and were more often from the poorer, if not the poorest, sections of English society. Yet about 70 per cent of Massachusetts migrants were married and were independent farmers and artisans, mostly of the reasonably prosperous 'middling sorts' of people. Most paid their own passages and thus began their lives in New England as independent farmers rather than indentured servants. New Englanders were not egalitarians, but the absence of the wealthiest and the poorest members of English society in the region meant the absence of both an overbearing aristocracy and a disgruntled and dangerous multitude of poor people.

Migrants to Massachusetts often arrived with their families and sometimes even in neighbourhood groups, bringing with them the kind of community bonds that took time to develop in other colonies. About a third of migrants were women, compared to 1-in-6 in Virginia and 1-in-14 in the Caribbean in the 1630s. The sex ratio in seventeenth-century New England was 3 men to 2 women, not the 9 men to 10 women that existed in England, but certainly more balanced than elsewhere in Anglo-America. Indeed, the idea of the family was so powerful that in early Plymouth, Massachusetts and Connecticut everyone had to live in a family home. Families were sometimes extended arrangements (unlike in England, where nuclear families were the norm), or at least with children living close by with their own families and creating complex, powerful, local, concentrated bonds of kinship. New England families were also highly patriarchal. In puritan communities fathers were spiritual as well as political, social and economic heads of their households, but if that was not sufficient to ensure obedience and deference, then long-living fathers in the healthy environment of early Massachusetts retained land until sons were more or less middle-aged. New Englanders married young too. Average age of marriage for women in the first generation was 19 and in the second 22, assuring a high birth rate and further extending the average length of parental and especially paternal authority. New England longevity was possible because there were few epidemic diseases and low infant mortality; life expectancy was just over 70 in the first generation, and was still 64 for men and 62 for women in the second generation.

As well as the covenanted family, New Englanders idealized and institutionalized the covenanted town, creating what they called 'peaceable kingdoms' and what historian Kenneth Lockridge called 'Christian Utopian Closed Corporate Communities'. There were no absolute geographic rules about the creation of towns, and settlement patterns often reflected a combination of what was familiar in England with adaptations to fit the new environment. Some towns were therefore scattered settlements, with families living on dispersed farms, similar to the practice in other colonies. Yet one of the most noted features of the region was the commonality of nucleated village settlements that reflected puritan religious corporatism. Characteristically, houses were arranged around a meeting house and common land, with front doors opening inwards to the village common and back doors opening on to the traditional open field system of farmland surrounding the settlement. Beyond that was the wilderness, a word that originally implied degeneracy into savagery and madness, not just unsettled land, and which had a particularly frightening resonance among New Englanders. New England utopianism was tempered by a fearful dystopianism.[9]

All early New England towns had covenants or mini-constitutions that directed who was allowed to live there and how they were supposed to conduct themselves. Town covenants required inhabitants to live in harmony with each other. This social cohesion rested to some extent on exclusion. Town populations were self-selecting in the first place, and second they 'warned out' undesirables and miscreants who came into their midst. But it was also based on consent. Freemen were allowed personally to covenant themselves and to vote at town meetings, and because they often constituted 60 to 70 per cent of the adult male population, the social cohesion of those towns was strong. Town government typically consisted of 'selectmen' who ran local institutions, made laws, dispensed justice and allocated land, although biannual town meetings attended by all inhabitants and at which freemen could vote ensured a kind of accountability. Town meetings, however, like covenants, were designed to manufacture consensus among the like-minded, not to provide forums for dissent for the fractious. In New England, local and, to a lesser extent, provincial leadership depended more on age and moral authority than on the ancient and hereditary wealth and social authority of English nobles and gentry. The social authority of early puritan local leadership was also extraordinarily strong compared to the emergent and improvised and often beleaguered leaders of other colonies in their early years.

As much as anything else, the church lay at the heart of New England town life. Colony law required that a Congregationalist Meeting House be built in every town and that towns financially support preachers through taxes that had to be paid by church members and non-members alike. The general court that governed the colony further buttressed local church authority with laws against blasphemers and dissenters. The colony's Body of Liberties of 1641 identified 12 capital crimes, including 11 from the Old Testament, among them idolatry and blasphemy. Though the clergy could not hold political office, their control of the church, in particular their ability to determine membership and non-membership, gave them a great deal of social and political influence. Among English puritans, there was a strong degree of lay control, but New England ministers sometimes insisted that their authority came from God rather than from congregational callings and they sometimes met in synods, undermining the puritan idea of congregational independence. Church- and town-imposed harmony were buttressed by the emphasis on education, especially religious education. Harvard College, for example, was established in 1636 and aimed to train and provide a plentiful supply of orthodox puritan ministers for the ever-growing number of towns in Massachusetts and the outlying colonies. From 1647, towns with 50 families were required to establish schools to inculcate in young people orthodox religion and traditional social values and behaviour.

Provincial politics

Government in early colonial Massachusetts was also based on covenanted ideals. Even so, in contrast to the cohesion of local communities in early New England, political tensions at the provincial level were almost inevitable among a predominantly moderately prosperous population for whom the very idea of going to New England was to attain political autonomy and rights. As in other colonies, therefore, a powerful provincial representative assembly soon emerged that sometimes challenged the province's leaders, John Winthrop in particular.

The Massachusetts Bay Company appointed John Winthrop as the colony's first governor, and he ruled initially in an autocratic fashion with a council of magistrates of seven or eight company members, elected by the shareholders. Winthrop determined that although freemen could vote for members of the general court, which became the assembly, only the court could vote for the governor and deputy, and only the governor and deputy could pass laws. After two initial meetings, attended by more men than Winthrop thought were entitled to be present, the governor did not call a general court for a year and a half. He ruled instead with a small cadre of directors who called themselves 'assistants'. In early 1634, though, the assembly proved its troublesome potential again when Thomas Dudley, Roger Ludlow and Israel Stoughton led demands to see the charter, hitherto kept secret (a rather striking abandonment of covenant principle). They thereby discovered the general court's right to make laws, including its exclusive right to impose taxes on the towns. The charter also revealed that not all freemen needed to attend the general court but could instead vote for two or three 'deputies' from each town. There followed two successive gubernatorial defeats for Winthrop, in 1635 by John Hayes and in the following year by Henry Vane. For the next decade, deputies' decisions were subject to governors' vetoes, but in 1644 the assistants and deputies split into two separate houses, though each still required the assent of the other for legislation to pass. From that point, though, the deputies, with popular support to assist them against council veto powers, elected a speaker, developed a committee system, kept their own minutes and, in general, institutionalized parliamentary rules and acted like a local version of the English House of Commons.

Experience with John Winthrop as well as the puritan penchant for covenants inclined the assistants to demand for Massachusetts a written legal code. In 1636, John Cotton produced his 'Moses his Judicials', revised in 1639, modified and published as the Body of Liberties in 1641. In 1646, however, Massachusetts faced a threat to its form of governance. A Presbyterian minister named Robert Child had visited the colony in 1641 and later complained that the colony's laws, in particular church regulations that excluded him from taking the sacrament, were not compatible with those in England and that his rights as an Englishman had therefore been violated. Child's challenge forced limited revisions of the Body of Liberties, some based on local precedent and some on the English common law, resulting in the 1647 *Book of General Lawes and Libertyes* that included some secular incursions on puritan divine authority. It was followed up, however, with the Cambridge Platform of 1648 that warned secular and rival religious authorities not to interfere with the colony's religious affairs. The Platform made no concessions on the exclusivity of church membership, but did drop the church membership requirement for minor officers such as constables and jurors.

If there was some political conflict at the provincial level in the early years, it was minor compared to that which afflicted most other colonies. Yet religious disharmony was almost inevitable in an environment of semi-independent congregations that elected their own ministers, and among puritans whose powerful sense of religious imperative could create bitter contestation over any theological disagreement. One solution to the problem was expulsion of the unorthodox from the colony. One early dissenter was Roger Williams, originally a Plymouth Pilgrim, later minister at Salem, who became a fierce critic of the Massachusetts establishment's continued attachment to the Church of England and of the connection of Church and state more generally. In 1635, he apologized to the general court, but went on to preach the even more radical doctrine that government officials had no business meddling in matters of conscience. Authorities in England ordered him to be arrested, but John Winthrop advised him to flee, and he moved to Narragansett Bay and established a colony that would practise the religious toleration that was the logical outcome of Williams's thinking.

Another influential dissenter was Anne Hutchinson, who caused the

Antinomian controversy of 1637–38 by advancing radical views on justification and sanctification, arguing in particular that knowledge of divine
grace could only be revealed to the self and to God, and that good works,
prayer and obedience to God's commandments, supposed outward signs of
grace, proved nothing of the sort. This belief, of course, threatened one of
the Massachusetts establishment's most awesome powers: its role in judg-
ing church membership by assessing who had received divine grace and
who had not. When her brother-in-law, minister John Wheelwright, went
public from the pulpit with these Antinomian ideas, the general court found
him guilty of sedition and banished him to New Hampshire. Then, when
former support waned – John Cotton withdrew his protection and Henry
Vane went back to England on family business – Thomas Shepard and
other ministers turned on Hutchinson, who was tried in the general court
in November 1637 and in her own church in March 1638. Hutchinson
incriminated herself by declaring that her knowledge of God was 'an immediate revelation', effectively rejecting the organized Church and indeed any
religious authority that pretended to intervene in any individual's relationship with his or her maker. She was excommunicated and banished from
Massachusetts for blasphemy. Like Williams, Hutchinson and her followers found refuge in Rhode Island, though she later moved to Long Island
and was killed by Indians who were resisting English encroachment.[10]

Population growth, new towns and new colonies in New England

By 1640, New England's population reached some 25,000, compared to
8000 in the longer-settled but still deadly Chesapeake. Migration then
slowed. Indeed, during the civil wars, as many as 1-in-10 residents of some
towns returned to England to join the puritan, parliamentary revolution.
After the civil wars and before the end of the century, only about 10,000 to
12,000 new arrivals appeared in New England. Even so, the region's population continued to increase. Demographic growth was attributable to the
relatively healthy environment of New England and consequent long life
expectancy, the high proportion of women and married migrants and to the
generally young age of marriage. The average family in seventeenth-century
New England produced seven children. The region's population thus
reached over 33,000 by 1660, 115,000 by 1710 and, after renewed migration, almost 460,000 by 1760.

This growing population, though, needed new places to live, and New
Englanders spread into the hinterlands of initial settlements along the coast
and then into inland valleys, a 'hiving out' that eventually contributed to
the undermining of puritan communitarianism. This process was evident
from the very beginning, when Winthrop immediately moved south from
Salem and founded Boston as the commonwealth's capital (named for the

Lincolnshire home of many of the migrants). There were 11 towns by the end of 1630, 21 in 1641 and 33 in 1647. By 1700, there were some 120 towns in the colonies of Massachusetts, Connecticut, Rhode Island and New Hampshire.

In some respects, this rapid development of new towns reinforced religious and communitarian values in New England. The general court issued town grants, but early new towns usually replicated the patterns of local church and civic authority and local identity upon which puritan corporatism depended. Also, under the first New England headright system, land devolved directly to individuals, but this was replaced by a system in which land grants were made to towns, which then allotted land to individuals. The new system therefore invested town authorities with considerable power. Land was allotted according to rank, gentlemen being granted 200 acres and others between 30 and 100 acres, though no one was given any great tracts of land. In time, however, wealthier families accumulated larger holdings, leasing surplus land and creating a population of tenants. As some moved away from the original town centres, they came to resent paying taxes for facilities that were some miles away, and either petitioned to be incorporated as separate towns or moved still further away. As the second and subsequent generations established new towns and farmsteads, furthermore, parental and clerical authority began slowly to diminish.

Besides the formation of new towns, another early sign of the 'declension' from corporatism that historians identify as a key feature of New England history was the creation of new colonies. New colonies were formed in part simply because of the growth and spread of population, but also in part because of religious dissension. In turn, the creation of new colonies engendered new kinds of conflicts. Connecticut came into being as a result of puritans moving into the Connecticut River valley from 1634 to seek new land and trading opportunities and to escape from religious repression in Massachusetts. In 1636, some groups of settlers from Cambridge and Newtown, Massachusetts, led by Reverend Thomas Hooker, established towns such as Hartford, Windsor and Wethersfield on the Connecticut River, some 100 miles from Boston. Hooker and many of his followers, though not necessarily Antinomians or believers in toleration, felt that communion should be more widely accessible and generally disliked the authoritarianism of the general court, especially that of John Cotton. Massachusetts claimed jurisdiction in the newly settled region, although it had no chartered right to these lands, but suffered a setback in 1635 when a group of English peers obtained the right to establish a separate colony and sent John Winthrop, Jr. to found one. In 1639, after the Pequot War destroyed the Amerindian threat to settlement (see below), Connecticut settlers established the Fundamental Orders, declaring their settlements a separate colony, although its political autonomy was not recognized by the parent colony or the crown for over 20 years. It finally received a crown charter in 1662, incorporating lands south of Massachusetts and west of Narragansett Bay, though the borders remained disputed for some time. John Winthrop, Jr.'s argument to the sensitive new court of Charles II was that the moderate colony of Connecticut would provide a counterbalance to the dogmatic colony of Massachusetts, which was still some months away from declaring acceptance of the king's Restoration.

As early as 1622, the first European settlers of what became New Hampshire had already moved on to lands between the Merrimack and Kennebec rivers, claimed by Sir Fernando Gorges and John Mason as the 'Province of Maine'. And the early residents were not puritans. Plans for an Anglican colony eventuated in nothing more than a few small settlements: the region west of the Piscataqua River devolved on Mason as 'New Hampshire' in 1629 and, with West Country settlers centred on Portsmouth, the colony developed enterprises in fishing, furs, timber and shipbuilding, and was a nominally Anglican but essentially secular society. In 1641, the small and insecure New Hampshire settlements accepted administration and protection from Massachusetts, and those of Maine did the same in 1652, although the descendants of Gorges and Mason sued to recover their losses. New Hampshire once again became a separate colony, with a royally appointed governor, in 1679. By that time, migrants from Massachusetts dominated the new colony's population, although they included religious dissidents such as Reverend John Wheeler, brother-in-law of Anne Hutchinson, exiled after the Antinomian controversy of 1637. Even when it shared a governor with Massachusetts from 1689, the lower Piscataqua region of New Hampshire retained a separate and Anglican identity, and the increasingly wealthy mercantile gentry of Portsmouth managed to secure full autonomy for New Hampshire once again in 1741. Maine retained a sense of difference too. When Cotton Mather urged a congregation of these far-northerners not to 'contradict the main end of Planting Wilderness', one resident replied, 'Sir, you are mistaken, you think you are Preaching to the People of the Bay; our main End was to catch Fish.'

The favourite destination for religious exiles from Massachusetts was Rhode Island. Roger Williams and Anne Hutchinson both moved there, as did Baptists, familists, millenarians, Quakers and spiritists. Williams founded the town of Providence in 1644, and with the support of the Earl of Warwick secured the sectarians' independence by obtaining a patent from parliament for 'Providence Plantations'. Williams obtained a new one for Rhode Island from Charles II in 1663. Williams's Acts and Orders of 1647 gave the colonists an elected legislature and governor, a broad franchise and freedom of conscience. Rhode Island therefore attracted a diverse and often fractious population. In 1657, Quakers who had been persecuted in the orthodox New England colonies began moving to Rhode Island, and they soon converted some prominent pre-existing residents. In 1659,

George Fox, founder of the Society of Friends, visited Rhode Island. In the eighteenth century, a community of Sephardic Jews who settled in Newport enriched the Rhode Island mix. Rhode Island, though part of New England, differed profoundly from Massachusetts.

New Haven was the last and shortest-lived of all New England's colonies. Reverend John Davenport and a congregation of radical puritans arrived in Boston in 1637, during the Antinomian controversy. He, his flock and London merchant Theophilus Eaton were horrified by the discord and moved almost immediately to Quinnipiac, on Long Island Sound, to form a purified puritan settlement. Ironically, Davenport and Eaton soon began rivalling each other, and other colonists squabbled among themselves too. One merchant group broke away to found the port of New Haven. New Haven colonists attempted to resist incorporation into Connecticut when the latter received its royal charter in 1662. But the annexation of New Netherland two years later made them accept amalgamation into Connecticut as preferable to absorption into the new colony of New York. One group that could not accommodate this new arrangement, though, moved on to New Jersey and founded the town of New Ark, later renamed Newark. The Long Island settlements, previously partitioned between Connecticut and New Netherland, were allocated to New York in the settlement of 1664.[11]

Conflict with Amerindians

The spread of Euro-Americans throughout New England eventually brought settlers into conflict with Amerindians. New Englanders initially had good intentions for Amerindians, judged by seventeenth-century European standards. The Massachusetts Bay Company seal depicted a Native American with the legend 'come over and help us', indicating a more than usual determination to convert Indians to Christianity and English civility. Like English colonists elsewhere, though, they had no doubt about the rightness of their claims to Amerindian land. In his 1629 'Reasons to be considered for justifieinge the undertakers of the intended Plantation in New England', John Winthrop cited Genesis 1:28, which directed people to 'Increase & multiply, replenish the earth & subdue it.' He therefore shared, but with perhaps greater than usual conviction, the agriculturalist inclinations characteristic of European colonizers in general. Furthermore, Winthrop shared William Bradford's providentialist belief that God cleared the way for English settlers, having recently 'consumed the natives with a great plague'.[12]

Another source of instability in Anglo-Amerindian relations was in the fur trade. The English wanted to exclude the Dutch from this lucrative business and allied with Narragansett and Mohegan Indians against the Pequot, trading partners of their New Netherlander rivals. In the resulting Pequot

War (1636–37), Plymouth, Massachusetts and Connecticut formed the Confederation of the United Colonies of New England and, allied with the Narragansett, killed, enslaved and exiled thousands of Pequot, giving the English control of southern New England. The war gave rise to some horrendous atrocities and puritan religious certainties permitted some peculiar reactions. After 400 Pequot men, women and children were burned alive in their fort by the Mystic River on 26 May 1637, William Bradford described the 'fearful sight to see them thus frying in the fire and the streams of blood quenching the same, and horrible was the stink and scent thereof; but the victory seemed a sweet sacrifice, and [the soldiers] gave praise thereof to God who had wrought so wonderfully for them'. Meanwhile, 'those that scaped the fire were slain with the sword, some hewed to pieces, others run through with their rapiers'. Those Pequot who survived the war became slaves of the Mohegans, though they later negotiated a grant of 214 acres on the west bank of the Thames River: America's first Indian reservation. Subsequent Indian dependence on the English fur trade and ever-dwindling resources of fur and land resulted in intertribal wars and further diminution of Indian numbers. The 70,000 Amerindian population of New England in 1620 was reduced to 12,000 in half a century.[13]

The difficulties of settlement, including treating with and sometimes fighting Amerindians, put the aim of Christianizing and civilizing the Indians in abeyance for a while. But after the Pequot War, minister John Eliot (who translated the Bible into Natick Algonquin) established a mission that inspired the Massachusetts General Court in 1646 to establish 'praying towns' that attempted a thoroughgoing conversion of Massachusett Indians to English civilization as well as to their strict version of Protestant Christianity. Their reasoning was that Indians were animalistic, governed by passions rather than reason, and thus they needed to be civilized before they could be Christianized. There were 14 'praying towns' by 1670, where Amerindians were forced to speak English, wear English clothes, eat English foods and adopt English manners as well as learn the fundamentals of Calvinism.

This kind of cultural imperialism led to bitter antagonism with the Wampanoag and Narragansett, who were already aggrieved by the continuous expansion of English settlement and by English support for their enemy, the Iroquois, in their war with the Susquehannock. Tension erupted in Metacom's War (also known as King Philip's War) in 1675–76. When Wampanoag chief Massasoit died in 1662, colonists rightly suspected his eldest son and successor, Wamsutta (Alexander to the English), of harbouring strong antisettler sentiments. They summoned him for interrogation, whereupon he was questioned but allowed to go home. When he subsequently died, the Wampanoag suspected foul play. This was the poisonous atmosphere in which Wansutta's brother, Metacom, succeeded to tribal leadership. Metacom (King Philip to the English) was even more hostile than his brother to English incursions and impositions. His 1660s' efforts to defer settlement and land speculation had failed, and in 1672 he was forced into a humiliating treaty with Plymouth that prevented him from making war and from selling land without English permission. In June 1675, the English hanged three Wampanoag for murdering a Christianized Indian spy named Sassamon, an extension of English jurisdiction that made Metacom finally call to arms the Algonquin-speaking coalition he had been forging for some years.

In late June, Metacom and his allies began attacking towns across New England. The colonists were sufficiently panicked to attack other tribes indiscriminately in retribution. The English eventually prevailed, first by allying with the Mohegans and their former enemies the Pequot, who taught the English the arts of wilderness warfare. The English, with the help of Governor Edmund Andros of New York, also formed an alliance known as the Covenant Chain with the five-nation Iroquois League in June 1676. The war was concluded with help from the Mohawk of New York in August 1676, and with the assassination of Metacom by a Christian Indian mercenary (Metacom's skull was publicly displayed in Plymouth for the next 20 years). Some 3000 Narragansett, Nipmuck and Wampanoag had died, and many more were executed, sold into slavery in the West Indies (including Metacom's wife and son) or exiled to French Canada. One way and another, Metacom's War resulted in the halving of New England's Indian population. Six hundred New England colonists also died, 1200 homes were destroyed and 52 towns – half the towns in the region – were attacked – 12 completely destroyed – and it took 30 years to regain the ground lost in this war.[14]

'Declension' in New England

The New England experiment in religious corporatism was the most successful and longest lasting of all the American charter groups' colonizing schemes, and yet it was almost bound to fail, certainly judged by the puritans' own impossible standards of success. These standards were upped in the 1640s. The first generation saw themselves as reforming the English Church from afar. But when the puritan revolution back home finally reformed English religion, most chose not to return. They therefore had to rethink what they were doing in America, and they reconceptualized themselves as nothing less than latter-day Israelites, a chosen people building Jerusalem in the New World.

The puritans also institutionalized the decline of the authority of their Church, for the rise of a second generation of New England colonists presented a predictable problem: a fall in the number of church members when membership was, in effect, largely restricted to an ageing population of visible saints. Numbers of church members declined because obtaining church membership was no easy business. From the mid-1630s, people had to prove that they were saved and were therefore qualified for full church membership in front of the minister and church members in extraordinarily exacting examinations. Church membership declined so drastically that a synod of 1662 decided upon what critics condemned as a 'Half-Way Covenant' that allowed unconverted children of full church members to be halfway members of congregations when they reached 16 years of age, allowing them to have their children baptized but not to take full communion or to vote. Many congregations resisted this apostasy and this imposition upon congregational independence, but, grudgingly and gradually, most relented by the end of the century.

The next church crisis arose from an influx of religious dissenters from puritan Congregationalism, including Baptists, Presbyterians and Quakers, in the 1650s. Although these new arrivals encountered severe repression, their presence eventually forced their toleration, encouraged by imperial intervention. After four Quakers were hanged in Massachusetts between 1659 and 1661, the newly restored king Charles II pressured the colony to permit private worship by dissenters. Most significantly, perhaps, the Anglican Church became a major force in New England life during the eighteenth century. In the 1720s, some Congregationalist ministers converted to Episcopalianism and took their members back into the Church of England. By 1770, there were up to 25,000 members of 74 Anglican congregations in New England.

These compromises, however, reflected a more general diminution of puritan religious zeal. The decline in puritan perfectionism was almost inevitable given the puritan belief in human imperfection. Aboard the *Arbella*, John Winthrop leavened his idealistic hopes with grim warnings, foreseeing the possibility of decline. His famous evocation of a city upon a hill, derived from Matthew's Gospel, was as much a caution against failure as an imperative to success:

> . . . . wee must Consider that wee shall be as a citty upon a hill. The eies of all people are uppon us. Soe that if wee shall deale falsely with our God in this worke wee haue undertaken, and soe cause him to withdrawe his present help from us, wee shall be made a story and a by-word through the world. Wee shall open the mouthes of enemies to speake evill of the wayes of God, and all professours for God's sake. Wee shall shame the faces of many of God's worthy servants, and cause theire prayers to be turned into curses upon us till wee be consumed out of the good land whether wee are a goeing. . .

These agonies over moral and spiritual declension made puritans anxiously alert to apostasy from the moment they arrived in New England. As early as 23 July 1630, John Winthrop complained to his wife Margaret that 'I thinke heere are some persons who never shewed so much wickednesse in England as they have doon heer.' As time passed, the problem grew worse. By the time the second generation came of age, Cotton Mather was expressing fears of 'creolean degeneracy'.[15]

The puritan idea of the covenant or contract between God and people encouraged the belief among New Englanders that every major storm, drought, crop failure, fire, epidemic, shipwreck, war or any other kind of disaster was perceived, in a common contemporary phrase, as a 'token of God's displeasure' at declining spiritual and moral standards. To assuage God, churches in various towns called days of humiliation, fast days, to reassert the virtues of devotion and good behaviour. On occasion, the general court declared fast days for the whole colony. One such occasion was 19 October 1652, when the court listed various afflictions, including storms, the recurrence of civil war in the British Isles and, significantly, 'the worldly mindedness, oppression, & hardhartedness feared to be among us'. This declaration was significant because for the first time sinful behaviour was noted not merely as a cause of calamity but as a calamity in and of itself. Though ministers had bemoaned the declension of puritan ways on previous occasions, this new development inspired the great jeremiads delivered and often published by preachers for the edification of New England's second and third and, supposedly, slacking generations.

The jeremiads

The titles of jeremiads, the most popular published works of their time in New England, often neatly captured their general message and powerful sense of imperative. The great New England historian Perry Miller noted, for example, Michael Wigglesworth's *God's Controversy with New England* (1662) as the first great jeremiad and Increase Mather's *The Day of Trouble is Near* (1673) and *A Discourse Concerning the Danger of Apostasy* (1677) as among the greatest. In 1679, after Metacom's War and an alarming upsurge in fires, shipwrecks and disease, the general court called a synod to investigate 'the provoking evils of New England'. The synod's deliberations were recorded in a *Result*, authored primarily by Increase Mather, which encapsulated the content of previous jeremiads and provided a model of the form that ministers could, and according to the synod should, emulate. The *Result* enumerated 10 categories of enormity, the first being 'a great and visible decay of the power of Godliness amongst many Professors in these churches'. After blaming their own, the clerics moved on to blaming others, first for pride. This sin was manifest in the failure of the poor to defer to their betters, and in the betters by their 'excess, gaudiness & fantasticality'. The latter was no trivial thing, for early setbacks in Metacom's War were attributed to 'monstrous and horrid Perriwigs, . . . and such like whorish Fashions'. Massachusetts (though not

Plymouth) had sumptuary laws that restricted what the poor could wear. Even church members, the saved, were guilty of 'Sinful Heats and Hatreds . . . evil Surmises, uncharitable and unrighteous Censures, Back-bitings, hearing and telling Tales'. The third problem was heresy, not just by non-puritans but also by ministers who 'hearken & adhere to their own fancyes and Satans delusions'. The next categories were swearing and sleeping in church, Sabbath breaking, inconstant parental discipline, fornication and drunkenness and untruthfulness.

The synod's tenth category of 'provoking evils' was headed 'Inordinate affection unto the world': in other words, the love of wealth. The synod bemoaned 'an insatiable desire after Land . . . that many hundreds, nay thousands of Acres, have been engrossed by one man, and they that profess themselves Christians, have forsaken Churches, and Ordinances, and all for land and elbow-room enough in the World'. Complaints about merchants 'price gouging' dated at least to the fining of Robert Keayne in 1639 for hoarding grain to create a shortage that would raise its price. He apologized, but other merchants pleaded in his mitigation that 'a certain rule could not be found out for an equal rate between buyer and seller'. John Cotton on that occasion enforced the notion of a 'just price' (as judged by the community on grounds of affordability and fairness rather than a price determined by the market or its manipulation), but four decades later the synod found reason to complain about the abandonment of the just price for the best price and the rise of usury. The synod also noted that poorer people were getting greedy too, bemoaning that 'Day-Labourers and Mechanics are unreasonable in their demands'. In this final category, the synod identified the most fundamental of the forces that were changing New England: the temptations of individual material betterment that were taken for granted in other colonies.[16]

Witchcraft

Antagonism between puritan religiosity and Yankee worldliness manifested itself most terribly in Salem, Massachusetts, in 1692. The witchcraft accusations and trials of that year represented not only tensions between diverging communities but also, and perhaps this is why they were so violent, within the guilt-ridden minds of individuals. Of course, belief in witchcraft was perfectly normal in early modern Europe and America, and although witchcraft accusations were on the decline in late seventeenth-century England, that belief provides the general context for explaining the Salem witch-hunt. New England's first witch execution took place in Connecticut in 1647, and dozens more witches were hanged (no New England witches were burned or drowned), and others accused but exonerated, in the succeeding half-century. In January 1692, though, several young girls from Salem were examining a glass for images of their future husbands. When one saw a coffin, the group panicked and accused a half-Indian half-African servant named Tituba of witchcraft. Tituba confessed. It did not end there, however, for Tituba, the girls and others subsequently made scores of denunciations, resulting in some 43 trials, 19 public executions, 4 deaths in custody and the crushing to death of one man as he was being 'pressed' between huge stones in a vain attempt to extract a confession. Eventually the sheer number of accusations aroused alarm among provincial leaders, and after Increase Mather expressed doubt on the sightings of witches in spectral form (agreeing with the defence of Rebecca Nurse, who was hanged for witchcraft on 19 July, that the devil could produce visions of the innocent to fool the credulous), the newly arriving governor, Sir William Phips, ordered that this evidence could no longer be used in court. Only three women were convicted thereafter, and Phips pardoned them and all those previously found guilty. The general court later issued compensation to the bereaved.

The Salem accusations followed patterns that were familiar elsewhere but which also reflected problems peculiar to the locality. Most of the accused were women, reflecting general fears of maternal authority (witchcraft was a particular threat to children), but the fear of female sexuality and power was particularly strong in puritan and patriarchal New England. Also, many of Salem's accused women had modestly independent means, threatening a patriarchal order that was particularly pronounced in New England. Quite a few of the accused had reputations for cantankerousness, and such awkward characters were a particular threat in a society where harmony was so highly prized. Others were slightly resentful beggars. Many accusers testified to beggars leaving their homes 'muttering', again offending notions of harmonious neighbourliness, but also arousing a dangerous guilt in the accuser at their own apparent absence of Christian charity. Furthermore, historians Paul Boyer and Stephen Nissenbaum found that what distinguished the Salem episode was the identification of accusers with Salem Village (now Danvers) and the accused with Salem Town. The semi-subsistence agricultural village held strongly to traditional New England mores, while the town was an increasingly prosperous commercial port, and the two locations thus respectively represented the New England past and its potential but, for some, dreaded future. A sense of the nature of the change is reflected in the fact that in 1661 the wealthiest 10 per cent of Salem residents owned 21 per cent of its wealth, but in the commercial expansion that was happening at the time that figure rose to 62 per cent on the eve of the outbreak of the witchcraft accusations. Many of the accusers were associated with the Putnams, a village farming family of declining fortune, and many of the accused with the Porters, a rising family connected to the town. The two families had been running a feud since at least 1689, since when the Putnams had supported and the Porters had opposed the retention of the services of the minister, Samuel Parris. Parris's daughter and niece were among the girls who initiated the witchcraft denunciations, and Tituba was Parris's slave. After Tituba and the girls made their accusations, it was the Putnams who called in the magistrates. Salem thus represented in miniature but stark form the changes and associated tensions that were occurring throughout much of New England.

In the eighteenth century, New England remained a distinctly religious and even puritan region, but the trauma of Salem undoubtedly diminished the power of religious certitudes. The disjuncture between old ideals and new behaviour continued to generate a sense of guilt and therefore an atavistic potential that manifested itself in a ministry-supported Great Awakening beginning in the 1740s. Yet this religious revival, though it provoked at least a temporary return to intense public piety, unforeseeably contributed to the further diminution of puritan ways. The revival, appealing to individual consciences and thus further reifying the self above the community, deepened more often than it healed religious disagreements, sometimes splitting congregations and further disaffecting dissenting elements in the laity from the ministry. Furthermore, religious contention manifested itself in politics, further legitimating modern political factionalism and contestation in the place of the puritan ideals of political harmony and deference.[17]

Political change in New England

What also undermined puritanism were developments in the relationship between Massachusetts and the empire in the late seventeenth century. During Metacom's War, the newly formed Lords of Trade and Plantations sent an emissary, Edward Randolph, to investigate New Englanders' notorious levels of political independence from England, evasions of the Navigation Acts that regulated trade by direct colonial exports through London (see chapter 8) and refusal to tolerate Anglicanism. The Massachusetts General Court gave Randolph a chilly reception, but in 1684 the Court of Chancery in London annulled the Massachusetts charter, breaking the covenant bond between rulers and ruled in the colony, and the next year James II incorporated the region with New York in the Dominion of New England. The Glorious Revolution saw the overthrow of the Dominion and its governor, Sir Edmund Andros, as well as James II, but new reforms were soon to follow. While Connecticut and Rhode Island retained locally elected governors (the only colonies to do so throughout the colonial period), in 1691 Massachusetts became a royal colony with a crown-appointed governor. The new charter abolished the church membership requirement for voting and allowed freedom of conscience to all Protestants, thereby eliminating the freedom to be intolerant that had been essential to attempts to create a monolithic puritan commonwealth. And so Massachusetts became less religious but at the same time more religiously heterogeneous. In 1718, the governor of Massachusetts even began encouraging immigration of non-puritan Protestants, especially Ulster (Scotch-Irish) Presbyterians. If they converted to Congregationalism they were allowed to stay in previously settled puritan areas, though most remained loyal to their denominational identity and settled instead on the western frontiers of Massachusetts, New Hampshire and Maine.

The new charter of 1691 not only undermined the puritan experiment but also reflected the interests of a new class of entrepreneurs. The new Massachusetts incorporated Plymouth and the islands of Martha's Vineyard and Nantucket, originally settled by puritans but included in New York in 1664. These acquisitions doubled the colony's size, added 10,000 people to its population and provided several new harbours for the colony's growing class of merchants to enhance further their increasingly vigorous trade.[18]

From puritan to Yankee: the commercialization of New England

What probably undermined puritanism more than any other single thing was the gradually increasing commercialization of New England's economy and the consequently expanding opportunities for individual material betterment. Even early on, some puritans were less keen than others on Christian commonwealths, and some towns were more loose affiliations than corporate communities. Always a commercial port, for example, Boston was never a covenanted community. Springfield, Massachusetts, was founded in 1636 as a company town run by and for the Pynchon family. Thomas Pynchon owned the only store and all the mills of this highly commercial and socially stratified town. By 1680, half the town's men were dependants – tenants and wage earners – many of them employed by Pynchon. Over time an increasing number of new towns more closely resembled Pynchon's Springfield than they did Christian, utopian, closed, corporate communities.

Even in the mid-seventeenth century, the spread of population into new towns and colonies began to loosen the bonds of puritan corporatism. As time passed, the process accelerated. From the late seventeenth century, land grants were given to speculators and even companies who were more interested in reselling at a profit than in settling tightly-knit religious communities. Land speculation became one of the biggest businesses in New England. Increasingly, they sold not just to puritans but also to Protestants of various denominations. New Englanders founded over 100 towns between the end of Queen Anne's War in 1713 and the end of the French and Indian War 50 years later. In the eighteenth century, settlers spread from the increasingly densely populated eastern regions into the Green Mountains, the upper Hudson Valley and the Lake Champlain region, lands claimed by New York. New Hampshire governors encouraged this migration as a means to extend their charter rights and land speculation opportunities at the expense of New Yorkers. Whitehall decided in favour of New York and then suspended grant giving by all parties, but attempts by New York to obtain fees from settlers led to outbreaks of violence between Yorkers and Yankees. There was talk of creating a new colony of Verd-Mont, though the state of Vermont did not come into existence until the Green Mountain Boys' rebellion following American Independence.

In the eighteenth century, community and family ties were less binding than they were in the seventeenth. Parental control of marriage declined, resulting in later ages of marriage, more companionate rather than pre-scribed relationships, less parental and biblical naming of children and a rise in premarital pregnancies and divorces. As third and later generations broke away from their parents, those parents did less to impose authority on their children and did more, as in other colonies, to imbue them with the qualities of individual assertiveness more appropriate to an increasingly secular, materialistic and competitive world.

Another sign of changing times and ways was a rise in criminal prosecu-tion and in litigation, in particular in disputes over property. Whereas in Virginia and Maryland the development of a court system and the growth of litigation represented new impositions of order where once there was dis-order, the growing court system and volume of cases in New England rep-resented the breaking down of an old order based on private, town- or church-based face-to-face conflict resolution. The end results were institu-tionally essentially the same: a legally codified system of justice presided over by neutral third parties in which criminal justice was administered and civil disputes were arbitrated. But how the Chesapeake and New England arrived at this convergence reflected their very different histories.

What spurred the ever more rapid spread of New England settlements and the new forms of behaviour that went with it was the increasing inte-gration of New England in the Atlantic economy. Without staple crop agri-culture, early New England had depended on the capital that came with new arrivals to keep its economy going. When immigration all but ceased at the beginning of the civil wars, a credit crisis and depression ensued that were severe enough to inspire the general court to offer bounties for the local production of goods that had hitherto been imported. It took time, but by the turn of the eighteenth century New England was as fully inte-grated into the Atlantic economy as other colonies were.

The puritans' work ethic was powerful enough that, notwithstanding their misgivings over certain economic practices, for many it was a short step from industriousness to entrepreneurship. Even before the puritans arrived, fishing and fur trading were big businesses in the region, and the puritans began to dominate them soon after their arrival. By the mid 1640s, New England already dominated cod fishing in the North Atlantic, and that enterprise, encouraged by abundant forests, spawned a busy shipbuilding industry. That in turn saw a rise in New England participation in Atlantic commerce. A growing class of merchants developed a large and lucrative trade, exchanging fish for wines in the Azores, Canaries and Madeira, and selling fish, meat, livestock, maize and barrel staves to the West Indians in return for sugar and molasses. New Englanders also established a rum distilling industry. This commerce brought increasing numbers of farmers out of semi-subsistence systems of local exchange into an increasingly elaborate market economy. Wheat became increasingly blighted and New Englanders added flax, maize and rye to their arable range, developed more orchards and horticulture and increased emphasis on pastoral agriculture to supply the provisions trade in the West Indies. New Englanders also began trading in slaves.

New England's economic output increased threefold between 1650 and 1710. The region's exports were worth £440,000 by 1770, not as much as staple-producing regions, but still impressive. Fish and whale products comprised almost half of those exports, meat and livestock another fifth, and then there were grains, timber products, potash and rum. Almost two-thirds of these goods went to the West Indies, a fifth to the British Isles and the rest to southern Europe and Africa. The coastal carrying trade was probably worth another £200,000 to New England merchants.

The wealth generated by this new commerce allowed a new class of merchants and lawyers to replace the declining clergy as the region's social and political elite. As elsewhere in British America, a commercial elite, albeit comprising lawyers and merchants rather than lawyers and planters, gained control of local and provincial political, judicial and administrative offices. Tellingly, among the new elite were many Anglicans. Other sorts of classes also contributed to the make-up of an increasingly economically variegated society. In the larger towns new kinds of artisans appeared. In addition to the blacksmiths, tanners, shoemakers, coopers and carpenters who already serviced urban and agricultural economies, in the eighteenth century there appeared more and more shipwrights, iron manufacturers, printers and silversmiths, servicing the more rarefied and even genteel needs of a more wealthy and cosmopolitan society. In place of the wilfully unostentatious abodes and attire of the earlier settlers, appeared Georgian houses and sartorial adornments that demonstrated a growing attachment to English genteel fashions.

The increasing gentility of New England merchants and lawyers was an outward sign of another new feature of New England life: growing economic inequality. By time of the American Revolution, 30 per cent of rural New Englanders owned up to 75 per cent of the wealth. Rural inequality was greatest in the large landed estates of Rhode Island, agricultural enterprises that rivalled in size, complexity and profitability the plantations of the Chesapeake. Wealth concentration, though, was greatest in the port towns, especially with the growth of slavery in the eighteenth century. Poverty increased substantially in New England, and by the middle of the eighteenth century up to a third of adult men owned no land and little other property, although in many cases they could expect to inherit property, or else were apprentices and journeymen aiming to become independent craftsmen. Many New Englanders still enjoyed propertied independence and a relatively high standard of living. Nevertheless, poverty was rising, assisted in New England by the high rate of losses among seafarers leaving many families destitute. In many communities in the eighteenth century, 5 to 7 per cent of households received poor relief, though that was substantially less than in Europe. Transient poor people were warned out if they could not find employment, while others were registered on the expanding poor relief rolls. Larger New England towns built workhouses in the mid-eighteenth century so that the poor could defray the growing costs of alms.

Even slavery began to grow in importance in New England in the early eighteenth century. In 1690, fewer than 1000 black people constituted less than 1 per cent of the region's population, though by 1720 there were over 6000 blacks and they constituted about 3 per cent of the population. By 1770, there were some 15,000 Africans or African-Americans in New England, though they remained only about 3 per cent of the region's population. Slavery was quite different in New England than in the plantation colonies. Slaves were concentrated in urban areas, especially in seaport towns, working as sailors, shipbuilders, dockworkers, artisans and domestic servants, rather than being primarily agricultural field workers. In 1755, slaves formed 18 per cent of the population of Newport, Rhode Island, the largest port in the least orthodox New England colony, and 30 per cent of households employed enslaved workers. In the countryside, slaves were usually distributed in ones and twos as farm labourers, though in Rhode Island some larger farms employed dozens of slaves as stockmen and dairy workers, emulating some of the smaller plantations of the south. Overall, 14 per cent of Rhode Island householders held slaves.[19]

New England's founders aimed to create harmonious religious communities that contrasted with the individualistic and commercialized world that they saw developing around them. They were remarkably successful for quite a long time. While most charter groups' ambitions were undermined within a generation, if not immediately, those of the Pilgrims and the puritans lasted much longer. The large majority of New England migrants shared the ideals of their leaders, rejected the individualism and materialism that drew other migrants to other parts of Anglo-America and managed to pass their ideals on to their descendants for at least two or three generations. Even so, some challenged the New England way from early on; the spread of population and the growth of commerce both reflected and promoted a declension from puritan ideals; and certainly by 1720 even Massachusetts was not the Bible Commonwealth its founders had imagined and crafted almost a hundred years before. The New England colonies were becoming increasingly thriving, entrepreneurial market societies, resembling ever more those of the Chesapeake, the West Indies and, in turn, the Middle Colonies and the Lower South.

Notes

1 Jack P. Greene's *Pursuits of Happiness: The Social Development of Early Modern British Colonies and the Formation of American Culture* (Chapel Hill, 1988) argues that the market-orientated and individualistic Chesapeake colonists most typified the values and behaviour of early British Americans.

2 *A Description of New England* (1616) in Philip L. Barbour, ed., *The Complete Works of Captain John Smith (1580–1631) in Three Volumes* (Chapel Hill, 1986), I, pp. 291–363.

3 D.W. Meining, *The Shaping of America: A Geographical Perspective on 500 Years of History* Volume I *Atlantic America, 1492–1800* (New Haven, 1986), p. 33.

4 Cited in Jack P. Greene, ed., *A Documentary History of American Life* Volume 1: *Settlements to Society, 1584–1763* (New York, 1966), p. 29.

5 Samuel Eliot Morison, ed., *Of Plimouth Plantation, 1620–1647 by William Bradford, Sometimes Governor Thereof* (New York, 1952), pp. 61, 77, 270, 271.

6 Eugene Aubrey Stratton, *Plymouth Colony: Its History and People, 1620–1691* (Salt Lake City, 1986).

7 Both quotes in Alison Games, *Migration and the Origins of the English Atlantic World* (Cambridge, MA, 1999), p. 19; figures from Henry A. Gemery, 'Emigration from the British Isles to the New World, 1630–1700: Inferences from Colonial Populations', *Research in Economic History* V (1980), p. 212. See also David Cressy, *Coming Over: Migration and Communication between England and New England in the Seventeenth Century* (New York, 1987); Virginia DeJohn Anderson, *New England's Generation: The Great Migration and the Formation of Society and Culture in the Seventeenth Century* (New York, 1991); Stephen Foster, *The Long Argument: English Puritanism and the Shaping of New England Culture, 1570–1700* (Chapel Hill, 1991).

8 'Reasons to be considered for justifieinge the undertakers of the intended Plantation in New England', The First Massachusetts Charter, 'A Modell of Christian Charity', in Greene, *Settlements to Society*, pp. 20–4, 66–9, 62–3.

9 Kenneth A. Lockridge, *A New England Town, The First Hundred Years: Dedham Massachusetts, 1636–1736* (New York, 1970), p. 16.

10 Edmund S. Morgan, *The Puritan Dilemma: The Story of John Winthrop* (Boston, 1956); *Visible Saints: The History of a Puritan Idea* (Ithaca, 1963).

11 Charles E. Clark, *The Eastern Frontier: The Settlement of Northern New England, 1610–1763* (New York, 1970), p. 13; John Frederick Martin, *Profits in the Wilderness: Entrepreneurs and the Founding of New England Towns in the Seventeenth Century* (Chapel Hill, 1991); Richard L. Bushman, *From Puritan to Yankee: Character and the Social Order in Connecticut, 1690–1765* (Cambridge, MA, 1967); Sydney V. James, *Colonial Rhode Island: A History* (New York, 1975).

12 Greene, *Settlements to Society*, pp. 62–3.

13 Morison, ed., *Of Plimouth Plantation*, p. 296.

14 Neal Salisbury, *Manitou and Providence: Indians, Europeans, and the Making of New England, 1500–1643* (New York, 1982); William Cronon, *Changes in the Land: Indians, Colonists, and the Ecology of New England* (New York, 1983); Russell Bourne, *The Red King's Rebellion: Racial Politics in New England* (New York, 1990); Patrick M. Malone, *The Skulking Way of War: Technology and Tactics among the New England Indians* (Baltimore, 1993); Jill Lapore, *The Name of War: King Philip's War and the Origins of American Identity* (New York, 1998); Daniel R. Mandell, *Behind the Frontier: Indians in Eighteenth-Century Massachusetts* (Lincoln, NB, 1996).

15 Greene, *Settlements to Society*, p. 68; Karen Ordahl Kupperman, 'The Beehive as a Model for Colonial Design', in Karen Ordahl Kupperman, ed., *America in European Consciousness, 1493–1750* (Chapel Hill, 1995), p. 282; Jack P. Greene, *The Intellectual Construction of America: Exceptionalism and Identity from 1492 to 1800* (Chapel Hill, 1993), p. 68.

16 Perry Miller, *The New England Mind: The Seventeenth Century* (New York, 1939); *The New England Mind: From Colony to Province* (Cambridge, MA, 1953), esp. chapters 1 and 2; Sacvan Bercovitch, *The American Jeremiad* (Madison, 1978).

17 Paul Boyer and Stephen Nissenbaum, *Salem Possessed: The Social Origins of Witchcraft* (Cambridge, MA, 1974); John Putnam Demos, *Entertaining Satan: Witchcraft and the Culture of Early New England* (New York, 1982); Richard Godbeer, *The Devil's Dominion: Magic and Religion in Early New England* (Cambridge, 1984); Carol F. Karlsen, *The Devil in the Shape of a Woman: Witchcraft in Colonial New England* (New York, 1987); Peter Charles Hoffer, *The Devil's Disciples: Makers of the Salem Witchcraft Trials* (New York, 1996); *The Salem Witchcraft Trials: A Legal History* (Lawrence, KS, 1998).

18 T.H. Breen, *The Character of the Good Ruler: Puritan Political Ideas in New England, 1630–1730* (New Haven, 1970); Richard R. Johnson,

Adjustment to Empire: The New England Colonies, 1675–1715 (New Brunswick, NJ, 1981).

19 Bernard Bailyn, *The New England Merchants in the Seventeenth Century* (Cambridge, MA, 1955); Stephen Innes, *Labor in a New Land: Economy and Society in Seventeenth-Century Springfield* (Princeton, 1983); *Creating the Commonwealth: The Economic Culture of Puritan New England* (New York, 1995); Christine Leigh Heyrman, *Commerce and Culture: The Maritime Communities of Colonial Massachusetts, 1690–1750* (New York, 1984); Greene, *Pursuits of Happiness*, pp. 55–80; Winifred Barr Rothenberg, *From Market Places to a Market Society: The Transformation of Rural Massachusetts, 1750–1850* (Chicago, 1992); Daniel Vickers, *Farmers and Fishermen: Two Centuries of Work in Essex County, Massachusetts, 1630–1850* (Chapel Hill, 1994).

6

The Middle Colonies, the Lower South and the West

The Restoration of Charles II in 1660 inaugurated a new phase of English colonization. The 'Restoration colonies' of the North American mainland between New England and Maryland, known nowadays as the Middle Colonies, comprised New York and New Jersey, won from the Dutch in 1664, the Quaker colony of Pennsylvania, granted to William Penn in 1681, and Delaware, which broke away from Pennsylvania 20 years later. Although these colonies had distinct histories in many respects, what they eventually had in common were ethnically and religiously heterogeneous populations and vigorous economies based mainly on grain production but which were also highly diversified. The other Restoration colonies were in the Lower South. Originally one colony, founded in 1663, Carolina soon cleaved into two separate geographical, economic, social and, eventually, political entities. North Carolina, above Cape Fear, remained part of 'greater Virginia', though its tobacco plantation economy was mixed with one based on grain, lumber and naval stores. Southern North Carolina and South Carolina eventually developed a highly articulated and extremely wealthy slave-plantation society, based primarily on rice but including indigo and other products. Georgia, founded in 1732, eventually resembled South Carolina.

Though these regions were quite different from each other, and though the colonies within each of them had their own distinct characteristics, the origins of all these colonies were profoundly shaped by recently shared historical experience. The proprietors of the Restoration colonies were all aware of and all conceived elaborate plans in the hope of avoiding the anarchic beginnings of previous colonizations and the continued political and economic semi-autonomy of those colonies. Those plans, furthermore, were shaped by the experiences of civil war, although not everyone perceived those experiences in the same way. James, Duke of York, the second son of the king who lost his throne and his head, attempted a form of absolutism in his proprietorship of New York. Others tried, in different ways, to impose more balanced political constitutions founded on carefully crafted social orders. New Jersey, Pennsylvania and, to some extent, Delaware were planned in accord with the religious principles of Quakers; New York adapted to the patroon system pioneered by the Dutch, Carolina was grounded first on a headright system and then on hierarchical ideas about landownership, and Georgia was founded in a fit of philanthropic egalitarianism. In common with each other and with earlier colonies, though, these proprietorial plans were soon cast aside or undermined by migrants and settlers who had their own more individualistic and materialistic visions and ambitions.

New Netherland

While the English were settling the Chesapeake, New England and the West Indies, the Dutch were settling what is now New York, what to them was New Netherland. In the early seventeenth century, Dutch merchants began trading in French fish and furs, and in 1609 English navigator Henry Hudson traversed the river to be named in his honour on behalf of the Netherlands. In 1613, the Dutch East India Company founded fur trading posts at Nassau, near what is now Philadelphia, and Orange, now Albany, at the junction of the Hudson River and Mohawk Valley. Trade increased once the Mohawk, the easternmost of the Iroquois tribes, drove the Mahican out of the upper Hudson Valley. In 1624, the Dutch West India Company, founded three years earlier and already active in Caribbean and Brazilian trade, sent 30 Dutch and Walloon families to Orange and Nassau. Another 200 went the following year, and a year after that Peter Minuet, the colony's first director-general from 1626–31, made a land purchase from the Manhate Indians and built a fortified village named New Amsterdam at the tip of Manhattan Island.

Initially the company ran the colony with little thought to establishing anything more than a set of trading posts, not wishing settlers to undermine their trading monopolies. Haltingly, though, an embryonic Dutch polity and society began to form. Indian resistance prompted the creation of a council, though it was allowed to do little more than report on colonial affairs to the company. Peter Stuyvesant, director-general from 1647 to 1664, even created a body of representatives and the offices of sheriff and burghermaster for New Amsterdam, though he soon abandoned these. If New Netherland was politically oligarchical, it was economically and socially hierarchical too. Killian Van Rensselaer proposed the establishment of manors similar to those in Maryland to settle the colony's interior. The company duly issued the Charter of Freedoms and Exemptions, affirmed by the Dutch government in 1629, authorizing a system of company-owned four-mile land grants managed by 'patroons', worked by tenants and exempt from taxes for a decade. The company created 10 patroonships, the most successful and the only one to last through the colonial period being Rensselaerwyck, near Albany.

Dutch religious toleration encouraged settlement, and New Netherland had the most heterogeneous population in North America. Besides the Dutch, settlers included Walloons, Brazilian and Caribbean blacks, French, Germans, Portuguese, Scandinavians, Sephardic Jews and English from the mother country, various colonies and of numerous Protestant denominations. By mid-century, the colony comprised a small settlement of about 1500 people on Manhattan Island (stretching inland only as far as present-day Wall Street), and a few small settlements up the Hudson River. New Netherland's population was still only around 9000 in 1664, however.

The Dutch colony was constantly under threat from Amerindians but ultimately fell to the English. Indian relations were complicated by the existence of at least 15 different Algonquian-speaking tribes, all with conflicting interests and land claims. In the early years the Dutch tried to stay neutral, but, when the Mohawks defeated their rival Mahicans, the Europeans treated with the winners. The Mahicans then attacked outlying farms, and Director-General Willem Kiefft (1638–47) inaugurated a three-year war (1642–45) by launching an appalling assault even by the standards of the time, killing 110 peaceful Indians encamped near New Amsterdam. This war spread to eastern Long Island, where the Massachusetts Antinomian Anne Hutchinson had finally settled, and she and her family were killed. Afterwards, New Netherland Amerindians could only resist the Dutch effectively with English assistance, and the English, for their own reasons, were not unforthcoming.

The 1650 Treaty of Hartford had established a border 10 miles east of the Hudson River between New Netherland and the expanding settlements of Connecticut, so that west Long Island was Dutch while the centre and east were English. The treaty did not end rival claims, however. Maryland settlers in the disputed region along the Delaware River occasionally revolted against the Dutch, joined from 1655 by Connecticut settlers exploiting a new Indian uprising. Encouraged by the Dutch loss of Brazil to Portugal, which near-bankrupted the Dutch West India Company, and by the policy of religious repression in favour of Dutch Reformed Calvinism by dictatorial Peter Stuyvesant, the English became minded to overthrow the Dutch altogether. They initially planned to capture New Netherland during the first Anglo-Dutch War (1652–54), but were thwarted by Massachusetts delaying its assistance of the invasion. Cromwell was also half-hearted about war with fellow Protestants, especially Dutch Calvinists.

The second Anglo-Dutch War (1664–67) was another conflict that neither Charles II nor the Earl of Clarendon especially wanted, but mercantile interests by now were forcing the issue. Courtiers and merchants sought

New World profits and saw the Dutch as rivals, in particular Royal African Company shareholders who wanted to nose into the Dutch-dominated African slave trade. Its chief executive, furthermore, was the Duke of York. Combined with an early 1660s' depression, these pressures forced a second Dutch war in which New Netherland capitulated. In March 1664, Charles II granted the colony to his brother James, Duke of York, and when Richard Nicolls led an expedition to capture the colony, its inhabitants urged Stuyvesant to surrender without a struggle. Nicolls, a pro-Stuart civil war soldier and interregnum exile, became the Duke's first deputy governor. The Dutch formally accepted English possession in the Treaty of Breda of 1667 (the English ceded Surinam, which the Dutch had recaptured during the same war). In 1673, the Dutch recaptured New Amsterdam during the third Anglo-Dutch War, but ceded the colony to England again in the Treaty of Westminster in 1674. In 1664, the colony and its major port were restyled New York and the capital was renamed Albany, following James's ducal titles. Long Island also became 'Yorkshire', complete with three ridings, though these appellations failed to stick. The land between the lower Hudson and Delaware rivers was to form New Jersey. The English confiscated the assets of the Dutch West India Company but left alone the private property of Dutch individuals, now designated 'denizens' of the English Empire, although considerable tensions remained between the two communities.[1]

Early New York

The Duke of York, the future James II, hoped to practise absolute rule over his colony. Indeed, New York was sometimes called 'the Duke's Province'. Accordingly, in 1665, Richard Nicolls implemented the 'Duke's Laws', the most authoritarian form of colonial rule in Anglo-America, though not quite absolutist in practice. James, who did not share other Englishmen's reservations about the existence of a standing army in peacetime, also established a garrison in New York – the first regular troops on the North American mainland and, apart from during Bacon's Rebellion, the only ones in peacetime before 1763. Equally significantly, there was no representative assembly. As Nicolls wrote to Clarendon: 'Our new Lawes are not contrived soe Democratically as the rest' of the colonies. From 1668 Colonel Francis Lovelace ruled the same way, but, like Nicolls, he allowed considerable local governing autonomy within the colony.

Less amenable to local wishes was Sir Edmund Andros, sent to reinstate the Duke's Laws following the third Anglo-Dutch War and the Treaty of Westminster. When Andros reported colonial demands for representative assemblies, James replied as his father's son, stating that 'I cannot but suspect they would be of dangerous consequence, nothing being more knowne than the aptness of such bodyes to assume to themselves many priviledges wch prove destructive to, or very oft disturbe, the peace of the governmt wherein they are allowed.' Andros ruled with courts of assize appointed by and answerable to himself alone. He had no truck with local autonomy, threatened to outlaw the Long Island puritans if they caused problems and forced Connecticut farmers to abandon their land claims in eastern New York. Complaints against Andros's arbitrary rule grew so multitudinous that even the Duke of York became alarmed and recalled the deputy governor in 1682. His replacement, Thomas Dongan, immediately found it necessary, as had other Stuart monarchs and minions, to call an assembly to raise revenue. New York's first assembly sat for three weeks in October 1683 and passed a 'Charter of Libertyes and Priviledges' that would have overturned some of the Duke's Laws, forbidden taxation without representation and instituted trial by jury. Dongan approved it, as did the Duke, but it became a dead letter when Charles II died and James became king.[2]

With James's accession to the throne in 1685, New York became a royal colony rather than a proprietorship. A new assembly met in October 1685, but then another the next year was first prorogued and then dissolved, and no other sat until after the Glorious Revolution. In 1688, Edmund Andros returned to rule over the Dominion of New England that incorporated New York, the Jerseys and all the New England colonies into what looked like a Spanish colonial viceroyalty. Andros governed without a representative assembly. In early 1689, however, news reached America of the Glorious Revolution of the previous December, and local militias throughout the colony began gathering around the merchant Jacob Leisler, who proclaimed William and Mary king and queen and reasserted Protestantism (many in James's government in Albany had been Catholic). Leisler's Rebellion, along with contemporaneous uprisings in New England colonies, overthrew Andros and the Dominion. Ultimately, though, the fact that Leisler was Dutch did not help him. He and a coterie of fellow Netherlanders held power until early 1691, when Captain Richard Ingoldsby arrived and insisted that Leisler hand over power to a new crown governor, Henry Sloughter. When Leisler refused, on the grounds that Ingoldsby had no commission papers, and when he delayed handing over power until a day after Sloughter's arrival, he and his associate and son-in-law Jacob Milborne were hanged as traitors. New York retained a powerful tradition of factional politics thereafter. After the Glorious Revolution, though, the colony's politics followed the same basic pattern of governance adopted in other colonies, with a royal governor, a council, and an assembly that allowed its political contentions to be channelled more peacefully.

Despite the political vexations of James's time, New York began to prosper. The deputy governors had improved anchorage and built public warehouses, mills and a mercantile exchange. The city remained small through the seventeenth century, continuing to trade primarily in furs, but the foundations of its eighteenth-century expansion as a port provisioning the West

Indies were laid. To be a successful entrepôt, though, New York needed a prosperous agricultural hinterland. Andros established a lasting relationship with the Iroquois, the Covenant Chain, which opened the interior to potential settlers. Yet economic growth in inland New York was slower than it might have been because the English retained the Dutch system of enormous patroonships, giving land to those who had little capital or inclination to develop their semi-feudal estates. Much of this land remained in the hands of speculators until population spread in the early eighteenth century.

Early New Jersey

In July 1664, the Duke of York sold some of his outlying New York territories to two old friends. During the interregnum Lord John Berkeley and Sir George Carteret had been exiled respectively to Paris and Barbados, and at the Restoration they cashed in their loyalty for the 5,000,000 acres between the Delaware and Hudson rivers that constituted New Jersey. There was confusion over their authority because while Charles II acknowledged his brother's right to grant land he did not concede the right to rule. Nevertheless, the proprietors (who were among the lords proprietors of the Carolinas) pushed ahead as if they had such a right. They aimed to attract settlers through their 'Concessions and Agreements' that guaranteed an assembly, free trade and toleration of Protestant religious dissent. The Concessions also offered generous headrights of 150 acres to migrants who paid their own way and 150 more for each dependant they brought with them, while servants would get 75-acre tracts at their end of their four-year terms.

Land titles remained in dispute, however. Baptists, puritans and Quakers on Long Island who had land titles under Nicolls of New York refused to accept the authority of the first governor, Philip Carteret, the proprietor's cousin, established their own towns in defiance of land grants and refused to pay quitrents and taxes. In 1674, a despairing Berkeley sold his western Jersey rights to a group of English Quakers who hoped to find sanctuary there. The new leaders were John Fenwick and Edward Billing, though their mutual hostility and financial problems soon ensured that the Society of Friends devolved control on Gawrin Lawrie, Nicholas Lucas and William Penn, the Quaker son of the Admiral who captured Jamaica, with financial backing from over 100 shareholdings. In 1676, the territory was divided into West Jersey for the Quakers and East Jersey remaining under Carteret's control.

The first Quakers to migrate in 1675 numbered about 100 and they formed 'Fenwick's Colony' at Salem in West Jersey. When West Jersey became a colony in 1676, however, Edmund Andros in New York refused to recognize it and had Fenwick arrested. In 1677, Penn and his fellow proprietors issued their 'Laws, Concessions, and Agreements', offering settlers similar terms to those offered by Berkeley and Carteret. Like Berkeley and Carteret, however, the new proprietors' right to rule was open to contest, and in 1683 the assembly, arguably illegally created by the proprietors, then appropriated the right to rule to themselves, deposing Governor Edward Billing and appointing their own governor and council. The assembly of East Jersey acted in much the same way, and Governor Philip Carteret was further burdened by Edmund Andros's demands for taxes. In 1680, Andros claimed the governorship for himself and had Carteret arrested.

That same year, proprietor George Carteret died, and a group of 11 Quakers, again including Penn, purchased the East Jersey proprietary. Philip Carteret returned to govern after Andros was recalled in 1682, but he antagonized his assemblies. That and antiproprietary and anti-Quaker violence became pretexts for the crown to revoke the Jersey charters and incorporate the colonies in the Dominion of New England in 1688. The proprietors got their colonies back in 1692, but establishing social and political order was by then more difficult than ever. When the Quakers bought East Jersey in 1682, they sold some shares to 12 others, half of whom were Scottish and who sold their shares on to another and larger group of mostly Scottish investors. Among the East Jersey proprietors were the Scottish Quaker Robert Barclay and James and John Drummond, earls of Perth and Melfort, all prominent men at the courts of Charles II and James II. Thereafter, southern East Jersey took on a Scottish character. Over several years, this group sent more than 700 Scottish settlers who, rather than mixing with others, formed separate colonies within the colony. The main settlers were Episcopalians from the north-east coastal region between St Andrews and Fife, though Presbyterians came to dominate East Jersey later. Perth and Melfort fled to France after the Glorious Revolution, leaving other Scottish proprietors and residents in a weaker position. Then, when the 1696 Navigation Act threw further doubt on Scottish proprietary claims by excluded Scots from imperial trade, the proprietors hoped to appease opposition by appointing as governor Jeremiah Basse, an Anabaptist and ally of Edward Randolph, England's surveyor-general of customs. Unfortunately for them, Basse denounced the Scots as smugglers and pirates and launched a campaign against the 'Scotch yoak'. Subsequent disorder prompted the proprietors to request the imposition of crown rule in 1702, when both Jerseys were reconstituted as the single province of New Jersey. The proprietors retained their private land rights but finally lost their right to rule, if they ever had it.

Disputed jurisdictions and land claims, and the political and social instabilities and economic insecurities that resulted, meant that settlement had not proceeded far by the time the crown took over the colonies. The East Jersey proprietors organized their territories into 2000-acre estates and discouraged the sale of tracts of less than 500 acres, in the hope of recreating a hierarchical landed order in the Scottish fashion. As a result, they attracted fewer settlers than did other colonies, only about 1000 Scots altogether. When the crown claimed the colony, the population of East Jersey was only around 7000. West Jersey had been similarly underdeveloped, although that was in part because from 1682 Quakers began settling on the other side of the Delaware River.[3]

Early Pennsylvania

From their first appearance in the 1650s, in the wake of civil war, Quakers suffered persecution due to their withdrawal from the state church, anti-Calvinist theological beliefs, minimalist church organization, opposition to oath-taking, adherence to freedom of conscience and to pacifism and, not least, their refusal to demonstrate deference towards supposed social superiors. Nevertheless, by the late 1670s there were 50,000 Quakers in England, Wales and Scotland, and a few in Continental Europe and the colonies, especially West Jersey. Persecution had recently grown worse, with some 1400 jailed in England and Wales in the late 1670s for attending their own services rather than Anglican ones; others had property confiscated in lieu of fines that many could not afford to pay.

On the face of it, therefore, it seems odd that in 1681 Charles II should grant a charter for Pennsylvania to Quaker William Penn. It was no small territorial accession. Constituting all the remaining unclaimed land in the known parts of North America, it was the largest American proprietorship ever granted, comprising some 29 million acres from the 40th parallel to New York. In addition, the Duke of York granted Penn the three lower counties that were later to become Delaware, giving Pennsylvania a Delaware River front and therefore greater access to Atlantic trade. A variety of considerations probably explain the Stuarts' generosity to these extreme Protestant dissenters. Penn was son of Admiral Sir William Penn, whose naval exploits helped earn England enormous wealth and power, who himself wielded considerable influence at court and to whom the king personally owed £16,000, though the whole of Pennsylvania seems a disproportionate discharge of this debt.

At the time, though, a formidable coalition of Protestant dissenters was forming and threatening the succession of the king's brother. The Popish Plot and Exclusion Crisis from 1678 focused establishment hostility on Catholics rather than dissenting Protestants. The Whig party that emerged during the Exclusion Crisis called for reconciliation of Protestant dissenters, even putting to parliament a bill allowing Quakers to affirm rather than swear their loyalty to the crown. The Whigs won both general elections of 1679, and consequently Charles prorogued parliament and sought a means to divide so that James could rule. One such means may have been the granting of Pennsylvania to William Penn, who was in league with a number of Levant Company merchants who, with Ottoman trade suffering as a consequence of Turkish taxes, wanted Atlantic trading opportunities (as soon as Penn received the grant he established the Free Society of Traders, of which many such merchants were members). A powerful faction had good reason to be grateful to the Stuarts.

Like the puritans, the Quakers migrated for religious reasons, both to escape actual or potential persecution and to follow Penn's dream of a Holy Experiment. But Quaker religious belief and practice was quite unlike that of the Congregationalists. The Quaker notion of an inner light, God's voice in every individual, meant they believed that all had access to salvation, in contrast to the Calvinist belief that God's voice could only be found in scripture and that only the elect were predestined for salvation. Quakers further differed from puritans in their toleration of others, and in that their church government was opposed to the kind of hierarchy favoured by puritan theocrats. In social make-up, though, the Quakers resembled the puritans, which helps to explain the early successes of Pennsylvanian colonization. The bulk of Quaker migrants both to West Jersey and Pennsylvania were middling property owners (though many Quakers in England were quite poor), who were literate and generally came in family units.

In 1682, Penn sent 23 ships and 2000 migrants to the colony, followed by 50 ships and 3000 more migrants in 1683. By 1700, the colony had some 21,000 inhabitants. Thanks in part to the mild winters and to growing seasons that allowed two and sometimes three harvests a year, Pennsylvania suffered none of the early demographic catastrophes endured elsewhere. Also, Penn cultivated good relations with Amerindians. The Pennsylvania Charter aimed 'to reduce the savage natives by gentle and just manners to the love of civil society and Christian religion'. Despite these condescending presumptions, rather than forcing Christianity on Amerindians or else enforcing their removal, Penn formed a covenant of friendship with the Leni Lenape of the Delaware Valley, and he became known to them as 'Brother Miquon'. In 1701, he signed a treaty with the Susquehannocks that kept Pennsylvania safe during King William's and Queen Anne's wars. The initial period of peaceful Anglo-Amerindian relations that characterized most English colonizations thus lasted much longer in Pennsylvania than elsewhere. Penn's descendants, however, were nowhere near so scrupulous. In 1686, the Lenape had agreed to cede to Penn lands west of Neshaminy Creek 'as far as a man can go in a day and a half'. The expansion of settlement by the second quarter of the eighteenth century, however, led to the 'walking purchase' of 1737, in which Penn's sons employed athletes who managed 64 miles in 36 hours, obtaining by these means some 1200 acres of land. Pennsylvania had hitherto escaped the triangular wars between the English, their European rivals and Amerindian allies on either side, but the legacy of bitter tension following the 'walking purchase' meant that in 1755, at the beginning of the French and Indian War, Indian invasions of western Pennsylvania saw 3000 settlers captured or killed, and 1000 more in 1756, with others fleeing over the Susquehanna River.

Penn also ensured a widely skilled settler population, calling on 'Industrious husbandmen and day labourers . . . carpenters, masons, smiths, weavers, taylors, tanners, shoemakers, shipwrights' to move to his colony. Wanting no slackers, he also warned, 'I desire all my dear country folks, who may be inclin'd to go into those parts, to consider seriously the premises, as well as the present inconveniences.' Penn's Concessions also granted 50 acres of land to servants after their terms were finished. His establishing of a Free Society of Traders, made up of many merchants already experienced in overseas trade, at least to the Levant, ensured Pennsylvanian produce would reach its markets. 'I had in my view,' he wrote in 1685, 'Society, Assistance, Busy Commerce, Instruction of Youth, Government of People's Manners, Conveniency of Religious Assembling, Encouragement of Mechanicks, distinct and beaten Roads.' Unlike the puritans, Penn saw no contradiction between establishing his Holy Experiment and making money. Nor did he attempt to hide his materialistic ends, writing that 'Though I desire to extend religious freedom, yet I want some recompense for my trouble.' The proprietor was astute enough to realize that others shared this kind of ambition, but that did not mean he could always control their aspirations when they conflicted with his own. The kinds of people he wished to attract were not those likely to submit to his will if it did not suit them. The hard-working and ambitious types he advertised for were never likely to give up too many of the fruits of their labours, and Quakers were naturally wary of authority and more jealous than most of their religious, political and economic rights. The colonists of Pennsylvania were therefore every bit as contentious and fractious as others elsewhere.[4]

The willingness of colonists to suit themselves was manifest in the way they settled the land. Penn attempted to use land allocation powers to avoid 'Wilderness Vacancies', believing that 'ordered space would mean orderly and happy lives'. Before sending settlers, therefore, Penn sent agents, including his cousin, William Markham, to survey land patents and to find a spot for a capital of Philadelphia at the confluence of the Delaware and Schuylkill rivers. Philadelphia was modelled on Turin, which Penn had visited, with grid streets and piazzas, and was built at roughly the same time as the planned capitals Annapolis and Williamsburg. Penn originally envisioned a 'greene Country Towne' in which all homeowners would have a 'Garden and small Orchard' and wealthier ones a countryside estate just beyond the city bounds. Yet merchants congregated at the waterfront, creating a more compact kind of settlement than Penn intended. The city prospered, as Penn hoped, soon challenging Boston and New York for the distinction of being the principal port in North America, but the City of Brotherly Love looked little like Penn envisioned it. Nor were Penn's plans for close-knit colonization of the countryside fulfilled. Most immigrants were independent farmers and artisans who spread themselves about the landscape as others did in other colonies. Villages appeared when and where required, as did many churches, taverns and mills, often threaded along the byways. In others words, as in other colonies, the landscape was fashioned by settlers' aspirations rather than by a pre-ordained plan.[5]

Colonial, national and religious rivalries meant that the settlement of the Quaker colony was not always peaceful. Penn and the Calverts of Maryland, for example, disputed the border of Pennsylvania and Maryland. Penn sold land in the south-west and Delaware region mainly to Welsh settlers, and in the Welsh Tract there were murders and house-burnings as the dispute between Pennsylvanians and rival Marylanders turned ugly. Only in the middle of the eighteenth century did surveyors Charles Mason and Jeremiah Dixon draw the border at the 40th parallel (the 'Mason-Dixon Line') – a significant victory for the Penns over the Calverts. Further resentment arose over Penn's sale of 25,000 acres to German Pietist Daniel Pastorus in 1686, allowing him and his followers to found 'Germanopolis' or Germantown, where 'we High-Germans may maintain a separate little province, and thus feel more secure from all oppression'. Religious toleration meant that Pennsylvania was settled by Anglicans, Presbyterians, German Lutherans, Moravians and others as well as Quakers. Most participated fully and equally in the colony's public life, although Jews and Catholics, while free to practise their religions, were barred from voting and office holding. As this policy indicates, Pennsylvanians had conflicting feelings over their population's heterogeneity. J. Hector St John de Crevecoeur celebrated the 'mixture of English, Scotch, Irish, French, Dutch, Germans, and Swedes', because 'from this promiscuous breed, the race now called Americans have arisen'. On the other hand, Benjamin Franklin asked 'why should Pennsylvania, founded by the English, become a colony of Aliens, who will shortly be so numerous as to Germanize us instead of us Anglifying them'.[6]

Even within the English Quaker community there were schisms. The first dispute of note came via the agency of George Keith, who was appointed surveyor for Robert Barclay and the East Jersey proprietors in 1685 and who later moved to Philadelphia, where he became embroiled in disputes with the Quaker establishment. Keith wished to reinvigorate the individualistic and egalitarian kind of Quakerism that existed before men like Penn and George Fox imposed a more organized, coercive religious regime organized by meetings dominated by Friends of high status. Hailing from Aberdeen and an associate of eminences in the early Scottish Enlightenment, in 1692 Keith published his 'Confession of Faith'. He and his 'Christian Quaker' followers left the Society of Friends in objection to the continuing activities of quarterly and yearly meetings, taking with them a sizeable number of poorer and middling Friends, especially in East Jersey and Long Island, who shared his attitude to what they saw as the increasing elitism of leading Quakers. In fact, Keith saw the likes of Penn as 'fools, idiots, silly souls, hypocrites, hereticks, heathens, rotten ranters, tyrants, and Popes'. The Keithian schism led to some violence, but soon fizzled out when he and many of his followers simply joined the Anglican Church.[7]

Many of Pennsylvania's early vexations, though, were political rather than religious. Many of his fellow Quakers despised and eventually undermined Penn's proprietorial authority. Penn's original draft charter granted him palatine powers, like those of the Bishop of Durham and the Baltimores of Maryland, but the Privy Council vetoed them. He had the right, however, to establish any form of government he pleased, within the confines of English laws, and the right to pass laws of his own making, subject to assembly and crown veto. His first constitution, The Frame of Government of the Province of Pennsylvania, reflected the contradictions between Penn's Quakerism on the one hand and his belief in hierarchy and authority, certainly his own proprietorial authority, on the other. The Frame of Government explicitly and firmly guaranteed freedom of conscience and allowed for extensive suffrage and a popular assembly. Yet in contrast to the 'Concessions and Agreement of West Jersey', which provided for a powerful legislature, the Pennsylvania Frame directed that the governor and council were to formulate legislation that the assembly could then approve or reject, but not discuss or amend. Part of the reason Penn retained these extensive executive powers and powers of patronage was to attract wealthy investors. Another reason, though, was to provide a check against what he saw as the potentially ruinous 'ambitions of the populace'. On the other hand, the Frame also reflected the Quaker experience of oppression by guaranteeing religious toleration of all Christians, trial by jury, protection from arbitrary searches and seizures and a much less violent penal code than existed anywhere else in the Anglophone world.

As in other colonies, however, the populace, or some of it at any rate, made its ambitions felt. Almost immediately after settlement, Quaker opponents teamed up with assemblymen from the Lower Counties that later became Delaware to vote down the Frame of Government, obliging Penn in 1783 to reduce the number of executive councillors from 72 to 18. Thereafter, Penn faced one challenge after another from those who wished to enhance assembly power. He attempted a very personalized form of rule during his time in the colony from 1682 to 1684, but then had to remain in England until 1699 to explain his loyalty to James II, defend his proprietorial conduct and rights and straighten out his financial affairs. Political factions did not hesitate to form in his absence. Early in the 1690s, less wealthy Quakers under the leadership of David Lloyd (originally appointed by Penn as his attorney-general) joined the antiproprietary party, previously led by wealthier men, and established the tradition of popular politics for which Pennsylvania became renowned. In 1692–94, Pennsylvania briefly became a crown colony and, under royal governor Benjamin Fletcher, the assembly debated as well as voted on legislation. When Penn was restored, assemblymen were determined to hold on to this right, and in 1696 the House of Representatives claimed the right to initiate legislation itself by simply amending legislation in spite of the Frame of Government and by challenging Penn's title to undistributed land. Eventually the opposition forced Penn to agree to a new constitution. In 1701, a joint committee of the Council and House drafted a Charter of Liberties that served as Pennsylvania's constitution until 1776. The Council was removed from the legislative process, leaving it an executive function as assistant to the governor, creating America's only unicameral legislature. The governor, but not the king, lost veto power over assembly legislation. The oath of allegiance to William Penn was also abolished. The vote remained limited to freemen, but freemen's rights were extended to those owning 50 acres of land or more in the counties (previously 100 acres were required for voting). In Philadelphia, the franchise, previously extended to all taxpayers, was restricted to those with property worth £50. Also, the assembly instituted annual elections by secret ballot. Penn retained his land titles and his power to appoint governors until he died in 1718, but his original political powers were severely circumscribed. He had even tried to sell his colony back to the crown.

William Penn's death led to a decade-long conflict between the children of Penn's first wife, Guilielma Springet, and those of his second, Hannah Callowhill, over ownership of the proprietorship. The courts eventually ruled in favour of the children of the latter, John, Richard and Thomas Penn, despite attempts to undermine the proprietorship. The final challenges to proprietorial power came from Benjamin Franklin, appointed by the Pennsylvania assembly to report to English authorities in 1757 and 1764. On the first visit, Franklin sought a diminution of Penn power and on the second advocated Pennsylvania's becoming a crown colony. Both missions failed and the Penns retained their proprietorship until American Independence.

Early Delaware

The Delaware Valley had originally been part of the grants given to the Dutch West India Company, though the English also claimed it. But when the company failed to develop the area, other Netherlands entrepreneurs obtained the blessing of King Augustus Adolphus for the creation of New Sweden in 1637. The first settlement, Fort Christina (now Wilmington), was founded the following year. Thereafter, a number of Swedish, Finnish and Dutch settlements appeared along the Delaware River, centred mainly on New Amstel (later New Castle), just south of Fort Christina and 40 miles south of the Schuylkill junction. Settlers there established a farming economy, mainly in wheat, rye, maize and tobacco, supplemented by timber and fur trading. And these Scandinavians brought to America the log cabin. The English soon tried to muscle into the area. In 1641, settlers from New Haven attempted to establish among the mostly Lutheran and Reformed population a puritan foothold at Salem Creek, though they were forced by the Dutch to accept Swedish rule. In 1655, the Dutch commandeered the Delaware Valley territory, renamed it New Amstel, and incorporated it within New Netherland, only to have it taken from them by the English in 1664. In 1682, the three 'Lower Counties' became for a short while part of Pennsylvania, granted to William Penn by the Duke of York.

In 1692, the region only had about 3000 people, mostly descendants of earlier English, Swedish and Dutch settlers who resented being part of a new Quaker colony, but also including some who had claims under the authority of James, Duke of York, and others claiming rights derived from the proprietors of Maryland. They were not Quakers either, and one of their dissatisfactions with Quaker rule was Pennsylvanian reluctance to establish a militia to protect settlers against Amerindians. In 1692, after the Glorious Revolution had removed his foothold in the English court, Penn appointed a deputy governor for the lower counties, and from 1701 dissidents formed their own assembly and created the separate colony of Delaware, though still under the proprietorship of Penn. Even after Delaware's peaceful secession, trade rivalry remained between Philadelphia and New Castle. In 1705, Delaware passed a law requiring ships passing up the Delaware to the rival city to pay duties. When one sailed by regardless, Pennsylvania Governor Evans (an Anglican who was sympathetic to Delaware) fired on the offending vessel, for which overreaction Pennsylvania's angry assembly successfully demanded his recall.[8]

Economy, society and population in the eighteenth-century Middle Colonies

It is fitting that one of the most serious outbreaks of hostility between Pennsylvania and Delaware colonists was over trade. The economies of the Middle Colonies became among the most robust and diverse in British America. Pennsylvania produced an economic surplus in the first year of its existence, and agricultural productivity grew at a rate of 2 to 3 per cent per annum in first three-quarters of the eighteenth century – a very high growth rate for a pre-industrial economy – even though the region produced no great staple. Without the staple-producing plantations that tended to amass wealth, Pennsylvania attracted settlers for its reputation as a 'best poor man's country'.

The Middle Colonies, Pennsylvania in particular, produced vast amounts of grain, but the region's mixed agriculture included orchards and garden produce, hemp, flax, livestock and, in southern Delaware, tobacco (making that corner of the Middle Colonies really a part of the 'Greater Chesapeake'). Almost three-quarters of the Middle Colonies' exports were grain and grain products, exported in roughly equal measures to southern Europe and the West Indies. These colonies also exported livestock and meat to the islands and flaxseed to Ireland. There was also a coastwise trade. Up to 40 per cent of Pennsylvania farmers' produce was surplus that went to market. These market-orientated agricultural economies were highly diverse, with over a third of rural household heads in some areas involved in services rather than farming. Merchants further diversified into flour milling, meatpacking and extractive and manufacturing industries in wood, potash and iron. Imports rose from just less than £100,000 per year in the 1720s to near £700,000 in the 1760s. As elsewhere, Middle Colony merchants gained control of shipping. Local merchants owned 60 per cent of New York ships and 75 per cent of Philadelphia ships by the 1760s. Shipbuilding and overseas and intercolonial trade led to rapid urbanization. In the middle of the eighteenth century, Philadelphia and then New York overtook Boston in terms of volumes of trade and population size. The population of the former in 1774 was near 30,000 and of the latter near 25,000. Older and smaller centres of population were growing rapidly too, as the colonial hinterlands quickly filled up. Albany's population reached near 4000 in 1774, and as early as 1765 a remarkable 20 per cent of Pennsylvanians lived in towns.

Though wealth distribution was more even and economic opportunity was more widespread in the Middle Colonies than in other regions, there was nevertheless growing inequality in the late colonial period. As territory filled up in the east, land prices rose and farm sizes fell. Farms of over 500 acres were quite common in Penn's day, but median farm size fell to between 100 and 200 acres, although family farms remained the most efficient means of agricultural production because of the shortage of and therefore relatively high cost of labour. Land speculation and development continued to be highly profitable to the descendants of Penn and the Jersey proprietors, and to those who purchased vast tracts in New York from them or from the crown after 1688. Even so, rapid building of roads, bridges and ferries in the interior meant that farm purchasing was attractive to ordinary settlers who could afford it, at least in Pennsylvania where western settlement was not inhibited by a large-scale presence of French settlers and Amerindians. Nevertheless, in parts of south-west Pennsylvania and New Jersey half of residents were renters by the 1750s, though in many cases they could expect to accumulate capital and purchase land later in life.

New York was most renowned for tenancy. In that colony there were 30 baronial estates, although this was a legacy of the Dutch mode of settlement more than British colonial development. Half these estates were manorial, with feudal rights to hold civil and criminal courts and to extract rents in produce and labour as well as money from tenants. Court functions had been taken over by local government responsible to the colony by the 1720s, however. Fowl and labour rents remained, if inconstantly collected, but in general landlords had to offer incentives to make tenants remain when there were alternative sources of land in neighbouring colonies. Inducements included a year's provisions, equipment, housing, free or low rents for a while, cheap and easy access to stores and milling facilities and equity in farm improvements. Some tenants were able to use these terms profitably and purchase land for themselves. There were tenant uprisings in the 1750s and a widespread revolt in 1766, though these were connected to competing land claims on the Massachusetts border and were complicated by conflicts with the British over taxes. Historians of these events, however, have found that the riots were less about tenants overturning the social order than about seeking more secure title to their lands or improvements in their lease terms.

Inequality was most pronounced in cities. By the 1770s, in rural areas, the wealthiest 20 per cent held 53 per cent of the wealth, while 10 per cent of urbanites possessed 65 per cent of wealth. The poorest 30 per cent in the cities possessed just 2 per cent of the wealth, and increasing numbers were working for subsistence wages or receiving poor relief. Even so, by the 1760s all but the poorest third of the population enjoyed significantly enhanced standards of living. As in other colonies, those who could afford it emulated English styles of gentility. The wealthiest had brick houses in the latest English fashions and often filled them with imported fineries.

Indentured servitude remained more important in the Middle Colonies, especially Pennsylvania, than it did elsewhere. Also, although the Middle Colonies never became slave societies in the manner of the more southerly and island colonies, they were nevertheless societies with slaves. Slave numbers rose from just over 6000 in 1710 to 35,000 in the Middle Colonies by 1770, although the climbing white population meant that of the whole population the proportion of blacks fell from 9 per cent to just over 6 per cent. As in New England, slavery in the Middle Colonies was primarily an urban institution. Slaves generally made up only around 2 or 3 per cent of rural communities, although they could constitute as much as 9 per cent of the population in some rural parts of Pennsylvania, and some countryside iron foundries had up to 50 slaves, though most northern slave-holders held only one or a few slaves, sometimes just as status symbols. Slavery was particularly important in New York. In some rural parts of that colony and in eastern New Jersey slaves constituted 15 to 30 per cent of the population, and they formed a third of the labouring population of New York City in the mid-eighteenth century. From the 1740s, New York and Philadelphia merchants found that demand was sufficient to begin importing slaves directly from Africa, and some 7400 slaves came to America via New York in the period 1770 to 1774.

Slaves worked at all kinds of tasks in northern cities. In the 1750s, more than two-thirds of Philadelphia master artisans employed slaves. Many others were domestic servants, shipbuilders and sailors. Slave numbers and the nature of slave work meant that African-Americans did not form the kind of tightly-knit and distinctive communities that were a feature of life in the plantation colonies, but rather were spread out in different households and relatively isolated from each other. Slavery was not necessarily less brutal in the northern colonies than it was in the southern plantation colonies, where the worst potentialities of enslavement were mitigated by masters' greater dependence on slave labour and the consequent development of paternalistic racial customs that slaves themselves helped to shape. Certainly northern slaves resisted the institution, sometimes violently. The New York slave revolt of 1712 was the first uprising of slaves anywhere in North America, and there was a further suspected plot in 1741. Eighteen slaves were executed in 1712. In 1741, 4 whites and 31 slaves were executed and a further 70 slaves were transported to and sold in the West Indies.

The Quakers were famously early opponents of slavery. In 1676, William Edmundson in Newport, Rhode Island, launched one of the very earliest attacks on the institution. Twelve years later, four Germantown Quakers declared slavery to be in violation of the 'Golden Rule': 'do unto others as you would that they should do unto you'. Other antislavery statements and pamphlets appeared occasionally in subsequent years, especially from Keithian quarters, but it was not until the second half of the eighteenth century that meetings began requiring members to renounce their human possessions. It was no doubt the influence of Quakers that made Pennsylvania the first state to abolish the institution after American Independence.

In 1710, the population of the Middle Colonies was around 63,000, but in the 1760s it passed the half-million mark. Pennsylvania was by some distance the most populous of these colonies, with a population of just over 180,000 in 1760, followed by New York, with near 120,000, New Jersey with almost 94,000 and Delaware with just over 33,000. By 1760, settlers had spread throughout the Middle Colonies and were beginning to reach into the far west. By 1727, New Yorkers had spread from the Hudson River Valley along the Mohawk River as far as Lake Ontario, where they built Fort Oswego and threatened the St Lawrence link between Quebec and the Ohio region. Rival French and British settlers and their Indian allies and enemies would contest this region for keeps in the French and Indian War that broke out less than 30 years later. Also, by the end of the 1720s, Pennsylvania settlers had colonized much of the Schuylkill and Susquehannah river basins. The following decade, German settlers moved out of Pennsylvania and into the Shenandoah Valley in Virginia and eventually further south to the backcountries of the Carolinas and Georgia.[9]

Political conflict in the early Carolinas

The other 'Restoration colonies' were South and North Carolina, although there were earlier efforts to colonize the region. From the middle of the sixteenth century various European interests made several failed attempts to settle the region between Florida and Virginia. The Spanish sent missions to the region and for some time settled what later became Port Royal, and French Huguenots attempted to establish religious refuges. As for the English, in 1629 Charles I granted his attorney-general Sir Robert Heath the territory of 'Carolana' between 31 and 36 degrees latitude, where he planned to settle French Huguenots who had fled to England following the fall of La Rochelle. Although agents scouted the region and secured supplies from Virginia, they made no settlement at this time. Indeed successful colonization finally occurred only after the Restoration of Charles II. Even then, as in the Chesapeake and the West Indies, but unlike New England, its beginnings were hesitant, marked by false starts, failures and adaptations, before a successful settler population finally created a viable society and polity in place of the most elaborate proprietorial plans thus far conceived.

In exile during the interregnum, the future king Charles granted seven of his followers 5,000,000 acres of land in the northern neck of Virginia between the Potomac and Rappahannock rivers. Plans to colonize this region, though, were eventually forgotten in favour of a more southern venture after the Restoration. In 1663, Charles annulled the Heath charter and issued a new one to eight lords proprietors, including courtiers such as the Duke of Albemarle, Earl of Clarendon, Sir George Carteret, William, Lord Craven and Earl of Shaftesbury, Anthony Ashley Cooper, and experienced colonizers such as Sir John Colleton, a Barbadian planter, Lord John Berkeley and his brother, William, governor of Virginia. Some of the proprietors were involved in other colonial and ancillary activities in New Jersey, the Bahamas, the Hudson's Bay Company and the slave-trading Royal African Company; they were not a mercantile house or company but an affiliation of aristocrats, civil war royalists who stuck by Charles in exile or who assisted his Restoration. Charles hoped they would be able to establish a colony that acted more in accord with English interests than the others did. The Carolina charter initially covered the same region previously granted to Heath, but a new charter in 1665 extended it southwards to 29 degrees latitude, to include the Spanish settlement of St Augustine and part of the region of the Gulf of Mexico, as a way of stymieing Spanish expansion.

Though there were, therefore, imperial aims behind the chartering of Carolina, once again the crown left it to proprietors to finance and organize the venture. As well as territory, the lords proprietors received the right to govern in a manner 'most agreeable' to the 'Monarchy under which we live', to make laws with the 'advice, assent, and approbation of the

Freemen', to establish a judiciary, a military and a nobility and to grant religious toleration. They initially drafted 'A Declaration and Proposals to All That Will Plant in Carolina' that allowed for an elected assembly that would have exclusive taxation powers, only with proprietorial veto rights over provincial lawmaking, and a form of county government similar to that in England. It also allowed for freedom of religion and instituted a headright system that granted 150 acres of land to every family member who moved there, though it also anticipated a large rent-paying population and reserved some large estates for slave plantations.

These plans proved financially unworkable, however, and in 1669 the Earl of Shaftesbury and his secretary, the philosopher John Locke, reorganized the enterprise under the 'Fundamental Constitutions of Carolina'. The new framework reaffirmed religious freedom, English law and local government, but instituted sponsorship in the form of shareholding. This new method of financing freed the proprietors from heavy dependence on headrights, allowing them, or so they thought, to create a hierarchical land and social system modelled on James Harrington's *Oceana*. Two-thirds of the land would belong to a carefully graded three-tiered aristocracy of great proprietors or seigneurs, with 12,000-acre landholdings each, baronies, middling 'landgraves' (holding a total of 48,000 acres) and smaller 'caciques' or 'cassiques' (holding a total 24,000 acres). Two-fifths of the land was to be reserved for these aristocrats, ensuring their domination locally as well as provincially. Below this aristocracy there were meant to be freemen or 'leetmen', tenants and even a class of serfs. The polity was carefully designed too, allowing for even greater executive power than originally envisioned. Laws were to be made by a council of nobles, with an assembly to meet every second November and assent to or reject laws, but which would not initiate or discuss legislation. Courts were to be run by seigneurs, with other landowners as magistrates. Lord Shaftesbury was explicit in his wish to 'avoid erecting a numerous Democracy'. Even so, the Fundamental Constitutions balanced its idealized oligarchic system with some popular and even innovative measures, with the franchise extended to those with 50 acres of land and the institutionalization of a secret ballot, pre-dating that of Pennsylvania. Furthermore, councillors, who were also judges, were required to swear to 'doe equall right to the rich and poore'.[10]

Though this charter remained formally in effect until royal rule (in South Carolina in 1719 and North Carolina in 1729), it never became law and was never instituted. The colonization of Carolina depended on the wide availability of land to attract settlers, as was the case elsewhere and as in fact Carolina's original 'Declaration and Proposals' had anticipated. A large, ambitious, immigrant population was unlikely to accept the political arrangements of the 'Fundamental Constitutions'. The first meeting of the governor, council and elected representatives in Charles Town rejected the document and later meetings refused to accept proprietorial compromises.

In the 1690s representatives began meeting separately, referring to themselves as a Commons House of Assembly. The system of government that thus emerged in South Carolina was much like that of other colonies, consisting of a governor, appointed by the proprietors, who consulted a council, with a separate assembly of elected representatives who insisted upon their right to independent existence and to increasing responsibility and power.

The pre-eminent opposition to the aims of the proprietors came from the Goose Creek men, mostly wealthy Barbadians who settled on a tributary of the Cooper River, who, to Shaftesbury's chagrin, wished to make Carolina serve 'the Interest of Barbados'. Nor were poorer Barbadian migrants held in high regard. Governor Joseph West in 1671 requested that the proprietors send more migrants directly from England, as 'one of our Servants wee brought from England is worth 2 of ye Barbadians, for they are soe much addicted to Rum, yet they will doe but little whilst the bottle is at their nose'. The proprietors attempted to nurture a rival population by supporting a Scottish settlement at Stuart's Town near Port Royal, only for the settlement to fail in the face of disease and Spanish assault. Alliances with Quakers and other dissenters failed to prevent the establishment of the Anglican Church in 1706, another of the aims of the Goose Creek men.

There were occasions when Carolinians worked together and a combination of external and internal enemies helped draw them together to some extent by this time. During the War of the Spanish Succession there was an increased threat of attack by the Spanish or their French allies. The English took the initiative in this corner of the war, though. In 1702 South Carolina governor James Moore attacked St Augustine, though he failed to capture it, and in 1704 he launched a more effective expedition to destroy Spanish missions in northern Florida. By this time, too, relations with the Tuscarora and then the Yamassee degenerated into warfare, and the growing slave majority in the population necessitated greater white cooperation. Even then, though, such contingencies could cause conflict between Carolinian interests. For some South Carolinians these conditions meant that the time had come to end proprietary rule. Alarmed by rumours of an impending Spanish assault in 1719, the assembly, declaring itself to be a Convention, as had the English Parliament during the Glorious Revolution of 1688–9, ousted Governor Robert Johnson in favour of James Moore (son of the James Moore who had attacked Spanish Florida); this antiproprietary revolt resulted in the imposition of royal rule.[11]

In the early years North Carolinian government developed in a similar fashion to that of South Carolina, though conflicts lasted longer, perhaps because the relative lack of wealth to be had from the economy made political office all the more attractive to the ambitious. The proprietors supposed initially that northern settlers would send representatives to Charles Town. Distance made this arrangement impracticable, however, and before the mid-1690s the northern region was governed in a unicameral meeting of the deputy governor, his appointed council and elected representatives. These arrangements did not ensure political stability, however. John Culpeper, the proprietors' own southern surveyor-general, in the early 1670s led a failed conspiracy in the south to secede from the proprietary. Fleeing to the Albemarle region, he joined with local forces resisting the proprietors' support of the Navigation Acts. In December 1677, Culpeper's Rebellion peaked when the insurgents imprisoned the governor and established a new administration 'by their owne authority & according to their owne modell'. The rebels dispatched Culpeper to England to plead their case. When he was tried for treason his acquittal was secured, ironically, by the support of Shaftesbury, who wished to make light of events in case the impression of disorder inspired the crown to revoke the proprietors' charter. The next governor, Seth Sothel, proved so unpopular that the northern assembly banished him from the Albemarle region in 1689. As a proprietor he then claimed the governorship of South Carolina, but once again was so objectionable that the other proprietors removed him in 1691. John Gibbs then led a rebellion against the next northern governor, Philip Ludwell, but he had too little popular support and had to flee to Virginia.

In the years that followed, Quakers and other dissenters who moved to North Carolina in great numbers resisted successive attempts to establish the Anglican Church in defiance of the proprietors' guarantee of religious liberty. In 1708, both the pro- and anti-establishment factions had rival claimants to the governorship and rival delegates to the assembly. Attempting to suppress a potential civil war, the proprietors appointed Edward Hyde, distantly related to Queen Anne, as governor. Hyde's first assembly in 1711 annulled all legislation passed under his predecessor, Thomas Cary. Cary's ship fired on the assembly house, but then ran aground. The rebels escaped to Virginia. After that, in a climate of growing political and social stability, successive assemblies established the Anglican Church, instituted constitutional procedures that made the assembly increasingly resemble the English House of Commons and promoted the economy with various infrastructural improvements. The lords proprietors held on in North Carolina until 1729, when the crown purchased seven of the eight proprietary shares. Sir George Carteret, Earl Granville, refused to relinquish his North Carolina title and held on to the Granville district until American Independence.[12]

Economy, society and population in the Carolinas

The first European residents of the Carolinas were Virginians who, encouraged by Governor Sir William Berkeley on behalf of his brother and the other Carolinian lords proprietors, settled around Albemarle Sound in the north, although some Virginians began colonizing the area as early as 1650.

The area lay within the earlier Virginia charter and its occupants resented the appropriation of their lands into Carolina, but were placated by the use of the deputy governor as a de facto governor and by the right to have their own representatives. The capital of the new colony eventually settled on New Bern, a compromise between northern and southern interests in the colony. Another group of early settlers were Massachusetts Bay puritans who migrated to the Cape Fear River region, again in what became North Carolina. Soon disillusioned, most returned north, though some visited Barbados and persuaded planters there that Carolina offered them opportunities.

In 1663, the self-styled 'Barbadian Adventurers' dispatched Captain William Hilton to explore the region and the following year about 800 Barbadians arrived in the Cape Fear valley, without licence from the lords proprietors, aiming to produce wine, olive oil and fruit. After three years of internal squabbling and Indian harassment, though, these settlers moved to Virginia. Some Barbadian and English colonists were prepared to make another effort, however, and the next settlement was at Port Royal, already favoured by Barbadian migrants encouraged by Sir John Colleton. Shaftesbury sent 300 settlers aboard three ships there in 1669 and 1670, but a series of calamities meant that only about a third of them survived the journey. In any case, settling inland and out of the range of the Spanish, they put themselves beyond the reach of ocean-going trade and established only subsistence farms. Eventually, however, at the advice of local Cusabo Indians, settlement began to focus on a location 60 miles north of Port Royal on the Ashley River. Spanish colonists from St Augustine attacked their fort unsuccessfully later in August 1670. At the behest of the proprietors, the settlers later moved to a peninsula at the junction of the Ashley and Cooper rivers, where they were safer from the Spanish and had better access to oceanic vessels, and which offered two routes into the Carolinian interior. Charles Town (renamed Charleston after the American Revolution) attracted increasing numbers of settlers. Successful settlement in the Carolinas had finally begun. By 1683 the port had 1000 inhabitants and a growing and increasingly prosperous hinterland.

The most dominant group of settlers were Barbadians, who constituted about half of all incomers in the 1670s. Pre-eminent among them were the aforementioned Goose Creek men, who had no interest in proprietorial land-holding plans. For the sake of attracting settlers and securing peace, the proprietors all but abandoned their neo-feudal dreams, granting headrights of manageable proportions on which colonists quickly used the slave labour, rather than tenants and serfs, that they had been accustomed to in the West Indies. They also sold local Amerindians into slavery, against proprietorial strictures. Also, while the proprietors aimed to avoid the 'Inconvenience and Barbarisme of scattered Dwellings', insisting on town settlements 'that hath given New England soe much advantage over Virginia', settlers simply sought out the best lands along the rivers, just as had the settlers of Virginia. Colonists also established the Anglican Church, despite the charter's promise of religious toleration, allowing wealthier men to build bases of authority in parishes and vestries as the Virginia elite had done, although in South Carolina social and political authority became uniquely centred in the capital of Charles Town.

Besides Englishmen from home and others from New England and Barbados – some Anglicans, some puritan – another large group of settlers were French Huguenots, some of whom were survivors from Florida who, via Virginia, settled the lower Pamlico River and laid out the town of Bath in 1704. Others came via the Netherlands, which acted as a refuge for French Protestants as it had earlier for English puritans. The Santee River Huguenot community continued to speak French for at least a generation, but most French settlers gradually acculturated to English ways. Most Huguenot churches became formally Anglican by the second generation, with services in English and ministers trained in England. Huguenots integrated with English settlers in other ways too, participating in South Carolina's economic, social, cultural and political life in Charles Town. A variety of other small groups followed, including a Swiss Protestant refugee colony established near New Bern in North Carolina in 1710. The Scots of Stuart's Town disappeared after the Spanish attack of 1686, but later an early settlement of Gaelic Scottish Highland Presbyterians appeared on the upper Cape Fear in North Carolina in 1739, presaging a huge influx that would follow the post-Culloden clearances. Welsh Baptists settled by the Peedee River in the 1730s too. There were numerous Quakers in South and, especially, North Carolina. Further west, in 1753, Moravians from Bethlehem, Pennsylvania, purchased 100,000 acres to form their settlement of Wachovia, centred on the town of Salem, North Carolina.

From the original roughly 200 settlers at Albemarle Point in 1653, the population of the Carolinas grew to about 1000 in 1660, mostly around Charles Town. That population grew to 26,000 by 1710, but Queen Anne's War and the Yamasee War discouraged immigration, at least to South Carolina. In 1730, South Carolina's population was still less than 10,000, while North Carolina's was approaching 30,000. After that, South Carolina's population grew more rapidly. In 1760, including Georgia, the region's population reached just over 214,000, and by 1770 some 350,000. The low population growth of the early years is attributable in part to the male-dominated migration that was common during early colonization almost everywhere. As well as a sex imbalance that lasted well into the eighteenth century, the Carolina environment, especially the coastal lowlands, was deadly for many. Slaves brought forms of malaria and yellow fever to which whites were not immune. A large and growing proportion of the Carolinian population, however, was black and enslaved. The Virginians living around Albemarle Sound in 1660 had about 20 slaves with them. A 1708 census counted 4080 whites and 4100 black plus 1400 Indian slaves. By 1760 the region had almost 95,000 Africans and African-Americans, and South Carolina's 57,334 blacks outnumbered its 36,740 whites.[13]

This population was notably more diverse than in all other regions except the Middle Colonies. Carolinian migrants came from all social groups, including younger scions of the English gentry. Just over a third arrived as indentured servants, a lower proportion than in the Chesapeake, and perhaps half of them could sign their names, indicating that they had the will and skills to get ahead after their terms of servitude. As an inducement to migrate, servants received land at the end of their terms, on average just over 100 acres. The average landholding at death of former servants was 369 acres. Four ex-servants eventually became assemblymen. The hardships of the Carolina environment meant fewer migrants, but those who took the risks and survived seem to have enjoyed greater opportunity for material success than those who went to the Chesapeake.

The spread of population, in particular the depletion of hunting grounds and the settlers' habit of enslaving Amerindians to sell in the Caribbean, eventually led to war, although early Amerindian–Anglo-American relations were relatively peaceful. Early settlers in the south forged an alliance with local Yamasee and Creek Indians, meaning an unusually long period of peace after initial white settlement. Early peace was also possible because 'the Hand of God', in the view of Governor John Archdale in 1707, was 'eminently seen in thinning the Indians, to make room for the English'. Indeed the Amerindian population in the Carolinas, east of the Appalachians, fell from around 20,000 in 1685 to 10,000 by 1700. Those who remained were 'serviceable to kill Dear, &c. for to procure Skins for Trade with us'. In 1711, though, the Tuscarora Indians attacked New Bern and killed its residents, but massive retaliation with help from Virginia prevented any further resistance. The survivors moved north to join the Iroquois in New York. The Yamasee also assisted against the Tuscarora, but in 1715 they joined with neighbouring Creeks and began attacking plantations around Port Royal, killing some 400 settlers, and at one point in the Yamasee War pushed the Carolinians as far back as Charles Town. Eventually, however, the colonists, armed slaves and their Cherokee allies pushed those Yamasee they did not kill or enslave beyond the Savannah River. In 1770, Governor William Bull reported that of the Amerindians who once dominated the region nothing remained 'but their names'. Anglo-Amerindian relations in North Carolina were more peaceful, as the Catawba confederation adopted a policy of negotiation with arriving colonists. Disease and growing dependence on European goods ensured that negotiations were far from equal or advantageous, however, and these people, too, found themselves removed further and further from their ancestral lands.[14]

The Carolinas initially developed slowly, though South Carolina eventually became mainland North America's wealthiest province. Early experiments with tobacco, cotton and sugar produced no satisfactorily profitable staple. Proprietors hoped to profit from goods otherwise only available by import, such as olive oil, silk, wine and citrus fruits. This attempted Mediterranean economy failed to develop, however, and early commerce largely served the Barbadian economy, as some Barbadian planters had in mind. One of Carolina's principal early exports to the West Indies was livestock. Cattle and hogs were branded, allowed to forage freely in the woods and on the savannahs, then rounded up and driven to pens before being sold to market, and in these ways seventeenth-century Carolinians pioneered the cattle industry and cowboy working life that we normally associate with the 'Old West' of the late nineteenth century. Many of the early Carolina cowboys were black, as were a third of the cowboys of the Old West. These goods were exchanged for West Indian sugar, which was then exported to England. Carolinians also made some profits provisioning privateers and pirates and selling Indian slaves to island planters. They also traded deerskins with Indians, exporting to England over 50,000 a year, worth up to £30,000, before the Yamasee War.

In 1705, parliament added naval stores to the items that, under the Navigation Acts, colonists could only export within the empire, and enacted bounties to encourage their production. Carolinians thus developed a reasonably lucrative line in lumber, tar and pitch. The bounty expired in 1724 as English rope makers continued to prefer the Scandinavian method of using resins from live pine trees (Carolinians used dead trees as that method was less labour-intensive). Lobbying by Carolinian and English merchants, however, persuaded parliament in 1729 to reintroduce bounties for Carolinian naval stores and to add a premium to Scandinavian ones, and naval stores thereafter became a mainstay of the economy of northern North Carolina (hence the nickname 'tarheels'). North Carolinians also retained a tobacco economy that made that section of the region part of 'greater Virginia'. Besides tobacco and naval stores, North Carolinians also exported grains, livestock, meat, lumber and barrel staves to the West Indies and Britain. North Carolinians made a virtue of their relative modesty, likening their colony, in relation to its grander northern and southern neighbours, to 'a vale of humility between two mountains of conceit'.

South of the Cape Fear River valley, in the first few years of the eighteenth century, a staple began to emerge in the form of rice. Rice was first successfully cultivated in the 1690s, after traders discovered larger and superior varieties of the grain in the East Indies and Madagascar. Exports grew slowly at first, as planters experimented, with the help of slaves, with different methods of cultivation. It was probably slaves who introduced paddy-field as opposed to dry-land production. By 1700, Carolinians were producing close to 270,000 pounds of rice annually, rising to 1.5 million pounds by 1710, near 20,000,000 pounds by 1730, and 72,000,000 pounds by the 1770s. By then, two-thirds of the Carolina rice crop was exported to Britain, the rest to southern Europe and the West Indies, and rice constituted the fourth great New World staple, along with sugar, tobacco and wheat.

Unlike West Indians with sugar, the Lower South did not develop a monoculture in rice. South and, especially, North Carolinians continued to export Indian slaves, deerskins, naval stores and foodstuffs to the West Indies. In 1748, parliament established a bounty of sixpence per pound of indigo produced, and South Carolinians renewed their experiments in and successfully cultivated the dye. Rice therefore made up 55 per cent of exports in the late colonial period, indigo 20 per cent, with the rest mostly naval stores and foodstuffs. South Carolina, therefore, never became a Barbadian-style society consisting almost exclusively of rich planters and slaves. Opportunity for others existed and was lauded as loudly as it was in other colonies. As early as 1666 Robert Horne appealed to 'all Artificers, as *Carpenters, Wheel-rights, Joyners, Coopers, Bricklayers, Smiths*, or diligent Husbandmen and Laboureres, that are willing to advance their fortunes' to move to Carolina 'where Artificers are of high esteem, and used with all Civility and Courtesie imaginable'. One of the best known examples of promotional literature from the region was Thomas Nairne's 'A Letter from South Carolina' (1710), which claimed that 'modest Industry' would secure 'all the Necessaries of Life' and that there was 'no Place in the Continent of America, where People can transport themselves to greater Advantage'.[15]

Yet South Carolina was markedly both more wealthy and unequal than other mainland colonies. By 1774, per capita wealth in the Charles Town district was over £2300: four times higher than in the Chesapeake and six times higher than in Philadelphia and New York City. Among whites near Charles Town the slave-holding rate was a remarkable 97 per cent, with average holdings of 43 slaves per free household head. One reason why wealth was so concentrated near Charles Town was that the city was the major point of import and export for the region. South Carolina merchants owned up to 40 per cent of shipping traffic in the port, worth about £100,000 by the 1770s. Furthermore, wealthier planters congregated in the city, especially in summer, to escape the stifling and disease-ridden swamps of the countryside. Located between the Ashley and Cooper rivers, it was relatively cool in summer and had a temperate winter too. Residents enhanced its climatic moderation and its renowned elegance with tree-lined avenues and close-set Georgian houses with Barbadian piazzas. By 1775, Charles Town had 12,000 inhabitants, making it the fourth largest city in North America, after Boston, New York and Philadelphia. Endowed with all the kinds of crafts and services the population needed, its wealth and, from the mid-eighteenth century its residents' powerful improving impulse, meant it was also blessed with a library company, a theatre, benevolent groups, fraternal clubs and horse races. Despite the attractions of Charles Town, however, some of the wealthiest South Carolinians made their way to Britain. They did not go there with the frequency of their West Indian counterparts, but, even so, in the 1770s, there were some 50 absentee South Carolinians in London alone.

The allure of Charles Town was so great, and the white population of the countryside so small, that in South Carolina there were no county courts or county-based politics and little county society. The countryside was divided into counties, parishes and townships, but only for record-keeping purposes, and not to extend gentry rule throughout the colony's localities. Plantations tended to be run by overseers. Local life was thus highly attenuated compared with that in other mainland colonies. In the 1750s, furthermore, other smaller towns came into their own throughout the region: Wilmington and Edenton, as well as New Bern, in North Carolina; Georgetown and Beaufort in South Carolina, and Savannah, Georgia. By this time, too, inland towns were developing, including Salisbury, North Carolina, Camden, South Carolina, and Augusta, Georgia.

Rice shaped the region south of Cape Fear as surely as tobacco shaped the Chesapeake and sugar the West Indies, although sometimes in quite distinct ways. Unlike tobacco, for example, rice could be planted in the same fields for several years, so settlement did not spread so rapidly inland as was the case in Virginia. Nevertheless, while the naval stores and deerskins industries encouraged extensive exploitation of land throughout the region, even into the lower Mississippi valley, rice allowed the countryside to become dominated by intensive agriculture and, in turn, allowed the creation of a more settled aspect to the landscape. By 1722 Carolinians claimed almost 1.2 million acres of land, reaching 2.5 million acres in the 1740s. Rice did encourage a lack of towns, however, and Charles Town remained the only urban settlement in the southern region until the establishment of Beaufort further down the coast in the 1720s, and then of inland towns in subsequent decades. Though not as lucrative as sugar, rice was even more lucrative than tobacco, making South Carolina by far the wealthiest of the mainland colonies. Above all, however, like tobacco and sugar, rice lent itself to plantation cultivation and large-scale slavery. One distinction in the rice economy, though, was that a crucial factor in its emergence and success was reliance on African expertise. That expertise allowed slaves to shape methods of cultivation to a far greater extent than elsewhere, with significant impacts on African-American and white society and culture in the region.

Slavery in the Carolinas

Slavery arrived at an earlier point in the development of Carolina than it did in the Chesapeake largely because of Barbadian migration, but also because of the known qualities of enslaved labour (more than half of early Carolinian slaves came from Barbados). As in Virginia, race relations took time to develop. Frontier conditions created what historian Peter Wood called a kind of 'sawbuck equality' in early Carolina, as black and white men felled the forests together. Low numbers of slaves and relatively relaxed interracial relations meant that Carolinians did not adopt a comprehensive set of slave laws until 1696. That year, however, the colony adopted the Barbadian code, the harshest in all of Anglo-America. By then, though slaves were used extensively in all forms of economic endeavour, especially in naval stores, rice was coming under cultivation, encouraging plantation production with a fully articulated slave system. The revocation of the Royal African Company's slave trade monopoly in 1698 encouraged slave importations to the Carolinas, as traders were free to explore new markets and local merchants were better able to attract them. The slave population of 1500 in 1690 grew to 4100 by 1710. By 1708 slaves were a majority of the South Carolina population, excluding Amerindians, and by 1720 they constituted a two-thirds majority. Parts of the low country, near the sea, had slave majorities of eight-to-one, resembling conditions in the West Indies.

Even so, in some respects South Carolinians were surprisingly permissive towards their slaves. African, specifically Senegambian, expertise in rice cultivation permitted the development of a task system of production, in which slaves were able to negotiate what was a reasonable amount of work – a task – to accomplish in a day. In contrast to the tobacco colonies' gang system of labour, which forced slaves to work from dawn till dusk, South Carolina slaves often completed their tasks by late afternoon, leaving them considerably more time to themselves than Chesapeake slaves enjoyed. In that time they cultivated extensive garden plots, both for subsistence and for sale. The Charles Town food market was dominated by an entirely illegal but tolerated and even much appreciated trade by slaves. The task system also allowed slaves more time for socializing as well as for working for themselves. Furthermore, the frequency of absenteeism and the indifference of non-slave-owning managers or overseers meant there was less paternalistic interference in slave life in the Lower South than was sometimes the case in the Chesapeake. What also helped enrich the South Carolina slave culture was its constant replenishment with new arrivals from Africa. South Carolina slaves achieved natural population increase and were on the way to becoming a Creole-dominated people before 1720, but thereafter an intensification of agriculture meant natural population decrease until the 1760s. Both these phenomena meant growth in the South Carolina slave trade, and some 20,000 slaves were imported in the 1730s alone.

The slave majority and the large number of Africans in South Carolina was so striking that Samuel Dyssli, a Swiss migrant who arrived in 1732, described the colony five years later as 'more like a negro country than like a country settled by white people'. Not surprisingly, many white people saw the colony's slave majority as a problem, especially considering the presence of Spanish colonists in Florida. For some years the Spanish had helped to destabilize southern Anglo-North America by harbouring runaway slaves. Slaves ran to a community they founded in Mose, near St Augustine, where, from as early as 1683, the Spanish had given them wage work and organized them in militia units. In 1739, South Carolina slave rebels stole guns and ammunition from a store at the Stono River bridge, near Charles Town, and destroyed plantations and killed numerous whites on their way to Florida. The Stono Rebellion was brutally suppressed and followed by changes in the law. Slave-holders could thereafter be fined for their slaves' indiscipline, manumissions would require legislative assent and taxes were imposed to slow down though not to stop slave importations.

Even before the Stono Rebellion, the assembly attempted to induce planters to import greater numbers of indentured servants. When these inducements failed, South Carolinians concocted a 1730 'Scheem . . . for Settling Townships' that attempted to ensure settlement of blocks of land at regular and strategic intervals in the colonial interior. Migrants were offered free transatlantic transportation, a farm and town lot, and supplies and tools. The scheme attracted several thousand settlers, including French and German Swiss Protestants, Ulster Scots, Welsh, Irish and Pennsylvania Quakers, as well as English migrants. Yet the numbers of migrants and the 10 townships founded in the 1730s were fewer than expected, partly because of lack of inland access to transatlantic shipping and partly because, though some land was good, much of the interior comprised sandy pine barrens. In the meantime, others attempted to create a white population in the region by founding the colony of Georgia.[16]

Georgia

The first plan to settle the area that became Georgia comprised a grant given in 1717 to Sir Robert Montgomery for a Margravate of Azilia, but Montgomery did nothing to settle the area. In 1732, though, George II granted General James Oglethorpe (a former military man and then a Member of Parliament) and 20 trustees, proprietorship of Georgia – named after the king – carved out of South Carolina between the Savannah and Altamaha rivers. The charter directed that the proprietors would make no profits and that the colony would come under crown rule after 21 years. The most significant directive, though, was that slavery was initially forbidden in colonial Georgia.

The imperial aim was to provide a white population in the new colony to provide a buffer against Spanish Florida and to counterbalance the slave majority in South Carolina. The trustees added an element of idealism to these plans. Some were opposed to slavery in principle, both because it was cruel to slaves and because it encouraged indolence and luxury among slave-holders. Furthermore, instead of a slave society, the trustees intended that Georgia provide a sanctuary for Protestant refugees and for debtors, and that it be a relatively egalitarian society of independent producers. To that effect, each male settler was to receive 50 acres of land, tools and a year's worth of supplies on arrival, though women were forbidden from owning land. Recipients were prohibited from selling land and from amassing more than 500 acres. Inheritance practices were controlled to prevent accumulation, and indeed land titles remained ultimately with the trustees. Settlement was supposed to be concentrated in planned villages and staked-out farm tracts. The trustees' philanthropic idealism manifested itself in other ways too. Trade with Amerindians was restricted to those granted licences and was regulated by law. Finally, the proprietors forbade the importation, manufacture and consumption of rum and other spirits.

Oglethorpe supervised settlement himself, making several lengthy visits to the colony, offering a uniquely hands-on approach to proprietorship. Settlement was initially successful, helped by the £136,608 that parliament spent on the colonization of Georgia between 1732 and 1752, the first government-subsidized colonization that Britain had ever undertaken. With Amerindian advice, Oglethorpe selected Savannah as the colonial capital, 10 miles up the eponymous river, with forts guarding the coast and a garrisoned outpost at Augusta further upriver as an Indian trading post. He negotiated eastern land rights with the Creek Indians, reserving to them coastal locations for seasonal use and upriver land. Most colonists initially settled between the lower Savannah and Ogeechee rivers, not far from Savannah. In 1733 the first 114 settlers disembarked at the mouth of the Savannah River, accompanied by Oglethorpe, and parliament and the trustees subsidized the migration of some 2500 people in the next decade, with other self-financed settlers arriving too. Colonists came from various backgrounds. About one-third of the subsidized settlers were German Moravians, Austrian Lutherans and a small group of around 40 Sephardic Jews. Others included Scottish Highlanders, who settled New Inverness, now Darien, on the Altamaha border.

The trustees attempted rationally and systematically to search for a useful staple, learning from the slow and halting efforts of other colonies. They established a nursery, the Trustee's Garden in Savannah, to experiment with wine, silk and other Mediterranean and exotic products, even employing European experts. As in South Carolina, this Mediterranean economy failed to take hold, but rice and indigo thrived. Without slaves, however, production levels remained low, and soon Georgians began to balk at the ban on slavery and other limits on their freedoms, including the

rights to own land and to produce and drink rum. Within five years of colonization settlers secured the modification of restrictions on landownership. In subsequent years settlers would acquire unlimited tracts of land in
fee simple. Rum and slaves were imported and used by some settlers,
despite proprietorial law, in particular by migrating South Carolinians.
Settlers also complained that the prohibition on rum restricted their marketing of produce in Barbados where rum was currency. The dead-letter
law was repealed in 1742. In 1747 Georgia's antislavery laws were tacitly
relaxed and in 1750 the trustees revoked the ban on slavery: another proprietorial big idea cast aside by settlers. The following year the trustees gave
in altogether and surrendered the colony to crown rule, a year earlier than
required. Slave numbers rose rapidly from 500 in 1751 to 15,000, near half
the colony's population, by 1775. Between the legalization of slavery and
American Independence, rice production increased tenfold.[17]

East and West Florida

In the Peace of Paris that concluded the French and Indian War of 1754 to
1763, Spain ceded Florida to Britain in exchange for Britain returning
Havana, its key Cuban base, to Spain. Florida would remain a British possession for just 20 years. Settlement there proceeded only slowly and Britain
ceded the colony back to Spain in the Treaty of Paris in 1783. The crown
organized the province into two colonies, East Florida, comprising the
peninsula that we call Florida now, and West Florida, along the Gulf of
Mexico, now the southern parts of Alabama and Mississippi, though the
border was soon moved to the Yazoo River to take in a fledgling settlement
at Natchez. Although Britain promised to respect Spanish residents' property rights, almost all 3000 of them (including those of African descent and
converted Amerindians) took up the encouragement and assistance offered
by Spain to move to Cuba.

   Treating with the Lower Creek Indians, the British planned plantations
along the St Johns River in East Florida. The crown gave over 200 grants
but, with emigration from England now officially discouraged, only about
20 were taken up, and those mostly by Scottish soldiers who had distinguished themselves during the late war. About 40 families arrived from
Bermuda in 1766. One of the most successful was Andrew Turnbull, a
Scottish physician, who established a Greek, Corsican and Italian tenant
colony at New Smyrna in 1768. By 1775 there were around 3000 colonists,
no more than there had been Spanish 12 years before. The province had the
beginnings of a plantation economy, with planters spreading along the
rivers in similar fashion to previous plantation settlements, but remained
heavily dependent on land speculation and Indian trade, with Scottish factors trading mostly out of Charles Town rather than St Augustine.

   The Spanish of West Florida moved to Vera Cruz, and the British reorganized the new colony into land divisions, with Pensacola as its capital. This region remained even more embryonic than its eastern namesake. Some French Louisiana settlers remained in the region and some new migrants made attempts to settle the area, such as the Company of Military Adventurers, largely New England military leaders, who settled over 100 families near Natchez in 1774. But most of the land remained in the hands of speculators and the main trade was with Indians. In 1775, the colonist population was around 5000, including about 1200 slaves.

Authorities in London hoped to use Florida to rein in the growing and notoriously troublesome population of British America. One official advocated 'a western boundary to our ancient provinces' so that eastern populations 'would emigrate to Nova Scotia or to the provinces on the southern frontier where they would be useful to their mother country instead of planting themselves in the heart of America beyond the reach of governments'. This proved to be yet another unfulfilled imperial aspiration, for although a few went to the Floridas and more went to Nova Scotia, far greater numbers moved to the backcountries of pre-existing colonies. Beyond 'reach of governments' was precisely where many of them wished to be.[18]

The backcountries and the trans-Appalachian west

By the middle of the eighteenth century much of the eastern seaboard of North America was densely populated and colonists were encroaching ever further into the interior. Pennsylvanians, New Yorkers and, behind them, New Englanders had for some time been hemmed in by the French and their Indian allies in the north-west, a region also claimed by Virginia. By 1754, competing encroachment resulted in the outbreak of the French and Indian War, a conflict that soon became part of the Seven Years War of 1756–63. By 1760, the French had been defeated (their concession of Quebec was formalized in the Peace of Paris of 1763; see chapter 7). After that, settlers moved with remarkable rapidity into the backcountries of the settled colonies and even into the trans-Appalachian west.

Expansion into the backcountries and further west meant new negotiations and confrontations with Amerindians. In 1758, Pennsylvania agreed that the Delaware could settle the Wyoming Valley. Even so, in 1763, the Paxton Boys cleared their way into western Pennsylvania with a brutal attack on peaceful Conestoga Indians. The Cherokee War of 1760–61 resulted from settlers increasingly impinging on the Indians' hunting land and, although the Indians won some significant victories, ultimately resulted in Cherokee removal further west. Other Amerindians accommodated further encroachment by acculturating into Euro-American society (a much understudied phenomenon), retreating into reservations or receding into unsettled areas in Florida or beyond the Appalachian mountains.

From the 1740s, then, and in growing volume in subsequent decades, settlers poured into the west. Colonists from New York and New England
moved further and further inland to the heads of the Connecticut River and
the junction of the Hudson and Mohawk rivers, though until the 1760s
Amerindians and rival French colonists hemmed them in there. From
Pennsylvania, colonists migrated into the southern backcountries, moving
down along the Great Wagon Road, an old Indian trail through the
Appalachian valleys, filling the backcountries of Maryland, Virginia, the
Carolinas and Georgia. By the 1750s, some 2000 families a year were
moving into the Shenandoah Valley, and the population of south-western
Virginia was doubling every eight years in the 1760s. J. Hector St John de
Crevecoeur left us a sense of the movement of people in the mid 1770s:
'Every spring the roads were full of families travelling towards this New
Canaan', he wrote, 'without law or government, without any kind of social
bond to unite them.' Crevecoeur was awestruck by 'the prodigious number
of houses rearing up, fields cultivating, that great extent of industry open'd
up to a bold indefatigable enterprising people' moving west from
Connecticut into the Wyoming Valley of Pennsylvania. The backcountry
received not only people moving from the eastern sections of long-established colonies but from Europe too, especially from the Celtic fringes of
the British Isles. Between 1750 and 1775, following the Highland clearances, around 20,000 Scottish highlanders arrived in North America, many
of them Gaelic speakers, most of them settling on the frontiers. There were
10,000 Scottish arrivals or first-generation descendants in Cumberland
County, in what is now mid-North Carolina. Among their number from
1774 was Flora MacDonald, who had harboured Bonnie Prince Charlie on
the Isle of Skye as he fled the scene of the failing Jacobite rebellion of 1745.
Even larger numbers, around 100,000, came from Ulster.

Wherever they came from, migrants sought land and therefore the kind
of economic and social independence that America had by now long
offered. Georgia Governor James Wright negotiated a series of treaties in
1763, 1766 and 1773, freeing up 5,500,000 acres for peaceful white settlement in the west of that colony. Wright advertised his newly acquired territories to prospective settlers in the same way that colonial promoters had
always done, as 'lands . . . of the most fertile quality' that 'will be parcelled
out in different tracts . . . from 100 to 1,000 acres, the better to accommodate the buyers'. He marketed lands as 'well watered', with accessible markets and free of royal quitrents for 10 years. He also helped show new
settlers the way to their promised land, providing a map denoting timber,
cane brakes, springs and well sites. As Bernard Bailyn wrote in his epic
study of late colonial migration: 'Every detail of this well-publicized adver-
tisement went straight to the hopes and desires of migrants everywhere.'
Selling western land often involved speculators, giving elites a chance to
enrich themselves even while offering opportunities to traditionally less

privileged people. One major agent in the new wave of western settlement was Lord Fairfax, America's only resident noble and a proprietor of Virginia's Northern Neck, who, in 1753, established his seat at Greenway Court near Winchester, a convenient spot from which to launch westward ventures. Fairfax and other speculators sold land on to others in smaller parcels at good profits. Another of the great speculators was George Washington, who wrote in 1767 of 'opening the backcountry for adventurers, where numbers resort to, and where an enterprising man with very little money may lay the foundation of a noble estate'.[19]

Western settlers' aspirations often put them at odds with their eastern counterparts. In the Carolinas discontent manifested itself in a 'Regulator' movement. Like Bacon's Rebellion in seventeenth-century Virginia, the movement originated in defence against Amerindian resistance, but soon became a focus of wider grievances. The Regulator movement was in part a response to the absence of governmental and judicial institutions, though its methods were sometimes brutal and lawless. Regulators also struggled for equal representation and political rights for westerners against indifferent eastern elites. In these ways their existence mirrored the kinds of social and political problems and processes that occurred in the initial settlement of the eastern seaboard: the movement from an inchoate society towards a new social settlement defined by settlers themselves. Sometimes, early western settlers created radical and even utopian ways of social and political life. In north central Pennsylvania, for example, 40 families formed the Fair Play system, a democratic form of law and government that existed until Pennsylvania incorporated the area in 1784.

Most western settlers, especially in the south, were beyond the easy reach of Atlantic commerce. Livestock was therefore a practical pursuit and enclosed 'cowpens' of a few hundred acres became a distinctive feature of the country, though cattle also ranged into the forests and swamps. Cowpens and cattle and hog ranges were often an early form of pre-settlement exploitation, managed by agents of land speculators before tracts were sold on to planters and farmers. Eventually, however, except in the upper reaches of the Appalachian piedmont where the ground was too high and the land was too rocky, new elites would later emerge with the eventual incursion of plantation agriculture and large-scale slavery. The west would ultimately, therefore, come to resemble the east.

The colonization of the backcountries, then, was characterized by the same features that characterized colonial settlement from the beginning. People were moving for their own betterment, sometimes engaging in idealized social and political experimentation, often in defiance of government. After a period of social and political contestation, however, the backcountries began to settle as new elites emerged. By the 1750s, that process was beginning to replicate itself yet again, this time beyond the backcountries, in the trans-Appalachian west.

Even after the French and Indian War there were still Amerindian claims to western lands that inhibited westward expansion, symbolized by the bloody Pontiac Rebellion from 1763. The end of the war and the driving out of the French offered such terrifying prospects that they inspired a kind of millennialism among some Amerindians. Pontiac, an Ottawa leader, believed that the Great Spirit, Manitou, spoke through him when he urged his people to drive the British from their lands. Pontiac's Rebellion began in May 1763 and consisted mostly of a series of sieges of north-western British forts. The British retaliated with attacks on villages and gradually wore the coalition down until Pontiac's allies sued for peace in May 1765, as did Pontiac himself in July 1767. Yet British authorities in London had already made a significant concession to Amerindian land rights. On 7 October 1763, George III issued the Great Proclamation. As well as defining the boundaries and confirming the traditional civil government of Quebec, and establishing government for and boundaries of East and West Florida and the newly captured Lesser Antilles, the royal pronouncement forbade incursions beyond the heads of rivers that emptied into the Atlantic Ocean (following a Pennsylvanian ban on settlement beyond the Alleghenies). The establishment of this Proclamation Line was one of the most significant statements of imperial policy that any British authority had yet made, and in setting a limit to further British colonization it was fundamentally anti-imperial. The Proclamation Line, however, only imperfectly inhibited western expansion during the short period of its existence (from an American perspective it was abolished by the Declaration of Independence in 1776 and from a British one it was abandoned under the Treaty of Paris of 1783). Over the years, like all imperial and proprietorial impositions, the Line bent and buckled under pressures from local, colonial interests, in this instance the western land companies that claimed vast tracts of trans-Appalachian territory and from settlers who had already moved there, or who moved there later, royal proclamation or no royal proclamation.

The first problem was that the Proclamation Line contradicted the land grants of the original colonial charters. Several colonies held land claims that stretched all the way to the Pacific Ocean, all under earlier royal imprimatur. Some colonies had already begun to put these claims into practical effect. In 1748, Virginia had granted the Ohio Company of Virginia all the lands between the Monongahela and Kanawha rivers, and, although the company failed to develop these lands, its activities encouraged speculators to invest heavily in it and prompted at least some settlers to move into the region. In 1753, the Susquehannah Company laid claim to a large portion of the Wyoming Valley in northern Pennsylvania, also claimed by Connecticut. By the early 1760s, therefore, there were several thousand Euro-American colonists already living west of the Line. These settlers proved unwilling to move back east, despite the Proclamation's injunction to 'remove themselves from such settlements'. A further way in which the Proclamation imperfectly reflected territorial realities was that some Amerindians still controlled lands to the east of the line of demarcation. Also, British authorities were nothing if not inconsistent. In the wake of Pontiac's Rebellion, British army Colonel Henry Bouquet, for example, knowingly gave blankets infected with small-pox as gifts to Indians, deliberately spreading the deadly disease among the Amerindians of the Ohio Valley.

In the event, it was the responsibility of William Johnson and John Stuart, respectively superintendents for Indian affairs for the Northern and Southern departments, the newly created departments of state responsible for colonial affairs, and whose jurisdictions were divided at the Ohio River, to manage these kinds of complications. In effect, that meant the gradual and regulated loss of Indian land and the movement of the Proclamation Line westwards over the next decade. In 1771, for example, the Line was renegotiated to give to Europeans the whole region south of the Ohio River between Fort Pitt and the Kentucky River. One company obtained London's permission to establish a colony called Vandalia in this region, but the project collapsed when America declared its independence. Western trailblazers (who earned that name by burning the foliage around old Indian paths to widen them for wagon traffic) discovered the Cumberland Gap through the mountains in 1750, and gradually settlers followed the rivers and valleys into what became Kentucky and Tennessee. British Americans first reconnoitred the Kentucky Stations of the Bluegrass Country (the grass itself was another European invader) in 1766, and in 1775 Daniel Boone and his 'long hunters' blazed the trail from Cumberland Gap across the Cumberland Plateau to Kentucky, where he planned to establish the proprietary of Transylvania. In 1774, the Virginia militia defeated local Indians attempting to prevent these latest intrusions, despite their illegality under the Proclamation. By 1776, several hundred settlers claimed over half a million acres of land in the region. Others moved into what were known as the Watauga settlements from 1772, on Indian lands near the Tennessee River at the end of the Great Valley between the Appalachians and the Cumberland Plateau. In the absence of any supervising colonial or imperial authority, these settlers formed their own governmental 'Association'. The British government declared the settlements unlawful, but the land was purchased from the Cherokees by North Carolina land speculators anyway.[20]

From the 1490s and through the sixteenth century the intellectual vanguard of English imperialists imagined what an Anglo-American Empire might be. But they got nowhere with kings, queens and parliaments who were interested in their ideas but not interested enough to put them into practice. In the second half of the sixteenth century, English merchant adventurers began looting French and Spanish New World colonies and ships, muscling in on their imperial trade and exploring the possibility of an actual Anglo-American plantation. The first attempted English colonizations ended in catastrophe at Roanoke, but from 1607 private companies and colonial proprietors initiated the English and, from 1707, British colonization of eastern North America and much of the West Indies. Monarchs and parliaments remained semi-detached from the process, granting charters to various groups who had plans for colonization that ranged from the prosaic to the fantastical. But in every case, even in New England, proprietors' corporate visions sooner or later succumbed to the individual ambitions of migrants and settlers.

The early empire was thus created from the bottom up, in the first place by a sort of public-private partnership between governments and proprietors, and in the second by private individuals for their own purposes. In fact, there was barely any such thing as 'empire' in Anglo- or British America. Rather, there was a congeries of colonies, each serving their own and their inhabitants' interests rather than any greater corporate aim. If there was any sense of corporatism at all within the colonies, once proprietors were dispatched, it was a centrifugal one based on the idea that what free Englishmen had in common with each other was the liberty to go abroad to pursue their material ambitions, practise their religions and generally go about their lives with minimal and at most local governmental encumbrance.

Yet if the creation of colonies pre-dated that of empire, it also almost preordained it. Authorities in England began to notice the colonies, at least once those colonies became conspicuously populous and wealthy, especially as the colonists so manifestly acted in their own interests, often to the detriment of English or British interests. Gradually, therefore, English and then British authorities began to imagine how an empire might be forged out of a disparate collection of colonies. The chapters that follow trace how that imagining developed, how colonial administrators and eventually monarchs and parliaments attempted to turn the empire into a more unified entity, how their plans fell apart as surely as did those of colonial proprietors and how British authorities subsequently attempted to pick up the pieces and create a new kind of empire altogether.

Notes

1 Oliver A. Rink, *Holland on the Hudson: An Economic and Social History of Dutch New York* (Ithaca, 1986).
2 Robert C. Ritchie, *The Duke's Province: A Study of New York Politics and Society, 1664–1691* (Chapel Hill, 1977), pp. 34, 101–2; Allan Tully, *Forming American Politics: Ideals, Interests, and Institutions in Colonial New York and Pennsylvania* (Baltimore, 1994); Patricia U. Bonomi, *A Factious People: Politics and Society in Colonial New York*

(New York, 1971); Michael Kammen, *Colonial New York: A History* (New York, 1975); Simon Middleton, *Privileges and Profits: Tradesmen in Colonial New York City, 1624–1750* (Philadelphia, forthcoming).

3 John E. Pomfret, *Colonial New Jersey: A History* (New York, 1973); Ned C. Landsman, *Scotland and its First American Colony* (Princeton, 1985).

4 D.W. Meinig, *The Shaping of America: A Geographical Perspective on 500 Years of History* Volume I: *Atlantic America, 1492–1800* (New Haven, 1986), p. 133; Gary Nash, *Quakers and Politics: Pennsylvania, 1681–1726* (Princeton, 1968), p. 10.

5 James T. Lemon, *The Best Poor Man's Country: A Geographical Study of Early Southeastern Pennsylvania* (Baltimore, 1972), p. 98; Joseph E. Illick, *Colonial Pennsylvania: A History* (New York, 1976), pp. 30–7; Frederick B. Tolles, *Meeting House and Counting House: The Quaker Merchants of Colonial Philadelphia* (Chapel Hill, 1948); Thomas M. Doerflinger, *A Vigorous Spirit of Enterprise: Merchants and Economic Development in Revolutionary Philadelphia* (Chapel Hill, 1986); William M. Offut, Jr., *Of Good Laws and Good Men: Law and Society in the Delaware Valley, 1680–1710* (Urbana, IL, 1995).

6 Meinig, *Shaping of America*, p. 133.

7 Peter Charles Hoffer, *The Brave New World: A History of Early America* (Boston, 2000), p. 241.

8 John A. Munroe, *Colonial Delaware: A History* (New York, 1978).

9 Sung Bok Kim, *Landlord and Tenant in Colonial New York: Manorial Society, 1664–1775* (Chapel Hill, 1978); Jean R. Soderland, *Quakers and Slavery: A Divided Spirit* (Princeton, 1985).

10 Robert M. Weir, *Colonial South Carolina: A History* (New York, 1983), p. 75; Weir, '"Shaftesbury's Darling": British Settlement in The Carolinas at the Close of the Seventeenth Century', in Nicholas Canny, ed., *The Oxford History of the British Empire* Volume I: *The Origins of Empire: British Overseas Enterprise to the Close of the Seventeenth Century* (Oxford, 1998) pp. 381, 384.

11 Weir, '"Shaftesbury's Darling"', p. 384; Aaron M. Shatzman, *Servants into Planters: The Origin of an American Image: Land Acquisition and Status Mobility in Seventeenth-Century South Carolina* (London, 1989), p. 154; Joyce E. Chaplin, *An Anxious Pursuit: Agricultural Innovation and Modernity in the Lower South, 1730–1815* (Chapel Hill, 1993).

12 William S. Powell, *Colonial North Carolina: A History* (New York, 1973); A. Roger Ekirch, *Poor Carolina: Politics and Society in Colonial North Carolina, 1729–1776* (Chapel Hill, 1981).

13 Meinig, *Shaping of America*, pp. 174, 177; Jack P. Greene, *Pursuits of Happiness: The Social Development of Early Modern British Colonies and the Formation of American Culture* (Chapel Hill, 1988), pp.

178–9; Peter H. Wood, *Black Majority: Negroes in Colonial South Carolina from 1670 through the Stono Rebellion* (New York, 1974), pp. 143–55.

14 Weir, '"Shaftesbury's Darling"', p. 378.

15 Horne, 'A Brief Description of the Province of Carolina', in Weir, '"Shaftesbury's Darling"', p. 393; Jack P. Greene, ed., *Selling a New World: Two South Carolina Promotional Pamphlets* (Columbia, SC, 1989), pp. 38, 35.

16 Wood, *Black Majority*, p. 132; Ira Berlin, *Many Thousands Gone: The First Two Centuries of Slavery in North America* (Cambridge, MA, 1998), pp. 64–76, 142–76; Philip D. Morgan, *Slave Counterpoint: Black Culture in the Eighteenth-Century Chesapeake and Lowcountry* (Chapel Hill, 1998).

17 Harold E. Davis, *The Fledgling Province: Social and Cultural Life in Colonial Georgia, 1733–1776* (Chapel Hill, 1976); Kenneth Coleman, *Colonial Georgia: A History* (New York, 1976); Betty Wood, *Slavery in Colonial Georgia, 1730–1775* (Athens, GA, 1984).

18 Meinig, *Shaping of America*, p. 283; Daniel H. Usner, Jr., *Indians, Settlers, and Slaves in a Frontier Exchange Economy: The Lower Mississippi Valley before 1783* (Chapel Hill, 1992); Paul E. Hoffman, *Florida's Frontiers* (Bloomington, IN, 2002).

19 Bernard Bailyn, *Voyagers to the West: Emigration from Britain to America on the Eve of the Revolution* (London, 1987), pp. 10, 8, 27, 19, 23.

20 Meinig, *Shaping of America*, p. 284; Marjoleine Kars, *Breaking Loose Together: The Regulator Rebellion in Pre-Revolutionary North Carolina* (Chapel Hill, 2002); Ronald Hoffman, *A Spirit of Dissension: Economics, Politics, and the Revolution in Maryland* (Baltimore, 1973) p. 243; Woody Holton, *Forced Founders: Indians, Debtors, Slaves, and the Making of the Revolution in Virginia* (Chapel Hill, 1999), pp. 215, 220.

7

The politics of empire, 1607–1763

Population, economy and society in British America

At the time of the death of Elizabeth I, British America was nothing more than a figment of some men's imaginations. In May 1607, it emerged as something more real: a small fort by the James River off the Chesapeake Bay. Over the next century and a half, though, it grew rapidly. By the time the Peace of Paris settled the French and Indian War in 1763, an imperial conflict that began over possession of lands in the Great Lakes region, Britain possessed vast territories encompassing all of North America from the Atlantic coast to the Mississippi River, and from Hudson's Bay in the north to the Floridas in the south: everything, in fact, except for the still tiny port of New Orleans, which passed from France to Spain in 1763. Britain also added Dominica, Grenada, St Vincent and Tobago, collectively called 'the Ceded Islands', to its empire in the Caribbean, and expelled the French from Senegal and Goree in Africa and from Pondicherry in India.

The earliest inhabitants of England's first permanent colony numbered only 105 when they arrived in the Chesapeake in May 1607, and the Jamestown population halved by the end of the summer. Most colonial populations needed rapid replenishment by new migrants in their early years, but within a decade or two sufficient numbers of women arrived and sufficient numbers of families formed for populations to grow naturally, and within a few more decades those populations became predominantly Creole. In the early 1660s, the Anglo-American population passed the 15,000 mark. By 1710, British America's population reached just over half a million, and by the end of the French and Indian War it was well over 2,000,000. By then it was rising more rapidly than ever, reaching almost 3,000,000 by the time of American Independence.[1]

By the 1770s, the colonies were conspicuously prosperous. Wealth in New England amounted to £19,000,000 in 1774, or £33 per head of the free white population at time of death. In the more commercial Middle Colonies, the total in the same year was £30,000,000, or £51 per head among free whites. Wealth was considerably greater in the tobacco and rice plantation colonies of the southern mainland, amounting to £86,000,000, or £132 per free white head, largely because of slave property. Information on the islands is patchy, but in sugar-growing Jamaica alone wealth amounted to £18,000,000, a staggering £1200 per free white person. This wealth translated into an enormously valuable and rapidly growing trade network between the colonies and Britain. In 1700, the colonies supplied about a fifth of British imports, rising to over a third by mid-century. The value of those imports tripled to over £1,000,000 during the same period. Also, in 1700 the colonies consumed only a tenth of British exports, but by mid-century that proportion was just over a third, and by 1770 colonists were spending up to 30 per cent of their incomes on goods imported from Britain. We can gain a sense of the volume of trade by the fact that in 1775 Lloyd's of London recorded ships with a total carrying capacity of 979,263 tons.[2]

As the colonies grew wealthier, they became more genteel, and the development of gentility fed the colonial consumer boom. From the 1690s, in the earliest settled colonies, wealthy elites spent lavishly to emulate English styles of architecture and landscape gardening and English fashions in household accoutrements and clothing. From about the 1720s, the middling sorts could afford to follow and, although relative inequality grew, many among even the lower sorts started to acquire basic comforts, if not necessarily anything refined. Growing civility was manifest in sociability extended to outsiders. In the 1740s, Scottish traveller Alexander Hamilton commented extensively on the hospitality he received and the conversation he enjoyed in the colonies, even if he sometimes made invidious comparisons with what he would have expected in the metropolis. Increasing refinement manifested itself in civic improvements. As early as the 1690s, Annapolis and Williamsburg advertised the growing wealth and civic sophistication of Maryland and Virginia, even if they were built in part to counter the perceived rusticity of these colonies. These and other towns and cities during subsequent decades were blessed with newly built theatres, library companies and other public institutions. Philadelphia boasted the American Philosophical Society, founded in 1743 and refounded in 1766. Even in the countryside, growing numbers of impressively decorated brick courthouses, churches and taverns adorned the crossroads of rural counties throughout the colonies in the eighteenth century. As time passed, in social and cultural terms and in appearance, the provinces increasingly resembled the mother country.

With all this territory, all these people, all this trade, wealth, grandeur and sophistication, how could Adam Smith possibly say that the British Empire in America 'existed in imagination only'? The answer lies in Edmund Burke's perceptive observation that the 'settlement of our colonies was never pursued upon any regular plan; but they were formed, grew, and flourished, as accidents, the nature of the climate, or the dispositions of private men happened to operate'. As we have seen in previous chapters, the crown claimed nominal ownership of North American territories and Atlantic and Caribbean islands. Yet, except in the cases of Jamaica, Georgia and Nova Scotia, the crown handed over the responsibility of conquering territories and organizing and financing colonization entirely to private companies and proprietors. Those charter holders got precious little reward for their troubles and expense, however, because in very short order the mass of colonists whom they encouraged to follow them appropriated the polities, economies, societies and cultures of the colonies for themselves. The historical processes by which the colonies were created thereby resulted in the kind of loosely federated empire to which Adam Smith referred. Indeed, Smith himself acknowledged that the success of Britain's colonies was attributable to the easy and wide availability of land and to colonial self-government. By the middle of the eighteenth century, though, British government officials were beginning to notice the by then large and still rapidly growing populations and wealth of the American colonies. They were also becoming increasingly alarmed at the degree of economic and political autonomy the colonies seemed to exercise. By then, they resolved to do something about these problems. In turn, the colonists resolved to resist.[3]

Two views of the imperial constitution

The fact that the colonies were self-created and, in turn, self-governing had profound implications for colonists' views on the constitution of the empire. Because the British constitution was and is unwritten, the nature and extent of the obligations it imposes and the liberties it extends in many cases emerge from happenstances that turned into customs which then became conceptualized as customary rights. In certain circumstances, some even became conceptualized as natural rights. It was in these ways that colonial self-government became the cornerstone of colonists' concept of Britain's imperial constitution. In the 1760s, Stephen Hopkins, a merchant from Providence and sometime governor of Rhode Island, expressed the historical justification of colonial rights as follows: 'To the infinite advantage and emolument of the mother state', migrants had 'left the delights of their native country, parted from their homes and all their conveniences . . . searched out . . . and subdued a foreign country with the most amazing travail and fortitude.' But they retained 'all the rights and privileges of freeborn Englishmen'. Indeed, a condition of their continuing membership of the British Empire was 'that they and their successors forever should be free, should be partakers and sharers in all the privileges and advantages of the then English, now British constitution'. Furthermore, their transplantation had taken place 'at the expence of the planters themselves' and under 'the protection of heaven and their own efforts', not those of the mother country. If the colonists had done all this for themselves, then they earned the right to rule themselves. Colonists thus believed in what they came to call 'diffused sovereignty'. That is, their own representative institutions, the colonial lower houses of assembly, had the exclusive right to rule within their own domains. These assemblies were, in the view of colonists, local equivalents of the English or British House of Commons. The British crown and parliament had the right to legislate for the empire as a whole, in matters such as intercolonial trade and imperial defence, but not on domestic matters within the colonies. As Hopkins allegedly declared in 1757, 'the King and Parliament had no more right to make laws for us than the Mohawks'. The imperial connection thus consisted of common allegiance to the crown and common enjoyment of the rights of freeborn Englishmen or Britons.[4]

The likes of Edmund Burke notwithstanding, most metropolitans saw things rather differently. Some even denied the very history upon which the colonists' concept of empire was based. Charles Lloyd, secretary to George Grenville, the first minister who introduced the Sugar and Stamp Acts in 1764, wrote that 'the Americans, under the shade and protection of Great-Britain, have made rapid advances in population, commerce and wealth'. Charles Townshend, president of the Board of Trade in 1763, chancellor of the exchequer in the government of William Pitt from July 1766, and de facto first minister when Pitt's mental health deteriorated later that year, argued that because the English state had founded the colonies to further its own interests, it had the right to 'power and dominion, as well as trade'. Even some who acknowledged early provincial self-government saw it as a political happenstance or a mere exigency of early colonization and not as a customary right or natural right. In 1679, the Lords of Trade, while attempting to impose Poynings' Law on Jamaica and Virginia, argued that the colonies' self-governing pasts were 'temporary and experimental constitutions' that did not represent 'a resignation and devolution to them of the royal authority', and that colonists should not 'regard as a right what was granted as a favour'. Massachusetts governor Thomas Pownall knew perfectly well the history of that colony, yet he wrote in 1768 that colonies were '*mere plantations*, tracts of foreign country, employed in raising certain specified and enumerated commodities, solely for the use of the trade and manufactures of the mother-country'. Pownall's views were extreme, or at least the bluntness of his expression of them was, and he made this statement at a time of particularly intense conflict between colonists and British government. But he nevertheless represented an old and widely shared mercantilist belief that the colonies should serve the economic interests of the mother country and an equally deep constitutional conviction that the colonies were politically subordinate to the mother country.[5]

Colonists' and British officials' interpretations of the imperial constitution were, clearly, entirely incompatible and represent what historian Jack P. Greene has called a 'latent dysfunction' at the heart of the early empire. As Greene also says, the reason the dysfunction remained latent was that English and British authorities did not push their mercantilist or their constitutional claims too far, at least before 1764. There were, broadly, four distinct periods of imperial relations between 1607 and 1763. From the founding of Virginia in 1607 to the passing of the first Navigation Act in 1651, English authorities barely had anything to do with the fledgling colonies, and it was during this time that habits of self-government set in. From 1651 to 1721, there were various attempts to impose imperial authority upon the colonies, although imperial intervention waxed and waned during these years, peaking in the later part of the reign of Charles II from 1675 and through the reign of James II to 1688. Edmund Burke memorably labelled the period from 1721 to 1748 – the premiership of Robert Walpole and the six-year power vacuum that followed his fall – one of 'wise and salutary neglect'. Finally, in 1748, the more interventionist Henry Pelham became first minister and he gave his blessing to more activist administrators at the Southern Department and the Board of Trade. This new imperialism, in part inspired by the aforementioned growing population and wealth of the colonies, was undermined by the necessities of the French and Indian War, but one of the products of that war was a renewed determination in Britain to impose imperial authority in the recalcitrant colonies. Moreover, this time parliament would be the initiator of efforts at economic and political reforms, aimed at creating the kind of corporate or unitary empire that imperialists had long envisioned.[6]

One of the problems of imperial governance before 1763, and even in the period 1651 to 1721, was the lack of coordination between the different bodies that exercised various forms of authority in the empire. Within the colonies, there were governors, councillors (who usually formed the upper houses of legislatures) and other executive officers, though the power to appoint some of those other officers remained in the hands of authorities at home, depriving governors of patronage powers. From home, the Treasury ran the customs system and appointed its officers. The Admiralty policed and enforced the Navigation Acts. The secretary of state for the Southern Department was the Cabinet office that had power of political oversight of the colonies, although where its responsibilities ended and those of the Privy Council began was not always clear. Various committees, most notably the Lords of Trade (1675 to 1685) and then the Board of Trade (1696 to 1782), reported to and recommended actions to the Privy Council. At certain times, also, monarchs, especially the later Stuarts, attempted to meddle in imperial and colonial affairs. And then there was parliament, which regulated intercolonial trade but which otherwise largely left the colonies alone, much to the frustration of imperialist reformers at the Lords and Board of Trade.

From 1764, however, parliament finally began making sustained efforts to reform the empire, inspiring a series of rebellions that eventuated in the American Revolution. That, though, is the subject of the next chapter. This one is about imperial relations from 1607 to 1763, and it focuses on how the two different and incompatible views of empire evolved and coexisted in the context of the changing nature of imperial relations during that time.

The origins of colonial self-government, 1607–1651

The origins of colonial claims to political autonomy lay in the manner of their founding by private companies and proprietors and, in turn, in the appropriation of colonial polities, economies, societies and cultures by the settlers who turned the colonies into viable entities. The first significant colonial claim for self-government came during the first meeting of the Virginia assembly in 1619. That meeting petitioned the Virginia Company to guarantee that no London-made company laws would take effect in Virginia unless ratified by the House of Burgesses. This claim was met with the first British concession to colonial self-government, albeit a private one, for the company accepted the petition in 1621. After the abolition of the Virginia Company in 1624, governor Lord Mandeville sent John Pory and John Harvey as commissioners to the colony. The assembly presented the two men with an account of the maladministration of governors under the *Lawes Divine Morall and Martial*, a 'Brief Declaration' asserting its own right to exist and an ordinance declaring that 'the governor shall not lay any taxes or impositions upon the colony, their lands or commodities other than by the authority of the general assembly'. The first actions of the first assemblies of Virginia thus reflected the kinds of legislative rights that Jacobean parliaments were petitioning for at exactly the same time, stoking the controversy that would soon engulf England and then the British Isles in civil war. They also set the agenda, albeit unknowingly, on which American colonists would rebel and then revolt against Britain a century and half later.

In 'A Proclamation for Settlinge the Plantations of Virginia' of 13 May 1625, which made Virginia a royal colony, the crown threatened this already firmly established principle of Virginian and colonial self-government by stating its intention to settle 'one uniforme Course of Government' in the burgeoning empire. Yet colonial self-government continued. Sir Francis Wyatt, the first royal governor of Virginia, pragmatically sought assemblymen's opinions, and in any case had at his disposal no administrators to advise him or soldiers to support him. Charles I gave his consent to the existence of the general assembly until 1639, when, despite a decade of ruling without parliament at home, he explicitly authorized Wyatt to summon the burgesses 'as formerly once a year or oftener, if urgent occasion shall require it'. Sir William Berkeley's commission as Wyatt's successor stated that the assembly 'together with the governor and council shall have power to make acts and laws for the government of that plantation, correspondent as near as may be to the laws of England'.[7]

Other contemporaneous threats to colonial autonomy were similarly warded off because of various political expediencies and other contingencies. The sub-patenting of Massachusetts by the Council of New England to John Winthrop's puritans, for example, invited crown suspicion. In 1634, the Privy Council created a committee to examine the colony and disbanded the Council of New England. Furthermore, Charles I issued a writ of *quo warranto*, requiring the Massachusetts Bay Company to justify its jurisdiction, and appointed Fernando Gorges as, in effect, royal governor. Gorges cried off, citing his age, and the writ was never delivered. Soon thereafter the king found himself too preoccupied fighting parliament for his own authority to worry about Massachusetts.

The chaos of civil wars throughout the British Isles between 1642 and 1651 allowed habits of self-government to develop yet further, although the highly unregulated state of affairs that colonists took advantage of ultimately attracted the attention of interregnum and Restoration authorities. In 1643, for example, parliament appointed the puritan Earl of Warwick to head a commission on colonies and trade, and he reported the provinces to be ungovernable. The execution of Charles I in 1649 brought matters to a head, as Antigua, Barbados, Bermuda, Virginia and Maryland declared allegiance to Charles's son, but the restoration of peace throughout most of the British Isles allowed the Commonwealth and Protectorate to negotiate and occasionally enforce political relations that were more suitable to England. In 1652, the Council of State sent a fleet with a new governor to Barbados to enforce acceptance of its rule and to reorganize local government, although Barbados kept its assembly and even its exemption from the Navigation Acts that allowed it to trade with friendly foreign nations. Virginia accepted the Protectorate, but was able to keep its assembly. In Maryland, the civil wars were replicated by puritan revolutions against the Catholic proprietor in 1655 and 1658, although Cromwell restored Lord Baltimore in 1657 and Charles II confirmed his proprietary rights in 1660. By this time, though, metropolitan concern about provincial economic and political autonomy was prompting imperial authorities to subject the colonies to more systematic oversight.

The navigation system

Before and during the civil wars, colonists traded with whomever it suited them to trade with, in particular the Dutch. The Dutch rivalled the threat to English interests posed by France and Spain in the West Indies, and exceeded it on the mainland through their presence in New Netherland. Parliament therefore began constructing the navigation system that a century or so later free-trade critics would call 'mercantilist'. This system, a set of navigation laws designed to ensure that colonial trade benefited the mother country and not its rivals, became a crucial part of the fabric of empire. Indeed, considering the extent of political autonomy that the colonies possessed, if the empire existed in anything more than an imaginary sense then it was as a maritime empire, a sea-born trading network. However, colonists resented and often evaded the navigation laws, prompting English and British authorities to attempt to exercise greater political oversight of the colonies.

In 1651, Cromwell's Rump Parliament passed a Navigation Ordnance that declared the colonies subordinate to parliament, limited the carrying of goods to and from the Americas to English or colonial ships and required that ships' masters and three out of four of their crew be English (the Scots were not allowed to trade freely in the empire until the 1707 Act of Union). The Act also identified 'enumerated articles' that could only be exported by colonists to other colonies or else to England from where they would be re-exported, to the benefit of crown coffers and English merchant middlemen. Enumerated articles initially included the most valuable colonial commodity staples of tobacco, sugar, ginger and dyes, though the list was extended from time to time later. The Ordnance was revived as a Navigation Act at the Restoration of Charles II in 1660, at the behest of a king who saw an opportunity to make himself slightly more financially independent of parliament.

The Staple Act of 1663 forbade colonists from importing goods that had not been produced in England or carried from English ports, giving English merchants a monopoly of exports to colonies just as the Navigation Act established an English monopoly of exports from colonies (the act excluded servants, horses and provisions from Ireland and Scotland, wine from Madeira and the Azores and salt for the northern fisheries). Finally, the Plantation Duties Act of 1673 closed a loophole in the developing navigation system by requiring that enumerated articles exported from colony to colony be taxed within the colonies – a measure aimed primarily at New Englanders. Within five years, English customs officers were collecting revenues throughout the empire, or in some cases collecting bribes from colonists who wished to evade the taxes. In 1696, after the overthrow of James II in the Glorious Revolution of 1688, a new Navigation Act codified all of the above, added the requirement that ships involved in colonial commerce had to be registered as well as built in England or the colonies, obliged governors and other officials to swear to uphold the navigation system or else forfeit bonds of £1000, created Admiralty courts (with no juries) to enforce the navigation system, authorized customs officials to use warrants known as 'writs of assistance' to board and search ships suspected of carrying smuggled goods and declared invalid colonial laws that conflicted with English trade laws. This system remained in place until 1849.

Although the Navigation Acts were only intermittently enforced, they reflected a mercantilist notion that the provinces should be of economic benefit to the mother country, even at the expense of the colonies themselves, and thus represented the beginnings of a corporate or unitary notion of empire. This idea informed later trade laws too. The 1699 Woollen Act protected English textile manufacturers and merchants by limiting the sale of colonial finished woollen products to local markets. Similarly, the Hat Act of 1732 and the Iron Act of 1750 protected domestic producers at the expense of colonial ones by prohibiting colonial exports of these products. A 1705 Naval Stores Act was designed to encourage production of supplies and to reserve North American pine trees for use as masts in the hope of reducing English dependence on the Baltic for naval stores. If the interests of colonists collided with those of other colonists, then the wealthier and often London-residing sugar planters of the West Indies gained the advantage over North American mainlanders. In 1733, parliament passed the Molasses Act, placing a prohibitive sixpence per gallon duty on raw sugar, rum and molasses imported from the French West Indies, where sugar was produced more cheaply and from where New England rum makers in particular purchased their raw materials. There were occasions when colonists got what they wanted, as South Carolina rice planters did in 1730, when they persuaded parliament to allow them to export directly to southern Europe. They gained again in 1748, when parliament established a bounty of sixpence per pound for indigo production. Crucially, though, on both occasions they had support from interested parties in Britain: rice merchants in 1730 and woollens manufacturers who needed dyes in 1748.

Colonists objected that the Navigation Acts would lower prices for their commodities at the same time as raising taxes, pinching their profits at both ends. Yet their objections were not merely based on economic self-interest, although their material interests happily coincided with their political principles. When Edward Randolph asked the assemblymen of Massachusetts in 1676 to enforce the Navigation Acts, they told him that 'laws made by your Majesty and your Parliament obligeth' them 'in nothing but what consists with the interests of that colony; that the legislative power is and abides in them solely to act and make laws by virtue' of their royal charter. Massachusetts was not alone in arguing for its trade rights on the grounds of political principle. In 1675, Virginians requested a colonial charter guaranteeing their rights as free Englishmen; the Jamaican Assembly's 1677 Bill of Privileges demanded that their rights be regarded as equal to those of all Englishmen, as did the New York Assembly's Charter of Libertyes in 1683. In the wake of the English Bill of Rights of 1689, Virginia, Maryland, Massachusetts, New York and South Carolina passed similar declarations in attempts to gain explicit parliamentary recognition of colonists' claims to their rights. Edward Littleton, a Barbadian planter, published a pamphlet unambiguously entitled *The Groans of the Plantations* (1689), in which he elevated free trade to a matter of natural rights. Before the Navigation Acts, he wrote, 'we were under the pleasing sound of Priviledges and Immunities, of which a free Trade was one, though we counted That, a Right and not a Priviledge', adding that 'without such Encouragements, the Plantations had been still wild Woods'. Through the Navigation Acts, however, colonists were '*commanded as Subjects . . . crusht as Aliens*. Which condition is the most dismal and horrid, that people can be under.'[8]

Nevertheless, in the main, colonists accommodated themselves to the navigation system. Benjamin Franklin even conceded that the right of parliament to enact the navigation laws was as great as the right of colonial assemblies to exclusive jurisdiction within their own domains. He told parliament in 1766 that 'the sea is yours'. 'You maintain, by your fleets', he continued, 'the safety of navigation in it, and keep it clear of pirates; you may have therefore a natural and equitable right to some toll or duty on merchandizes carried through that part of your dominions.' For others, accommodation to the Navigation Acts was more about expediency than principle. Some saw that a closed system of trade gave them what amounted to a monopoly over potential foreign competitors in English markets. In any case, the Navigation Acts were difficult to enforce and colonists ignored them when they could. Only Carolinians responded with any enthusiasm to the naval stores acts, while New Englanders felled trees reserved for masts for their own purposes whenever they wanted to. Traders routinely evaded the Molasses Act through bribes of 1 to 1½ pence to customs officers. If traders were caught and tried for evading taxes, local juries often acquitted them because they liked the cheaper goods that smuggling guaranteed.[9]

The Lords of Trade, James II and the empire, 1676–1689

Faced with colonists' objections to and evasions of trade laws, English authorities sensed a need for closer political oversight of the empire. Those authorities had already experimented with various forms of imperial bureaucracy. As early as 1625 there was a Privy Council subcommittee on trade, and a Commission for the Plantations sat between 1634 and 1641. There was also, during the same period, a Committee of Trade, then a Council of Trade from 1650 to 1653, a variety of trade-inspecting subcommittees during the rest of the interregnum and a Council for Trade and Plantations from 1660 to 1665. Then there was another Council of Trade and a Council for Plantations, respectively created in 1668 and 1670, which were combined in 1672 as the Council of Foreign Plantations and given an annual budget of £7400. This was the immediate precursor to the Lords of Trade, which became a longer-lasting and much more purposeful imperial administrator. In the royal colonies of Virginia, Jamaica, Barbados and the Leeward Islands, the Lords gave governors broader and more detailed instructions and demanded that they report back regularly on the progress of implementation. The Lords also attempted to make the governors of Virginia and Jamaica more independent from their legislatures by insisting that the assemblies vote for a permanent revenue for the salaries of governors and their officers and for the ordinary expenses of government (as Barbados and the Leeward Islands had already done in 1663 and 1664). Virginia agreed a levy of two shillings per hogshead on exported tobacco, but Jamaica refused. The Lords also applied Poynings' Law to these colonies, insisting that their legislative bills require crown approval and asserting that those legislatures existed at crown discretion, not as of right.

The Lords also attempted to turn private colonies into crown ones and to prevent the creation of any new private colonies. The creation of Pennsylvania as the proprietorship of William Penn in 1681 represented a setback for imperial hardliners, although Penn had fewer chartered priveleges than previous proprietors. On the other hand, the Lords and Privy Council issued writs of *quo warranto* requiring the proprietors of the Carolinas, Connecticut, Maryland, Massachusetts, New Jersey, Pennsylvania and Rhode Island to justify their authority. Furthermore, the New Hampshire towns were separated from Massachusetts and made a crown colony in 1679. But, as Edward Randolph recommended, the main target was the virtually independent and virulently anti-Catholic colony of Massachusetts. When hardliners in the colony persuaded the majority to ignore the writ of *quo warranto*, they gave British authorities the pretext they needed to revoke the charter and make Massachusetts a crown colony in 1684. Bermuda became a crown colony the same year.

The following year, James II acceded to the English throne and subsequently abolished the Lords of Trade and attempted a more direct form of crown government in the colonies. New York ceased to be a proprietary and became a crown colony by virtue of James's accession in 1685. But the king extended his direct jurisdiction hugely. His most significant action in the colonies was to create the Dominion of New England, a giant entity that included all of New England and eventually New York and the Jerseys. Had James II not been overthrown in the Glorious Revolution of 1688, he would most likely have followed an earlier Lords of Trade recommendation that other colonies be amalgamated into similar Spanish-style imperial vice-regencies.

Tempered imperialism, 1689–1721

Imperial impositions were more tempered after the Glorious Revolution, but administrators nevertheless pushed hard for enforcement of the Navigation Acts and political reform. The overthrown Dominion of New

England was not revived, but in 1691 Massachusetts received a new charter that significantly enhanced the power of the governor in relation to the
assembly and, more fundamentally, that broke forever the covenant
between puritan New Englanders and their God. Massachusetts gained
from its absorption of Plymouth Colony, although some of the descendants
of the Pilgrims were less than pleased. In 1692, the crown took over
Pennsylvania, but then gave it back to William Penn two years later. The
Calverts lost Maryland, though that had more to do with domestic religious and political struggles and the Calverts' Catholicism than with royal
ambitions to gain control of the colony's affairs. The Calverts eventually
got their colony back when Benedict Leonard Calvert became the fourth
Lord Baltimore and converted to Anglicanism in 1715.

   During these years, furthermore, administrators made serious attempts
to reform colonial trade and politics and thereby create a more coherent
empire. In 1696, a new institution, the Lords Commissioners of Trade and
Plantations, commonly known as the Board of Trade, was created with
more or less the same responsibilities as the old Lords of Trade. The Board
also faced more or less the same problems as the Lords, complaining in the
first year of its existence, the eighth year of the Nine Years War, that the
colonies 'refuse each other mutual assistance, minding more their present
profit than the common defence'. The Board consequently attempted to
amalgamate some jurisdictions and make colonies act more in accordance
with the interests of each other and of England, albeit unsystematically and
only temporarily. In the 1690s, Sir William Phips governed Massachusetts
while simultaneously controlling the militias of the other royal colonies of
Connecticut, New Hampshire and Rhode Island. In 1698, Lord Bellomont
was governor of New York, Massachusetts and New Hampshire and controlled the militias of Connecticut, New Jersey and Rhode Island as well.[10]

   The Board tried even harder to deal with the more general underlying
problem of the independent behaviour of the private colonies. In March
1701, the Board recommended the forfeiture of all colonial charters, noting
in addition the particular problems constantly complained of by governors
that none of the charter colonies had ever fulfilled the imperial purposes
'for which such large tracts of land, and such privileges and immunities
were granted'. It therefore recommended that the private colonies be 'put
into the same state of dependency as those of your Majestie's other
Plantations' and, moreover, that this be done 'by the Legislative power of
this Kingdom'. Calling on parliament to pass laws affecting the private
colonies' constitutions was new and its significance can hardly be overstated. Colonists already subscribed to the view that parliament had a
general supervisory authority over imperial matters such as war and intercolonial and international trade, but had no right to intervene in the internal affairs of colonies, much less to determine modes of colonial
governance. In accord with colonists' belief in their right to govern them-

selves, these matters belonged within the remit of their own provincial assemblies. As Governor Sir William Beeston of Jamaica reported to the Board of Trade in 1701, colonial assemblymen believed 'that what a House of Commons could do in England, they could do here, and that during their sitting all power and authority was only in their hands'. Fortunately for the colonies, and perhaps fortunately for peaceful relations within the empire too, especially after the beginning of Queen Anne's War, parliament rejected the Board's recommendations in 1701, and then again in 1702 and 1706.

Between 1688 and 1721, numerous domestic and international matters kept parliament and monarchs more distracted from colonial affairs than they might have been otherwise. After the civil wars and the political instabilities and crises that followed, it was imperative that the settlement following the Glorious Revolution worked, and William and Mary and their parliaments paid due attention to this matter. There was still the legacy of the Stuarts to worry about, especially as James II invaded Ireland in 1690 and his son invaded Scotland in 1715. These were not the only issues of succession to cause concern. William and Mary had no children and Princess Anne's only living child, William, Duke of Gloucester, died on 30 July 1700, leading to a preoccupation with the Act of Succession of 1701 and with ensuring the accession of the House of Hanover when Anne died in 1714. In the meantime, the politics of Queen Anne's reign were blighted by party conflict as intense as anything seen since the Whigs and Tories first emerged during the attempts to exclude James, Duke of York from the throne between 1679 and 1683. Also during Anne's reign there were complex negotiations between the English and the Scots over the Act of Union that abolished the Scottish Parliament and created a politically unified Britain in 1707. The international scene was unfavourable too. The overthrow of James and accession of William set England at conflict with France in the Nine Years War of 1688–97, shortly followed by Queen Anne's War, or the War of the Spanish Succession, of 1702–13.

In the imperial power vacuum thereby created, provincial self-government extended itself further and further, as colonial governors constantly complained. Lord Cornbury, governor of New York, wrote that 'as the Country increases' colonists 'grow saucy, and noe doubt but if they were allowed to goe on, they will improve upon it'. Robert Hunter wrote to the Board in 1712 that the colonists of New Jersey were determined 'to make themselves an independent people, and to that end . . . to divest the administration . . . of all the Queen's power and authority and to lodge it in the Assembly'. The same year Robert Lowther in Barbados noted that

> This project hath been a long time on foot and a great progress hath been made in it, for they have extorted so many powers from my predecessors, that there is hardly enough left to keep the peace, much less to maintain the decent respect and regard that is due to the Queen's servant.[11]

The 1713 Treaty of Utrecht introduced an interlude of peace between the European powers that might have allowed attentions to turn to the colonies. However, it proved difficult enough to get George I, after his accession in 1714, interested in British domestic affairs, the more so imperial ones, as opposed to those of Hanover. Also, in the early Hanoverian years, the collapse of the South Sea Bubble speculative frenzy and its economic and political fallout distracted the attentions of many parliamentarians. In 1720, though, crown advisors responded to the rebellion against the South Carolina proprietors by asking the Board for recommendations for reforming government in all the colonies. The Board responded by proposing comprehensive economic and political management, but once again its urgings went largely unheeded.

'Salutary neglect', 1721–1748

Hitherto, governments had neglected the colonies because of other preoccupations, but when Robert Walpole became first minister in 1721, laissez-faire government became a principle of policy. Indeed, the kind of hands-off administration that Walpole adopted within Britain, his colonial administrators adopted across the empire. As Charles Delafaye, secretary to the lords justices, wrote to Governor Francis Nicholson regarding the governor's relationship with colonists in South Carolina in 1722: 'One would not Strain any Point where it can be of no Service to our King and Country, and will Create Enemys to one's Self.' Under the Walpole premiership from 1721 to 1742, therefore, the colonies enjoyed a period of what Edmund Burke would later call 'wise and salutary neglect'.

Nevertheless, the Board of Trade attempted even in Walpole's years to find means to uphold trade laws and to enforce imperial political authority. The aforementioned Hat Act (1732) and Molasses Act (1733) represented efforts at economic management, although they were both passed after lobbying by special interest groups. The implementation of royal rule in the Carolinas in 1729 was an attempt at political management, although, again, circumstances rather forced administrators' hands. Otherwise, appeals for assistance by colonial officials on the ground fell on deaf ears in England. In 1723, Governor Samuel Shute travelled to England to plead with the Board because the Massachusetts Assembly showed 'little or no defference to any opinion or orders . . . from the Ministry at Home', but the Board could do little because parliament declined to intervene. Soon, governors lost even the little support they had from the Board. In 1729, the next governor of Massachusetts, William Burnet, requested that the Board ask parliament to force the assembly to vote him a permanent revenue, but the secretary of state for the Southern Department, Thomas Pelham-Hollis, the Duke of Newcastle, was unwilling to take 'things to that extremity'. Hitherto, colonial ministers and bureaucrats had been dedicated if often frustrated characters. But, as secretary from 1724 to 1746, Newcastle turned the Southern Department into a little empire of his own, dispensing patronage for political favours and with little regard for effective administration in the larger empire overseas. Indeed, by controlling patronage himself, he deprived governors of the opportunity to create power bases of their own within the colonies and thereby to govern more effectively. By 1746, Newcastle controlled 92 colonial 'patent offices', many of them held by men who worked with assemblies against governors. How frustrating this was is clear in the complaint of Lieutenant-Governor William Gooch of Virginia: 'how despicable the governor of a province must be when stript of the Power of disposing of the few places that fall within his Government, and how little serviceable to the Crown, when deprived of the only means of rewarding Merit and creating Influence'. The best that most governors could hope for in these circumstances was to become political managers rather than executives or representatives of royal power. Indeed, many governors opted barely to govern at all, leaving most business to the houses of assembly. What Jack P. Greene has called the 'domestication of the governors' still further advanced colonists' habits of autonomy. Lord Monson, President of the Board of Trade from 1737 to 1748, was similarly ineffective, and by 1748 colonial governors were writing to each other in dismay, as Cadwallader Colden did to George Clinton, that officials in England were 'too busily employ'd another way to mind Such Trifles' as colonial affairs.[12]

Even in these years of salutary neglect, British politicians did consider if only briefly how they might bring the colonies under better order. In 1734, the House of Lords considered but did not propose a bill to give the crown a veto on colonial laws, and in 1744 and 1749 the House of Commons considered making royal instructions to governors legally binding, but again backed down. In the event, the only major parliamentary political intervention in the empire was the creation and financing of the colonization of Georgia in 1732. Although the charter directed that Georgia would become a royal colony after 21 years (it actually did so in 1751), the fact that it was initially a proprietary under General James Oglethorpe and 20 trustees indicated, once again, that colonization was a private business. The fact that proprietors' plans gave way to settlers' ambitions also reinforced customs of colonial self-government and the notions of customary and natural rights that developed with the practice.

A new imperialism, 1748–1754

In the 1740s, however, the growth of colonial populations, wealth and trade noted at the beginning of this chapter was becoming increasingly apparent. With that came a growing awareness that colonial economic and political autonomy meant that Britain was gaining less from the empire than it might have done. Gubernatorial power had become virtually non-existent in many colonies and factionalism put an end even to legislative authority in New Hampshire and North Carolina, and caused civil war to break out in New Jersey. Governor Lewis Morris of the latter colony was still only one of several governors who felt that 'The too great and unwarrantable encroachment of the Assemblies make it necessary that a stop some way or other should be put to them, and they reduced to such propper and legall bounds as is consistent with his majestie's Prerogative and their dependence.' In the late 1740s, then, the Board of Trade developed a more activist kind of imperialism once again. In 1746, the Duke of Bedford took over the Southern Department from the lackadaisical Duke of Newcastle, and when Lord Monson died in 1748 Bedford took the opportunity to appoint George Dunk, Earl of Halifax, in Monson's place. Newcastle had lobbied for his brother-in-law, the Duke of Leeds, a man much like Monson, but Bedford considered it 'Highly improper, considering the present Situation of things, to have a nonefficient Man at the head of that Board'.

Halifax, president of the Board from 1748 to 1761, was not a 'nonefficient' man, though he still could not bring the colonies sufficiently to heel. In 1748 he persuaded parliament to vote substantial sums to secure Nova Scotia as a British colony. Though the province had been a British possession since 1713, it was still economically underdeveloped and demographically predominantly French. He also had prepared a series of reports and recommendations 'to revise the Constitutions of the Settlements abroad' and 'to regulate them, that they may be usefull to, & not rival in Power and Trade their Mother Kingdom'. Although he failed in a bid to have his office converted into that of a secretary of state, he did get the Board's powers significantly enhanced. His practical efforts consisted primarily in pressuring governors to control the assemblies, revise their colonies' laws, and 'strictly to adhere to your instructions and not to deviate from them in any point but upon evident necessity justified by the particular Circumstances of the case'. He also required them to report regularly and organized a packet boat system for that purpose.[13]

Like previous industrious administrators, however, Halifax was largely disappointed with his results, especially once the French and Indian War of 1754–63 necessitated the end of political reform and once again offered colonial assemblymen opportunities to extract political concessions from governors in return for wartime appropriations. The Board of Trade, the Privy Council and others made some piecemeal attempts at reform during the war. In 1754, for example, the Board and the Privy Council upheld Virginia Governor Robert Dinwiddie's 'Pistole Fee', a hefty 16 shillings and 10 pence levy for issuing land grants. The burgesses made the usual kind of colonial complaint about the governor's greed and corruption, admonishing the imperial authorities with the warning that 'If your Lordships do not restrain [such] officers within due bounds, they will abuse their authority.' Dinwiddie's lawyer's response was that 'the king is absolute proprietor of these lands' and 'may act by his substitute'. The Board also persuaded the Privy Council to veto Virginia's 1758 Two Penny Act. This act of price-fixing was the burgesses' response to a drought that had caused the price of tobacco to rise to 4½ pence per pound, which, because tobacco certificates were used as a form of exchange in the Chesapeake, augured serious inflation. Among the main losers from the act were Anglican clergymen, who were paid in certificates of quantities of tobacco that were now worth much less than they might have been. With the backing of the Board and the Privy Council, from 1759 the clerics started suing their vestries for back payment. The 'Parsons' Cases' were lost causes, however, because the juries were made up of Virginia colonists who supported their assembly's anti-inflationary measure. The cases brought to prominence a young lawyer named Patrick Henry, who argued in *Reverend James Maury* v. *Fredericksville Parish* in December 1762 that only a tyrant would disallow the acts of a colonial assembly. Henry would become a leading light of the revolution in Virginia.[14]

There was even more trouble in Massachusetts. In 1760, the general court passed an act setting the fees of imperial officials without the 'clause of suspension' that prevented the act becoming law until approved by the Privy Council. The Board attempted to intervene by forcing the general court to include a suspension clause in all its legislation. The general court objected on the grounds that English liberties could only be secured through bodies to which men gave their consent. In other words, only the general court and not the English parliament or any other body could make law in Massachusetts. The same year saw the beginnings of the writs of assistance controversy. As these warrants to search ships for smuggled goods were issued under the authority of the king, after the death of George II in 1760 Massachusetts customs officials requested that the superior court of judicature issue new ones. Chief Justice Stephen Sewall refused to issue any until a full meeting of the court ruled whether his court or vice-admiralty courts had the authority to issue such writs. Sewall subsequently died, and Governor Francis Bernard appointed Thomas Hutchinson in his place, much to the chagrin of James Otis of Barnstaple, who had been promised the post by previous governors William Shirley and Thomas Pownall. Subsequently, Oxenbridge Thacher argued against the writs on the technical grounds that they were too general and not specific for Massachusetts, but future revolutionary firebrand James Otis, Jr., son of the snubbed Otis of Barnstaple, added the assertion that parliament had no right to issue the writs because its supremacy did not extend to violating the rights of freeborn Englishmen through illegal searches and seizures. The court hesitated in the face of Otis's radical arguments, initially requesting clarification from England and only later ruling the writs legal. That delay was enough to destroy the authority of the writs as legal instruments in Massachusetts from thereon in.

Tensions between mother country and Massachusetts had a religious dimension to them too. Henry Caner, Anglican Vicar of Boston's King's Chapel, persuaded Archbishop of Canterbury Thomas Secker of the need to advance the cause of Anglicanism in the puritan colony. One means of doing so was building Christ Church, Cambridge, in 1761, in sight of Harvard College, where the colony trained its Congregationalist ministers. Another was to persuade the Privy Council to disallow general court legislation that impeded the activities among the Indians of the Anglican Society for the Propagation of the Gospel. The veto of 1763 triggered a newspaper controversy in which Boston Congregationalist minister Jonathan Mayhew raised the spectre of an American bishopric, the alleged possibility of which continued to poison imperial politics in Massachusetts until Independence.

The Board's and others' attempts to enforce imperial law and will in the colonies during the French and Indian War were therefore patchy, ineffective and, in some instances, alienating and counter-productive. Only after the war would the Board be able to resume systematic efforts at reform. That conflict, though, would help the Board convince hitherto reluctant MPs that they must throw the full weight of parliament behind their endeavours.

The French and Indian War and its consequences, 1754–1763

The beginnings of the French and Indian War in 1754 illustrate the growing importance of colonies and empire in London's view of Britain's interests. Previous wars between European powers had their American theatres and indeed some began in the colonies. The War of Jenkins' Ear that turned into the War of the Austrian Succession (1739–48), or King George's War, began with outrage at the removal of a British ship's captain's ear, for alleged smuggling, by Spanish West Indian authorities. As historian Eliga H. Gould has said, however, as that war progressed it became more about the balance of power in Europe than anything imperial.

The French and Indian War, on the other hand, marked a new British isolationism from Europe and the rise of a new 'blue water' policy of imperial conquest. The war began in the forests of the north-west of North America and became, as contemporaries put it, a 'great war for empire' in which Britain expelled the French from Canada, Senegambia, India and, temporarily, Guadeloupe and Martinique, and the Spanish from Florida. At the beginning of the war, Newcastle was said to have responded to the new French threats in North America with a sarcastic tirade: 'Annapolis, Annapolis! oh! yes, Annapolis must be defended; to be sure Annapolis should be defended – where is Annapolis?' The story illustrated the patronizing disdain for provincials that remained a part of metropolitan political culture, but it also demonstrated Newcastle's out-of-date and out-of-touch attitude towards the importance of empire. A more typical attitude at the time was that of commentator John Shebbeare, who argued that 'whatever is expended in the Defence of English plantations, returns to England again'. According to J. Payne's *The French Encroachments Exposed*, 'what money is laid out in this way . . . will return to us with Double interest'.[15]

The 1748 Treaty of Aix-la-Chapelle had left open the question of whether the Ohio River valley belonged to British North America or French Canada, but within five years that issue could no longer be set aside. After 1748, the French built a line of forts southwards from the Great Lakes, including forts Le Beouf and Machault on the Allegheny River and Fort Duquesne where the Allegheny and Monongahela rivers meet, near present-day Pittsburgh. It was this fort, with its location at the forks of the Ohio River, which alarmed the British more than any other, and made even Newcastle determined to push back the French. With Newcastle's blessing, Governor Robert Dinwiddie of Virginia despatched 22-year-old George Washington to demand French withdrawal from the Ohio valley in October 1753; after the French refused, Britain backed attacks on French troops in the north from 1754.

This first phase of the British campaign went extraordinarily badly. Washington lost his Indian scouts and allies after he inadvertently attacked a French diplomatic mission and then, learning his error, alienated his Indian allies by preventing Indian leader Half-King and his warriors from killing the prisoners and collecting their booty. Washington's militiamen were no match for the regulars of the French *troupe de la marine*, backed by their Indian allies, who knew the region's geography and how to fight in it. On 3 July, they attacked Washington and his men at the newly built Fort Necessity, forcing their surrender the following day. Then things got worse. General Edward Braddock had agreed with several colonial governors to attack four forts between the Ohio River and Lake Ontario. On 9 July 1755, Braddock and an advance force of 1373 men were surprised a few miles from Fort Duquesne by a small body of around 630 Indians and 36 French officers and men. Braddock attempted to make his men fight in European formation, only to see them slaughtered by a mobile and all but invisible enemy firing at them from the forest. After two hours, he finally ordered a retreat, but was shot before he could organize it. His men promptly panicked and ran, abandoning the dead and dying by the banks of the Monongahela. The Battle of the Wilderness cost the British the lives of 814 men and 63 out of 86 officers, including Braddock. The French and Indians lost fewer than 50. The defeat prompted a moral as well military ignominy, for the British responded to it by expelling the Acadians from Nova Scotia in September and October 1755. It also inspired the formal declaration of war made by George II in May 1756.

The next winter, the British under John Campbell, Lord Loudoun, built Fort William Henry, at the southern end of Lake George. On 3 August 1757, the French under Count Louis de Montcalm began a siege that forced its surrender six days later. Montcalm guaranteed the British safe passage out of the fort, much to the chagrin of his Indian allies, who expected to extract spoils from the defeated enemy and who attacked 60 or 70 British Americans as they retreated, before the French could becalm them. The story of the massacre was later exaggerated, not least in James Fenimore Cooper's *The Last of the Mohicans*, but did much to encourage the subsequent merciless warfare against France's Indian allies, in particular by Major General James Abercrombie and Lord Jeffrey Amherst.

After the accession of William Pitt as prime minister as well as secretary of state for the Southern Department in June 1757, however, the conflict turned in Britain's favour. Once Pitt put money and men behind the war effort, there was little the French could do. Their army was top class and well led, but with too few habitants and with Indian allies who were unwilling to take on the British in set-piece battles, they were ultimately unable to resist. In the second half of 1758, British soldiers, American militia and their Cherokee allies captured Louisbourg at the mouth of the St Lawrence River, Fort Frontenac, Fort Duquesne and, in November, recaptured Fort Ticonderoga (which the French had captured in July and which they called Fort Carillon). The following July, the French lost Fort Niagara, Lake Champlain and, on 18 September, all of Quebec except Montreal, which finally surrendered on 8 September 1760. The capture of Detroit on 29 November capped the British conquest of French North America. At the Peace of Paris of 10 February 1763, France recognized British possession of Quebec (in return for withdrawal from the sugar islands of Martinique and Guadeloupe) and all American territories east of the Mississippi River (the French retained Louisiana to the west), and Spain ceded East and West Florida to Britain.

Victory in the French and Indian War renewed colonial patriotic feeling towards Britain and the empire. But the British view at the end of the conflict was that colonists had contributed little to the war effort and had in fact impeded it at times. In the early stages of the conflict, no colony complied entirely with Whitehall's requisitions of men and supplies and some, notably Maryland, North Carolina, Pennsylvania and Georgia, contributed very little. British commanders in the field also bemoaned the shortage of equipment provided by colonists, the short terms of militiamen's service and what they saw as the ill-disciplined behaviour of the provincial servicemen under their command. They also resented local citizens who resisted the requisitioning of supplies and the billeting of soldiers, and British officers often could do little against them because local authorities tended to sympathize with them. Furthermore, every assembly took advantage of the wartime emergency to use its money-raising powers to force governors to sign laws that further eroded their prerogatives and violated the Navigation Acts. In particular, assemblies passed paper money laws creating currencies that tended to depreciate in value, to the gain of American debtors and the cost of British creditors. Paper money emissions grew by 355 per cent between 1754 and 1764. Also, colonial evasions of the Navigation Acts were costing the British Treasury around £700,000 per year by the end of the war. When caught, American smugglers claimed to be acting under a flag of truce and exchanging prisoners with the enemy, and even sometimes carried French men with them to make the scam convincing.

For their part, colonists in general resented requisitions and billeting, especially as, in the early years, the American war seemed to be serving no good purpose. Masters so resented their servants being requisitioned for military service without compensation that in Pennsylvania the British army's recruiting officers were arrested, while the assembly formally objected 'to the very great Oppression of the said Masters, and Injury to the Province'. Ordinary soldiers resented being retained longer, sometimes more than a year longer, than their periods of enlistment. Maryland's governor, Horatio Sharpe, warned that 'an Insurrection of the People is likely to ensue'. Colonial officers, members of provincial elites in most cases, deplored the 12 November 1754 War Office directive that gave British officers from the rank of major downwards precedence over American officers of the same rank, and made all British majors of regular forces superior to the highest-ranking Americans.

Mutual resentment diminished somewhat from 1757, however. Pitt, besides stirring patriotic feelings at home and in the colonies with his inspiring oratory, promised to reimburse the assemblies for the costs of raising men, promoted colonial field officers to brevet colonel to exempt them from taking orders from lower-ranking British officers and supplied troops, provincial and British, with superior equipment. The building of new barracks and improvement of supply networks resulted in a diminution of civil disaffection over billeting and requisitioning. At this point the colonists got behind the war, providing in all some 60,000 fighting men in provincial units and another 12,000 who joined British units before the war's end, compared to 21,000 British regulars who fought in the Canadian campaign. The colonies also spent some £2,500,000 on provisions and equipment.[16]

Colonists were proud that the capture of Quebec was a largely American effort and that their contributions in the North American theatre freed British forces to make their distinguished efforts elsewhere in this global conflict. Yet many Britons continued to resent the early underperformance of the colonists. Many also felt aggrieved that even if the colonies had provided men, it was the British who bankrolled them. The Treasury spent £7,500,000 prosecuting the war in American alone, including £1,000,000 reimbursing the colonies for their troops. The cost of the war as a whole was an average £13,700,000 per year. Britain's national debt almost doubled after 1756, reaching £132,600,000 in 1763, with annual interest payments of £5,000,000, despite the fact that land taxes rose to 25 per cent of annual income and governments had imposed regressive excise duties on beer and cider that respectively caused riots in London in 1760 and the West Country in 1763. A further £250,000 would be required annually to station 10,000 troops in Canada and Florida to protect these acquisitions during the first year after the war and 7500 troops thereafter. It seemed only fair to many Britons, ranging from First Minister George Grenville to John Ploughshare, a fictitious Hertfordshire tenant farmer and newspaper correspondent, that colonists themselves should help pay for 'that army which defends them against the savages'.[17]

During the frustrating early years of the French and Indian War, Lord Granville, president of the Privy Council, told Benjamin Franklin, representing Pennsylvania in London, 'you contend that the King's Instructions to his Governors are not Laws, and think yourselves at Liberty to disregard them at your own Discretion'. Granville continued, according to Franklin, 'The King and Council is THE LEGISLATOR of the Colonies; and when his Majesty's Instructions come there, they are the LAW OF THE LAND; they are, said his L—ship, repeating it, the Law of the Land, and as such *ought to be* OBEYED.' This was one of the most strident assertions, in word or deed, of royal authority made by a British official to a colonial for a very long time. Yet by the time the war was over, many in Britain concluded that the colonies were so ungoverned that the full weight of parliamentary authority would finally have to be brought to bear on the American provinces. Royal authority expressed through the Privy Council and governors was no longer considered adequate. As one Board of Trade policy paper of 1763 put it: 'no other Authority than that of the British Parliament' would be 'regarded in the colonys or be able to awe them into acquiescence'.[18]

The Glorious Revolution and the British constitution

The quote is a revealing one, for it demonstrates the enormous regard that Britons had been gradually developing for the authority of parliament since the Glorious Revolution of 1688. When William of Orange invaded England on 5 November 1688 and James II vacillated and then fled to France on 22 December, parliamentarians stepped into the breach. William, European champion of Protestantism and husband of Mary, James's eldest daughter, took executive authority in consultation with informal meetings of lords and former MPs who had already decided that an elected convention would determine the future shape of English government. Only the more extreme Whig members of the convention that met in early 1689 envisioned a constitutional monarchy limited by means of parliamentary sovereignty, but, deliberately or not, the convention nevertheless laid the foundations for this order of things to emerge in subsequent years.

Indeed, the very existence of an elected convention that considered who shall be king and under what conditions was itself of enormous symbolic importance, implying that ultimate power lay with the people. It is true that in practice the options open to the convention were limited. Reinstating James II was unacceptable to too many Englishmen unless he had powers that were so diminished that James would not accept them. A regency of James's son was too risky. In any case, William made it clear that he found these alternatives unacceptable and set conditions on his own acceptance, including one that monarchical authority would rest with him and not with Mary. Nevertheless, the 6 February offer of the throne to William marked a significant moment in British constitutional history. William did not consider his accession to the throne as being subject to contractual obligations, and Tories believed for another generation in the divine right of kings, but the events of 1688 and 1689 were nevertheless significant moments in England's progress towards parliamentary supremacy and limited monarchy. The simultaneous publication of a Declaration (later Bill) of Rights that listed the unacceptable misdeeds of the previous king, and that asserted the necessity of free elections, frequent parliaments and other liberties, further promoted the message that parliament was the repository for and the guardian of the rights of free Englishmen.

Although William and Mary and even Anne retained considerable prerogative powers, parliament accrued increasing control over the monarchy during their reigns. The Bill of Rights directed that parliament should meet 'frequently'. In practice, it met annually. First, MPs pushed for a legislative guarantee of frequent elections. After unsuccessful attempts in 1689, 1693 and 1694, parliament finally overcame William's resistance and passed a Triennial Act on a second attempt in 1694. This guarantee of elections every three years represented a major restriction of the crown's prerogative power to dissolve parliament. The Septennial Act of 1716 stretched the maximum period between parliaments to seven years, though that certainly did not undermine the principle of guaranteed meetings of parliament. The Elections Act of 1696 attempted to ensure the 'free' elections that the Declaration of Rights called for, though it did not entirely eliminate intimidation, bribery and treating. Place Bills in 1692, 1694, 1699 and 1701 removed land tax collectors, salt duty commissioners and customs and excise officers from the House of Commons, thereby limiting the number of placemen and restricting crown patronage in the House of Commons, even if the monarch continued to exert sufficient patronage power to control the House of Lords. Though dating to Commonwealth days, parliamentary committees grew in number and strengthened in importance after 1689, enhancing legislative oversight of executive action. In turn, executive oversight of the legislature diminished. The crown retained the right to veto parliamentary legislation, but only used it rarely and did not use it at all after 1708.

The Act of Settlement of 1701 further enhanced parliamentary power.

That act is best remembered today for excluding Catholics from the throne, re-enforcing the intolerance of the 1689 Toleration Act that allowed freedom of worship for Protestant dissenters but not for Catholics. Even that measure, though, however illiberal it may now seem, represented a powerful assertion of parliamentary control over the monarchy. These acts also represented, according to contemporary Protestant sensibilities, victories for a liberty-loving religion over papist absolutism. Furthermore, after the experience of King William's War and with the throne due to devolve on the Elector of Hanover after the putative reign of Anne, the Act of Settlement directed that parliament's permission be granted before military forces were committed to protect any foreign king's overseas possessions, a major and novel incursion on executive control of foreign policy. The act also forbade monarchs from going overseas without parliamentary consent, although this provision was not enforced and in 1716 was repealed. It also excluded foreigners from membership of parliament and the Privy Council, from receiving civil and military posts and land grants (especially foreign ones) – further limiting patronage opportunities of kings – and excluded all placemen from parliament, though, again, this provision was not enforced and was replaced by the less prohibitive Regency Act of 1706. More significantly, the crown was forbidden from removing judges without parliamentary consent.

Furthermore, the near continuous state of warfare between 1689 and 1713 meant that the crown constantly needed money and, therefore, parliament. In the 1690s, furthermore, MPs secured increasing control over military expenditure and used the power of appropriation to direct government spending more generally. The 1698 Civil List Act granted William £700,000 per annum for life to cover household and executive expenditure (including ministerial salaries, pensions and secret service costs) and made all military and naval expenditure the sole responsibility of parliament. Parliament entrenched its economic powers during the 1690s' 'financial revolution', in which it took control of government debt. In 1693, parliament began raising loans from private investors and repaying the debt through annuities. Thousands of investors thereby developed a personal economic interest in parliament. Also, in 1694, parliament created the Bank of England, which could raise its own capital and lend money to the government. In turn, government guaranteed that it would pay regular interest on the debt. The scale of and technicalities involved in this financial revolution required that the Treasury was, by 1714, presenting a yearly budget to parliament, making annual meetings of parliament a necessity.[19]

Parliamentary authority thus increased immensely between 1689 and 1715. As many of these acts indicate, though, what the Glorious Revolution settlement actually created was a less adversarial and more cooperative and indeed collusive relationship between crown and parliament. The 'principle of coordination' meant, in practice, that sovereignty was exercised by the 'crown-in-parliament', which controlled the crown but also meant executive control of a majority in the legislature. 'Real' Whigs or 'True' or 'Country' Whigs, as opposed to the 'Court' Whigs aligned with Robert Walpole from 1721, condemned the use of patronage as a means of achieving 'coordination' as conspiratorial and corrupt. Among the most strident critics were John Trenchard and Thomas Gordon, and their pseudonymous *Cato's Letters* (1724) were widely read in the American colonies. Nevertheless, most people accepted that some means of achieving governmental stability was essential, or at least acknowledged that the accommodation of crown and parliament was vastly preferable to the struggles and often bloody strife that had afflicted the country from the Addled Parliament in 1614, through the Petition of Right of 1629, the civil wars of 1642 to 1651 and the uncertainties of the interregnum, Restoration, Exclusion Crisis and yet another revolution in 1688. The tumults of 1745 reminded some of how far Britain had come, but how much of a threat of a return to tyranny and civil strife remained. An anonymously written pamphlet of 1746 noted that 'It was reserved for our Times to see that the greatest Struggles for Power may be carried on, without any of those Violences, and without producing any of those Mischiefs, which deform our antient Chronicles, and which are not absolutely effaced in the Stories of later Times.'

Furthermore, while some criticized the particular practices of government, few attacked the principles of the new constitutionalism. Indeed, in many people's minds the post-1689 constitution created stable and effective government while simultaneously guaranteeing the rights and liberties of free Britons as set out in vestiges of the ancient (pre-1066) constitution and various charters, starting with the Magna Carta of 1215 and ending with the Bill of Rights of 1689. According to one Whig sermon of 1734, notwithstanding over 200 capital crimes on the statute books, Britain's 'System of wise human laws' showed that Providence had separated Britons from the 'rest of mankind' as the 'chosen People of God'. A little less hubristically, but equally tellingly, Horace Walpole wrote of a 'Constitution most admirably calculated for the Ease and Freedom of the Subject'. Sir William Blackstone wrote that the 'idea and practice of . . . political and civil liberty flourish in their highest vigour in' Britain, where they are 'deeply implanted in our constitution, and rooted in our very soil'. In particular, it was parliament that came to represent the perfect balance between liberty and law that the new constitutional arrangements created. As Edmund Burke said, by the middle of the eighteenth century, parliament had been transformed from 'a mere representative of the people, and a guardian of popular privileges for its own immediate constituents . . . into a mighty sovereign'.

As Linda Colley has said, such was the regard for the new political arrangements in Britain that from the early eighteenth century a 'cult of Parliament' increasingly prevailed, and not just among the lords, gentry and merchants who benefited most directly from the increasing power of parliament over the crown. In early eighteenth-century England and Wales, the franchise extended to a quarter of adult men, and although the proportion of the enfranchised declined, it never went lower than 14 per cent during the century. Though Britain was hardly a democracy, a higher proportion of its people voted than anywhere else, except in the British American colonies. Election days were civic festivities accompanied by waving of Union Jacks, marching bands playing patriotic tunes, drinking loyal toasts and other patriotic activities, such as the burning of pontifical effigies, even in rotten boroughs where MPs were selected, not elected. Even those who did not qualify to vote sometimes felt that MPs represented them. Hence the increasingly frequent petitioning of parliament by unenfranchised men and even women over issues of local importance.[20]

Britons were so pleased with their new constitutional arrangements that they tended to universalize their benefits. This tendency was partly attributable to the chauvinism engendered by the almost endless warfare of the years 1689 to 1763. It was also, though, inherent in the Whig ideology that perceived the Glorious Revolution as a major step in the progress of British history towards constitutionally guaranteed liberty. That Whig ideology, of course, was connected to Enlightenment notions that saw political ideas and practices as universal laws rather than as the outcomes of localized historical circumstances. The fact that some foreign commentators praised Britain's eighteenth-century political arrangements, as Charles Louis de Secondat Montesquieu did in his *Spirit of the Laws* (1748), encouraged the tendency among Britons to regard their constitutional arrangements as perfect and therefore universally applicable: applicable, indeed, throughout the empire.

The Glorious Revolution in America

Britons failed to see, therefore, that the American colonial experience of the Glorious Revolution and its consequences was quite different from their own (as indeed eighteenth-century Englishmen tended to forget that the warfare that resumed in other parts of the British Isles with the accession of William III meant that Ireland and Scotland experienced 1688 and its aftermath quite differently too). There are some remarkable similarities between the experiences of tyranny suffered by colonists and metropolitans in the later Stuart era, and some historians see the Glorious Revolution as a 'transatlantic phenomenon'. The most obvious parallel is that the future James II ran New York and did so under the Duke's Laws and without calling a representative assembly for 19 years. When Governor Thomas Dongan finally called an assembly in 1683 to raise revenue, it passed the Charter of Libertyes and Privileges that became a dead letter when James ascended to the throne and New York became a royal colony and, in turn, a part of the Dominion of New England. Under the Dominion, Edmund Andros ruled all the New England colonies from 1686, plus New York and New Jersey from 1688, without once calling a representative assembly. Another parallel is that the Catholicism of the Duke of York and a conspicuous number of his colonial officials added to the sense of grievance New Yorkers felt towards their proprietary and then royal masters. It was the same in Maryland, where resentment of the arbitrary, Catholic Calvert proprietors led to a rebellion and a *Complaint from Heaven with Huy and Crye* in Maryland in 1676. That, of course, was the year of Nathaniel Bacon's rebellion against Governor William Berkeley and the Green Spring faction in Virginia.[21]

Yet there were significant differences in the way colonists experienced Stuart rule, in the ways that the Glorious Revolution took place in the colonies and, most importantly, in the settlements that followed in the wake of the revolutions in the colonies and empire. These differences, in turn, meant that the descendants of the generation of 1689 would remember the revolution and assess its significance in profoundly different ways. As we have seen in previous chapters, many of the grievances that colonists felt in the years before the Glorious Revolution were specifically colonial and not just English. And colonists expressed those grievances not only in terms of the rights of Englishmen but also in terms of the rights of Englishmen abroad. When Virginians requested a colonial charter in 1675, they wished it to reflect 'those just rights and privileges as were their due whilst they lived in England, and which they humbly hope that they have not lost by removing themselves' to America. Increase Mather's *Vindication of New England* asserted that 'No Englishmen in their Wits will ever Venture their Lives and Estates to Enlarge the Kings Dominions abroad, and Enrich the whole English Nation, if their Reward after all must be to be deprived of their *English Liberties*.'[22]

Also, the events of 1689, or in some instances non-events, played out differently in each colony. When news of William's invasion of England and James's departure reached the colonies in early 1689, most colonial governors declared their colonies for William and Mary and thereby prevented popular revolts. Even in the three colonies where uprisings occurred – Massachusetts, New York and Maryland – the timing and nature of those revolts varied according to local circumstances. First to rise was Boston in April 1689, with a quick and decisive overthrow and jailing of Edmund Andros that returned Massachusetts, Connecticut, New Hampshire, Plymouth and Rhode Island to their previous conditions of virtual independence. Next month, Jacob Leisler's insurgents, mostly artisan militiamen, forced Lieutenant-Governor Francis Nicholson to flee New York and formed a Committee of Safety that partially implemented the Charter of Libertyes and thus gave New York regular representative government for the first time in its history. Yet the Glorious Revolution in New York was not only about James II but also about grievances Dutch people felt against the English and, even more important, recent erosions of artisans' trade privileges. As historian Simon Middleton has said, the Glorious Revolution in New York 'was a colonial rather than an Old World struggle'. If New England and New York moved away from royal rule, at least temporarily, Maryland moved towards it. On 1 August, after Lord Baltimore failed to proclaim William and Mary, John Coode's 'Protestant Associators' overthrew the proprietary and declared themselves for the Protestant king and queen. The fact that Marylanders preferred crown to proprietary rule demonstrates just how various and specific were the local circumstances of the Glorious Revolution as it happened in the colonies.[23]

More importantly, there was no single Glorious Revolution settlement in the individual colonies or in the empire as a whole. In contrast to the Glorious Revolution settlement in England, the outcome in the colonies was a series of compromises that once again reflected the peculiarities of local circumstances. Of the most rebellious colonies, only Marylanders got what they asked for from the Glorious Revolution, and that was the implementation of royal government. Even that was not permanent, though, because when Benedict Leonard Calvert converted to Anglicanism following the former proprietor's death in 1715, the Baltimores got their proprietary back. In New York, Jacob Leisler and his son-in-law, Jacob Milborne, were hanged as traitors for a slight delay in handing over power when the new royal governor arrived in 1691. New Yorkers did retain their assembly with royal rule, though. In 1692, a new charter reimposed royal rule in Massachusetts, breaking forever the puritan colonists' covenant with God, enhancing governors' powers and ending the independent existence of Plymouth Colony as it was absorbed into the Bay colony.

Furthermore, the new king and his parliaments failed to acknowledge the declarations of rights passed by various colonies, and so colonists did not receive the chartered rights guaranteed to Englishmen at home through Parliament's Bill of Rights. On the contrary, as we have seen, within a few years, English authorities once again began to assert imperial interests over colonial ones, in particular with the passing of the new Navigation Act of 1696 and the efforts of the new Board of Trade to enforce the act and, in general, to enforce imperial order from 1696. Those efforts often entailed the exercise of executive powers that the crown in England and Britain had abandoned or would soon forgo. Crown officials in the colonies continued to prorogue and dissolve legislative assemblies, determine the frequency of their meetings, veto acts passed by those legislatures, create courts and dismiss judges. Colonial laws were subject to Privy Council as well as gubernatorial review. To avoid this review, assemblies often passed temporary laws that would expire before imperial authorities had the opportunity to approve or veto them. From 1706, the Board of Trade allowed most colonial laws to 'lye by', tacitly approved unless specifically objected to by some interested party, although governors were instructed to impose a 'suspending clause' that prevented any legislation concerning private property and crown prerogative from coming into effect until after crown approval. In other words, while the Glorious Revolution settlement represented for Britons the beginning of the end of executive-legislative strife, in America the revolution marked just another moment in a continuing struggle to preserve and extend legislative rights against executive authority, proprietorial or imperial.

Colonists therefore remembered or interpreted the legacy of the Glorious Revolution quite differently from the way Britons at home did. Christopher Gadsden of South Carolina wrote in 1764 that the Glorious Revolution had rendered his colony's 'Liberties and Constitution . . . secur'd & establish'd upon . . . firm and lasting foundation'. But for Gadsden the firm and lasting foundation was not parliamentary supremacy but legislative supremacy. For colonists, the Glorious Revolution represented the affirmation of the right to self-government through representative assemblies in the colonies. Gadsden was about to discover that his liberties were not based on a firm foundation but were about to come under assault from British attempts to assert parliamentary supremacy in America. Ten years later, Pennsylvania's John Dickinson would complain that parliament's actions in the previous decade were 'a total contradiction to every principle laid down at the time of the [Glorious] Revolution'.[24]

If British and British American constitutionalism diverged after the Glorious Revolution, so did their political practices and, in turn, their political cultures. As a result of 1689 and subsequent reforms, the orientation of political antagonism in Britain shifted on its axis. The principle of coordination, the operation of the crown-in-parliament, created a collusive relationship between the executive and the legislature, so that in the eighteenth century there was less vertical conflict between crown and parliament than there was horizontal conflict between parliamentarians. Even that horizontal conflict was less destabilizing and dangerous in the eighteenth century than it had been in the seventeenth. The Toleration Act and the Act of Settlement lessened the potential for the extreme religious sectarianism that had previously existed among MPs, a feature of the civil war era in particular. Equally important, eighteenth-century political antipathies were expressed through but also institutionalized in and therefore controlled by political parties. However vicious British party politics may have been at times, the very fact that the Whigs and Tories existed guarded against the kind of dangerous legislative instability that existed in the seventeenth century. As David Hume noted at the time of the fall of Robert Walpole, it was in the interest and it was the practice of Britons 'not to contend, as if they were fighting *pro aris et focis*', but to seek consensus or at least compromise. 'Moderation', as Hume said elsewhere, 'is of advantage to every establishment.'[25]

American colonial political practices and political culture, however, remained firmly tied to their seventeenth-century moorings. As there had not been a single Glorious Revolution settlement in the colonies or for the empire, as no principle or practice of coordination was established or practised in British America, the primary axis of political antagonism remained the vertical one between executives and legislatures. As governors and assemblies continued to confront each other in a polarized fashion, colonists did not learn the kind of institutionalized collusion that operated within Britain. They thus retained a seventeenth-century kind of political culture: fractious, suspicious and aggressive. When British governments finally made a concerted and sustained effort to impose imperial authority from 1764, therefore, they found themselves confronted by unreconstructed Roundheads.

Before 1764, imperial officials at the Southern Department and the Lords and Board of Trade only occasionally succeeded in persuading a majority of parliamentarians of the necessity of passing and enforcing trade laws and disciplining and controlling colonial assemblies. By the middle of the eighteenth century, the growing population and wealth of North America began to attract metropolitan attention, and when the French and Indian War highlighted problems in imperial governance, many politicians and commentators concluded that it was time to act. For Edmund Burke, colonial autonomy was irreducible; a historical fact that could not be altered even if it were desirable to do so. For most metropolitans by 1763, however, it was both desirable and doable. Political economist Malachy Postlethwayt made the same historical observation that Burke did in the same year, but, unlike Burke, he still believed that a corporate or unitary empire could be created out of the disparate one that existed. 'Let us revive the consideration of our ancestors', Postlethwayt wrote,

> and grow wise by their misfortunes. If the English colonies in America were wisely consolidated into one body, and happily united in one common interest . . . ; if their united forces were framed to act in concert for the common safety, and their commercial councils regulated for the general prosperity; would not such political concord and harmony establish invincible strength and power?

Like the members of the Board of Trade of 1763, Postlethwayt had no doubt that parliament had the right and the power 'to determine upon such a union in government and constitution . . . as may tend to strengthen the whole British empire'. Like the men at the Board of Trade, he was wrong.[26]

Notes

1 Jack P. Greene, *Pursuits of Happiness: The Social Development of Early Modern British Colonies and the Formation of American Culture*

(Chapel Hill, 1988), pp. 178–9; Robert V. Wells, *Population of the British Colonies in America before 1776: A Survey of Census Data* (Princeton, 1975), p. 284.

2 John J. McCusker and Russell R. Menard, *The Economy of British America, 1607–1789* (2nd edn, Chapel Hill, 1991), pp. 57, 61, 280; Jacob M. Price, 'The Imperial Economy, 1700–1776', in P.J. Marshall, ed., *The Oxford History of the British Empire* Volume II: *The Eighteenth Century* (Oxford, 1998), p. 97.

3 *An Account of the European Settlements in America* (2 vols, London, 1757), 2, p. 288 (written by William Burke, but, historians believe, with considerable input from Edmund Burke); *An Inquiry into the Nature and Causes of the Wealth of Nations* (1776), in R.H. Campbell, A.S. Skinner and W.B. Todd, eds, *The Glasgow Edition of the Works and Correspondence of Adam Smith* (2 vols, Indianapolis, 1976), 2, pp. 946–7.

4 *The Rights of the Colonies Examined* (1764), in Jack P. Greene, 'Empire and Identity from the Glorious Revolution to the American Revolution', in Marshall, *The Eighteenth Century*, p. 228; *The Grievances of the American Colonies Candidly Examined* (1766), in Eliga H. Gould, *The Persistence of Empire: British Political Culture in the Age of the American Revolution* (Chapel Hill, 2000), p. 130; Jack P. Greene, *Peripheries and Center: Constitutional Development in the Extended Polities of the British Empire and the United States, 1607–1788* (New York, 1986), p. 58.

5 Charles Lloyd, *The Conduct of the Late Administration Examined, relative to the American Stamp Act* (1767), in Gould, *Persistence of Empire*, p. 118; Lords of Trade to Privy Council, 28 May 1679, in Greene, *Peripheries and Center*, p. 34; Thomas Pownall, *The Administration of the Colonies* (1768); Townshend, speech, 6 February 1765, in Greene, 'Empire and Identity', p. 224.

6 James A. Henretta, *'Salutary Neglect': Colonial Administration under the Duke of Newcastle* (Princeton, 1972).

7 Jack P. Greene, 'Metropolis and Colonies: Changing Patterns of Constitutional Conflict in the Early Modern British Empire', in Jack P. Greene, *Negotiated Authorities: Essays in Colonial Political and Constitutional History* (Charlottesville, 1994), p. 45; Warren Billings, ed., *The Old Dominion in the Seventeenth Century: A Documentary History of Virginia, 1606–1689* (Chapel Hill, 1975), pp. 51–8.

8 Greene, 'Metropolis and Colonies', pp. 46, 59; *Peripheries and Center*, pp. 20–1.

9 'Examination of Benjamin Franklin', 13 February 1766, in Gould, *Persistence of Empire*, p. 124.

10 Board of Trade Report to Lords Justices, 30 September 1696, in Greene, 'Metropolis and Colonies', p. 49.

11 Board of Trade to Queen, 26 March 1701; Beeston to Board of Trade, 19 August 1701; Cornbury to Board of Trade, 6 November 1704; Hunter to St John, 1 January 1712; Lowther to Board of Trade, 16 August 1712, in Greene, 'Metropolis and Colonies', pp. 50, 51.

12 Delafaye to Nicholson, 16 January 1722, William Gooch, 'Some Remarks on a Paper Transmitted into America, Entitled a Short Discourse on the Present State of the Colonies in America with respect to Great Britain', in Greene, *Peripheries and Center*, pp. 46, 47; Shute to Crown, 16 August 1723; Newcastle to Burnet, 26 June 1629; Colden to Clinton, 8 December 1748, in Greene, 'Metropolis and Provinces', pp. 63, 68–9, 65.

13 Lewis to Board of Trade, 20 October 1748; Bedford to Newcastle, 11 August 1748; 'Some Considerations Relating to the Present Condition of the Plantations. . . .'; Board of Trade to Governors, in Greene, 'Metropolis and Provinces', pp. 71, 72, 72–3, 73.

14 Robert M. Calhoon, *Dominion and Liberty: Ideology in the Anglo-American World, 1660–1801* (Arlington Heights, IL, 1994), p. 38.

15 Horace Walpole, *Memoirs of King George II*, John Shebbeare, *Three Letters to the People of England* (1756), J. Payne, *The French Encroachments Exposed* (1756), in Gould, *Persistence of Empire*, pp. 62, 65; Daniel Baugh, 'Great Britain's "Blue-Water" Policy, 1689–1815', *International History Review* X (1988), pp. 33–58; 'Withdrawing from Europe: Anglo-French Maritime Geopolitics, 1750–1800', *International History Review* XX (1998), pp. 1–32.

16 Pennsylvania House of Assembly to Robert Hunter Morris, 11 February 1756 and Sharpe to William Shirley, 2 February 1756, in Gould, *Persistence of Empire*, p. 67.

17 Julian Gwyn, 'British Government Spending and the North American Colonies, 1740–1775', in Peter Marshall and Glyn Williams, eds, *The British Atlantic Empire before the American Revolution* (London, 1980), p. 77; Gould, *Persistence of Empire*, pp. 74, 103; John Ploughshare, 'I Am Old for England' (1766), in Gould, *Persistence of Empire*, p. 119.

18 Franklin to the Proprietors, 20 August 1757, 'Hints Respecting the Civil Establishment in Our American Colonies' (1763), in Greene, *Peripheries and Center*, pp. 52, 69.

19 Mark Kishlansky, *A Monarchy Transformed: Britain, 1603–1714* (London, 1996); Jennifer Carter, 'The Revolution and the Constitution', in Geoffrey Holmes, ed., *Britain after the Glorious Revolution, 1689–1715* (New York, 1969).

20 *Power and Patriotism: A Political Epistle, Humbly Inscribed to the Right Honourable H.P. Esq. . . .* (1746), Reverend James Bate, *An Assize Sermon Preach'd at Maidstone in Kent. . .* (1743), Horace Walpole, *A Second and Third Letter to the Whigs. . .* (1748), in Gould, *Persistence*

of *Empire*, pp. 18, 4, 22; William Blackstone, *Commentaries on the Laws of England* (1765), in Greene, 'Empire and Identity', p. 212; Edmund Burke, Letter to the Sheriffs of Bristol, in Greene, *Peripheries and Center*, p. 57; Linda Colley, *Britons: Forging the Nation, 1707–1837* (New Haven, 1992), p. 56.

21 Richard S. Dunn, 'The Glorious Revolution and America', in Nicholas Canny, ed., *The Oxford History of the British Empire* Volume I: *The Origins of Empire: British Overseas Enterprise to the Close of the Seventeenth Century* (Oxford, 1998), p. 446.

22 David S. Lovejoy, 'Two American Revolutions, 1689 and 1776', in J.G.A. Pocock, ed., *Three British Revolutions: 1641, 1688, 1776* (Princeton, 1980), pp. 246, 254.

23 Simon Middleton, *Privileges and Profits: Tradesmen in Colonial New York City, 1624–1750* (Philadelphia, forthcoming), p. 128.

24 Christopher Gadsden, *South Carolina Gazette*, 17 December 1764, John Dickinson, *An Essay on the Constitutional Power of Great Britain over the Colonies in America* (1774), in Greene, 'Metropolis and Colonies', p. 90.

25 David Hume, 'That Politics May Be Reduced to a Science' (1741), 'Of the Coalition of Parties' (1759), in Gould, *Persistence of Empire*, pp. 17, 18.

26 Malachy Postlethwayt, *Great-Britain's True System* (1757), in Gould, *Persistence of Empire*, p. 68.

8

The American Revolution,
1764–1783

The end of the Seven Years War was a triumphal time in Britain. William Pitt, chief architect of the great victory, gave a sense of the historical nature of the achievement when he proclaimed in parliament in 1763 that in the preceding three years of the war Britain 'had over-run more world' than the Romans had 'conquered in a century'. There was to be no complacency, however. The new first minister, George Grenville, did not doubt that France and Spain would recover from their 'distress' and assert their ambitions in America again. He was determined, therefore, to protect Britain's possessions overseas. The maintenance in North America of 10,000 troops in the first year after the war and 7500 troops thereafter would, however, be expensive, expected to cost upwards of £250,000 annually. With a national debt of over £130,000,000 and with clamour for a reduction of wartime taxes, few Britons doubted that colonists should pay for the soldiers in North America. Soame Jenyns, president of the Board of Trade, asked in 1765: 'Can there be a more proper Time to force [the colonists] to maintain an Army at their Expence, than when that Army is necessary for their own Protection, and we are utterly unable to support it?'

Colonists did not see these things the same way, though. William Bollan of Massachusetts responded to Jenyns directly with the observation that 'for one hundred years past, while Canada and Louisiana were in the hands of France, the colonies wanted no such defence or security from England; but, on the contrary, they defended themselves'. Americans, in fact, were deeply suspicious of British motives in maintaining troops in America. Many Britons may have become more accustomed to the idea of the state maintaining a standing army in peacetime, confident that the Glorious Revolution settlement guaranteed their liberties. American colonists, however, had not experienced the Glorious Revolution as an event that settled the conflict between crown and parliament, but as just another in an ongoing series of battles between the forces of liberty and those of tyranny. Therefore, they still held to the old axiom that the existence of a standing army in peacetime was inherently a threat to liberty.

The colonists were right to be suspicious about the intentions of British imperial authorities at the end of the 'great war for empire'. That war had not only made those authorities determined to impose direct taxes on the colonies, but it had also created a majority in parliament willing to assert its supremacy to create the more corporate or unitary empire that imperial officials at the Privy Council, the Lords and Board of Trade and the Southern Department had been imagining for many years. Few in Britain doubted that parliament, the repository of British liberty and sovereignty, had the right to tax the colonies and even to reform their constitutions. Colonists disagreed, first because natural rights to property entailed freedom from taxation without representation and second, but equally importantly, because of customary constitutional rights. As Benjamin Franklin put it in a newspaper letter of 1766, the colonies were 'Planted in times when the powers of parliament were not supposed so extensive as they are become since the [Glorious] Revolution . . . in lands and countries where the parliament had not then the least jurisdiction'. Furthermore, all but Georgia and Nova Scotia were planted without '*any money* granted by parliament', but by people who had, with 'permission from the crown, purchased or conquered the territory, at the expence of their own private treasure and blood'. 'These territories thus became *new* dominions *of the crown*', Franklin went on, 'settled under royal charters, that formed their several governments and constitutions, on which the parliament was *never consulted*; or had the *least participation*.' The colonies indeed had their own 'separate parliaments, called modestly assemblies'.

Colonists' allegiance to Britain and the empire therefore depended not on common subjection to parliamentary authority but on common loyalty to the crown. As we have seen, however, loyalty to the crown by no means entailed obeisance. On the contrary, colonists' commitment to empire was contingent upon the king's commitment to the maintenance and protection of the colonists' rights as freeborn Englishmen or Britons. One of those rights was to government by consent. A related one was the right to withdraw consent if government broke the social contract with the governed by violating people's natural or constitutional rights. After 12 years of acts and actions by parliament that colonists interpreted as violations of those rights, 13 mainland colonies did precisely that. The Declaration of Independence of 1776 expressed their withdrawal of their consent to be governed by Britain. Some British American colonists could not afford to follow suit, even if they wished to. The Canadian colonies and the Floridas were too economically underdeveloped to contemplate independence from Britain and, in any case, the predominantly French population of Quebec and even some of the English inhabitants of the Canadian colonies had never become accustomed to extensive self-government. The colonies of the Atlantic and Caribbean islands, with their huge slave majorities, could not risk the instabilities associated with revolution or forgo British military protection from this internal enemy or from potential invasion by other European powers. This chapter examines the reasons why and the means by which 13 colonies broke away from Britain to form the United States. The next explores how Americans created new constitutions for their new country, and how Britain reformulated what remained of its empire in light of the experience of the American Revolution.[1]

'No taxation without representation'

On 5 April 1764, parliament passed the American Duties Act or American Revenue Act, better remembered as the Sugar Act. Although it raised the duty on various colonial imports and added several export commodities to articles enumerated in the Navigation Acts, it was most infamous for imposing a threepence per gallon duty on molasses, rum and sugar imported into the colonies, replacing the sixpence duty of the Molasses Act of 1733. The Molasses Act was designed to deter trade with the French sugar islands, but had been rendered ineffective by colonists' paying customs officials bribes of 1 to 1½ pence. Halving the duty, First Minister George Grenville hoped that colonists would obey the law and pay the tax. For those who did not, the legislation empowered the Royal Navy, with assistance from the army, to board ships to check for papers or contraband. Grenville put 8 warships and 12 armed sloops to sea to detect smugglers, and reminded customs officers in the colonies that they would lose their livings if they colluded in illegal trade. The act also empowered vice-admiralty courts to try those caught smuggling, sidestepping colonial juries that tended to be sympathetic to the smugglers from whom they purchased their cheap, low-tax goods. To make matters worse, the tax and fines for evasion were payable only in specie – gold or silver – and not in paper money, which tended to depreciate in relation to its face value. Parliament also passed a Currency Act that forbade the circulation of paper money altogether, first in New York and later elsewhere, so that British merchants and tax collectors would receive revenues and payments from colonists at full rather than below face value.

Colonists complained bitterly in a flood of pamphlets about the inequities of the Sugar Act and of the increasing insistence on payment in specie, linking their objections to the military enforcement of these impositions. Yet they took little further action at this stage. Americans agreed that parliament had no business meddling in internal colonial affairs and that they should not be taxed directly without their own consent, and, of course, with no representatives in parliament they could not possibly give their consent there. Having had little reason to articulate systematically the precise limits of parliamentary authority, however, there was some confusion and disagreement among colonists in 1764 about the legitimacy of the Sugar Act. It had long been understood that parliament had the right to regulate trade in the empire and had other supervening powers in larger imperial matters, hence general, albeit grudging, acceptance in theory of most of the Navigation Acts and other trade regulations. There was no doubt that the Sugar Act, unlike the Molasses Act, was intended to raise revenue rather than regulate trade. Yet some accepted the Sugar Act as an 'external' tax on imports and exports, as distinct from an illegitimate 'internal' tax on local transactions within individual colonies.

There was little confusion or disagreement among colonists about the Stamp Act, which was clearly a revenue-raising measure on colonists' local transactions. The act directed that as of 1 November 1765 all legal documents, including private contracts, plus newspapers, pamphlets, broadsides and even cards and dice had to be written on or accompanied by stamped paper issued from London. Colonists could obtain the paper by buying it from local officials. Grenville announced his intention to impose this Stamp Act on the colonies on the same day that parliament passed the Sugar Act, in April 1764, which proved to be an epic tactical blunder. Colonists, well informed in advance, rendered the measure unenforceable by the time it was supposed to come into effect. Bostonians were the first to take direct action. The radical Samuel Adams and the Loyal Nine organized a South End mob under cobbler and known troublemaker Ebenezer Mackintosh. On the morning of 14 August, the crowd hanged an effigy of the colony's stamp collector, Andrew Oliver, from a 'Liberty Tree' and made it clear they expected no one, the sheriff included, to take it down. In the evening they paraded it in front of government house, in sight of Governor Francis Bernard, Lieutenant-Governor Thomas Hutchinson and the council, and then destroyed Oliver's administrative building and burned his house down. Oliver resigned the next day. The crowd also demolished Hutchinson's mansion 11 days later. Threats and actions like these across the colonies meant that by the day colonists were supposed to start using stamps, there was not a single stamp tax collector still in office in any of the continental provinces. Colonists then just went about their business as if the Stamp Act had never been passed.

Also, organizations calling themselves Sons of Liberty sprang up in towns and counties throughout the colonies, and over the next several years would organize and coordinate actions against other British measures. Politicians from 10 of the 13 North American mainland colonies that later claimed Independence met in New York as the Stamp Act Congress from 3 to 25 October 1765, an early instance of intercolonial cooperation (there was a precedent in the Albany Congress that met to discuss mutual defence issues at the beginning of the French and Indian War). Furthermore, merchants in various colonies made non-importation agreements directed at British exports. Merchants and manufacturers in Britain began petitioning MPs about the danger to their pockets. The Duke of Newcastle feared unemployment in Britain leading to 'Riots, Mobbs, & Insurrections'. Under these different forms of pressure, and after Grenville had been replaced as first minister by Charles Wentworth Watson, Marquis of Rockingham, parliament repealed the Stamp Act on 16 March 1766, having not made a penny from it. A month later, furthermore, parliament passed an Indemnity Act, promising not to prosecute anyone involved in anti-Stamp Act protests, except a few of the most troublesome agitators. Another month on, parliament reduced the sugar duty to one pence per gallon, to make it competitive with the traditional bribe in the hope of getting at least some revenue from a tax that was still being evaded.

Colonial traders were notorious tax evaders, but objections to the Sugar and Stamp Acts were founded on deeply held principles. The most basic but least important argument against these measures was that Britain did not need to tax colonists as the mother country profited handsomely from 'the general benefits of trade'. Those benefits were both private and public, for the Navigation Acts provided British merchants with a near monopoly on colonial trade and a source of tax revenue for the Treasury. The Resolutions of the Stamp Act Congress noted that 'as the profits of the trade of these colonies ultimately center in Great Britain, to pay for the manufactures which they are obliged to take from thence, they contribute very largely to all supplies granted there to the Crown'. Some Britons conceded as much. William Pitt reckoned that Britain profited to the tune of 'two millions a year' from 'the trade of the colonies'.

But colonial objections to parliamentary taxation went beyond issues of utility and raised the cry of 'no taxation without representation'. The fact that colonists had no representation in a parliament that was attempting to tax them was an important grievance in and of itself, but it mattered so deeply because of the relationship, as colonists perceived it, between property and personal and political liberties.[2]

American Roundheads and British Whigs

Colonists used a language about the taxes imposed on them that appears on the face of it absurdly hyperbolic. Time and time again after 1764 colonists claimed that Britain was destroying American 'liberty' and imposing 'tyranny' and 'slavery' on the colonies. Thomas Jefferson was not the first when he wrote in his *Summary View of the Rights of British America* (1774) that Britain's 'series of oppressions . . . too plainly prove a deliberate systematical plan of reducing us to slavery'. Two years later, Congress approved Jefferson's Declaration of Independence, with its references to Britain's 'design to impose absolute despotism' and 'an absolute tyranny over these States'.[3]

This kind of language was in part inspired by a Whig ideology that perceived politics and history as a perennial battle between virtuous, republican liberty on the one hand and corrupt, conspiratorial tyranny on the other. Some of the colonists' revolutionary thought and discourse thus resembled that of Britain's 'eighteenth-century commonwealthmen', especially that of John Trenchard and Thomas Gordon, English opposition or 'Country' or 'True' Whigs, whose *Cato's Letters* lambasted the corruption of 'Court' Whigs in the age of Robert Walpole. Yet the feelings colonists expressed were really more like those of seventeenth-century English revolutionaries. As Jonathon Sewall, a contemporary and friend of John Adams, who became loyalist, wrote in a private letter of his fellow colonists, in particular those of Massachusetts,

> there is an enthusiasm in politics like that which religious notions inspire, that drives men on with an unnatural impetuosity that baffles and confounds all calculation based on rational principles. Liberty . . . is a word whose very sound carries a fascinating charm. The colonists fancy this precious jewel in danger of being ravished from them.

Later in the revolutionary crisis, Britons began to understand how the colonists had never adopted the kind of consensual mode of political behaviour that had developed in Britain since the Glorious Revolution had changed the nature of constitutionalism and political discourse and conflict, and how eighteenth-century American political constitutionalism and behavioural norms resembled those of their ancestors in the English revolutionary era. As one British officer wrote in 1777, the colonists 'have an inveterate hatred to our constitution both in church and state, the principles they suck in with milk naturally lead to rebellion . . . whilst they pretend, in the canting style of the last century, to exalt the dominion of king Jesus, [but] have nothing really at heart but to erect their own'. Reflecting on events in 1780, Joseph Galloway wrote that the American Revolution 'has arisen from the same source, and been conducted by the same spirit with that which effected the destruction of the English government in the last century'.[4]

Underlying American objections to taxation without representation was a concept of the relationship of property and a form of liberty that dated to the seventeenth century. For colonists, the essence of personal liberty was independence from the will of others, a kind of independence that required ownership of property. In particular, ownership of a farm or an artisan shop meant that a man (women were deemed, mostly by men of course, to be naturally incapable of exercising independence) was free of landlords or wage payers. So when colonists argued that parliament, by taxing their property without their consent, was taking away their 'liberty' and reducing them to 'slavery', they meant it almost literally. Property was the means to personal independence, the foundation of liberty. Lack of property meant dependence, the foundation of slavery. Deprivation of property through arbitrary taxation thus threatened to reduce colonists to slavery. When the British were using the navy, the army and courts without juries to enforce arbitrary taxation, colonists perceived a systematic conspiracy to destroy American liberty and impose on Americans a form of slavery.

There were leading British figures willing to heed the colonists, if not necessarily to agree with them. Isaac Barré doubted the legitimacy of parliamentary taxation on the same historical grounds that colonists did, asking rhetorically during the Stamp Act debate whether the colonies had been 'planted by your care . . . nourished by *your* indulgence . . . [and] protected by *your* arms' and suggested that in fact they had gone to America because of 'your oppressions' and developed freely and prosperously 'by your neglect'. Barré's assessment of colonial history was similar to that of Edmund Burke. Burke actually thought that parliament's right to tax the colonies was 'clear beyond a contradiction'. It was the expediency of it that worried him. William Pitt also questioned the constitutionality of the Stamp Act, although only after it became clear that the act was unenforceable. Most Britons, however, steadfastly held to the view that parliament had the right to tax the colonies and indeed must do so. The mainstream British response to colonists' arguments about taxation without representation once again revealed metropolitan regard for the institution of parliament. Britons replied that if colonists were not represented directly in parliament they nevertheless enjoyed 'virtual' representation, as did residents of rotten boroughs, women, children and other dependants. Thomas Whately addressed the colonists directly on this matter, arguing in 1765 that

> all *British* Subjects are really in the same [condition]; none are actually, all are virtually represented in Parliament; for every Member of Parliament sits in the House, not as Representative of his own constituents, but as one of that august Assembly by which all the Commons of *Great Britain* are represented.

Whately further maintained that while the colonies had their own assemblies, America was nevertheless 'one Nation' with England, Scotland, and Wales 'govern'd by the same supreme Authority'.[5]

The British theory of virtual representation also rested on the notion that all British people at home and overseas shared the same interests. For colonists, Americans and Britons shared the rights of freeborn Englishmen, but they did not have the same kinds of particular needs, as was becoming increasingly clear from British legislation. In any case, the colonists had their own elected legislatures that represented them directly and in the 'actual' sense. These colonial assemblies were thus the only bodies that could legitimately tax them. It was this point that the argument over taxation connected seamlessly with one about the constitution of the British Empire.

The constitution of the empire

Indeed, arguments over the legitimacy of the Sugar and Stamp Acts had already raised the issue of the constitution of the empire. When George Grenville introduced the Sugar Act to parliament on 9 March 1764, he said he 'hoped that the power and sovereignty of Parliament, over every part of the British dominions, for the purpose of raising or collecting any tax, would never be disputed'. He hoped in vain. The Virginia Resolves of 30 May 1765 stated that

> taxation of the people by themselves, or by persons chosen by themselves to represent them, who can only know what taxes the people are able to bear . . . and must themselves be affected by every tax laid on the people, is the only security against a burthensome taxation, and the distinguishing characteristick of British freedom.

Therefore,

> the General Assembly of this Colony have the only and sole exclusive right and power to lay taxes and impositions upon the inhabitants of this Colony, and that every attempt to vest such power in any person or persons whatsoever other than the General Assembly aforesaid has a manifest tendency to destroy British as well as American freedom.

The next day, the burgesses rescinded some of the resolves, but they were nevertheless printed in full in newspapers throughout British America and emulated by the assemblies of other colonies.

Similarly, the 19 October Resolutions of the Stamp Act Congress, after admitting allegiance to the crown and 'all due subordination' to parliament (what was 'due' was, of course, limited), stated:

> II. That His Majesty's liege subjects in these colonies are intitled to all the inherent rights and liberties of his natural born subjects within the kingdom of Great Britain.
> III. That it is inseparably essential to the freedom of a people, and the undoubted right of Englishmen, that no taxes be imposed on them but with their own consent, given personally or by their representatives.
> IV. That the people of these colonies are not, and from their local circumstances cannot be, represented in the House of Commons in Great Britain.
> V. That the only representatives of the people of these colonies are persons chosen therein by themselves, and that no taxes have ever been, or can be constitutionally imposed on them, but by their respective legislatures.

Examined by parliament in 1766 on how the British government was to recoup the costs of the war, Benjamin Franklin replied that 'when aids to the crown are wanted, they are to be asked for of the several assemblies, according to the old established usage, who will, as they always have done, grant them freely'. To say that the colonial assemblies had given money 'freely' was far from the truth, but the larger point was true: historically, in the main, colonists had been left to tax and govern themselves.

In response to these kinds of claims, Governor Francis Bernard had the following to say to the assembly of Massachusetts:

> In an empire, extended and diversified as that of Great Britain, there must be a supreme legislature, to which all other powers must be subordinate. It is our happiness that the supreme legislature, the parliament of Great Britain, is the sanctuary of liberty and justice; and that the prince, who presides over it, realizes the idea of a patriot King. Surely, then, we should submit our opinions to the determinations of so august a body; and acquiesce in a perfect confidence, that the rights of the members of the British empire will ever be safe in the hands of the conservators of the liberty of the whole.[6]

Arguments over where sovereignty lay within the empire came to the fore of the growing dispute between provincials and metropolitans on the day the Stamp Act was repealed. On 16 March 1766, First Minister Lord Rockingham, not himself unfriendly to the colonists, put through parliament a Declaratory Act, similar to the Declaratory Act of 1720 concerning Ireland, stating that parliament had the right to legislate for the colonies 'in all cases whatsoever'. The Declaratory Act helped Rockingham gather a majority for repeal of the dead-duck Stamp Act by helping parliament save face. But the act also made explicit for the first time MPs' claims that colonial assemblies were subordinate to parliament and that parliament was sovereign throughout the empire.

Colonists made no immediate widespread or violent protest against the Declaratory Act, hoping it was a meaningless gesture, but were prepared to confront its constitutional implications should need or opportunity arise. Need and opportunity soon arose. In June 1767, parliament passed the Townshend Duties, requiring colonists to pay taxes on a wide range of everyday imported goods, including glass, lead, paint, paper and tea. In devising these levies, the new chancellor of the exchequer, Charles Townshend, attempted to exploit the distinction that some colonists drew, during the two previous tax revolts, between internal and external taxes. Townshend and other parliamentarians thought this distinction absurd, as did the more hardline colonists, but humoured the notion in the name of compromise. In an attempt to ensure compliance, Townshend also established a Board of Customs Commissioners to collect the taxes. Unlike the Stamp Act officials, these new commissioners were Britons, not colonials, and would therefore be less susceptible to local pressure, or so Townshend thought. The introduction of outsiders in fact aggravated colonists yet further. The new customs commissioners' remuneration would comprise one-third of revenue raised by duties and fines for tax evasion. The commissioners, soon nicknamed 'customs racketeers', notoriously practised laxity for a while, lulling traders into a false sense of security, and then pounced, lining their pockets with the greater profits to be made from fines. Townshend wished further to diminish imperial officials' dependence on colonial assemblies through 'independent Salaries for the civil officers in North America'. To colonists, that would make them unaccountable to the assemblies and was therefore unacceptable.

For most colonists, the Townshend Duties clarified the issue of whether 'external' taxes were a legitimate exercise of parliamentary power or not. They decided they were not. Colonial objections included the now familiar call of 'no taxation without representation' and, once again, colonists organized boycotts of British goods, with Sons of Liberty chapters intimidating colonial merchants into compliance when need arose. But, recalling the Declaratory Act, the colonists' objections also included explicit claims that political sovereignty was diffused throughout the empire and that therefore the colonial lower houses of assembly were equivalent to the House of Commons. John Dickinson's *Letters from a Farmer in Pennsylvania* (1768) led the colonial charges against the Townshend Duties. Defending the rights of colonial assemblymen, Dickinson wrote that

> These men, whose deliberations heretofore had an influence on every matter relating to the *liberty* and *happiness* of themselves and their constituents, and whose authority in domestic affairs at least, might well be compared to that of *Roman* senators, will *now* find their deliberations of no more consequence, than those of *constables* [7]

Even more consequentially, Samuel Adams made the case for 'diffused sovereignty' in his Circular Letter of 1767, passed by the Massachusetts General Court to be distributed for approval by all other assemblies throughout the colonies. At this point, theoretical debate turned into a very real dispute, because Massachusetts Governor Francis Bernard, on instructions from the Privy Council and Lord Hillsborough, the new colonial secretary and an imperial hardliner who had twice served as president of the Board of Trade, ordered the House to rescind the letter on pain of dissolution, an exercise of executive power not undertaken in Britain since the reign of James II. The House refused and Bernard dissolved it. The voters of Massachusetts then re-elected many of those members who had voted against rescinding and voted out many of those who voted for it. The newly elected assembly then met without the governor convening it, a harbinger of the extra-legal institutions that would emerge during the revolutionary crisis of 1774 to 1776.

Hillsborough also ordered other governors to prevent the assemblies in their colonies from replying to Massachusetts. Later, in 1769, Hillsborough pushed for reform of the Massachusetts charter. The 1691 charter had allowed the colony to have an elected council or upper house of assembly. In all the other colonies councils were appointed and Hillsborough felt that elections in Massachusetts made the council too susceptible to popular pressure. George III advised against this action for the time being, as 'altering Charters is at all times an odious measure', but the matter of the Massachusetts charter would arise again in another five years.

Despite setbacks in Massachusetts, it was now clear that the British were determined to impose their vision of imperial sovereignty. A similar but longer constitutional stand-off took place in South Carolina from 1769 to 1775. On 8 December 1769 the South Carolinian Commons House of Assembly authorized a £1500 donation to London's Society of Gentleman Supporters of the Bill of Rights in aid of John Wilkes, the English radical excluded from parliament. When Governor William Bull obeyed Colonial Secretary Lord Hillsborough's order to veto all appropriation bills until the Commons House withdrew its funding for Wilkes, he made a sharp break with local tradition. The Commons House had initiated legislation since 1691 and in 1756 the council acknowledged the Commons House's exclusive right to initiate appropriation bills. The Wilkes fund controversy dragged on until 1775, with the assembly issuing IOUs to keep the government functioning, creating increasingly rancorous relations between the colony and imperial authorities.

Parliament itself took a similar stand against the New York assembly in 1766 in defence of its Mutiny or Quartering Act, which billeted troops on unoccupied dwellings in New York City and required New Yorkers to pay for it. At first the colonial legislature refused to comply. The assembly finally caved in June 1767, but not before parliament passed the New York Restraining Act, directing the governor to veto all legislation passed by the assembly until it complied with the Quartering Act. During this controversy, the Earl of Shelburne, the colonial secretary (the Southern Department had been replaced by a new Colonial Department) even considered making it '*High Treason* to refuse to *obey* or *execute*' parliamentary legislation.[8]

The New York Restraining Act also focused attention once again on another sensitive issue: the existence of a standing army in peacetime. The new measures passed after the war seemed to substantiate suspicions that the army was there not to protect colonists against the French, the Spanish or the Indians, but to enforce illegitimate taxes and impose a new imperial order. In 1768, their suspicions seemed to be confirmed. In June that year, Boston's customs commissioners seized the sloop *Liberty* and fined its owner, John Hancock, one of Boston's favourite Sons of Liberty, for a technical violation of the Townshend Duties. What followed was the Liberty

Riot, in which an angry crowd went looking for customs officials to hang (and not necessarily in effigy). The customs officials fled to Castle William, a fortress in the middle of Boston Harbour, and from there they called for troops to restore order in Boston. Lord Hillsborough ordered General Thomas Gage, the British army's commander-in-chief in New York, to dispatch four regiments to Boston. The troops arrived there in October 1768 and camped on Boston Common, in full view of the whole town.

The arrival of the troops not only seemed to confirm that the British intended to deprive Bostonians of their property and liberty by force, but also caused trouble because poorly paid soldiers took part-time jobs in the city, as they had in New York, by undercutting local wages. This phenomenon helped unite ordinary people with wealthier merchants through similar material as well as ideological reasons to oppose the presence of troops. There was much at stake too, more in fact for poorer people than for the well heeled. Troops taking jobs deprived poorer Bostonians and New Yorkers of much if not all of their incomes. It gave even slaves a reason to side with their masters against British measures. A common way for slaves to gain freedom for themselves or for loved ones was to take part-time jobs for wages. When troops took those jobs, they deprived slaves of what was often their only route to freedom. So it was that poorer people were in the vanguard of harassing the troops in the streets, an activity that eventually led to tragedy. On 5 March 1770, a fight occurred between a local dockworker and an off-duty soldier looking for work in the shipyards, and that evening a crowd gathered outside the customs house on King Street. There was nothing too unusual in any of these events. The duty sentry that night, Private Hugh White, called for assistance and Captain Thomas Preston duly appeared with six more soldiers. Preston attempted to calm the crowd, but Private Hugh Montgomery was knocked over and fired his musket as he rose to his feet. No one knows for sure what happened next, but the soldiers claimed to hear someone shout 'Fire', a call that mob leaders used as a summons, and then they let a volley loose into the crowd, killing four men and a boy who had come to watch. The King Street Riot and the tragedy that followed it provided martyrs for the small but strident group of radicals who were leaning increasingly in favour of full and formal independence from Britain. They called the event the Boston Massacre and Paul Revere's famous engraving depicted mean-faced soldiers wilfully firing on defenceless innocents.

Even so, the shock of the killings made way for what Samuel Adams later called a 'period of quessence'. The most disaffected of colonists kept up agitation. Adams, for example, established the first of a network of intercolonial Committees of Correspondence to try to stoke up hostility towards Britain. But most colonists had little stomach for further trouble and simply went about their normal business. The British also kept a low-key presence. The troops withdrew to Castle William and officials made few attempts to enforce the remaining taxes. In May 1769, the new chancellor, Lord North (Townshend died in September 1767), proposed to abolish all the Townshend Duties except the one on tea, serendipitously for American radicals as the boycott against British merchants that had been in place since 1767 was on the brink of collapse. Parliament agreed in March 1770.

After less than two years, however, the British began trying again to get the colonies in order, but found the colonists as determined as ever not to be pushed around. A British navy revenue ship called the *Gaspée* spent the spring of 1772 harassing trading ships in Narragansett Bay and, making matters worse, the captain allowed his crew to supplement their provisions by going on land to steal cattle and crops from local farmers. On 10 June, the ship ran aground near Providence, Rhode Island, and that night a crowd of local merchants, fishermen, farmers and labourers burnt it to the waterline. Parliament set up a commission of inquiry and offered a £500 reward for information leading to the arrest of the perpetrators. No one said a word and no one was ever prosecuted: a warning to the British about the solidarity of colonial hostility to their recent actions, but a warning that ultimately went unheeded.

The road to revolution, 1773–1775: The Tea Act to the outbreak of war

Even after the *Gaspée* incident and all that went before it, the British might have backed away from further confrontations with their fractious colonial subjects. But, in May 1773, First Minister Lord North set in motion a train of events leading pretty directly to independence. He persuaded parliament to pass the Tea Act, exempting the East India Company from this last remaining Townshend duty, effectively giving the then financially troubled corporation a monopoly in the American tea market. Also, cheap East India tea could only be sold by company consignees, not passed on to local merchants. Predictably enough, colonial merchants found the Tea Act unacceptable. British officials hoped, however, that consumers, with new access to cheaper tea, would take a different point of view. That proved to be a miscalculation, for suspicious colonists felt that if East India tea was cheap in the short run, it would not be once local traders had been driven from the market. All over America, therefore, colonists acted to prevent the company from landing and selling its tea. In Philadelphia and New York, groups of residents threatened company consignees with death if they did not resign. They resigned. In Annapolis, a crowd of people burned an East India Company ship, the *Peggy Stewart*, to the waterline. Most famously, on the night of 16 December, in Boston once again, a large crowd of local people, dressed as Mohawk Indians and led by local Sons of Liberty, boarded the *Beaver*, the *Dartmouth* and the *Eleanor*, the three East India Company ships in the harbour, and threw all the tea – 90,000 pounds of it – into the water.

The British authorities believed that events such as the Boston Tea Party were promulgated by a small number of troublemakers, as opposed to the popular actions they actually were. They felt, therefore, that with a swift and decisive response they could stamp the problem out. In the spring and summer of 1774, parliament passed four punitive measures: the Coercive Acts. In them, the British repeated many of the mistakes they had made before in dealing with the colonies, only on an even grander scale. The Impartial Administration of Justice Act provided for trials of those involved in the Tea Party in England and without a jury. The Boston Port Act closed the harbour until the city paid £9000 compensation to the East India Company, which Bostonians had no intention of doing. This act further alienated not only merchants, but also, once again, working people, who depended on the harbour for a living. The Quartering Act billeted troops in people's homes in Boston, as distinct from previously when they were billeted on unoccupied buildings, bringing home to colonists, in the most literal sense, the implications of the presence of a standing army in peacetime. The Massachusetts Government Act annulled the colony's charter, an arbitrary violation of the colonists' self-governing rights, and imposed what amounted to martial law. Its provisions made General Gage governor of the colony and gave him power to appoint the upper house, finally eliminating its susceptibility to popular control. The governor also gained the power to appoint sheriffs, and sheriffs gained the power to appoint juries. As well as abolishing elected juries, the act outlawed town meetings – the ancient New England institution that was a foundation of local rule and that had recently provided a platform for radicals – unless they were authorized by the governor.

The Coercive Acts were known in the colonies as the Intolerable Acts. There was another act of parliament of 1774 that was not a Coercive Act, but which colonists counted among the Intolerable Acts. The Quebec Act finally established a constitution for the colony captured from France in 1763. The constitution of Quebec included everything the colonists despised: the legislature was not to be elected but appointed by the crown; all acts were subject to royal veto; taxes were to be raised by Westminster; French civil law, lacking basic English rights such as habeas corpus and trial by jury, was to be retained; Catholicism would be tolerated; and, menacingly, the southern border of Quebec was redrawn southwards to the Ohio river, on territory that various colonies claimed by right of their charters, so that this authoritarian colony, which might be used for military invasion, bordered the other colonies not only along the north but also in a huge arc around the west.

However, at the very point when Britain attempted to assert its authority most strongly, the North American mainland part of the empire began to collapse. For one thing, the members of the abolished Massachusetts House of Assembly simply carried on meeting in Cambridge, just outside Boston, and later a little further away in Concord and then Salem, despite the Massachusetts Government Act supposedly having put them out of business. Moreover, on 7 October 1774, it declared itself to be a Provincial Congress, proclaiming that its members derived their authority not from the British crown but from the towns that the members represented. This was a momentous act: the Massachusetts representatives were declaring themselves to be a government in direct defiance to the official British government in Massachusetts. It was, in effect, a revolutionary government. Many saw the self-proclaimed existence of the Massachusetts Provincial Congress as tantamount to a declaration of independence.

Furthermore, from 5 September to 26 October, another unofficial quasi-governmental institution constituted itself. The Continental Congress comprised delegates from all the colonies that would later become part of the United States except Georgia. Its first action was to warn the Massachusetts colonists against taking aggressive measures, although it promised aid if the colony was attacked and called on people across the colonies to arm themselves in readiness for any British assault. The Congress also adopted the 'Declaration and Resolves', endorsing the Massachusetts Provincial Congress's Suffolk Resolves, which repeated objections to taxation without representation, reaffirmed commitment to the notion of diffused sovereignty and listed objections to the Intolerable Acts. The Continental Congress also adopted the Continental Association, an intercolonial non-importation agreement against British goods, under which local committees of inspection – another form of authority constituted in defiance of Britain – had enforcement power. In taking these actions, although it genuinely professed subordination to the king, the Continental Congress was acting, in effect, as a revolutionary government. It was a self-appointed body that made demands of Britain; it adopted a policy, the non-importation pact; and it franchised local committees to enforce its orders, to act, effectively, as its own police force. A series of rebellions was now turning into a full-blown revolution. The last thing the Congress did before adjourning was resolve to meet again the following May.[9]

The outbreak of war, 1775–1776

Before the Second Continental Congress could convene, however, war broke out. Parliament rejected compromise proposals from Edmund Burke and from former first ministers William Pitt and Lord North, all of which would have more or less accepted the colonists' terms. Instead, Colonial Secretary Lord Dartmouth ordered General Gage to get the colonies under control with a show of force. Gage knew that parliament was underestimating the extent of discontent and the resolve of the colonists. His request for 20,000 men, a massive force capable of all-out war, was, however, refused by London. He had at his disposal since he began governing Massachusetts in 1774 just 3500 troops, enough to infuriate but not to intimidate the colonists. Once again, the British administration at home misunderstood the nature of the problem they were dealing with.

Gage sent 700 men from Boston to hunt down Samuel Adams and John Hancock and capture an illegal arms cache in Concord. The soldiers set out on the night of 18 April 1775, but the colonists had a communication network at the ready, headed by Boston silversmith Paul Revere, who rode through the Massachusetts countryside that night warning that 'the Redcoats are coming' or 'the regulars are coming' (these words are commonly recalled as 'the British are coming', but this is a post-revolutionary recollection and likely a wrong one, for Revere's midnight ride pre-dated Independence and the colonists still considered themselves British). The British soldiers were thus met by a troop of civil militia at Lexington Green. The British killed 8, wounded 10, and moved on. Militiamen who had gathered from towns in the area then launched a surprise attack that killed 14 British soldiers at Concord Bridge. The redcoats were then subjected to sniping and surprise attacks on the march back to Boston. Altogether, around 275 British soldiers and 101 colonists lost their lives. These kinds of civil militiamen would prosecute the American war effort on their own until Congress adopted them as the core of a regular army, the Continental Army, under George Washington. Even afterwards, independent militias would serve an important role in the war, especially in suppressing loyalists and supporting the revolutionaries' new civil institutions.

After the battles of Lexington and Concord, militiamen from all over New England joined the Massachusetts forces besieging the British in Boston. With the arrival of reinforcements under generals William Howe, Henry Clinton and John Burgoyne, the British tried to break the siege. Gage chose to assault Breed's Hill on the Charlestown peninsular north of Boston (the ensuing battle would be named after nearby Bunker Hill). On 17 June, Gage sent 2200 troops up the hill to engage the entrenched Americans. When they neared the top, the colonists inflicted heavy casualties on the first few rows and the remainder panicked and hastily retreated. Half an hour later, having reformed their lines, the British attacked but were forced to withdraw once again. By the time of the third assault, though, the Americans were short of gunpowder and some resorted to throwing stones. The British took this as the signal for a bayonet charge that ousted the colonists and finally claimed the hill. The colonists lost 400 men, but the British lost 1054: a terribly expensive victory and, ultimately, a futile one. In early 1776, American forces occupied Dorchester Heights, south of Boston, and once again bombarded the British with cannon and mortar fire. On 17 March, Howe, who replaced Gage as British commander, withdrew his forces to Halifax, Nova Scotia, abandoning the city his soldiers had fought so hard for; he now faced the prospect of invading a continent.

Meanwhile, fighting broke out elsewhere too. On 10 May 1775 (the day the Second Continental Congress convened), a force of Green Mountain Boys under Ethan Allen of Vermont and Massachusetts militia under Benedict Arnold (later a traitor to the patriot cause) took Fort Ticonderoga and, two days later, Crown Point, gaining control of northern New York and forcing the British back over the Canadian border. In July, Congress ordered an invasion of Quebec, hoping to inspire an anti-British uprising by the *Canadiens*. The American invaders captured Montreal but were repelled from Quebec City on 31 December, as the cold northern winter was setting in. Further south, it was the British and their loyalist allies who took military initiatives, though they failed to suppress what was rapidly turning into an armed uprising on a continental scale. On 17 November 1775, Virginia Governor John Murray, Lord Dunmore, issued a proclamation offering freedom to slaves who would join him and fight against their disloyal masters. He raised a loyalist force but, after a defeat in December, he fled to a battleship off the coast and the most he managed to do from there was launch a naval assault on Norfolk, burning most of the port town on New Year's Day. In North Carolina, a combination of loyalist Scottish Highlanders and former Regulators attempted to join with a British expeditionary force under Lord Charles Cornwallis and Sir Henry Clinton at Wilmington, but were defeated at the battle of Moore's Creek on 18 February 1776. The British then moved down to South Carolina, hoping to capture Charleston, and on 28 June attacked a partially completed fort on Sullivan's Island (later named after its revolutionary war commander William Moultrie). The spongy palmetto log walls of the fort easily absorbed the British fire and the colonists were able to fire back at will, inflicting over 200 casualties and damaging every British ship present. The British then withdrew from the south, not returning for over two years.[10]

In the vacuum of power and under these wartime circumstances the Continental Congress inevitably took on yet more of the functions of government. It engaged in diplomacy, publishing a 'Declaration of the Causes of Taking Up Arms', but also offering the 'Olive Branch Petition' that called on George III to persuade parliament to end hostilities. On 23 August 1775, the king rejected it, instead proclaiming the colonies to be 'in open and avowed rebellion', which was true, and later that the rebels intended 'establishing an independent empire', which was not yet true. At the 26 October opening of parliament, the king stated his intentions and revealed his interpretation of imperial history. 'The object is too important', he said,

> the spirit of the British nation too high, the resources with which God hath blessed her too numerous, to give up so many colonies which she has planted with great industry, nursed with great tenderness, encouraged with many commercial advantages, and protected and defended at much expence of blood and treasure.

In December, parliament passed a Prohibitory Act, outlawing all colonial trade. Consequently, Congress began seeking alliances with other countries, eventually forming its decisive league of friendship with France. Congress carried out military policy, ordering the invasion of Canada, formed a regular army, the Continental Army, and appointed a commander-in-chief, George Washington. It also raised money to fight the war, printing £2000 in paper notes initially.[11]

Loyalism

Despite years of controversy over issues as fundamental as property, liberty and the constitution of the empire, and despite warfare that spread like wildfire from April 1775, it took some time for Congress to resolve on Independence. As natural as American independence may seem to us now, claiming it was a momentous step to take at the time. No other colony or group of colonies had done anything like it before in the modern age, and it took almost 30 years more for a second New World colony to gain its independence from a European power, when Haitian slaves revolted from 1794 and won freedom and independence from France 10 years later. Furthermore, colonists would be ensuring a long and, for all they knew, futile struggle against the mightiest power on earth. Moreover, American colonists still felt a powerful affinity with the mother country. Though migrants left or in some cases fled England or Britain to make a new life in America, they continued to consider themselves English or British. The societies and polities they established were recognizably British in form. Their economies, religions, cultures, architecture, clothes and books were almost all British in origin, and whatever adaptations colonists made to New World circumstances, colonial America remained and indeed became increasingly British in character. Colonists, including those who never set foot in Europe, commonly called Britain 'home'. Even after 1764, Americans defended their rights as colonists as the rights of freeborn Englishmen or Britons. John Dickinson saw no contradiction in opposing British policies while still proclaiming that 'every drop of blood in my heart is *British*'.[12]

 It was therefore difficult for colonists to abandon their Britishness, and many never did. Some one-third of colonists in what became the United States remained loyal to the crown even after Independence. Reasons for remaining loyal varied widely. Some had always deferred to British authority because they believed in order and obedience to the king, others because, like Britons at home, they revered parliament as the guarantor of the rights of freeborn Britons in America as well as in the home islands and therefore believed in parliamentary supremacy. Others still had been as vehement in their objections to British imperial policies as those who went on to fight the patriot cause, yet simply could not choose to become deadly enemies of their mother country when the moment of decision arrived. Some stayed loyal to Britain for reasons of particular exigency, most notably the slaves who ran to join Governor Dunmore and Amerindians whose best interests lay with British regulation of colonial territorial expansion. Western Carolina Regulators and New York tenants chose to oppose what local leaders and landlords supported. Remaining loyal required as much courage as turning patriot. Since 1764, those inaccurately deemed 'Tory' for defending or for inadequately opposing British policy were subjected to hangings in effigy, tarring and feathering and other forms of harassment and violence by 'Whig' opponents of British measures. When independence came, they first faced test acts and loyalty oaths, and then confiscation of property and expulsion from their homes. Few of those who stayed eventually got their property back. Many left: between 80,000 and 100,000 resettled in Britain or, more often, in Canada and the Caribbean during or at the end of the war.

The bulk of loyalists, in the larger imperial context, were those in the colonies north of New England, in the Floridas and in the islands of the Atlantic Ocean and the Caribbean Sea. Most of these colonists disliked taxation without representation and notions of parliamentary supremacy every bit as much as did those in the 13 colonies that declared independence. But the sparsely populated provinces of Canada and Florida were in no position to challenge the mother country militarily for independence or to survive economically without its support. In any case, most Quebecois were French or of French ancestry, and the rights of freeborn Britons meant little to them. Accustomed to the centralized constitution of New France and unaccustomed to habeas corpus, trial by jury and other liberties, they were not much affronted by parliamentary supremacy, and as long as they were left free to practise their Catholic religion they generally accommodated themselves to British imperial rule. In any case, they found the virulently anti-Catholic puritans of New England deeply unattractive. On the islands, with their enormous slave majorities and tiny white populations, vulnerability to invasion by rival Europeans or privateers and dependence on Britain and on other colonies for even such basic essentials as food, independence might well have been suicidal. For one reason or another, only the economically self-sufficient and demographically and politically stable colonies of the mainland from New England to Georgia could afford to consider independence.[13]

The Declaration of Independence

Those who finally did declare American Independence did not do so lightly. Some of those in the 13 colonies that became the United States had favoured independence for some time, but the best chance of victory required a critical mass of support that would obviate a civil war within the colonies and instead create mass support for a war of independence. For those in favour of independence, choosing the right moment meant the difference between victory and defeat, life and death. As Benjamin Franklin wittily warned his fellow signers of the Declaration of Independence, 'we must all hang together or, most assuredly, we shall hang separately'. For some time after war broke out then, Congress professed colonists' loyalty to king and mother country.[14]

Gradually, though, the idea of independence began to catch on. On 16 May 1775, soon after war broke out, the Massachusetts Provincial Congress requested that Congress draft a model constitution for all the colonies. New Hampshire's Provincial Congress did the same on 18 October. At this point, the Continental Congress refused to be pushed into sanctioning de facto declarations of independence. Massachusetts radically amended its constitution (abolishing its governor and creating a council appointed by the Congress) and on 5 January 1776 New Hampshire produced a brand new constitution for itself. South Carolina followed on 25 March, Virginia on 29 June (with a Declaration of Rights passed on 27 June) and New Jersey on 2 July. Other assemblies to declare themselves Provincial Congresses and repudiate their allegiance to the crown before 4 July included Georgia, North Carolina and Rhode Island. On April 12, North Carolina became the first to instruct its delegates in Congress to vote for independence if in concert with others, followed by Virginia on 15 May.

The Continental Congress was undoubtedly further emboldened by the impact of Thomas Paine's *Common Sense*, published on 10 January 1776. Paine, a Thetford-born radical and former excise man who had emigrated to Philadelphia only 13 months previously, launched a vitriolic attack on the institution of monarchy and recent British actions, and with its strident calls for immediate independence and the establishment of an American republic, it either captured people's imaginations or, more likely, articulated what many were already thinking or feeling. Either way, it went into 25 reprint editions and sold as many as 150,000 copies, when most pamphlets and newspapers sold only a few thousand. Its sales were only part of the story. As Philadelphia physician and politician Benjamin Rush wrote, 'Its effects were sudden and extensive upon the American mind. It was read by public men, repeated in clubs, spouted in Schools, and in one instance, delivered from a pulpit instead of a sermon by a clergyman in Connecticut.' One of those 'public men' was General George Washington, who, though no admirer of Paine's more radical ideas, described *Common Sense* as 'working a powerful change in the minds of many men', persuading them of 'the propriety of separation'. By June 1776, then, there was not only the widespread support required for a declaration of independence, but considerable popular pressure in several colonies that forced political leaders to pass their own declarations of independence or to instruct their delegates in Philadelphia to do so in conjunction with others.[15]

One of the colonies where there was a popular push for independence was Virginia, and on 7 June 1776, Richard Henry Lee, a Virginia delegate in Philadelphia, proposed that Congress pass a 'resolution of independence' asserting that 'these United Colonies are, and of right ought to be, free and independent States, that they are absolved from all allegiance to the British Crown, and that all political connection between them and the State of Great Britain is, and ought to be, totally dissolved'. Three days later, Congress appointed a committee comprising John Adams, Benjamin Franklin, Thomas Jefferson, Robert R. Livingston and Roger Sherman to 'prepare a declaration to the effect of' Lee's resolution. Jefferson was chosen as principal author on account, according to John Adams's recollections, of his 'peculiar felicity of expression'. After submitting his work first to Adams and Franklin, then to the rest of the committee, the five men handed their draft to Congress on 28 June. On 2 July, Congress voted in favour of Lee's resolution, although Americans celebrate their independence on 4 July, the day Congress approved the final and in some ways significantly redrafted declaration.

The Declaration of Independence represented certain shifts in American political thought and language that were necessitated by the fact of independence. Colonists, as colonial subjects, had previously rested their arguments against British measures on the basis of the rights of free Englishmen or Britons. In declaring themselves no longer British, however, they could not very well continue to do so. Instead, the Declaration referred to the natural rights of all mankind. Hence Jefferson employed what have become the most famous words of the Declaration: 'We hold these truths to be self-evident, that all men are created equal, that they are endowed by their Creator with certain unalienable Rights, that among these are Life, Liberty and the pursuit of Happiness.'

Jefferson clearly drew on John Locke's *Second Treatise of Government*, with its claims about the rights to 'life, liberty, and property'. The aim of eighteenth-century rhetoric in general, and the purpose of the Declaration of Independence in particular, was not to say something new but to express the thoughts of others, and even if necessary the words of others. As Jefferson wrote to Richard Henry Lee almost 50 years later, his aim in writing the Declaration was not

> to find out new principles, or new arguments . . . but to place before mankind the common sense of the subject, in terms so plain and firm as to command their assent. . . . All its authority rests then on the harmonizing sentiments of the day, whether expressed in conversation, in letters, printed essays, or the elementary books of public right, as Aristotle, Cicero, Locke, Sidney, etc.

For American colonists, those sentiments were put into practice in their colonial charters, conceived in Lockean fashion as contracts between colonies and crown voluntarily entered into by American settlers and English kings, and equally binding still. Hence also the meaning of the words immediately following those above, also distinctly Lockean, would have been clear to all colonists:

> That to secure these rights, Governments are instituted among Men, deriving their just powers from the consent of the governed. That whenever any Form of Government becomes destructive of these ends, it is the Right of the People to alter or to abolish it, and to institute new Government, laying its foundation on such principles and organizing its powers in such form, as to them shall seem most likely to effect their Safety and Happiness.

After the preamble's enunciation of natural rights, the social contract and the right to revolt, the bulk of the Declaration of Independence comprises a list of calumnies the colonies suffered that justified this particular revolt. All the measures that American colonists objected to after 1764 were acts of parliament, and yet the 'history of repeated injuries and usurpations' that the Declaration listed were laid at the feet of the king. Parliament was mentioned only twice and even then obliquely. The Declaration begins a particular group of grievances with the words, 'He has combined with others to subject us to a jurisdiction foreign to our constitution, and unacknowledged by our laws; giving his Assent to their Acts of pretended Legislation.' That meant parliament, of course, though the word was evidently unprintable. Towards the end of the Declaration, drawing attention to times when colonists appealed to their 'Brittish brethren', the document states that 'We have warned them from time to time of attempts by their legislature to extend an unwarrantable jurisdiction over us.'

Yet, besides the obvious populist and propagandistic advantages of identifying a singular focus of blame, there was a particular American logic behind the apparent disjuncture between the Declaration's account and the actuality of recent events. Blaming the king converged with the colonial theory of empire wherein colonists felt they owed allegiance to the king, not to parliament. But that allegiance was contingent on his protection against oppression. If he failed to protect his colonial subjects against acts of oppression, he may as well have committed those acts himself. Jefferson's *A Summary View of the Rights of British America* (1774) and Congress's Olive Branch Petition had appealed to George III to override parliamentary taxes and other measures. Here, the colonists failed to understand the nature of eighteenth-century English constitutionalism. For a constitutional monarch, following the precepts of the Glorious Revolution, to override parliament would have been an outrage, something no monarch had done since 1708. George III was a law-abiding constitutional monarch. Yet the principle of coordination and the idea of the crown-in-parliament were alien concepts to the American colonists. There had been no Glorious

Revolution settlement in the colonies in 1689, and colonists continued to hold to a civil war concept of political separation and tension, not of collusion, between the executive and legislative branches of government. The Declaration of Independence thus implicitly acknowledged but entirely rejected the precepts of 1689, as those were understood in Britain.[16]

The War of Independence: the northern campaigns to 1778

For Americans, the Declaration of Independence changed the nature of the war that had begun on Lexington Green over a year earlier. Before 4 July 1776, the conflict was not a war for independence but an insurrection, an armed rebellion against government policies, a civil war at most. After the Declaration, the conflict was a fully-fledged revolutionary war for national liberation. The Declaration was less significant to the British, though, who felt both before and after 4 July that they were merely enforcing order upon truculent colonials. At the time that Americans declared their independence, the British were focusing their military attention on the north. On 2 July 1776, British forces landed at Staten Island, New York, the vanguard of some 32,000 troops who, by mid-August, gathered near New York under General William Howe and his brother, Admiral Lord Richard Howe, in command of 73 warships and 13,000 seamen. The plan was to capture New York City and isolate New England to the east, which they believed to be the heart of the rebellion.

Naturally, Congress and General Washington were eager to defend New York. In their first encounter on Long Island on 27 August, Howe surprised the Americans, inflicted 1500 casualties and divided their forces in two. Howe then hesitated, allowing Washington to escape to Manhattan Island, reunite his army, take on the British in some minor engagements and, above all, evade being encircled before retreating into New Jersey and then crossing the Delaware River into Pennsylvania to rest and recuperate. The British nevertheless captured New York and retained it throughout the war. Howe also established outposts in Newport, Rhode Island and various parts of New Jersey, and then settled down for the winter. Washington, however, ignored the European custom of settling down for winter. Wanting to end the year on a higher note than the Long Island defeat and subsequent retreat, he audaciously exploited the troops Howe had left isolated in New Jersey. On Christmas night, he slipped back across the Delaware River with fewer than 3000 men and surprised a camp of 1500 Hessian troops at Trenton, New Jersey, capturing or killing 1000 of them with only 6 of his own wounded. (In all, the British recruited some 30,000 German mercenaries during the war, adding significantly to American resentment.) At Princeton, a few miles north, the Americans defeated three regiments of redcoats on 3 January before retreating across the river to settle for the winter at Morristown, New Jersey, north-west of New York.

Despite these victories, the early campaigns had been demoralizing for the patriots. During the depressing September march through New Jersey, Thomas Paine, now a volunteer in the Continental Army, wrote a pamphlet entitled *The American Crisis*. Memorably and prophetically, it opened with these words:

> These are the times that try men's souls. The summer soldier and the sunshine patriot will, in this crisis, shrink from the service of his country; but he that stands it *now*, deserves the love and thanks of man and woman. Tyranny, like hell, is not easily conquered; yet we have this consolation with us, that the harder the conflict, the more glorious the triumph. What we obtain too cheap, we esteem too lightly: it is dearness only that gives everything its value.[17]

During the winter in the woods around Morristown, many soldiers did indeed desert, some simply leaving once their year-long terms were up, others only temporarily to care for their families. Only about 1000 Continental soldiers (those in the regular army) plus some militiamen stuck it out through the whole winter. Nevertheless, in the spring of 1777, new recruits began arriving, encouraged by the victories at Trenton and Princeton, inspired by Paine's words and attracted by bounties of $20 and 100 acres of land. By the time active hostilities resumed, the Continental Army was a force of 9000 men.

Washington's forces suffered badly in the Pennsylvania theatre the next year, though defeats there were far less significant than American victories elsewhere. In July, Howe took his forces south down the New Jersey coast, north up the Chesapeake Bay and inland to approach the American capital, Philadelphia. Washington failed to repel the British at Brandywine Creek on 11 September, and a week later Howe occupied Philadelphia, while Congress fled to Lancaster and then York, Pennsylvania. On 4 October, Washington attacked British positions north of Germantown, but was beaten back by British reinforcements from Philadelphia. After that, he and his men retreated to camp for the bitter winter at Valley Forge. Yet these engagements sapped Howe's manpower and morale more than they did Washington's. While Washington took about 2000 losses in the Pennsylvania campaigns and Howe half that number, the former's forces could be replenished more readily than the latter's. The Americans also improved their military practices while wintering at Valley Forge, in particular with standardized drill procedures introduced by Friedrich Wilhelm von Steuben.

Moreover, in taking most of his forces out of New York, Howe had effectively abandoned General John Burgoyne in the north. In June 1777, Burgoyne moved with 7000 men south from Canada and in early July recaptured Fort Ticonderoga. At that point, however, he delayed, allowing General Philip Schuyler to place obstructions on the route to the Hudson

Valley and a large American force to gather around General Horatio Gates in the Mohawk Valley. Attempting to move further south, Burgoyne was met and defeated twice, on 19 September and 7 October, at Bemis Heights, near the head of the Hudson River. Retreating north, Burgoyne then found himself besieged at the village of Saratoga. With no hope of rescue from the few forces left behind by Howe in New York, Burgoyne surrendered on 17 October. His 5700 troops captured, Burgoyne went home in disgrace. The military implications of the loss were bad enough, but the diplomatic ones were serious too. Burgoyne's submission to terms with Gates elevated the status of the Continental Army and Congress from that of traitors to that of sovereign authorities. A British critic of Burgoyne noted that the 'history of nations affords no instance of a convention or treaty, made with Rebels'. One in New York wrote that the British 'call the Americans, Rebels: yet in every instance they are treated like the Subjects of an Independent State'.

Saratoga turned out to be decisive because it finally brought France more fully into the war. France had already provided substantial supplies to the Americans, including most of their gunpowder. But, while hoping that the war would cause Britain significant difficulty, the French, like others, had not hitherto supposed that the Americans could win. When news of the American victory at Saratoga reached Paris on 4 December, though, it inspired jubilation and changed French minds about the potentialities of the American insurgency. On 6 February 1778, the French and the Americans signed the Treaty of Amity and Commerce in which France recognized the United States and granted it trading privileges. They also signed the Treaty of Alliance, in which both sides agreed to fight on until American independence was won, that neither would make peace with the British without the consent of the other, and that they would guarantee each other's territories in the Americas 'from the present time and forever against all other powers'. In 1778, naval war broke out between Britain and France, and Britain's military resources were stretched further still when Spain joined with France in the hope of regaining territories lost in previous wars, in particular Gibraltar. In 1780, Britain declared war on the Netherlands because the Dutch had continued trading with France and the United States. As the American War of Independence reached a crucial juncture, therefore, Britain found itself fighting in Europe, Africa, India and all across the world's oceans as well as in the Americas.

After Saratoga, the British were more willing to make concessions, short of recognizing American Independence. On 16 March 1778, parliament repealed the Tea Act, the Coercive Acts and the Prohibitory Act and passed a new Declaratory Act that renounced parliamentary taxation of the colonies, in effect promising to return to imperial arrangements as they had been before 1764, only with explicit acknowledgement of the rights that colonists demanded. Parliament also despatched a peace commission headed by the Earl of Carlisle. As with Burgoyne's surrender, some were appalled that the government should 'treat with those who denied, and took up arms in opposition to the authority of parliament . . . the *unlawful* and *vagrant* assembly, the Congress'. In the end it hardly mattered anyway, for the commissioners reached America after Congress approved the French Alliance that committed the United States to independence not only through their own Declaration but also by international treaty.[18]

The War of Independence: the southern campaigns to 1781

The peace commissioners were undermined in any case by a change in British military strategy. Following Saratoga, Clinton replaced Howe as commander-in-chief and was ordered to withdraw from Philadelphia, defend the north from New York and relaunch the British campaign in the south. Washington pursued Clinton across New Jersey and he and General Charles Lee caught up with the 12–mile long British lines and launched an assault at Monmouth Courthouse on 28 June. The battle was militarily indecisive, but much better for American morale than it was for British. Clinton withdrew to New York, exactly where the main British land forces had been located two years before, while Washington took up positions north of the city on White Plains. An occasionally violent stalemate then ensued until the end of the war.

In the meantime, Americans were winning significant victories in the west against the British and their Native American allies. Amerindians knew that independence would eliminate the Proclamation Line, and therefore had good reason to fight for the British against the Americans. Throughout the war, Daniel Boone and a small band of settlers resisted numerous attacks by the British and their Shawnee allies and thereby maintained an American toehold in the Kentucky region. On 4 July 1778, George Rogers Clark surprised and routed a British force at Kaskaskia on the Mississippi River in the Illinois region south of what would later be St Louis. In February 1779, he defeated the British again at Vincennes on the Wabash River and then moved east to defend settlers in western Pennsylvania, winning an important victory at Newton (now Elmira) on 29 August, with the assistance of 4000 men supplied by Washington. Clark and General John Sullivan then carried out Washington's wish that the Iroquois should not be 'merely overrun but destroyed'. Thereafter there was sporadic resistance by Native Americans, but their strength was broken and the way was clear for the massive westward migration of Americans that would take place once the war was over.

The Americans even won some victories on the seas, despite Britain's awesome naval power. In the spring of 1778, John Paul Jones, using a French sloop-of-war, the *Bonhomme Richard* out of Brest, began attacking British merchant ships in home waters. That year, he defeated the British warship *Drake* and attacked the Cumbrian port of Whitehaven. In 1779, he threatened Leith, near Edinburgh, and in September he captured two more British warships, *Serapis* and the *Countess of Scarborough*, off the Yorkshire coast. Jones's naval activities were more than a military nuisance. They sent insurance prices up, British morale down, further encouraged French naval expansion and engagement in the war and made the world more aware of American Independence and its potentialities.

But most of the fighting from 1778 occurred on mainland North America, south of the Potomac River. Despite Howe's warnings (Howe was now back in England), Colonial Secretary George Germaine, Viscount Sackville, chose to believe that loyalists could control large areas of the south while the British army could suppress the rest. At first, this new southern strategy seemed to work. In the winter of 1778–79, the British captured Georgia and French Admiral Charles Henri Comte d'Estaing's siege of Savannah failed to dislodge them. The French navy then retreated to the West Indies. On 12 May 1780, American General Benjamin Lincoln abandoned Charleston, South Carolina, with 5500 patriots captured. Following his triumph in Saratoga, Congress put Horatio Gates in charge of the southern forces, but after losing the battle of Camden, South Carolina, on 16 August 1780, he withdrew to North Carolina and left much of the south undefended. Then, however, the war turned against the British.

One problem was that before leaving Charleston Clinton issued a proclamation restoring citizenship to patriots who would take an oath of allegiance to the crown and assist in the subjugation of the South Carolina countryside, forcing rebels who might otherwise have gone home into continuing the struggle, while simultaneously infuriating loyalists with this overly forgiving act. The war in the South then turned especially vicious. Patriot 'overmountain men' destroyed Patrick Ferguson's 1000-strong loyalist forces at King's Mountain in the south-west of North Carolina on 7 October 1780. On 17 January 1781, Britain's Banastre 'Bloody' Tarleton (who earned that nickname by executing prisoners of war) suffered a decisive defeat by General Daniel Morgan's forces at nearby Cowpens, in the north-west of South Carolina, losing 900 men to Morgan's 72. Meanwhile, Congress appointed Nathanael Greene commander in the south, and he proved devastatingly adept at using guerrilla tactics to wear down the British in what was becoming a war of attrition. First, he lured the southern commander, Lord Charles Cornwallis, and some of his forces out of Charleston into a tiring and wasteful chase across the Carolinas before engaging them at Guilford Courthouse, North Carolina, on 15 March 1781. Losing 250 men, Greene withdrew, technically conceding the battle, but he had taken out a quarter of Cornwallis's forces, 100 killed and 400 wounded. Cornwallis retreated to coastal Wilmington. Greene then joined with guerrilla forces that had formed since King's Mountain and Cowpens to harass British soldiers with flash attacks that inflicted hundreds more casualties before the British retreated to Charleston and Savannah on the coast, back where they started.

Greene hoped the redcoats would chase him again, but Cornwallis made the fateful decision to subdue Virginia instead. Joining with Benedict Arnold, who turned Tory in September 1780, the combined force of 7200 men almost captured Governor Thomas Jefferson and the Virginia assembly in an attack on Charlottesville on 4 June 1781. On 1 August, however, Cornwallis settled his troops at Yorktown, a spot he chose as a naval base, thinking that with the British navy in command of the seas he was safe on this Chesapeake peninsula. Instead, he made himself and his men a sitting target and soon American and French forces were bearing down on them from all directions.

In 1780, Comte Jean Baptiste, Donatier de Rochambeau, and 5500 men had captured Newport, Rhode Island, and thereafter protected the town with a naval detachment under Comte de Barras. The next July, Rochambeau and Washington agreed to combine forces and attack New York. Before they did, however, news reached them that French Admiral Comte François Joseph Paul de Grasse was heading from the West Indies to the Yorktown peninsula with 20 ships of the line and 3000 troops. Marie Joseph, Marquis de Lafayette, and forces from Pennsylvania blocked Corwallis's route out of the peninsula while Washington and Rochambeau headed south, though they took a route that suggested an assault on New York, tricking Clinton into readying his defences rather than preparing an attack. At the same time, a naval squadron under de Barras trapped the British on land. On 6–9 September, de Grasse defeated an inadequate British naval force under Admiral Thomas Graves that had come down to the Chesapeake from New York, and then sent ships up the bay to collect the combined Franco-American forces of 17,000, who subsequently besieged Cornwallis and his 8000 men. The British held out until 17 October, when, four years to the day since Saratoga, a drummer beat the call for a truce and waved the white flag. On 19 October, Cornwallis and the British troops formally surrendered, while their pipers played 'The World Turned Upside Down', a song from the era of the English civil wars.[19]

The Treaty of Paris, 1783

Leading British politicians recognized right away the significance of Cornwallis's surrender and the defeat broke British resolve. Lord North is reported to have said as soon as he heard the news: 'Oh God, it's all over.' Lord Chief Justice Loughborough wrote that a 'general despondency was the first effect of Lord Cornwallis's surrender' and opposition MP, William Weddell, wrote to his wife that 'every Body seems really sick of carrying on ye American War'. New British commander, Sir Guy Carleton, kept troops in New York in the hope of forcing an exhausted American regime into retaining some connection with the crown, but few at home were interested anymore. On 27 February 1782, parliament voted against continuing the war, and on 5 March authorized the government to negotiate for peace. North and Germaine resigned and on 20 March the Marquis of Rockingham once again became first minister. Rockingham died in September, however, and was replaced by Lord Shelburne, who, as colonial secretary, had proved reasonably well disposed towards the colonists. It was he who oversaw the peace negotiations in Paris.[20]

The position of the American peace commissioners, John Adams, Benjamin Franklin, John Jay and Henry Laurens, was a complicated one. The United States was obliged to continue fighting until France made peace with Britain, but in a separate alliance France was obliged to fight on until Spain secured Gibraltar. By 30 November 1782, the Americans had negotiated a preliminary peace treaty with Britain, but it remained provisional. In early 1783, France and Spain gave up on Gibraltar and reached an armistice with Britain. The various parties finally signed the Treaty of Paris on 23 September. According to the treaty, Britain recognized the United States as an independent nation and acknowledged American claims to all lands east of the Mississippi River. Britain retained the Canadian colonies, but returned East Florida to Spain. The status of the largely unsettled lands of West Florida remained ambiguous. Britain agreed to withdraw its forces in the north-west into Canada, though it later reneged on this commitment. Britain also later reneged on promises to allow Americans to fish off Newfoundland and in the Gulf of St Lawrence and dry their catches on unsettled parts of the Canadian coast, and to allow American merchants to trade freely in the British West Indies. The British violated these parts of the treaty because the Americans were not entirely unshifty themselves. On the issue of pre-revolutionary merchant debts, negotiators agreed that British merchants would 'meet with no legal impediment' to repayment, which was something less than a promise that they would be paid. The Americans also agreed that Congress would 'earnestly recommend' that confiscated property would be returned to loyalists. It never was.

On 26 April 1783, 7000 loyalists were evacuated from New York, the last of those to flee to Canada, Europe and the West Indies from the loyalty oaths, test acts, disfranchisement, confiscations and expulsions imposed on them by the newly free American states after the Declaration of Independence. On 24 November, the last British troops left New York and on 4 December they left Long Island and Staten Island. Also, on 4 December, George Washington said farewell to his officers at Fraunces Tavern in New York, and on 23 December handed in his resignation to the Congress, then sitting in Annapolis, Maryland. He was home at Mount Vernon in time for Christmas.

Despite the immensity of its wealth and power, winning the War of American Independence was never going to be easy for Britain. Political and military authorities made mistakes, to be sure. One was in vacillating between a strategy of engaging in battles aimed at destroying the enemy with decisive blows and of engaging the enemy in a variety of actions aimed at wearing them down. The British therefore never exploited fully the benefits of either strategy. Worse, Howe and Clinton proved hesitant at key moments and let opportunities slip by, while Burgoyne and Cornwallis fatally overreached themselves. The British also failed to coordinate their land and sea operations. But the Americans had advantages that the British could do little about. The generalship of Washington and Greene, in particular, was at times inspired, as was the decisive coordinated assault of Washington, Rochambeau, Lafayette, de Barras and de Grasse on Cornwallis at Yorktown. As important, the Americans possessed the determination that came with defending their homeland and, in some cases, their homes. Furthermore, the terrain was unfamiliar and difficult for the British, especially as much of the fighting took place in areas of wilderness. Moreover, the territory that the British were required to subdue was vast, a thousand miles long and in places several hundred miles wide, and there was no vital centre from which they might control the whole. This problem became even worse when the war went global in 1778. Although the British committed 56,000 men to the field, they never had the numbers needed to hold down the rebellious colonies indefinitely.

Perhaps most of all, though, it proved impossible to suppress a people at arms who were convinced of their rights and determined to fight. The British finally learned that they could not govern the American colonies without the colonists' consent, however much force they tried to use and however well they might use it. In this respect, the outcome of the American war had little to do with the mistakes of politicians or military men in the 1770s and 1780s and more to do with the circumstances of colonial development and imperial government in the preceding century and a half. The colonists had created the American settlements by themselves and had throughout their histories more or less governed themselves. They were not about to sacrifice the rights and liberties they created and to which they had grown accustomed to the imperial imaginings of a new age of Britons. The British learned the lesson well. In the future, when and where possible, imperial authorities would endeavour to ensure that habits of colonial self-government would not become as entrenched as they did in the American colonies. Americans, meanwhile, had lessons to learn while creating new governments for a new republic.

Notes

1 William Pitt and George Grenville, speeches to parliament, 1763, 1764, Soame Jenyns, *The Objections to the Taxation of Our American Colonies, by the Legislature of Great Britain, Briefly Consider'd* (1765), William Bollan, *The Mutual Interest of Great Britain and the American Colonies Considered with respect to an Act Passed Last Session of Parliament for Laying a Duty on Merchandise, Etc., with Some Remarks on a Pamphlet, Intitled, 'Objections to the Taxation of the American Colonies, Etc. Considered'. In a Letter to a Member of Parliament* (1765), in Eliga H. Gould, *The Persistence of Empire: British Political Culture in the Age of the American Revolution* (Chapel Hill, 2000), pp. 106, 115, 116, 130; Benjamin Franklin, 'On the Tenure of the Manor of East Greenwich', 1766, in Jack P. Greene, *Peripheries and Center: Constitutional Development in the Extended Polities of the British Empire and the United States, 1607–1788* (New York, 1986), p. 67.

2 Newcastle to Archbishop of Canterbury, in Stephen Conway, 'Britain and the Revolutionary Crisis, 1763–1791', in P.J. Marshall, ed., *The Oxford History of the British Empire* Volume II: *The Eighteenth Century* (Oxford, 1998), p. 329; Samuel Eliot Morison, ed., *Sources and Documents Illustrating the American Revolution, 1764–1788, and the Formation of the Federal Constitution* (1923, Oxford, 1979), p. 33; *The Celebrated Speech of a Celebrated Commoner* (1766), in Gould, *Persistence of Empire*, p. 126.

3 *Summary View of the Rights of British America* (1774), Jefferson Papers, University of Virginia; Morison, *Documents*, p. 158.

4 Private letter (1775), in Robert M. Calhoun, *Dominion and Liberty: Ideology in the Anglo-American World, 1660–1801* (Arlington Heights, IL, 1994), p. 66; *A Letter from an Officer at New-York to a Friend in London* (1777), in Gould, *Persistence of Empire*, p. 189; *Historical and Political Reflections on the . . . American Rebellion* (1780), in Peter Charles Hoffer, *The Brave New World: A History of Early America* (Boston, 2000), p. 493.

5 Isaac Barré, speech in parliament, 1766; Thomas Whately, *The Regulations Lately Made concerning the Colonies*, in Gould, *Persistence of Empire*, pp. 130, 119; Edmund Burke, in Conway, 'Britain and the Revolutionary Crisis', p. 330.

6 George Grenville, speech to parliament, 1764, in Hoffer, *Brave New World*, p. 468; Morison, *Documents*, pp. 17–18, 33; 'Examination of Benjamin Franklin' and Bernard's speech to the Massachusetts General Court, 1765, in Gould, *Persistence of Empire*, pp. 128–9, 122.

7 Townshend to Duke of Grafton, 25 May 1767, in Conway, 'Britain and the Revolutionary Crisis', p. 332; *Letters from a Farmer in*

Pennsylvania, to the Inhabitants of the British Colonies (1768), in Paul Leicester Ford, ed., *The Writings of John Dickinson* (Philadelphia, 1895), p. 373.

8 Shelburn to Chatham, 18 March 1767, in Conway, 'Britain and the Revolutionary Crisis', p. 331.

9 Declaration and Resolves of the Continental Congress, 14 October 1774, The Association, 20 October 1774, in Morison, *Documents*, pp. 118–25.

10 David Hackett Fischer, *Paul Revere's Ride* (Oxford, 1994); Mark V. Kwasny, *Washington's Partisan War, 1775–1783* (Kent, OH, 1996); Don Higginbotham, *The War of American Independence: Military Attitudes, Policies, and Practice, 1763–1789* (New York, 1971) pp. 57–97.

11 Royal Proclamation, 23 August 1775, Address to Parliament, 26 October, 1775, in Francis D. Cogliano, *Revolutionary America: A Political History, 1763–1815* (London, 2000), pp. 61–2.

12 An Address to the Committee of Correspondence in Barbados (1766), in Gould, *Persistence of Empire*, p. 125.

13 Mary Beth Norton, *The British-Americans: the Loyalist Exile in England, 1774–1789* (Boston, 1972); Robert M. Calhoon, *The Loyalists in Revolutionary America, 1760–1781* (New York, 1973).

14 H.W. Brands, *The First American: The Life and Times of Benjamin Franklin* (New York, 2000), p. 512.

15 Benjamin Rush to James Cheetham, 17 July 1809, George Washington, reported by William Reed, n.d., in John Keane, *Tom Paine: A Political Life* (London, 1995), pp. 112, 111.

16 Declaration of Independence, in Morison, *Documents*, pp. 157–61; Lee Resolution (1776), Thomas Jefferson to Richard Henry Lee (1825), in Carl L. Becker, *The Declaration of Independence: A Study in the History of Political Ideas* (1922, New York, 1970), pp. 25–6. See also Garry Wills, *Inventing America: Jefferson's Declaration of Independence* (New York, 1978) and Pauline Maier, *American Scripture: How America Declared Independence from Britain* (New York, 1997).

17 Thomas Paine, *The American Crisis*, in Bruce Kuklick, ed., *Thomas Paine: Political Writings* (Cambridge, 1989), p. 40.

18 Anon., A Letter to Lieut. General Burgoyne, on His Letter to His Constituents (1779), anon. letter from New York (1778), Edmund Jenings, *Considerations on the Mode and Terms of a Treaty of Peace with America* (1778), in Gould, *Persistence of Empire*, pp. 194, 196.

19 Samuel Eliot Morison, *The Oxford History of the American People* (Oxford, 1965), p. 265; Higginbotham, *War of American Independence*, pp. 98–388.

20 Conway, 'Britain and the Revolutionary Crisis', pp. 342–3.

9

Afterword: The United States and the new British Empire

Between the middle of the seventeenth century and the middle of the eighteenth, imperial administrators attempted to create a coherent, corporate or unitary empire out of the diverse and disparate colonies in America. In those years they received occasional assistance from crown and parliament, but none that was sufficiently systematic or sustained to make the British Empire much more than an imaginary construct. From 1764, however, parliament asserted a new imperial order defined by its own supremacy and by the subordination of colonies to the mother country. In turn, Britons were astonished to witness a series of rebellions culminating with the Declaration of Independence and a successful revolutionary war.

British administrators learned from this experience that the root of the problem of imperial governance lay in the private and autonomous origins of colonies. Late in the day top-down solutions such as parliament declaring and asserting its authority did not work in an empire that was built from the bottom up and in which colonists therefore felt that self-government was a constitutional and indeed natural right. In the future, colonization would become part and parcel of a centrally controlled process of empire building. In the meantime, however, colonists in Canada, the Caribbean, Ireland and India were accustomed to or else aspired to the kind of self-government that characterized the first British Empire. Here, too, imperial administrators attempted to minimize colonial autonomy and maximize imperial authority, but they did so with a great deal of caution. This chapter traces how British authorities edged their way carefully towards a new imperial order.

The first part of this chapter, however, explores how the people of the new United States worked out what forms of government they would adopt for themselves. At the state level, they created new constitutions that redefined relationships between executives, legislatures and judiciaries. Also, having decided to form a United States as opposed to 13 separate nations, they had to define relations between these branches of government at the national level, and between central, state and local government. Furthermore, Americans had to craft a new relationship between government and the governed. The American Revolution, with its rhetoric of rights and liberties and with its success having depended on the contributions of ordinary people, politicized large numbers of people who had not normally participated in politics before 1763. As the historian Carl Becker put it in 1909, the American Revolution was not only about 'home rule', but became a domestic conflict over 'who shall rule at home'.[1]

Initially, experience with imperial governors and the popular nature of the Revolution inspired Americans to experiment with simple and responsive forms of state government. Some of the early state constitutions dispensed with governors altogether, two erected government by unicameral legislatures and most ensured annual elections. In time, however, practical problems of governance encouraged a retreat from this radicalism and the creation of more complex and remote governments. Most of the states revised their constitutions to create bicameral legislatures, extend executive power and make government more remote from and less responsive to the people; tendencies exemplified in the forming of the federal constitution that went into effect in 1789. The revised state and new federal constitutions ensured that the elites that dominated colonial political life before 1776 would dominate national political life after 1789. Yet those elites had to negotiate and compromise. To revise the state constitutions and to create the new federal constitution, reformers had to hold special conventions, ostensibly of the people. To get the new constitutions ratified, they had to hold plebiscites. As a result, while in practice the new systems of government shifted power away from the people, the reformers had to accede to a new principle that came to define American republicanism: the sovereignty of the people.

Social change in revolutionary America

The spirit of liberty that found expression in revolutionary pamphlets and the Declaration of Independence, also found expression in the streets. Without the participation of ordinary men and women, the 'lower sort' of people, the American Revolution would never have happened. It was they who participated in the Stamp Act riots, the Liberty Riot, the King Street Riot that preceded the Boston Massacre, the Boston Tea Party, and the multitudinous other actions carried out against British officials and their supporters. John Adams gave a sense of the popular composition of revolutionary crowds when he described those confronting the soldiers the night of the Boston Massacre as 'a motley rabble of saucey boys, runaway apprentices, negroes and mulattoes, Irish teagues and out landish jack tarrs'. As the Revolution progressed, these kinds of people began to institutionalize their involvement in politics. First, they joined or forced their ways into the Sons of Liberty chapters, originally composed mostly of well-heeled men who had the money, time and learning to engage in politics. Next, they comprised the bulk of members of committees of inspection that formed the Continental Association, which enforced the boycott of British trade after the Intolerable Acts of 1774, and then the committees of safety that appeared when fighting broke out in 1775. In some colonies it was popular pressure or fear of an uncontrolled popular rebellion that prompted political leaders into instructing their delegates in Congress to declare independence in 1776.[2]

Radical protest was not just directed at the British but at inequities at home as well. As John Adams observed to his wife, Abigail, in April 1776: 'We have been told that our struggle has loosened the bonds of government everywhere; that children and apprentices were disobedient; that schools and colleges were grown turbulent; that Indians slighted their guardians; that negroes grew more insolent to their masters.' Indeed, among the most significant advances of the Revolution were those made for and made by African-Americans. Colonists soon noticed the disjuncture between their calls for liberty and the existence in their midst of slavery. Reverend Jeremy Belknap noted retrospectively in 1795 that at 'the beginning of our controversy with Great-Britain, several persons, who before had entertained sentiments opposed to the slavery of blacks, did then take occasion publickly to remonstrate against the inconsistency of contending for our liberty, and at the same time depriving other people of theirs'. By that time, all the states north of Maryland had abolished or were about to abolish slavery, either with immediate effect or gradually by legislating that slaves born after a certain date were to be freed in early adulthood. Belknap's letter was written to St George Tucker, a Virginia jurist, and highlights the fact that slavery was not abolished in the staple plantation states of the South. Even so, southern state legislatures passed manumission laws that freed masters to liberate their slaves if they so wished.

African-Americans had more reason than anyone to grasp the full meanings of revolutionary rhetoric about liberty and they often liberated themselves. The death of Crispus Attucks, one of John Adams's 'Jack Tars' in the Kings Street Riot, though he was a free sailor and not a slave, gave notice that African-Americans were as determined to fight for freedom as anyone else. The thousands of southern slaves who fled their masters following Lord Dunmore's proclamation, some of whom fought for the British, confirmed this fact, to the point that George Washington was eventually persuaded to allow black men to fight for the patriot cause too. Other black people employed the political system to quicken the end of slavery, such as those who petitioned northern legislatures for their freedom from as early as 1774, in particular in Pennsylvania and Massachusetts. Also in

Massachusetts, Quock Walker attempted to end his own enslavement by the simple expedient of leaving his master, Nathaniel Jennison and hiring himself for wages to James Caldwell, brother of one of his family's former owners. When Jennison forced Walker back into his service in 1781, the latter took the former to court. In 1783, after various appeals, the Massachusetts Supreme Court decided that Walker and, by implication, all other Massachusetts slaves were entitled to liberty under the 'free and equal' clause of the state constitution.[3]

Yet there were limits to social and political change in revolutionary America. No southern state abolished slavery, and in the early 1800s manumission laws were hedged in with limitations, including the exiling of former slaves, as planters became alarmed at the numbers of free blacks in their midst and white artisans petitioned against those they saw as economic competitors. The Declaration of Independence of 1776 and the Constitution of 1787 reflected America's ambiguous attitude to slavery and freedom for African-Americans. In his first draft of the Declaration, Jefferson included a long and passionate attack on the slave trade, but it was excised from the final version at the request of delegates from South Carolina and Georgia. The only reference to slavery, as opposed to the slave trade, was an oblique criticism of Lord Dunmore's proclamation, whereby the king 'has excited domestic insurrections amongst us'. According to James Madison, the Founding Fathers in Philadelphia in 1787 did not wish 'to admit in the Constitution the idea that there could be property in men', so the Constitution mentions slaves and slavery only euphemistically while simultaneously upholding the institution. Under the Constitution, three-fifths of 'all other persons' besides free ones were to be counted for apportioning taxation and representation in Congress, fugitive 'persons held to service or labour' were to be returned to their states of origin and Congress was forbidden from banning the 'importation of such persons as the states shall see fit' for 20 years. The federal government finally abolished the slave trade in 1808.

Other groups also lost as well as gained from the American Revolution. Women contributed to the revolutionary effort, especially when non-consumption of British goods made women's domestic productivity a political act, though they did not get the vote (except temporarily in New Jersey). The Declaration of Independence stated that 'all men are created equal', but said nothing of women. On 31 March 1776, in a famous letter, Abigail Adams urged her husband to 'Remember the Ladies' when drafting 'a new code of laws' for America. In particular, she urged him to check 'the unlimited power' of husbands as men were 'naturally tyrannical'. Adams was not doing anything so radical as requesting votes for women, but she nevertheless warned that if attention was not paid to the ladies 'we are determined to foment a Rebelion, and not hold ourselves bound by laws in which we have no voice, or representation'. John Adams replied that he and his fellow congressmen 'know better than to rescind our masculine laws'. Indeed, during the war, courts upheld the law of 'coverture' whereby women were obliged to follow the political allegiance chosen by their husbands, even in cases of patriot-leaning women who wished to break from their husbands' loyalism. Margaret Livingston, wife of New York revolutionary Robert, commented that 'our sex are *doomed* to be obedient in every stage of life so that *we* shall be the great losers in this contest'.[4]

In fact, Amerindians were probably the greatest losers of the American Revolution. The elimination of the Proclamation Line of 1763 opened lands beyond the Appalachians to a massive influx of European American settlers after the War of Independence. Poorer white men probably gained the most from the American Revolution. After independence, the new states abandoned the traditional 40–shilling freehold voting requirement, initially extending the franchise to all taxpayers and eventually to all adult white men. Yet this enfranchisement was, in a sense, a compromise. As long as property restrictions remained in place, the proportion of white men who were able to vote declined, for the rise of poverty visible in the later colonial period continued unabated in the early national era. Gaining the vote was a new liberty, but for many it came in place of the personal independence that property ownership allowed. A similar kind of compromise emerged from the process of constitution making in the new nation.

The state constitutions

American Independence meant that almost all the former colonies had to create new forms of government. The exceptions were Connecticut, which retained the model of government established by the Fundamental Orders of 1639 and the Charter of 1662, and Rhode Island, which retained the government first established by the Acts and Orders of 1647 and the Charter of 1663. The distinction that allowed these colonial constitutions to keep operating as state constitutions was that the executive function of government was not fulfilled by proprietors or crown appointees but by elected governors. Other states had to write new constitutions. Asked his views on the matter by a North Carolina delegate, John Adams published his *Thoughts on Government, Applicable to the Present State of the American Colonies in a Letter from a Gentleman to his Friend* (1776), urging a 'mixed constitution' with an elected lower house of assembly, an independent executive and a legislative upper house that would mediate between the other powers. In the end, at state and federal levels, Americans moved towards Adams's model. In the beginning, though, they experimented with simple and highly responsive legislative government.

The earliest new constitutions appeared even before 4 July 1776. On 19 June 1775, the assembly that kept on meeting in defiance of the Massachusetts Government Act reformed the provincial constitution by electing a 28-member council as the executive and dispensing with the office of governor altogether. The New Hampshire assembly followed that of Massachusetts in declaring itself to be a provincial congress that derived its powers from the people and not the king. With no charter to revise, on 5 January following, the Congress drafted an entirely new constitution creating a directly elected House of Representatives that would, in turn, elect a council that would then elect a president to replace the royal governor. South Carolina made a similar arrangement on 25 March 1776. In May 1776, Virginia adopted a Declaration of Rights and a new constitution with an elected governor. New Jersey followed on 2 July.

After Congress declared independence, constitution making became even more radical. The next innovation was the election of legislatures whose first function was to draft constitutions, a step towards conventions whose sole purpose was to draft a constitution. The first state to create such a legislature was Pennsylvania, which held elections on 8 July 1776. The first to produce a constitution in this way was Delaware, which did so on 20 September. Delaware's new constitution reflected older practices, but Pennsylvania's was far more radical, emerging as it did from a revolution within the Revolution. After the 1 May 1776 elections failed to remove the anti-independence majority in the Pennsylvania assembly, the pro-independence party refused to take their seats, rendering the body inquorate. Then, the Philadelphia Committee of Inspection, which included radical intellectuals like Thomas Paine as well as urban artisans, called a convention of county committees in Philadelphia in June, which scheduled an election on 8 July for a new legislature to draft a constitution. The election limited the franchise to those who swore to support independence, but in a democratic manoeuvre the committee removed the property requirement for voting. On 28 September this extra-legal legislature adopted a Declaration of Rights and the most democratic state constitution drafted thus far. The new government would comprise an annually elected unicameral legislature only. Bills had to pass two consecutive legislative sessions before becoming law, effectively subjecting legislation to referenda. A council of censors would be elected every seven years to inspect all aspects of government activity. Georgia emulated Pennsylvania, although both states would later revise their constitutions and create bicameral legislatures and more powerful governors.

A further innovation appeared with Maryland's adoption of an electoral college to elect its senators in 1777. It was a cumbersome arrangement, but it did allow for more direct election of members of the legislative upper house than did selection by members of the lower house. On the other hand, Maryland's was the only state constitution that did not have annual elections and it had a higher property qualification for voting than any of the others. Indeed, by this time, constitution makers across the states were already devising ways of making government less not more responsive to the people. The New York constitution of April 1777 created a governor who, with a chancellor and a Supreme Court judge, was a member of a council of revision that could veto legislation, subject to an override by a two-thirds majority of the legislature. The governor, with four senators, was also part of a council of appointment, responsible for filling other posts in the executive branch. In 1780, Massachusetts revised its constitution and extended these powers, giving the governor exclusive veto power, though still subject to a two-thirds override, and exclusive power to make executive appointments, although subject to senate approval. Other states subsequently revised their constitutions in similar ways.

Yet in making government more remote from the people, reformers had to accept the principle of popular sovereignty. Some had argued already that no mere legislature, even if elected, had the authority to draft or vote on the implementation of something as fundamental as a constitution. Calls for a special convention (that would not subsequently become a legislature) to draft the constitution and for a popular vote of approval before implementation were especially strong in New York in 1777, though movements for them were defeated. It was thus Massachusetts that introduced the world to the constitutional convention and referendum. In September 1776, the general court proposed that it draft a new constitution and then subject it to inspection by the towns before legislative representatives voted on its adoption. The process was approved by 74 towns, but the disapproval of 23 towns prompted a rethink. Following Pennsylvania's lead, in March 1778 a specially elected House of Representatives submitted a new draft constitution for a referendum on ratification. Furthermore, rather than approval by a simple majority of towns, there was one man one vote, with property qualifications suspended and a two-thirds majority required for ratification. The voters rejected the constitution by 9972 votes to 2083, prompting another rethink. Again, the general court consulted the towns, which approved the idea that a new constitution be drafted not by a legislature but by a special convention sitting only once and for one purpose only. The convention, ostensibly a meeting of the people like the English Convention of 1689, finally gathered on 1 September 1779. The constitution was submitted to a referendum on 2 March 1780, although confusing returns from the towns threw the outcome into doubt. The convention eventually declared that two-thirds had voted to approve and the revised constitution began its operations on 25 October.

The Continental Congress and the Articles of Confederation

As soon as war broke out between Britain and the colonies in 1775, some members of the Continental Congress felt that a more formal confederation would give the United States more credibility in negotiating foreign alliances. Benjamin Franklin put a Plan for Union before Congress in August that year, but others still hoped for reconciliation and resisted a move they felt would be tantamount to a declaration of independence. At independence, therefore, Congress became the government of the United States. Moves were already afoot, though, to create a more formalized confederation. On 12 June 1776, five days after Richard Henry Lee tabled his motion for independence, a committee of 13 (1 member from each colony) began drafting Articles of Confederation under which the putative new nation might be governed. The committee presented a draft set of articles to Congress on 12 July, but disagreements over the number of votes each state should have in the central government and over the tax burdens each would undertake temporarily prevented agreement. On 15 November 1777, however, Congress approved the Articles of Confederation and sent them to the states for ratification. The limits the Articles set on central government were sufficient to secure the support of nine states by the middle of 1778. One of those limits held up ratification, however, for the 'landed' states had refused to relinquish their colonial charter claims to all territory westwards to the Pacific Ocean. The 'landless' states of Delaware, New Jersey and Maryland balked at the failure to create a national domain in the west, and only backed down when the landed states started to renounce their claims. The Articles finally went into effect on 1 March 1781.

Some already felt, however, that the Articles required revision. Like some of the new state constitutions, the Articles of Confederation created a simple unicameral legislative government. Congress was empowered 'to appoint one of their number to preside; provided that no person be allowed to serve in the office of president more than one year in any term of three years'. The legislative, term-limited president was given no special powers. The articles made no allowance for a national judiciary, though Congress had created admiralty courts that acquired appellate jurisdiction in state disputes from 1777. Furthermore, the Confederation Congress was subordinate to the states. The Articles did direct that the 'union shall be perpetual' unless all the states consented to its dissolution, and gave Congress sole responsibility for foreign policy, power to determine the size of the army, appoint its higher officers and run the navy and the right to arbitrate disputes between states. Congress could also set standards of weights and measures, regulate coin, issue paper money, borrow on the nation's credit and determine the quantity of common expenditure. Yet it could only employ these powers with the assent of 9 of the 13 states, had no tax raising powers of its own, and no means of coercing states into raising the revenues that it might requisition. Indeed, the Articles defined the United States as 'a firm league of friendship' that bound the states to each other in 'common defence, the security of their liberties and their mutual and general welfare' and a 'confederacy' in which 'Each State retains its sovereignty, freedom and independence, and every power, jurisdiction, and right, which is not by this confederation expressly delegated to the United States, in Congress assembled'.

Under both the Continental and the Confederation congresses, states failed to supply the men, supplies and money these bodies requisitioned. Congress had little choice but to keep printing paper money and bonds to raise war supplies, pay troops and cover the costs of government. But as these emissions grew in quantity, eventually to over $200,000,000, they lost their value, the currency collapsed in 1779 and Congress declared bankruptcy in 1780. Yet it proved impossible to amend the Articles to give the government some financial independence. Various attempts to revise the Articles to give Congress coercive powers over the states failed. A November 1781 proposal to give Congress the right to raise a 5 per cent import duty and an April 1783 attempt to give Congress a 25-year impost to be collected by states failed because of the dissent of one state. Other attempts to revise the Articles to make them easier to revise also floundered.

The congresses' financial problems led to political crises. In December 1782, a small group of Continental Army officers at Newburgh, New York, threatened a mutiny or worse if Robert Morris did not reverse his policy suspending army pay. Washington ended the crisis and set the terms of military subservience to civil authority with his Newburgh Address of 15 March 1783, but this winter of discontent heightened the sense that reform was required. Furthermore, unable to persuade the states to compensate loyalists and pay pre-revolutionary debts to British merchants, Congress was in turn unable to persuade the British to vacate forts in the north-west, respect American fishing rights off Newfoundland or allow American trade with the British West Indies. In 1784, Spain withdrew free navigation rights on the Mississippi River and free access to the port of New Orleans. Attempts to broker commercial treaties failed when the United States defaulted on its debts to France, Spain and the Netherlands in 1786.

The economic crisis raised domestic problems that furthered the imperative to create a more competent central government. First, there were fears that some states might raise tariffs or river navigation fees against the citizens of other states. The threat of interstate discord was greatest between Maryland and Virginia, as both claimed the Potomac River. At the Mount Vernon Conference that met at the home of George Washington from 25 March 1785, state commissioners resolved the matter by agreeing to share navigation rights and customs duties and to coordinate their currencies and private debt policies. When the proposals were ratified by the Virginia legislature, James Madison persuaded state lawmakers to invite commissions from other states to a meeting in Annapolis to discuss a wider trade agreement. Only five states sent commissioners to Annapolis in September 1786, so the attendees resolved instead to invite states to send representatives to another convention in Philadelphia the following May. The aim of the proposed convention would go beyond trade, in the words of Alexander Hamilton's resolution, 'to devise such further provisions as shall appear . . .

necessary to render the constitution of the Federal Government adequate to the exigencies of the Union'. Congress consented to the proposed meeting, but limited it to revising rather than overhauling the Articles of Confederation. Eight of the states, however, authorized their delegates to work towards Hamilton's broader aims.

The previous month, problems of governance came to a head in the form of farmers' revolts that spread across the country. The most significant was Shays's Rebellion of 1786–87, an uprising in western Massachusetts against state fiscal policy that required payment of taxes and debts in gold and silver. Rebels there and elsewhere closed courthouses to prevent forfeitures and auctions of debt defaulters' property and tarred and feathered government officers, just as patriots had done during the conflicts against Britain. Also, although the Massachusetts militia repressed the rebellion, only Virginia offered support and there was no national police or military authority to give assistance. The men who convened at Philadelphia had all witnessed their own revolution against Britain. They were determined that no similar revolution would succeed against them.[5]

The Philadelphia Convention and the United States Constitution

The Constitutional Convention that subsequently met in Philadelphia sat from 25 May to 17 September 1787 and comprised 55 delegates from 12 states (Rhode Island declined to participate). Most of the Founding Fathers were lawyers, planters and merchants – hitherto the elites of colonial societies and now the elite of the United States. Most had considerable experience in government, 42 having served in at least one of the national congresses that had sat before, and most broadly favoured the strengthening of central government. Among them were some of the most respected men of the Revolution, including George Washington, who presided, and Benjamin Franklin, whose support assisted eventual ratification, but the main players in the event were Alexander Hamilton and James Madison.

Madison, 'the Father of the Constitution', spent the winter and spring of 1786–87 studying political theory, contemplating recent state constitutional history and writing preparatory notes entitled 'Vices of the Political System of the United States'. The Convention rejected some of the details of the form of government Madison advocated, but most importantly it accepted his reformulation of American constitutionalism and republicanism. Madison wanted the national government to have authority directly over and be directly answerable to the people, so it could have concurrent jurisdiction with the states, rather than operating, as before, at one remove and through the states. In his view, the United States should be a nation, not a confederation. The Philadelphia meeting would therefore be a convention of the people, the document it produced would be subjected to a referendum and any later amendments would be made through special arrangements and not be acts of mere legislatures. The Constitution thus began with the words 'We the People of the United States'. Furthermore, this invocation of popular sovereignty legitimated the Convention's dismissal of the limited remit established by the Confederation and indeed its overthrow of the Articles of Confederation and (supposedly) Perpetual Union. It also legitimated the creation of a central government with a structure and with powers that would have been unthinkable when some of these same men sat in the Congress that declared independence 11 years earlier.

The Constitution created a complex bicameral legislature, in part to resolve the question of state representation in the central government. The Virginia or Large State Plan proposed representation according to population, but members from less populous states objected that their states would be underrepresented and the New Jersey or Small State Plan proposed one state one vote. The Convention agreed the Connecticut or Great Compromise of 16 July, creating a bicameral legislature with a number of congressmen in the House of Representatives in proportion to a state's population and two members from each state in the Senate. The lower house was to be the representative chamber, with congressmen elected by the people every two years. An important departure from the days when Congress was appointed by state legislatures, the House of Representatives reflected Madison's resolve that central government should belong in part to the people and thus share concurrent jurisdiction with the states. Senators, on the other hand, were to be appointed every six years by state legislatures, with one-third of them subject to reappointment every two years. The Constitution permitted states to regulate their own elections, and over the next half-century all of them opted for popular election of senators, something finally guaranteed via the 16th Amendment to the Constitution in 1913.

Though the Convention rejected Madison's proposition of a veto over state legislation, it also rejected a proposal by Luther Martin of Maryland for a 'supremacy clause' guaranteeing state sovereignty. Indeed, the Constitution gave Congress unprecedented powers. Congress's long list of 'enumerated powers' included the right to raise taxes, regulate trade, print money, raise an army and navy and use the militia to suppress domestic insurrections. Congress also had authority 'to make all laws which shall be necessary and proper for carrying into execution' its enumerated powers. The potential expansiveness of the 'necessary and proper' clause provoked particular controversy during the ratification debates and later formed the basis of 'loose construction' arguments for 'implied powers' after the Constitution came into effect. The Constitution also set out Congress's exclusive jurisdiction in areas such as foreign affairs and limited the rights of states.

Most delegates initially assumed they would create a weak presidency, but Alexander Hamilton led a faction that successfully pushed for an independent executive with extensive powers. The president would be selected by an electoral college, consisting of as many members per state as a state had in Congress (replicating the Connecticut Compromise), every four years and without a limit on numbers of terms (the two-term limit was finally enacted in the 22nd Amendment, adopted in 1951). Again, each state legislature could choose how its electoral college members were selected, making popular election possible, though there is still no constitutional guarantee that presidential elections must be decided by popular votes. Subjecting the president to independent election already gave the executive office a powerful mandate and the president's enumerated powers were also extensive. The president was to be commander-in-chief of the armed forces and was authorized to engage in diplomacy, make treaties and appoint ambassadors, executive secretaries and judges with the advice and consent of the Senate. The president could also recommend legislation to Congress and veto legislation from Congress, though executive vetoes could be overturned with a two-thirds majority of both houses. Nevertheless, the Founding Fathers retained enough of their seventeenth-century suspicion of executive authority not to create a president-in-congress that could control the legislature in the manner of Britain's crown-in-parliament. Indeed, the House of Representatives was empowered to impeach a president, and in that event the Senate could put him on trial and potentially remove him from office.

The Constitution's system of checks and balances was further supplemented by the expansion of the national judiciary. The Constitution said little specifically about the judiciary, except to create a Supreme Court consisting of a chief justice and an unspecified number of associate justices. Custom has since set the number at eight. The Founding Fathers laid down nothing regarding the Supreme Court's competence over interpretation of the constitutionality of executive actions or legislative acts, although 'judicial review' was practised in late colonial America and became established by later Supreme Court rulings. The Constitution also allowed for the creation of inferior federal courts, ensuring that federal laws would be interpolated by national rather than by state judicial authorities. The Judiciary Act of 1789 established the structure of the federal judiciary and directed that federal courts would have competence where state and federal law seemed to come into conflict.

The Convention delegates directed that their Constitution be 'submitted to a Convention of Delegates, chosen in each State by the People thereof' and that it would come into effect only when ratified by nine states. In a further concession to popular sovereignty, amendments could only be proposed by two-thirds of state legislatures or two-thirds of Congress, and would only come into effect when approved by three-quarters of the states, thereby preventing the people's constitution from fickle meddling by mere legislators. On 21 June 1788, New Hampshire became the ninth state to ratify, meaning that elections could take place in November and the new form of government would come into being the following March.

One reason why the advocates of the new Constitution won the debate over ratification was by grasping the initiative and determining the terms. In the winter of 1787–88, Alexander Hamilton, James Madison and John Jay, under the pseudonym Publius, published 85 pro-Constitution essays in newspapers and book form: the so-called 'Federalist' or *Federalist Papers*. The term 'federal' had previously been used to denote the central or national government, although more often, and in political theory, the term referred to devolution of power outwards from the centre. Yet by calling themselves the 'federalists' (as opposed to 'Nationalists' or 'Consolidators', as they were called in the Convention), Hamilton, Madison and Jay implied their devotion to devolved government and simultaneously lumbered their opponents with the negative appellation 'anti-federalist'. Further, in the papers, Hamilton's acerbic authoritarianism appealed to hardliners who feared the libertinism into which they thought America was descending, while Madison's reasoned liberalism mollified fears that the Constitution threatened states' rights and individual liberties.

To some extent, though, the 'federalists' were pushing at an open door, for many felt that the United States needed to be, as the Constitution put it, rather oddly, 'a more perfect Union'. Yet many found the Constitution less than perfect, and the 'federalists' had to make concessions to them to get their framework of government ratified. At the Constitutional Convention, Elbridge Gerry of Massachusetts and George Mason of Virginia called for a bill of rights to protect states' rights and individual liberties, and Madison promised to see that one was enacted, despite his fear that enumerated rights might be seen by some future tyrant as the states' or the people's only rights. In March 1788, Rhode Island rejected the Constitution as it had no provisions protecting states' rights and individual liberties, and in July North Carolina refused to ratify without amendments to those effects. Pennsylvania, Massachusetts, Maryland, South Carolina, New Hampshire, Virginia and New York made their ratifications conditional on such amendments. Only Delaware, New Jersey, Georgia and Connecticut ratified the Constitution unconditionally. Good as his word, Madison proposed a Bill of Rights to Congress on 25 September 1789. The states ratified 10 amendments by 15 December 1791. Eight enumerated various liberties and legal immunities. The ninth noted that the rights thus far enumerated were not the people's only rights. The tenth reserved the powers not expressly granted to Congress to the states or to the people, counterpointing Congress's 'necessary and proper' clause. North Carolina finally ratified the Constitution in November 1789 and Rhode Island followed the following May.

Unlike the British after 1688, the Americans after 1776 developed a constitutional system that did not attempt to eradicate the foundations of political tension that were the source of seventeenth-century revolutions. The American executive continued to operate outside the legislature, but relations between these two branches of government were balanced by a system of checks that were further supplemented by the mediating force of a judiciary. It is true that in practice the precise balance of powers between the branches of government was still to be established, and in subsequent years power shifted towards the president and Supreme Court at the expense of Congress, but the Constitution of 1787 provided a sound framework. The Constitution and its 10th Amendment also established a viable balance between federal and state authority, albeit a less clear one, and one that would break down in 1860–61, when the election of an antislavery president inspired 11 southern slave states to secede from the Union. It would only be made to work again by the agency of civil war. Even so, the Constitution and Bill of Rights created a balance of powers at the federal level and between the states that Americans in 1791 could live with.

Although the administrations of presidents George Washington (1789–1797) and John Adams (1797–1801) impinged on the powers of the legislature and violated the rights of individuals (most blatantly in the case of the Sedition Act of 1798), those who objected were able to form political parties that represented opposition mostly within the bounds of the political order, notwithstanding occasional antitax uprisings, such as the Whiskey Rebellion of 1794 and Fries' Rebellion of 1799, both in Pennsylvania. The notion persisted that political parties represented corrupt conspiracies that undermined the republican concept of the common good, and the elections of 1796 (after Washington's retirement) and, especially, 1800 were such vituperative campaigns that they renewed fears among some of social and political chaos. The depth of partisanship was expressed by Thomas Jefferson's characterization of his victory over incumbent President John Adams as the 'Revolution of 1800'. In fact, Jefferson's election was just a peaceful transfer of power from the Federalist to the Democratic-Republican Party that, on the face of it, does not seem to merit such a description. Then again, given the fractious nature of American political history hitherto, perhaps this demonstration that Americans had finally created a polity that could accommodate government and opposition and balance order and dissent was a sort of revolution after all.

A new British Empire

The American Revolution and War of Independence did not teach the British that it was wrong to impose metropolitan supremacy over what remained of the empire. But it did teach them to be more careful about how they went about it. As a result, British imperial policy after the Revolution appears hesitant and indecisive at best, confused and contradictory at worst. In fact, it was pragmatic and flexible, but it nevertheless headed in a clear direction, the same direction it had been taking since 1748 and especially 1764: towards the creation of a centralized and authoritarian empire. In the old Caribbean colonies of Barbados, the Leeward Islands and Jamaica, and in the 'Ceded Islands' of Dominica, St Vincent, Grenada and Tobago, acquired in 1763, British administrators had to accommodate and even allow the extension of local and legislative power during and for some time after the American Revolutionary War. Even so, as Caribbean economic power gradually waned during and after that war, the islands found their interests increasingly unheeded in the mother country. British governments ensured that traditions of representative self-government would not develop in the Caribbean and South American colonies, and in Mauritius and the Cape of Good Hope, by imposing 'Crown Colony' government, comprising a nominated council advising a royal governor, when these colonies were acquired during the French Revolutionary and Napoleonic wars. The Quebec Act of 1774 left the unrepresentative institutions of the French Empire intact, and even the Constitutional Act for Canada of 1791 created forms of government in which gubernatorial and thereby metropolitan power conspicuously outweighed that of provincial assemblies. While giving up some parliamentary powers in Ireland immediately after the American Revolution, the Act of Union of 1800 abolished the Irish Parliament just as that of 1707 had abolished the Scottish one. In a series of measures between 1767 and 1813, parliament gradually undermined the political and economic autonomy of the East India Company and moved towards metropolitan control of India. And parliament and ministries directly supervised the initial colonizations of Sierra Leone and Australia, controlling colonization there from the very beginning.

Although British imperialists self-consciously imposed a more centralized and authoritarian imperial regime, they did not think they were doing anything illiberal. On the contrary, Britons continued to believe that the blessings of the British constitution benefited white colonists throughout the empire. Furthermore, the elimination of abuses committed by the East India Company, the abolition of the slave trade and, ultimately, of slavery, and Christian missionary activities in Africa and Asia allowed Britons to believe that the new empire was beneficent towards non-white peoples too.

The West Indies

In the 1763 Peace of Paris, Britain gained the French West Indian islands of Dominica, St Vincent, Grenada and Tobago. Needing to attract settlers to the 'Ceded Islands', British authorities allowed the replication there of the system of self-government that had existed in other colonies, with all its limitations on imperial power. True, governors were commanders-in-chief in the islands, controlling fortifications and militias and possessing the power to declare martial law. They could also call, prorogue and dissolve assemblies and veto legislation. Yet the assemblies had power to initiate legislation, especially taxation, and governors of the new islands were thus as hamstrung as those of the old ones were. On the other hand, British administrators attempted to influence the process of settlement in the new islands in order to create a population that was more amenable to imperial rule. Commissioners sold land in limited lots at auction in the hope of preventing the accumulation of great estates that had given large planters enormous power both within the colonies and in Britain. In subsequent years, British imperial policy in the Caribbean would, because of the need to accommodate to local conditions, appear similarly ambiguous. But this was not due to confusion or lack of direction. Policy makers were feeling their way towards maximizing metropolitan power in the West Indies. That process would culminate with the imposition of Crown Colony government on colonies gained during the French Revolutionary and Napoleonic wars of 1793 to 1815.

From their beginnings in the 1620s, the West Indian colonists had enjoyed the same levels of autonomy and had developed the same habits of self-government as their North American counterparts. Even so, Caribbean colonists could not afford to react to British measures after 1763 as stridently as continentals did. There were anti-Stamp Act riots in the Leeward Islands, but the Leewards were more dependent than most on American imports and were thus susceptible to threats of American boycotts against colonies that complied with the act. Elsewhere in the Caribbean there was little disorder against this or the other British measures that caused such controversy on the continent, even after the Intolerable Acts of 1774. During the crisis caused by those acts, assemblies in Barbados, Jamaica, Tobago, Grenada and the council of St Vincent petitioned in support of the Americans, and the Barbadians even established a fund for the people of Boston. Nevertheless, Caribbean objections stressed the inexpediency and unenforceability of British measures as much as the rights of colonists. The reasons why West Indians were relatively circumspect in their responses to British measures after 1763 were quite simple. Across the islands, slave majorities were 6-to-1 in 1748, increasing to 12-to-1 by 1815, and as high as 20-to-1 in the Ceded Islands and 37-to-1 in Demerara. A slave insurrection in Jamaica in 1776 reminded West Indian whites of the dangers they faced. Caribbean planters were well aware of the influence that violent defences of their liberties might have among their slaves. In any case, the absence of British naval protection would have left islanders vulnerable to attack from the French, the Spanish and the Dutch.

Even if West Indian independence was out of the question, island colonists nonetheless took opportunities to extend their autonomy during the American revolutionary era, just as they had always done. In 1774, Grenadian planter Alexander Campbell challenged the right of customs man William Hall to collect duties without the colonists' consent. Lord Chief Justice Mansfield ruled in *Campbell* v. *Hall* that royal orders could not supersede local laws on the grounds that while the crown had the right to establish whatever form of government it saw fit on a new territory when it was first acquired, any changes thereafter could only be authorized by an act of parliament or a colonial assembly. This case tempered and yet strengthened imperialism in Britain. It limited what British authorities could do with colonies already acquired, but confirmed the developing imperative to direct colonization from the centre from the beginning.

During the War of American Independence, as with previous wars, West Indian assemblies used international conflict to extend their authority and limit that of governors. In 1778, the Jamaican Assembly declared itself as well as the council and governor to be commissioners for forts, fortifications and public works, leaving the governor only able to recommend actions in these areas. The following year, the assembly gained control of the militia and the power to declare martial law. The assemblies of Antigua, Barbados, Grenada, St Kitts and St Vincent gained the right to examine public accounts and authorize appropriations towards forts, fortifications and public works. The Jamaican Assembly also attempted to eliminate the right of governors to remove judges. When the governor dismissed four judges in 1778, a long controversy eventuated in the Judges Act of 1781. The Governor's instructions from 1783 included the proviso that judges would be appointed on good behaviour.

Caribbean planters were able to continue asserting assembly rights because they remained economically significant to Britain, although their power was beginning to diminish in the late eighteenth century. British sugar consumption doubled in the second half of the eighteenth century to 20 pounds per head by 1800, although it levelled at that point with a rise in import duties. British imports from the West Indies increased fivefold between 1748 and 1815, rising from 21 per cent to 28 per cent of total imports. Exports to the West Indies multiplied tenfold, from 5 per cent of exports to 12 per cent. The islands accounted for one-eighth of treasury income and employed half of Britain's long-distance shipping.

Nevertheless, the West Indian colonies were badly affected by the American War of Independence. The Restraining Acts of 1775 and the Prohibitory Act of 1776 cut the islands off from North American imports and exports. Some planters engaged in desultory efforts at food cultivation during the war, but mostly the islanders attempted to rely on imports from America via free ports in neighbouring foreign islands. The Jamaican Assembly enacted bounties for this purpose, despite their violating British commercial policy. Scottish merchants were eager for West Indian sugar to replace the tobacco trade that disappeared during the war, but depression reduced demand as the war went on. Wartime commerce with England and Ireland was rendered dangerous and uneconomical by American privateering and the consequent rise in insurance costs. American privateers captured hundreds of British vessels in the West Indies during the war and even launched military assaults on Tobago, Dominica, Barbados and Grenada. Food shortages caused deaths by malnutrition and reduced fertility among slaves. The slave population of Barbados fell from near 79,000 in 1774 to under 62,000 in 1784. The West Indies never regained the economic strength they had possessed before the American war.[6]

After the war, in an attempt to pressure the Americans into settling prerevolutionary merchant debts and compensate loyalists, the British cut off American trade with the West Indies. That measure was also designed to assist Canadian trade. Limited commerce reopened after the Jay Treaty of 1794, although by then some West Indian planters had diversified into food production, Scottish and Canadian fish supplies had to some degree replaced American ones and the growing whiskey distilling industry in the United States reduced American demand for rum and therefore for West Indian molasses. Subsequently, American–West Indian trade only reached half its pre-1775 levels. Another sign of declining influence was a huge rise in import duties on West Indian sugar. The duty on Muscovado sugar was 4 shillings and 10 pence per hundredweight, or 15 per cent, in 1759, but by 1815 it was 30 shillings, or 50 per cent.

West Indian interests were also starting to come second to those of others. The 1766 Free Port Act opened four Jamaican ports to foreign merchants, in particular Spanish ones, and later two Dominican ports were opened to attract French traders. These actions were taken in favour of British manufacturers who demanded easier access to sources of cheaper raw materials and to markets. Free or at least freer trade policy gained even greater favour after publication of Adam Smith's *Wealth of Nations* in 1776. Smith also criticized slave labour on grounds of its inefficiency. Others began to critique slavery on moral grounds too, auguring new challenges to West Indian interests. In 1788, parliament began regulating conditions on slave ships. A bill to abolish the slave trade passed the Commons but failed in the Lords in 1792 and the trade was abolished in 1807. West Indian planters began ameliorating the conditions of their slaves to prevent natural population decrease from depleting slave populations too severely. They could only go so far, however, without undermining productivity to the point of making agriculture unprofitable. In particular, planters could not afford to reduce significantly the labour of women and thereby enhance their ability to reproduce and to avoid miscarriages. The rate of natural population decrease per year was 3 per cent in 1748. The rate of decrease grew less drastic in subsequent years, but the slave population was still diminishing at a rate of 0.5 per cent per annum in 1815. Slavery was abolished in British dominions in 1833.

The declining economic power of the British West Indies allowed imperial authorities to make fundamental reforms of the imperial order, at least in newly acquired colonies. By the end of the French Revolutionary and Napoleonic wars in 1815, Britain had gained St Lucia and Trinidad from France and Spain, and the Guiana colonies of Demerara, Essequibo and Berbice from the Netherlands. Metropolitan authorities saw to it that these new colonies would be subjected to close imperial oversight from the beginning, and that no tradition of self-government would develop. Britain imposed on them Crown Colony government in which local representation comprised nothing more than a nominated council advising a governor. There were no elected assemblies.

The Canadian Colonies

Quebec, Newfoundland and Nova Scotia were all too demographically and economically underdeveloped to join their southern neighbours in declaring independence from Britain. And in any case, each of them for different reasons had not developed the habits of autonomy that characterized government further south. Even so, the American War of Independence created a crisis in the governance of these colonies, especially in Quebec when the Americans invaded. Furthermore, each colony was growing and developing, not least with the influx of thousands of loyalists from the United States after the Treaty of Paris. This growth and development, and the arrival of these new colonists in particular, presented imperial administrators with the familiar problem of growing demand for self-governing rights. Those authorities acceded to some extent when they had to, but nevertheless succeeded in imposing a considerable degree of imperial authority on these colonies' developing constitutional arrangements.

Even before American Independence, the Quebec Act of 1774 represented a new kind of imperialism. The Act allowed *Canadiens* to sit on a governor's council, but there was no elected assembly. The lack of representative institutions was not exactly welcomed, but nor was it, in a population accustomed to distant rule from Paris, considered an enormity. It helped that British authorities suspended the Test Acts, tolerated the Catholic Church and retained French civil law. The latter concession to French Canadians was convenient for British authorities who wished to stamp out colonial dissent, for in French civil law there was no habeas corpus or guarantee of trial by jury. Furthermore, Quebec's borders were redrawn to include all the lands south to the Ohio River and west to the Mississippi. Britain was attempting to write its new imperial constitutionalism on the largest possible scale.

French Canadians exhibited a partial and conditional loyalty towards the British Empire. During the War of Independence, the Quebecois failed to form militias to defend the colony against the American invasion of 1775–76 (it was defended instead by British regulars and Royal Highland Emigrants) and they sold provisions to the invading American army. On the other hand, they proved unwilling to rise against the British, despite the invitation of an American mission under Benjamin Franklin. The Quebecois showed some interest in a mooted French takeover of the colony when France joined the war with the Americans in 1778, but it was luke-warm. As France had ceded Quebec in return for keeping Guadeloupe in 1763, there had been little love lost between the *Canadiens* and French imperial authorities. In any case, Americans had little enthusiasm for a French Quebec and invasion plans were suspended in 1780.

The 10,000 loyalists who migrated to Quebec after the War of Independence were aggrieved at the absence of representative government and English civil law, as Governor Frederick Haldimand, who was initially reluctant to accept them, feared they would be. The return of early wartime Governor Guy Carleton, now Lord Dorchester, in 1786 boded ill for colo-nists who wished to see greater colonial autonomy and expanded legislative powers, especially as he was now governor of Quebec, Nova Scotia and New Brunswick, and military commander of these three provinces plus Newfoundland. But it proved impossible for Britain to continue ruling without an elected assembly. The colony was costing £100,000 annually to administer and Britain's national debt in 1784 stood at £243,000,000. The 1778 Renunciation Act meant that parliament could not tax the Canadian colonies directly. Also, since the Cochrane affair of 1781, in which John Cochrane, son of the Earl of Dundonald, had drawn bills of credit worth some £843,000, the colony was near bankrupt. With no assembly to raise remedial revenues, a new constitutional settlement was required. The new colonial minister from 1789, William Grenville, acknowledged that he needed assemblies with tax-raising powers in Canada, but he was deter-mined that those assemblies could not become as independent as the older ones had been.

The 1791 Constitutional Act for Canada divided Quebec into two colo-nies. The newly settled areas in the west became Upper Canada and the older settled region Lower Canada, with English civil and ecclesiastical law restored to the former and French retained in the latter. Both colonies were endowed with representative assemblies, though executive and therefore imperial powers continued to outweigh those of these legislatures. Lower Canada had an assembly of 50 members, but was balanced by an executive and legislative council in which membership was to be hereditary, giving political power to a developing aristocracy that was being created by the seigneurial land system. Land was also set aside for Anglican clergy, though religious tests were not applied to exclude the majority Catholics from voting or office holding. Asked during debates over the bill if he intended 'to assim-ilate the [French] Canadians to the language, the manners, the habits, and above all, to the laws and constitution of Great Britain', William Pitt replied 'that he certainly did mean to do so, though not by force'. The government and economy that emerged in Lower Canada thereafter certainly favoured the minority English speakers, of whom there were about 10,000 compared to a Francophone majority of 150,000 in 1791. The executive and legislative councils were peopled by a majority of Anglophones and even the 16 English-speaking assembly members of 1792 strongly overrepresented this relatively small constituency. The English were also taking over the *seigneuries*. By 1800, over a third of them were owned by Anglophones. Despite the extensive imperial powers retained by the Canada Act, then, political conflict in Lower Canada increasingly comprised contests between British and French Canadians, rather than between colonial and imperial interests.

Upper Canada was supposed to be a model for Britain's new imperialism. Constitutional arrangements were similar to those established in Lower Canada, except for the implementation of English rather than French civil law. J.G. Simcoe, the first lieutenant-governor from 1792 to 1796, intended 'that the utmost Attention should be paid that British Customs, Manners, & Principles in the most trivial as well as the most serious matters should be promoted & inculcated to obtain their due Ascendancy to assimilate the Colony with the parent state', though he only partly succeeded. The new settlers were a mixture of Catholic *Canadiens* and migrants from what was now the United States, who, though empire loyalists, were nevertheless mostly religious dissenters. Consequently, only about 2 per cent of the population was Anglican. Continued immigration by Americans in search of land exacerbated political as well as religious dissent as the colony developed. Even so, the colony remained small at this time, with a population of just 35,000 in 1800, and its economic development was just beginning. Montreal traders formed the North West Company in 1784 to rival the Hudson's Bay Company in the exploitation and settlement of western Canada. Alexander McKenzie reached the Pacific Ocean by land in 1793, and fur trading was extending further and further west. Even so, settlement had not yet reached Lake Winnipeg.[7]

British administrators had their travails in the maritime colonies during and after the American Revolution too. Nova Scotia had been governed directly by parliament since Britain conquered Acadia in 1710. After the defeat of General Edward Braddock at the Battle of the Wilderness in July 1755, the British decided to deal with one perceived problem of governance in the province. Governor William Shirley demanded that the French renounce Catholicism. When they refused, he had 10,000 of them removed. A few thousand escaped to Ile St Jean and Quebec and others were shipped to France, but many made their way to Louisiana where they became known as Cajuns. After that, though, British administrators introduced a potentially even more troublesome population to the colony.

In 1748, the Earl of Halifax persuaded parliament to subsidize the development of Nova Scotia, a form of imperial intervention only previously practised in Georgia. Halifax and his colonial administrators attracted settlers from New England, though these migrants predictably campaigned for an elected assembly. During the war, in 1758, the Board of Trade instructed Governor Charles Lawrence to allow one. Lawrence encouraged further New England immigration by offering toleration to dissenters and exemption from Anglican tithes. The fact that about half the colony's population in 1775 consisted of New England migrants from the previous decade unnerved Governor Francis Legge when war broke out in the colonies further south. He was positively alarmed by the militias' refusal to muster to defend Halifax in the autumn of 1775, although many simply wished not to abandon their families to American privateers marauding the Canadian coasts. Some Nova Scotians sent food supplies to Boston, but the fact that many went south when the war broke out left the colony inhabited by a mostly loyalist population. The Americans hatched no invasion plans to match those for Quebec. After the war, the pro-Britishness of the colony was assured by the in-migration of some 35,000 loyalist refugees, who tripled the colony's population and boosted its economy more than pre-war and wartime investment had done. Older Nova Scotians joined with former New England migrants and their descendants to push for assembly control of the colony's finances. They partially succeeded when they gained appropriation power over road money, the largest single sector of the colony's expenses.

Loyalist migrants to Nova Scotia did not always integrate well with older settlers, and some insisted on the creation of their own province in New Brunswick in 1784. The first governor of New Brunswick, Thomas Carleton, attempted to undermine local power by replacing New England-style towns with parishes. He also installed an Anglican Bishop, Charles Ingliss, a loyalist from New York. Although assemblymen continued to push for legislative rights, local government and the Church of England to a great extent subdued the local sources of pressure on assemblymen to assert colonial rights as strongly as had hitherto been the norm. In 1820, New Brunswick was reabsorbed into Nova Scotia.

St John's Island and Cape Breton were acquired from France in 1763 and, again, did not have a long history of self-government. Cape Breton was barely settled. St John's Island was surveyed, with towns and counties (including a capital at Charlottetown) laid out in 1764–69. Land lots were then sold by lottery in London. Most purchasers were speculators based in Britain, many of them wealthy men associated with the Earl of Egmont. Land was settled largely with Scottish tenants, some of whom went on to form a notably loyal regiment of Royal Highland Emigrants during the Revolutionary War, though there were still only around 1300 settlers in 1775. Newfoundland had no year-round government of its own and parliament had legislated for it since the mid-seventeenth century. Cut off from food supplies from New England and Ireland and largely prevented from fishing by privateers during the War of Independence, Newfoundlanders were too concerned with survival to pose any problems to the mother country. By 1800, the colony's population was still only around 16,000, and though it was gradually forming a settler population rather than just fishing bases, it only attained year-round government and a governor of its own in 1824.

Another change in the attitudes and practices of British imperial authorities in Canada had to do with slavery. Before the American Revolution, British authorities had blocked a number of colonies' attempts to ban the importation of slaves from Africa. Afterwards, however, in some places British officials and Canadians encouraged abolition not only of the slave trade but of slavery too. In 1793, Governor Simcoe made moves to abolish slavery in Upper Canada. The assembly, over a third of whose members were slave-holders, compromised with legislation prohibiting new imports and effecting gradual abolition. Judges in Lower Canada and Nova Scotia ruled that slavery was illegal. In 1800, four New Brunswick judges failed to agree on slavery's legality, but when one of the slave-holding judges freed his bondspeople after the case, slavery began to wither away, all but disappearing by 1820.

Among the loyalists who left the United States for Nova Scotia were some 3000 blacks, many of them former slaves. Constituting some 10 per cent of loyalists and many of them contributing to the British war effort, they might have expected to be treated as equals. Instead, they were the last refugees to receive provisions, clothing and housing. Many never received the land they were promised, and those who did were given an average of 50 acres compared to the 200 given to many white claimants. They also received lower wages than whites and were subject to segregation in religious and civil institutions. By January 1792, then, some 1200 of them had taken the offer of free passage to Sierra Leone. These black migrants, in poignant contrast to white ones, were seeking a better life by travelling eastwards across the Atlantic. They were also part of a new kind of British imperialism, one in which the government would attempt to engineer the character of colonial societies from the beginning of colonization.

Ireland

Early modern Ireland never enjoyed the levels of self-government that other British colonies did. Imperial relations were defined to a great extent by Poynings' Law (1694), which directed that legislation was initiated in the English Privy Council and not in the Irish parliament, and by the Declaratory Act of 1720, which asserted the principle of British parliamentary sovereignty in Ireland some 46 years before another one did the same for America. Imperial officials also tended to appoint Englishmen to judicial, church and military posts in Ireland, and to distribute Irish peerages to Englishmen who had little or no connection with Ireland. The Penal Laws passed between 1695 and 1704 imposed legal disabilities on the growing population of Presbyterians and other Protestant dissenters as well as on

Catholics. The Navigation Acts and the East India Company monopoly in India and China excluded the Irish from colonial trade and made the Irish economy heavily dependent on commerce with England. Between 1700 and 1800 the proportion of Irish imports originating in England rose from 54 per cent to 79 per cent, and the proportion of its exports destined for England rose from 45 per cent to 85 per cent.

These discriminations prompted an increasingly powerful 'Protestant' or 'colonial' nationalism in eighteenth-century Ireland. William Molyneux's *The Case of Ireland's Being Bound by Acts of Parliament in England Stated* (1698), which captured the growing sense of Irish grievance, called for access to imperial commerce, increased powers for the Irish parliament and, more generally, an equal partnership in empire deserved by what Molyneux regarded as a sister kingdom rather than a mere colony. The perceived dangers posed by the Catholic majority limited the potentials for Protestant anti-imperialism, however, and the 'Undertakers', Irish magnates and parliamentary leaders, were able to rule Ireland without too much difficulty, despite discontent. Furthermore, Poynings' Law and the Declaratory Act were not rigorously enforced, especially under Walpole. Indeed, like the American colonial assemblies, although perhaps less aggressively, the Irish parliament asserted and extended its influence, particularly in matters of finance, during the first half of the eighteenth century.[8]

When the British began recasting imperial rule from 1763, however, their plans for reform included Ireland. When Lord Lieutenant George Townshend (elder brother of Charles, the chancellor of the exchequer) arrived in Ireland 1767, his first aim was to persuade the Irish parliament to increase the number of troops it paid for from 12,000 to 15,325 and to increase the size of Irish regiments from around 280 to the British norm of 500 so that these military units could be 'rotated' around the empire. Townshend's difficulties in obtaining parliamentary agreement to this measure convinced him that rule through Irish 'Undertakers' was too indirect and from thereon Britain would rule more directly though resident lord lieutenants who would cultivate a 'Castle party' to dominate parliament. Irish Protestants were further alienated by the fact that the British began recruiting Irish Catholic soldiers to bolster the empire's military forces, especially after the American war broke out.

Controversies between Britain and the American colonies from 1764 further encouraged Irish political dissent. The Americans, seeing their situation as similar to Ireland's, attempted to drive a wedge between the British and the Irish by exempting Ireland from the boycotts imposed in response to the Stamp Act and the Townshend Duties. When the Americans included Ireland in the boycott following the Coercive Acts, the Irish tended to blame the British government rather than the American colonists. During the American war Irish protesters formed groups of 'Volunteers', originally to guard against possible French invasion after Saratoga. When a French invasion failed to materialize, they began expressing Irish grievances against the British, in particular by demanding 'A Free Trade' and by passing resolutions reflecting the aims and language of American revolutionaries. Led by Presbyterians, but with significant support from Anglicans and Catholics, and with their numbers peaking at 60,000, the Volunteers represented a formidable force. In November 1779, First Minister Lord North, facing failures in America and difficulties at home, conceded to their demands for direct and equal access to colonial trade and that future trade regulation would have to be approved by the Irish parliament. These concessions seemed to encouraged further dissent, however, for over the next few months Irish MPs pushed for an act of habeas corpus, an independent judiciary with judges appointed on good behaviour, an Irish Mutiny Act and the end of Poynings' Law. In April 1782, after Yorktown and the fall of North, the Irish parliament carried Henry Grattan's proposal for Irish legislative independence. Lord Lieutenant Richard Fitzpatrick saw little point in objecting and, in May, First Minister Lord Shelburne acceded. The king would retain a veto over Irish legislation, but the Declaratory Act was repealed and Poynings' Law amended to allow Irish initiation of some legislation; judges were to be appointed on good behaviour, appellate jurisdiction was restored to the Irish House of Lords and a Mutiny Act would be allowed.

As many perceived at the time, however, there was a contingent character to Ireland's 'Constitution of 1782', and many sensed that a 'final adjustment' would follow once Britain recovered from its losses in America. British imperialists' opportunities arose because of the ways in which the French Revolutionary War impacted on Ireland. When war broke out in 1793, some Irish groups hoped that they, like the Americans, might free themselves from the empire with French assistance. Initially the situation looked dire for imperialists. Presbyterians in the north formed the Society of United Irishmen in 1791 and, allied with disaffected Anglicans, believed they could both rebel against Britain and continue to control the Catholic majority. Some even felt, since the French Revolution of 1789 and subsequent French defiance of the Pope, that Catholics might yet become friends of liberty. Ireland might even have revolted in December 1796, had 20,000 soldiers under Lazare Hoche landed at Bantry Bay. The rebellion that did occur in 1798 received too little French assistance, with just over 1000 men under Joseph-Amable Humbert landing at Sligo in September. The British, however, learning from their American experience, had built up a military force of some 100,000 in Ireland during the 1790s, while naval squadrons guarded the coast. After hearing of the rebellion, Pitt sent Lord Cornwallis to Ireland to resolve the Irish situation through a Union similar to that attained with Scotland in 1707.

The 1800 Act of Union incorporated Ireland into the 'empire of Great Britain'. But it was the idea of equality within the larger empire that proved most compelling in persuading the Irish to sacrifice their self-government. Pro-Unionists pointed out that the Irish could benefit as the Scottish had from full and free access to the trading, administrating and military opportunities offered by Union (and even the republican Theobald Wolfe Tone advocated an Irish empire). Subsequently, Protestant nationalism all but disappeared and even Catholic soldiers and missionaries gained from the imperial connection. Catholics hoped that parliament in London would more likely bring about Catholic emancipation than would an Irish parliament, though the failure to establish equality would ensure problems for later imperial administrators. For the time being, however, the British felt they had solved the problem of colonial self-government by means of a Union that wrested control of Ireland from the Irish but gave the Irish a role in controlling the territories of others.[9]

India

Indian colonization, like American colonization, was initially a product of private enterprise. In the seventeenth and early eighteenth centuries the East India Company established several trading posts on the Indian coasts. Seventeenth- and eighteenth-century India was much more populous than North America, and its polities, societies and economies were more complex and organized than those of pre-conquest northern Amerindians. There was therefore no possibility of an immediate territorial takeover accompanied by removal or extermination of indigenous peoples, and until the middle of the seventeenth century the East India Company sought trading rights from local leaders who used East India Company money and military resources in their efforts to establish their own autonomy from the declining Mughal empire and to secure their own rule over the claims of local rivals.

The East India Company's power in India was strengthened by the ousting of the French from the subcontinent. Between 1748 and 1763 the British and the French continued to be partisans in Indian conflicts between rival successors to the position of Nawab of Arcot and then that of the Nizam of Hyderabad. The British championed Muhammad Ali as Nawab of Arcot. Britain's 1760 victory in the Battle of Wandiwash and subsequent expulsion of the French from Pondicherry allowed the British to install Ali as a British client. The East India Company finally formally annexed the territory at the end of the century. In 1756, the Nawab of Bengal, Siraj-ud-Daula, demanded redress for the East India Company developing trade links without his permission, especially in Calcutta, and for its exemptions from local taxes. When the British refused to cooperate, the Nawab captured Calcutta. Robert Clive recaptured the port in January 1757 and then defeated Sirja-ud-Daula's forces at the Battle of Plassey in June. Clive, the Company's Bengal Governor until 1760, suggested direct British rule to William Pitt in

1759, but the Company installed a succession of client Nawabs instead. One of those clients attempted to establish his independence by forming an alliance with the Mughal emperor and the Wazir of Oudh in 1763, but the British defeated these forces at Buxar the following year. Under the Treaty of Allahabad (1765), the Mughal Emperor Shah Allam II ceded the *diwani* to the Company (once again under Clive's governorship after his return in 1765), meaning that the British now possessed Bengal, including Bihar and Orrisa, a huge territory from Calcutta almost to Delhi, with direct rule over its 20 million people and control of its £3,000,000 of revenues. The Wazir of Oudh maintained his independence, but under British protection and in the presence of a British garrison.

The Maratha confederacy and Haidar Ali and then Tipu Sultan in the south-west continued to rival the British as successors to the Mughal Empire until the early nineteenth century. Even so, with direct or indirect control of the ports of Bombay and Surat and the regions of Oudh, Bengal, Bihar and the Carnatic, the East India Company was a great economic and political power in India by 1765. The profits it gained, not only in trade but also through its 'revenues' or taxes, increasingly attracted British governmental attention. Others worried about allegations of East India Company political oppression and economic exploitation in India, especially when parliamentary charges to these effects were laid against Robert Clive in the early 1770s and against Warren Hastings between 1787 and 1795. Expansion and war against the Maratha and in Mysore also created unease in the late 1770s and early 1780s. Others still worried about the corrupting influence, and not only of English 'nabobs', company servants who returned to England with ill-gotten gains. Lord Chatham famously complained in January 1770 that the 'riches of Asia have been poured in upon us, and brought with them not only Asiatic luxury, but, I fear, Asiatic principles of government'.

Attempts to reform the Company and to bring India under direct rule ran up against the Company's financial crises and accusations of undue interference with legitimate private enterprise. Some of the defences made for the Company mirrored the private property rights arguments made on behalf of the American colonists before and after 1763. India, however, was different from the American colonies in two fundamental and related ways. First, the dense populations and complex polities, societies and economies of India precluded the wholesale removal or destruction of Indian peoples. Second, the East India Company therefore required the assistance of the British army in establishing and maintaining its hegemonies. Some 900 British soldiers supported 2000 sepoys at Plassey and 850 British supported 5300 sepoys at Buxar. Though the empire in India was initially forged through private enterprise, it nevertheless depended on public resources. British imperialists could thus lay claims to governing rights in India that they were denied in America.[10]

In 1766 a parliamentary inquiry supported First Minister Chatham's claim that the government had a right to some of the tax revenues the Company was collecting. The Company and its supporters protested but nevertheless conceded a £400,000 annual bounty to the Treasury from its Bengal revenues. The subsidy was significant in the view of Alexander Dalrymple, as it showed that 'no part of this Nation, whether in a Corporate or Individual Capacity, is independent of the Supreme Jurisdiction of Parliament'. Subsequently, another parliamentary inquiry resulted in maladministration charges against Clive, and though he was acquitted parliament confirmed its authority to oversee Company executives. Meantime, a government-sponsored secret committee produced nine reports that provided ammunition for those wishing to reform the relationships between the crown, the Company and the empire in India. Lord North's subsequent attempts at reform once again were met with objections based on Company property rights, but were undermined mainly by the Company's parlous finances that prompted the prime minister to promote the Tea Act that precipitated the final stage of the American crisis. Nevertheless, temporarily having to forgo some of the Company's revenues allowed North to push for concessions. The subsequent Regulating Act brought Company management and Indian dispatches under close ministerial supervision and inspection. Also, the governor of Bengal, Warren Hastings, was made Governor-General of all the Indian territories and was to be assisted by four Company- and crown-appointed councillors. The Act appointed a Supreme Court of a chief justice and three assistant justices, all appointed by the crown.[11]

North saw these measures as compromises and intended to extend government intervention when the time came for the Company's charter renewal in 1780. The American War of Independence limited reforms included in the new charter, but Chatham's India Act of 1784 created a Board of Control of six Privy Councillors that would develop policy in civil, military and revenue affairs and that could review and revise all Company dispatches, although administration on the ground would remain in Company hands and its commercial autonomy was left intact. There remained disputes over the line between the powers of the government's Board of Control and the Company's Court of Directors, particularly over the intricate and interwoven issues of trade and revenue (tax) collection, but the act clearly made the government a partner in the administration of India to a greater degree than ever before, and a more than equal partner in the formulation of policy if not quite in its implementation.

At various points in subsequent years the Board of Control considered taking over local Indian administrative responsibilities from the Company, in particular in the matter of collecting and transferring revenues from India to Britain. The practical problems of creating a new bureaucracy and potential political and legal challenges prevented the implementation of these ideas, however, and the Company retained its administration powers in the charter renewals of 1793 and 1813. The Company nevertheless saw a diminution in its powers in these years in a surprising area: its commercial privileges. Since its first charter in 1600 the Company had held a monopoly in Asian trade. It kept that monopoly in its China trade, but lost it in India. The Company had previously been required to buy up and export manufactured goods, which it did with considerable mark-ups, but an increasingly powerful combination of free-trade advocates, British manufacturers and private merchants in India pushed for a significant enhancement in tonnage and, moreover, direct access to the trade. The 1793 charter obliged the Company to ship 3000 tons per year of manufactured goods for private British merchants and manufacturers. In 1813 the company lost even this 'regulated monopoly' as the charter renewal of that year gave individuals unlimited and open access to Indian markets. Furthermore, in 1813 the government marked out its claim of superordination over the Company by inserting a clause asserting the crown's 'undoubted sovereignty' in Britain's Indian territories.

After 1763, a broad consensus on imperial issues inspired parliamentary attempts to impose a new imperial order on the colonies, and its heavy-handed efforts led to disaster when 13 North American colonies broke away to form the United States. After 1776, British authorities were much more circumspect. Nonetheless, with a new pragmatism and flexibility, those authorities slowly and patiently reorganized their empire in the West Indies, Canada, Ireland and India from the centre and, increasingly, in alignment with the interests of the mother country. The old empire may still have been an imaginary construct in 1776, but by the early nineteenth century the imperial centre was exerting unprecedented levels of control over the colonial peripheries.

More fundamentally, in the late eighteenth century the metropolis began to take control of the process of colonization in newly acquired parts of the world. When James Cook explored the Pacific and claimed New Zealand and Australia (then New Holland) in the 1770s, he did so under the auspices of the British government, not on behalf of a private company or proprietor. The first government that the British established in New South Wales had a governor only, with no appointed council, much less a representative assembly. The First Fleet that arrived at Botany Bay in January 1788 consisted of government-owned vessels, not private ones. It carried convicts and their guards sent to colonize a new land, not migrants voluntarily taking their chances for their own purposes. Like their American forebears, these settlers were creating a colony. But, unlike their American forebears, they were creating a new kind of empire too.

Notes

1 Carl L. Becker, *The History of Political Parties in the Province of New York, 1760–1776* (Madison, WI, 1909), p. 5.

2 Jesse Lemisch, 'Jack Tar in the Streets: Merchant Seamen in the Politics of Revolutionary America', *William and Mary Quarterly*, 3rd Ser., XXV (July 1968), p. 399. For examples of popular pressure provoking revolution see Ronald Hoffman, *A Spirit of Dissension: Economics, Politics, and the Revolution in Maryland* (Baltimore, 1973); Woody Holton, *Forced Founders: Indians, Debtors, Slaves, and the Making of the Revolution in Virginia* (Chapel Hill, 1999); and Michael A. McDonnell, *Popular Mobilization and Political Culture in Revolutionary Virginia* (Chapel Hill, forthcoming).

3 John Adams to Abigail Adams, April 1776, in Eric Foner, *Tom Paine and Revolutionary America* (Oxford, 1976), p. xviii; Belknap response to St George Tucker, 'Queries Respecting Slavery and Emancipation of Negroes in Massachusetts', in T.H. Breen, 'Making History: The Force of Public Opinion and the Last Years of Slavery in Massachusetts', in Ronald Hoffman, Mechal Sobel and Fredrika J. Teute, eds, *Through a Glass Darkly: Reflections on Personal Identity in Early America* (Chapel Hill, 1997), pp. 73, 93–5.

4 Mary Sumner Benson, *Women in Eighteenth-Century America: A Study of Opinion and Social Usage*, (New York, 1935), p. 247; Joan Hoff Wilson, 'The Illusion of Change: Women and the American Revolution', in Alfred F. Young, ed., *The American Revolution: Explorations in the History of American Radicalism* (Dekalb, IL, 1976), pp. 383–445; Robert M. Calhoon, *Dominion and Liberty: Ideology in the Anglo-American World* (Arlington Heights, IL, 1994), p. 64.

5 Resolution of Commissioners at Annapolis, 14 September 1786, Congressional Resolution Calling the Federal Convention, 21 February 1787, in George Anastaplo, *The Constitution of 1787: A Commentary* (Baltimore, 1989), pp. 256–7.

6 J.R. Ward, 'The British West Indies in the Age of Abolition, 1748–1815', in P.J. Marshall, ed., *The Oxford History of the British Empire* Volume II: *The Eighteenth Century* (Oxford, 1998), pp. 415–39.

7 Cited in Peter Marshall, 'British North America, 1760–1815', Marshall, *The Eighteenth Century*, p. 385.

8 Jack P. Greene, *Peripheries and Center: Constitutional Development in the Extended Polities of the British Empire and the United States, 1607–1788* (New York, 1986), p. 58.

9 Thomas Bartlett, '"This famous island set in a Virginia sea"': Ireland in the British Empire, 1690–1801', in Marshall, *The Eighteenth Century*,

pp. 253–75; Nicholas P. Canny, *Kingdom and Colony: Ireland in the Atlantic World, 1560–1800* (Baltimore, 1988).

10 H.V. Bowen, 'British India, 1765–1813: The Metropolitan Context', in Marshall, *The Eighteenth Century*, pp. 542, 532; P.J. Marshall, *Problems of Empire: Britain and India, 1757–1813* (London, 1968).

11 *A General View of the East-India Company, Written in January, 1769* (1772), in Eliga H. Gould, *The Persistence of Empire: British Political Culture in the Age of the American Revolution* (Chapel Hill, 2000), p. 142.

Chronology

1536, 1543	Acts of Union of England and Wales.
1539–41	Hernando de Soto explores south-east of North America.
1540–42	Francisco Vásquez de Coronado explores south-west of North America.
1541	Cartier founds Charlesbourg-Royal, near Quebec.
1541	Irish Parliament declares Henry VIII king of Ireland.
1543–46	First Anglo-Scottish War.
1547–50	Second Anglo-Scottish War.
1547–53	Reign of Edward VI.
1551	Thomas More's *Utopia* in English.
1551–52	English wool trade collapses, merchants begin forming joint stock trading companies.
1553–58	Reign of Mary I.
1555	Richard Eden's translation of Peter Martyr's *Decades of the New World*.
1555–60	Chevalier de Villegagnon's Huguenot colony established near Rio.
1558	England cedes Calais to France.
1558–1603	Reign of Elizabeth I.
1559	Acts of Settlement and Uniformity establish Anglican Church.
1559	Treaty of Câteau-Cambrésis.
1559–60	Scottish Reformation.
1560s	English begin establishing plantations in Ireland.
1562–65	Huguenot colonies established in South Carolina and Florida; Spanish found St Augustine, Florida.
1562–98	French Wars of Religion.
1563	Jean Ribault, *The whole and true discovereye of Terra Florida*.
1564	John Hawkins begins slave trading.
1565	Humphrey Gilbert writes *Discoverie for a New Passage to Cataia* (1576).
1565	Beginning of Revolt of the Netherlands against Spain.
1570	First of Martin Frobisher's voyages of exploration in north-west.
1570s	Rise of puritan Congregationalism.
1570s–	Francis Drake and sea dogs attack Spanish ships and settlements.
1572	Puritan Admonition to Parliament.
1577	John Dee, *Memorials Pertayning to the Perfect Art of Navigation*.
1577–80	Drake's circumnavigation of the globe.
1578	Gilbert's 'Norumbega' settlement fails to materialize. James VI accedes to Scottish throne.

1580	Unification of Spain and Portugal.
1582	Richard Hakluyt the younger, *Divers Voyages*.
1583	Gilbert lost at sea before founding planned North American settlements; Bartolomé las Casas, *Brief narration of the destruction of the Indies*.
1584–87	Failed attempts to settle Roanoke Island.
1584	Hakluyt, 'Discourse of Western Planting'.
1585	Richard Hakluyt the elder, *Inducements Toward Virginia*.
1585–1604	War between England and Spain. Defeat of Spanish Armada, 1588.
1587	Execution of Mary, Queen of Scots.
1588	Thomas Hariot, *A Briefe and True Report of Virginia*.
1589	Hakluyt, *Principal Navigations*.
1590–96	Edmund Spenser, *The Faerie Queen*.
1594–1603	Nine Years War in Ireland.
1595	Death of Drake in the West Indies.
1595–1617	Walter Raleigh's Guiana expeditions (Raleigh executed in 1618).
1596	Raleigh, *Discoverie of the large and bewtiful Empire of Guiana*.
1598–1600	Hakluyt's *Principal Navigations* expanded to three volumes.
1600	Founding of East India Company.
1603–25	Reign of James VI and I, Union of English and Scottish crowns.
1604	Treaty of London; Charles Leigh attempts settlement on Wiapoco River; Pierre du Guast, Comte de Mont, founds first French colony in Acadia.
1606	Founding of the Virginia companies of London and Plymouth.
1607	First permanent English colony established at Jamestown, Virginia.
1607–08	Temporary settlement at Sagadahoc, Maine.
1608	Samuel de Champlain founds permanent colony in Quebec.
1609	Henry Hudson explores Hudson's Bay and Dutch claim New Netherland; *Sea Adventurer* wreck on Bermuda, inspires Shakespeare's *The Tempest*, 1611.
1609–10	Winter 'starving time' in Virginia.
1609–13	Robert Harcourt attempts settlement in Guiana.
1609–14	First Anglo-Indian war in Virginia.
1610–19	Lawes Divine, Morall and Martiall in Virginia.
1612	English settle Bermuda.
1613	First Dutch settlements in New Netherland (New York).
1614	Addled Parliament; marriage of John Rolfe and Pocahontas; first major tobacco exports from Virginia.

1618	Offers of headrights and private plantations in Virginia.
1618–48	Thirty Years War.
1619	First meeting of Virginia House of Burgesses; first slaves in Virginia.
1619–22	Amazon Company and Roger North attempt settlements in South America.
1620	'Pilgrim Fathers' found Plymouth Colony; Mayflower Compact.
1621	Founding of Dutch West India Company.
1622	Opechancanough's uprising in Virginia.
1623	Puritans settle Cape Ann for Dorchester Company.
1624	English and French colonize St Kitts.
1624–25	Dissolution of Virginia Company; royal rule in Virginia.
1625	Samuel Purchas, *Hakluytus Posthumous or Purchas his Pilgrims*.
1625–49	Reign of Charles I.
1626	Dutch found New Amsterdam on Manhattan Island.
1627	English settle Barbados; Harcourt and North attempt settlement in Guiana.
1628	Founding of Nevis; John Endecott's puritans settle Salem, Massachusetts.
1629	Petition of Right, beginning of Charles I's 'eleven years' tyranny'; Charles I grants 'Carolana' to Robert Heath; settlements in New Hampshire; formation of Massachusetts Bay Company.
1630–43	Founding of Massachusetts Bay colony and Great Migration; English settle Providence Island.
1632	Founding of Montserrat and Antigua; Maryland charter granted to Cecil Calvert, Lord Baltimore.
1634	First settlements in Connecticut and Rhode Island; founding of Maryland. Writ of *Quo Warranto* issued to Massachusetts Bay Company, unenforced.
1636	Founding of Harvard College.
1636–37	Pequot War in New England.
1637	Founding of New Haven, absorbed by Connecticut in 1662; founding of New Sweden (later New Amstel, then Delaware).
1637–38	Antinomian controversy in Massachusetts; Anne Hutchinson expelled.
1639	Fundamental Orders establish Connecticut, confirmed by crown in 1662; first meeting of Barbadian Assembly.
1641	New Hampshire accepts administration from Massachusetts; Massachusetts Body of Liberties.
1642–45	Dutch-Indian war in New Netherland.

1642–51	Civil Wars throughout British Isles.
1644	Opechancanough's second uprising in Virginia.
1644–46	Richard Ingle's Rebellion and 'plundering time' in Maryland.
1646	Rev. John Eliot translates Bible into Algonquin, promotes 'praying towns'.
1647	Roger Williams founds Rhode Island, confirmed by crown in 1663.
1647–48	Massachusetts *Book of General Lawes and Libertyes*; Cambridge Platform.
1648	Treaty of Westphalia; First English settlements in the Bahamas.
1649–60	Charles I beheaded; Commonwealth and Protectorate rule England.
1650	Treaty of Hartford.
1651	First Navigation Act; Thomas Hobbes, *Leviathan*.
1652	Barbados forced to accept parliamentary rule.
1652–54	First Anglo-Dutch War.
1654–57	Maryland's Civil War.
1655	Dutch capture New Sweden and rename it New Amstel; Cromwell's Western Design, failure to capture Hispaniola; English capture Jamaica.
1660	Second Navigation Act.
1660s	First slave laws passed in Barbados and Virginia.
1660–85	Restoration and reign of Charles II.
1662	Halfway Covenant in Massachusetts.
1663	Staple Act addition to Navigation Acts; founding of slave trading Company of Royal African Adventurers; Charter for Carolina by eight lords proprietors.
1664	English capture New York, New Jersey and Delaware.
1664–67	Second Anglo-Dutch War.
1665–66	Great Plague and Great Fire of London.
1665–71	Henry Morgan's buccaneers terrorize Central America.
1666–67	Anglo-French War.
1667	Treaty of Breda.
1669	Lord Shaftesbury and John Locke, 'Fundamental Constitutions of Carolina'.
1672	Founding of Royal African Company (monopolizes slave trade to 1698).
1672–74	Third Anglo-Dutch War.
1673	Plantation Duties Act.
1674	Treaty of Westminster; first Quaker settlements in New Jersey.
1675	Virginia requests charter of freedoms.

1675–76	Metacom's War (King Philip's War) in New England.
1675–86	Three large slave rebellions in Jamaica.
1676	English and Iroquois League form Covenant Chain; Bacon's Rebellion in Virginia; *Complaint from Heaven with Huy and Crye & a petition out of Maryland and Virginia*.
1676–86	Lords of Trade attempt to enforce Navigation Acts and reform colonial governance.
1677	Culpepper's Rebellion, North Carolina; Jamaica Bill of Privileges.
1679	New Hampshire becomes a royal colony.
1679–83	Exclusion Crisis.
1681	Quaker William Penn founds Pennsylvania.
1683	New York 'Charter of Libertyes and Priviledges'.
1684	Bermuda and Massachusetts become royal colonies.
1685	Revocation of Edict of Nantes, Huguenots migrate to colonies.
1685–88	Reign of James II.
1686	Creation of Dominion of New England.
1688–89	Glorious Revolution, James II overthrown, Convention Parliament and Declaration of Rights; uprisings for William and Mary in Maryland, Massachusetts, New York and Leeward Islands; Edward Littleton, *The Groans of the Plantations*.
1689–90	John Locke, *Two Treatises of Government*; *Essay Concerning Human Understanding*.
1689–97	King William's War; War of the League of Augsburg.
1689–1702	Reign of William III (to 1702) and Mary II (to 1694).
1689–1715	Royal rule in Maryland.
1690–91	Battle of the Boyne; Treaty of Limerick.
1690s	Keithian schism among Quakers in Pennsylvania and Jerseys.
1691	Massachusetts permanently becomes a royal colony.
1692	Witchcraft scare in Salem, Massachusetts; Maryland establishes Anglican Church; Irish servant and slave insurrection conspiracy in Barbados; earthquake destroys Port Royal, Jamaica
1692–94	Pennsylvania under royal rule.
1694	Triennial Act.
1695–1704	Irish Penal Laws.
1696	New Navigation Act; founding of Board of Trade.
1697	Treaty of Ryswick.
1698	Civil List Act; William Molyneux, *The Case of Ireland*.
1699	Woollen Act; founding of Society for Promoting Christian Knowledge.

1700	Founding of Society for the Propagation of the Gospel; Samuel Sewell, *The Selling of Joseph*;
1700–22	Maroon wars in Jamaica.
1701	Slave insurrection conspiracy in Barbados; Pennsylvania Charter of Liberties; founding of Delaware; Act of Settlement.
1701–06	Board of Trade unsuccessfully urges abolition of private colonies.
1702	East and West Jersey become royal colonies; Cotton Mather, *Magnalia Christi Americana*.
1702–13	Queen Anne's War, or War of the Spanish Succession.
1702–14	Reign of Queen Anne.
1704	South Carolinians attack Spanish Florida; Battle of Blenheim; British capture Gibraltar.
1705	Naval Stores Act; Virginia slave code; Robert Beverley, *The History and Present State of Virginia*.
1706	Board of Trade implements 'suspending clause' on colonial legislation.
1707	Act of Union of England and Scotland.
1710	Assassination of Governor Daniel Parke of Nevis.
1711–13	Tuscarora War, North Carolina.
1712	Slave uprising in New York City; formal division of the Carolinas.
1713	Treaty of Utrecht, Britain acquires Hudson's Bay, Newfoundland, Nova Scotia (Acadia), French half of St Kitts, Gibraltar and Minorca; *asiento* for slave trade to Spanish America.
1714–27	Reign of George I.
1715	Jacobite Rebellion in Scotland.
1715–16	Yamasee War, South Carolina.
1716	Septennial Act.
1718	Act for Transportation of Convicts to Colonies; founding of New Orleans.
1719	South Carolina becomes a royal colony.
1720	Declaratory Act for Ireland.
1721–42	Ministry of Robert Walpole.
1721–48	'wise and salutary neglect' of colonies.
1724	Thomas Gordon, John Trenchard, *Cato's Letters*; Duke of Newcastle appointed secretary of state for the Southern Department.
1727–28	Anglo-Spanish War.
1727–60	Reign of George II.
1729	North Carolina becomes a royal colony.
1729–39	Maroon wars in Jamaica, end with recognition of maroon community.

1732	Hat Act.
1733	Founding of Georgia; Molasses Act; first issue of Benjamin Franklin's *Poor Richard's Almanac*.
1734	Rev. Jonathan Edwards's conversions mark beginning of Great Awakening.
1736	Slave conspiracies in Antigua and Barbados; Rev. John Wesley tours America.
1737	'Walking Purchase' in Pennsylvania.
1739	Stono slave rebellion, South Carolina; George Whitfield tours America.
1739–48	War of Jenkins' Ear, or War of the Austrian Succession.
1741	'Negro Conspiracy' in New York City.
1743	Founding of American Philosophical Society (refounded 1767).
1745–46	Jacobite Rebellion and invasion of England, ends with Battle of Culloden.
1746	John Woolman begins persuading Quakers to forsake slavery.
1746, 1748	Lords Bedford and Halifax head Southern Department and Board of Trade.
1748	Charles-Louis Secondat de Montesquieu, *The Spirit of the Laws*; Treaty of Aix-la-Chapelle; government funding for colonizing Nova Scotia; Virginia allows Ohio Company to claim western lands.
1748–54	Ministry of Henry Pelham.
1749	Georgia trustees abandon prohibition on slavery.
1750	Iron Act; Currency Act; Jonathan Mayhew, *A Discourse Concerning Unlimited Submission*.
1751	Georgia becomes a royal colony.
1754	Albany Conference; death of Henry Pelham, ministry of Duke of Newcastle; Woolman, *Some Considerations on the Keeping of Negroes*, Philadelphia Yearly resolves against slavery, other Quaker meetings follow; Pistole Fee Controversy, Virginia.
1754–63	French and Indian War, Seven Years War (1756–63).
1755	Expulsion of French from Nova Scotia.
1757	William Pitt joins government; Edmund and William Burke, *An Account of the European Settlements in America*.
1758–63	Two Penny Act and Parsons' Cases, Virginia
1759–60	British capture Quebec, Montreal.
1760	Writs of Assistance controversy, Massachusetts; Tacky's slave rebellion, Jamaica; Battle of Wandiwash, British expel French from India.
1760–61	Cherokee War.

1760–1820	Reign of George III.
1761	Pitt resigns; Halifax becomes secretary of state for Northern and Southern Departments; slave conspiracy, Bermuda, rebellion in Nevis.
1762	Newcastle resigns, ministry of Lord Bute begins.
1763	Peace of Paris, England acquires 'ceded islands' (Dominica, Grenada, St Vincent, Tobago), the Floridas, Quebec, St John's Island, Cape Breton, trans-Appalachian west and Senegal; George III's Great Proclamation; Bute resigns, George Grenville ministry.
1763–67	Pontiac's uprising.
1764	American Duties (Sugar) Act; Currency Act; James Otis, *Rights of the British Colonists Asserted and Proved.*
1765	Stamp Act, Stamp Act riots, Sons of Liberty and Committees of Correspondence founded, non-importation agreement, Stamp Act Congress meets and issues 'Declaration of Rights and Grievances'; Grenville resigns, Lord Rockingham ministry; Treaty of Allahabad; St Mary's Revolt by slaves, Jamaica.
1765–67	Quartering Act and New York Restraining Act.
1766	Repeal of Stamp Act, Declaratory Act, American Trade and Free Port Act; Rockingham resigns; new Pitt (now Earl of Chatham) ministry; Pitt's mental health fails, Charles Townshend becomes de facto prime minister; founding of Kentucky Stations; East India Act and Parliamentary subsidy.
1767	Townshend Duties; Townshend dies, Lord Grafton ministry; Circular Letter; John Dickinson, *Letters from a Farmer in Pennsylvania.*
1768	Lord Hillsborough appointed secretary of state in new Colonial Department; Soame Jenyns heads Board of Trade; Liberty Riot, troops arrive in Boston, Massachusetts; slave rebellion in Montserrat; Captain James Cook's first Pacific voyage.
1769	Hillsborough resigns, Lord Dartmouth becomes colonial secretary.
1769–71	Regulator movement in North Carolina.
1769–75	Wilkes fund controversy, South Carolina.
1770	Grafton resigns, Lord North ministry, repeal of Townshend Duties, except on tea; Battle of Golden Hill, New York, King Street Riot/Boston Massacre.
1772	*Gaspée* incident; Somerset case sees beginning of end of slavery in Britain; Regulating Act for India; Cook's second voyage.
1773	Tea Act, Boston Tea Party and other protests.

1774   Intolerable Acts: Administration of Justice Act, Boston Port
            Act, Quartering Act, Massachusetts Government Act,
            Quebec Act; Thomas Gage becomes military governor of
            Massachusetts; Massachusetts General Assembly becomes a
            Provincial Congress, issues Suffolk Resolves; other legisla-
            tures follow and form new constitutions in 1774–76; first
            Continental Congress meets, issues Declaration and
            Resolves, forms Continental Association; Thomas Jefferson,
            Summary View of the Rights of British America; *Campbell
            v. Hall.*

1775   Dartmouth refuses Gage request for 20,000 troops;
            American War of Independence begins with Battles of
            Lexington, Concord, Bunker Hill, Ticonderoga, invasion of
            Quebec, Lord Dunmore's Proclamation; Second Continental
            Congress issues 'Declaration of the Causes of Taking Up
            Arms', Olive Branch Petition, forms Continental Army
            under General George Washington; Proclamation for
            Suppressing Sedition and Rebellion; Prohibitory Act;
            Dartmouth resigns, George Germain, Lord Sackville
            becomes colonial secretary.

1776   Thomas Paine, *Common Sense*, John Adams, *Thoughts on
            Government*, Adam Smith, *The Wealth of Nations*;
            Congress issues Declaration of Independence (4 July); British
            evacuate Boston and Charles Town; Washington loses New
            York but wins skirmishes at Trenton and Princeton;
            Hanover Revolt by slaves in Jamaica; Cook's third voyage.

1777   Thomas Paine, *The American Crisis*; Congress adopts
            Articles of Confederation; British occupy Philadelphia, win
            battles of Brandywine Creek and Germantown, but lose
            Saratoga.

1778   American Treaty of Amity and Commerce and Treaty of
            Alliance with France; Spain joins war against Britain; parlia-
            ment renounces right to tax colonies and sends peace delega-
            tion under Earl of Carlisle; British withdraw from
            Philadelphia, Battle of Monmouth Courthouse; British
            launch southern strategy; Irish 'Volunteers' protest British
            rule.

1779–80   Continental currency collapses, Congress declares bank-
            ruptcy.

1780   Massachusetts holds first constitutional convention and refe-
            rendum; Pennsylvania abolishes slavery, other northern
            states follow.

1780–84   Fourth Anglo-Dutch War.

1781   States ratify Articles of Confederation; siege of Yorktown,

	British General Lord Cornwallis surrenders; Cochrane affair, Quebec.
1782	'Constitution of 1782' in Ireland; North resigns, Rockingham then Lord Shelburne ministries; J. Hector St John de Crèvecoeur, *Letters from an American Farmer*.
1782–83	Officers mutiny, Washington's Newburgh Address.
1783	Treaty of Paris, Britain recognizes United States, cedes Floridas, Tobago and Senegal; British troops leave New York, but remain in north-west; Shelburne resigns, Duke of Portland ministry; defeat of Charles James Fox's East India Bill; William Pitt the younger becomes prime minister.
1784	Order in Council excludes American merchants from British colonial trade; Pitt's India Act; Council of Trade and Plantations replaces Board of Trade.
1784–1820	Colony of New Brunswick.
1785	Mount Vernon Conference.
1786	Annapolis Convention; Shays's Rebellion, Massachusetts.
1787	British begin settling Sierra Leone; North-west and South-west Ordinances; US Constitutional Convention.
1787–88	Constitutional ratification debates, Alexander Hamilton, James Madison, John Jay, *The Federalist Papers*.
1788	US Constitution ratified, elections for new government; formation of Committee for Abolition of the Slave Trade, Association for the Discovery of Africa; First Fleet arrives Botany Bay, New South Wales.
1789	US Constitution comes into effect; beginning of French Revolution
1791	US Bill of Rights; Constitutional Act for Canada; formation of Society of United Irishmen.
1792	Black loyalists settle in Sierra Leone.
1793	East India Company Charter renewal.
1793–1802	French Revolutionary Wars.
1794	Jay Treaty; beginning of slave revolution in St Domingue.
1798	Rebellion in Ireland.
1800	Act of Union with Ireland.
1802	Peace of Amiens, Britain gains Trinidad and imposes Crown Colony rule.
1803–15	Napoleonic Wars.
1803	Louisiana Purchase.
1804	St Domingue slave rebellion ends with Haitian independence.
1807	Sierra Leone becomes Crown Colony.
1807–08	Britain and USA abolish slave trade.
1812–14	War of 1812.

1813	East India Company Charter renewal.
1814	Treaty of Ghent.
1815	Treaty of Vienna, Britain retains Demerara, St Lucia, Tobago, Cape of Good Hope, Malta, Ionian Islands and Mauritius, imposes Crown Colony rule.

Select bibliography

Introduction

Useful reference books on the early British Empire and American colonies include Daniel Vickers, ed., *A Companion to Colonial America* (Oxford, 2003); Peter C. Mancall, ed., *Encyclopedia of American History* Volume I: *Three Worlds Meet (Beginnings to 1607)*, Billy G. Smith, ed., *Encyclopedia of American History* Volume II: *Colonization and Settlement (1608 to 1760)*, Paul A. Gilje, ed., *Encyclopedia of American History* Volume III: *Revolution and a New Nation (1761–1812)* (New York, 2003).

Among the most informative textbooks are R.C. Simmons, *The American Colonies: From Settlement to Independence* (London, 1976); Richard Middleton, *Colonial America: A History, 1585–1776* (Oxford, 1992, 3rd edn, 2002); Anthony McFarlane, *The British in the Americas, 1480–1815* (London, 1994); Peter Charles Hoffer, *The Brave New World: A History of Early America* (Boston, 2000); Alan Taylor, *American Colonies: The Settling of North America* (London, 2001); and Mary K. Geiter and W.A. Speck, *Colonial America: From Jamestown to Yorktown* (London, 2002). More thematic introductions to early America include Michael Kammen, *People of Paradox: An Inquiry Concerning the Origins of American Civilization* (New York, 1973); Gary B. Nash, *Red, White, and Black: The Peoples of Early America* (Englewood Cliffs, NJ, 1974); T.H. Breen, *Puritans and Adventurers: Change and Persistence in Early America* (New York, 1982); James A. Henretta and Gregory H. Nobles, *Evolution and Revolution: American Society, 1600–1820* (Lexington, KY, 1987); Esmond Wright, *The Search for Liberty: From Origins to Independence* (Oxford, 1994); Edward Countryman, *Americans: A Collision of Histories* (New York, 1996); Jon Butler, *Becoming America: The Revolution before 1776* (Cambridge, MA, 2000); Francis Jennings,

The Creation of America: Through Revolution to Empire (Cambridge, 2000); Ned C. Landsman, *From Colonials to Provincials: American Thought and Culture, 1680–1760* (Ithaca, 2000).

Classic interpretations of early American history include Charles M. Andrews, *The Colonial Period of American History* (4 vols, New Haven, 1934–38); Louis Hartz, *The Liberal Tradition in America: An Interpretation of American Political Thought since the Revolution* (1955, New York, 1991); Perry Miller, *Errand into the Wilderness* (Cambridge, MA, 1956); and Daniel J. Boorstin, *The Americans: The Colonial Experience* (New York, 1958). The 'new' economic and social histories from the 1950s called these interpretations into question, and a set of new syntheses appeared in the late 1980s, including Bernard Bailyn, *The Peopling of British America: An Introduction* (New York, 1986); D.W. Meinig, *The Shaping of America: A Geographical Perspective on 500 Years of History* Volume I: *Atlantic America, 1492–1800* (New Haven, 1986); Jack P. Greene, *Pursuits of Happiness: The Social Development of Early Modern British Colonies and the Formation of American Culture* (Chapel Hill, 1988); and David Hackett Fischer, *Albion's Seed: Four British Folkways in America* (Oxford, 1989). More often, perhaps, the broad sweep of British American history is captured in collections of essays. Some cover all aspects of early America, such as Jack P. Greene and J.R. Pole, eds, *Colonial British America: Essays in the New History of the Early Modern Era* (Baltimore, 1984) and David Armitage and Michael J. Braddick, eds, *The British Atlantic World, 1500–1800* (London, 2002). Others take particular themes, such as Nicholas Canny and Anthony Pagden, eds, *Colonial Identity in the Atlantic World, 1500–1800* (Princeton, 1987); Stephen Innes, ed., *Work and Labour in Early America* (Chapel Hill, 1988); Bernard Bailyn and Philip D. Morgan, eds, *Strangers within the Realm: Cultural Margins of the First British Empire* (Chapel Hill, 1991); Philip D. Morgan, ed., *Diversity and Unity in Early North America* (London, 1993); Ronald Hoffman, Mechal Sobel and Fredrika J. Teute, eds, *Through a Glass Darkly: Reflections on Personal Identity in Early America* (Chapel Hill, 1997); Carla Gardina Pestana and Sharon V. Salinger, eds, *Inequality in Early America* (Hanover, NH, 1999); and Christopher L. Tomlins and Bruce H. Mann, eds, *The Many Legalities of Early America* (Chapel Hill, 2001).

A famous exception to the rule that until recently historians of Britain have neglected British America is A.L. Rowse: see *The Expansion of Elizabethan England* (London, 1955) and *The Elizabethans and America* (London, 1959). Other historians, such as Kenneth R. Andrews, P.J. Marshall, J.R. Pole, David Beers Quinn and Glyndwr Williams, have long been acknowledged for their contributions to American and imperial history, but have only relatively recently received recognition of their contributions to British history. J.G.A. Pocock pleaded for histories of Britain to include colonies and empire in 'British History: a Plea for a New Subject', *New Zealand Journal of History* VIII (1974) and testaments to renewed British interest in the empire include Peter Marshall and Glyn Williams, eds, *The British Atlantic Empire before the American Revolution* (London, 1980); Angus Calder, *Revolutionary Empire: The Rise of the English Speaking Empires from the Fifteenth Century to the 1780s* (New York, 1981); Frederick Madden and David Fieldhouse, eds, *The Classical Period of the First British Empire 1689–1783* (Westport, CT, 1985); P.J. Marshall, ed., *The Cambridge Illustrated History of the British Empire* (Cambridge, 1996); Nicholas Canny, ed., *The Oxford History of the British Empire* Volume I: *The Origins of Empire: British Overseas Enterprise to the Close of the Seventeenth Century* (Oxford, 1998); P.J. Marshall, ed., *The Oxford History of the British Empire* Volume II: *The Eighteenth Century* (Oxford, 1998); Andrew Porter, ed., *The Oxford History of the British Empire* Volume III: *The Nineteenth Century* (Oxford, 1999); Judith M. Brown and William Roger Louis, eds, *The Oxford History of the British Empire* Volume IV: *The Twentieth Century* (Oxford, 1999); Robin W. Winks, ed., *The Oxford History of the British Empire* Volume V: *Historiography* (Oxford, 1999); Linda Colley, *Captives: Britain, Empire, and the World, 1600–1850* (London, 2002); Niall Ferguson, *Empire: How Britain Made the Modern World* (London, 2003); Simon Schama, *A History of Britain* Volume III: *The Fate of Empire, 1776–2000* (London, 2003).

Chapter 1 Foreword: Before the British Empire

Scholarship on European imperialism in general includes Glyndwr Williams, *The Expansion of Europe in the Eighteenth Century* (London, 1966); Samuel Eliot Morison, *The European Discovery of America: The Northern Voyages, AD 500–1600* (Oxford, 1971); *The European Discovery of America: The Southern Voyages, AD 1492–1600* (Oxford, 1974); G.V. Scammell, *The First Imperial Age: European Overseas Expansion, c.1400–1715* (London, 1989); Christine Daniels and Michael V. Kennedy, eds, *Negotiated Empires: Centers and Peripheries in the Americas, 1500–1820* (London, 2002); Geoffrey Parker, *Empire, War and Faith in Early Modern Europe* (London, 2002). For Spanish, Portuguese, French and Dutch empires in particular, see J.H. Elliott, *Imperial Spain, 1469–1716* (London, 1963); Bailey W. Diffie and George D. Winius, *Foundations of the Portuguese Empire, 1415–1580* (Minneapolis, 1977); Felipe Fernández-Armesto, *Before Columbus: Exploration and Colonization from the Mediterranean to the Atlantic, 1229–1492* (London, 1987); P.E. Russell, *Portugal, Spain, and the African Atlantic, 1343–1490* (Brookfield, VT, 1997); Olive Patricia Dickason, *The Myth of the Savage and the Beginnings of French Colonialism in the Americas* (Edmonton, Alberta, 1984); Philip Boucher, *Les Nouvelles Frances: France in America,*

1500–1815: An Imperial Perspective (Providence, RI, 1989); W.J. Eccles, *The French in North America, 1500–1783* (Ann Arbor, 1998); James Pritchard, *In Search of Empire: The French in the Americas, 1670–1730* (Cambridge, 2004); Oliver A. Rink, *Holland on the Hudson: An Economic and Social History of Dutch New York* (Ithaca, 1986); Jonathan I. Israel, *The Dutch Republic: Its Rise, Greatness and Fall, 1477–1806* (Oxford, 1995).

English expansionism within the British Isles is treated in T.C. Smout, *A History of the Scottish People, 1560–1830* (Edinburgh, 1969); Michael Hechter, *Internal Colonialism: The Celtic Fringe in British National Development, 1536–1966* (Berkeley, 1975); Arthur H. Williamson, *Scottish National Consciousness in the Age of James VI: The Apocalypse, the Union, and the Shaping of Scotland's Public Culture* (Edinburgh, 1979); Bruce Lenman, *Jacobite Risings in Britain, 1689–1746* (New York, 1980); L.M. Cullen, *The Emergence of Modern Ireland, 1600–1900* (London, 1981); Nicholas Canny, *Kingdom and Colony: Ireland in the Atlantic World, 1560–1800* (Baltimore, 1988); *Making Ireland British, 1580–1650* (Oxford, 2001); S.J. Connolly, *Religion, Law and Power: The Making of Protestant Ireland, 1660–1760* (Oxford, 1992); Glanmor Williams, *Renewal and Reformation: Wales c. 1415–1642* (Oxford, 1993); Christopher Whately, *Bought and Sold for English Gold?* (Edinburgh, 1994); Steven G. Ellis and Sarah Barber, eds, *Conquest and Union: Fashioning a British State, 1485–1725* (London, 1995); A. Grant and K.J. Stringer, eds, *Uniting the Kingdom? The Making of British History* (London, 1995); John McGurk, *The Elizabethan Conquest of Ireland* (Manchester, 1997); Michael J. Braddick, *State Formation in Early Modern England, c. 1550–1700* (Cambridge, 2000).

For the English economy and New World expansionism see Ralph Davis, *The Rise of the English Shipping Industry in the Seventeenth and Eighteenth Centuries* (Newton Abbot, 1971); David Beers Quinn, *England and the Discovery of America, 1481–1620* (London, 1974); Kenneth R. Andrews, Nicholas P. Canny, and P.E.H. Hair, eds, *The Westward Enterprise: English Activities in Ireland, the Atlantic and America, 1480–1650* (Liverpool, 1978); Joyce Appleby, *Economic Thought and Ideology in Seventeenth-Century England* (Princeton, 1978); Kenneth R. Andrews, *Trade, Plunder, and Settlement: Maritime Enterprise and the Genesis of the British Empire, 1480–1630* (Cambridge, 1984); C.G.A. Clay, *Economic Expansion and Social Change: England, 1500–1700* (2 vols, Cambridge, 1984); Karen Ordahl Kupperman, *Roanoke: The Abandoned Colony* (Totowa, NH, 1984); David Beers Quinn, *Set Fair for Roanoke: Voyages and Colonies, 1584–1606* (Chapel Hill, 1985); James D. Tracy, *The Rise of Merchant Empires: Long-Distance Trade in the Early Modern World, 1350–1750* (Cambridge, 1990); Robert Brenner, *Merchants and Revolution: Commercial Change, Political Conflict and*

London's Overseas Traders, 1550–1653 (Princeton, 1993); Stephen Coote, *A Play of Passion: The Life of Sir Walter Ralegh* (London, 1993); David Loades, *England's Maritime Empire: Seapower, Commerce and Policy, 1490–1690* (London, 2000).

Chapter 2 Visions and ambitions, 1516–1775

The most noted modern authority on the creation of nationhood is Benedict Anderson, *Imagined Communities: Reflections on the Origin and Spread of Nationalism* (1983, London, 1991). Modern critiques of imperialist ideology, in particular the creation of the native 'other', begin with Edward W. Said, *Orientalism: Western Conceptions of the Orient* (1978, London, 1995) and *Culture and Imperialism* (New York, 1993). Said's ideas have been most thoroughly applied to the New World in Tzvetan Todorov, *The Conquest of America: The Question of the Other* (New York, 1985) and in some of the works on Amerindians cited below. Other scholarship on European reactions to and perceptions of the New World and empire, and on developing American identity, includes Edmundo O'Gorman, *The Invention of America: An Inquiry into the Historical Nature of the New World and the Meaning of Its History* (1961, Millwood, CT, 1972); J.H. Elliott, *The Old World and the New, 1492–1650* (Cambridge, 1970); Stephen Greenblatt, *Marvellous Possessions: The Wonder of the New World* (Oxford, 1991); Anthony Grafton, *New Worlds, Ancient Texts: The Power of Tradition and the Shock of Discovery* (Cambridge, MA,1992); Jack P. Greene, *The Intellectual Construction of America: Exceptionalism and Identity from 1492 to 1800* (Chapel Hill, 1993); Anthony Pagden, *European Encounters with the New World: From Renaissance to Romanticism* (New Haven, 1993); *Lords of All the World: Ideologies of Empire in Spain, Britain and France, c.1500–c.1800* (New Haven, 1995); Karen Ordahl Kupperman, ed., *America in European Consciousness, 1493–1750* (Chapel Hill, 1995); Barbara Arneil, *John Locke and America: The Defence of English Colonialism* (Oxford, 1996); David Armitage, *The Ideological Origins of the British Empire* (Cambridge, 2000); Rebecca Ann Bach, *Colonial Transformations: The Cultural Production of the New Atlantic World, 1580–1640* (London, 2000); Andrew Fitzmaurice, *Humanism and America: An Intellectual History of English Colonization, 1500–1625* (Cambridge, 2003).

For reactions to and perceptions of Amerindians in particular, and for the nature of encounters between Amerindians and Europeans, see Francis Jennings, *The Invasion of America: Indians, Colonialism, and the Cant of Conquest* (Chapel Hill, 1975); Robert F. Berkhofer, Jr., *The White Man's Indian: Images of the American Indian from Columbus to the Present* (New York, 1978); H.C. Porter, *The Inconstant Savage: England and the North American Indian, 1500–1660* (London, 1979); Karen Ordahl Kupperman,

Settling with the Indians: The Meeting of English and Indian Cultures in America, 1580–1640 (Totowa, NH, 1980); *Indians and English: Facing Off in Early America* (Ithaca, 2000); Dorothy V. Jones, *License for Empire: Colonialism by Treaty in Early America* (Chicago, 1982); P.J. Marshall and Glyndwr Williams, *The Great Map of Mankind: Perceptions of New Worlds in the Age of Enlightenment* (Cambridge, MA, 1982); Anthony Pagden, *The Fall of Natural Man: The American Indian and the Origins of Comparative Ethnology* (Cambridge, 1982); James Axtell, *The Invasion Within: The Contest of Cultures in Colonial North America* (New York, 1985); *The European and the Indian: Essays in the Ethnohistory of Colonial North America* (Oxford, 1987); *Beyond 1492: Encounters in Colonial North America* (Oxford, 1992); *The Indians' New South: Cultural Change in the Colonial Southeast* (Baton Rouge, 1997); Timothy Silver, *A New Face on the Countryside: Indians, Colonists, and Slaves in the South Atlantic Forests, 1500–1800* (Cambridge, 1990); Robert A. Williams, *The American Indian in Western Legal Thought: The Discourses of Conquest* (New York, 1990); Stuart B. Schwartz, ed., *Implicit Understandings: Observing, Reporting, and Reflecting on the Encounters Between Europeans and Other Peoples in the Early Modern Era* (Cambridge, 1994); Patricia Seed, *Ceremonies of Possession in Europe's Conquest of the New World, 1492–1640* (Cambridge, 1995); Colin G. Calloway, *New Worlds for All: Indians, Europeans, and the Remaking of Early America* (Baltimore, 1997); Gesa Mackenthune, *Metaphors of Dispossession: American Beginnings and the Translation of Empire, 1492–1637* (Norman, OK, 1997); Gregory H. Nobles, *American Frontiers: Cultural Encounters and Continental Conquest* (New York, 1997); Gordon M. Sayre, *Les Sauvages Américaine: Representations of Native Americans in French and English Colonial Literature* (Chapel Hill, 1997); Michael Leroy Oberg, *Dominion and Civility: English Imperialism and Native America, 1585–1685* (Ithaca, 1999); Joyce E. Chaplin, *Subject Matter: Technology, the Body, and Science on the Anglo-American Frontier, 1500–1676* (Cambridge, MA, 2001). For general reference, see Bruce Trigger and Wilcolm Washburn, *The Cambridge History of the Native Peoples of the Americas* (3 vols., Cambridge, 1996).

Studies of early modern English and British population, economy, society and internal and overseas migration include Peter Laslett, *The World We Have Lost: England Before the Industrial Age* (New York, 1965); B.A. Holderness, *Pre-Industrial England: Economy and Society from 1500 to 1750* (London, 1976); Ann Kussmaul, *Servants in Husbandry in Early Modern England* (Cambridge, 1981); David W. Galenson, *White Servitude in Colonial America: An Economic Analysis* (London, 1981); E.A. Wrigley and R.S. Schofield, *The Population History of England, 1541–1871: A Reconstruction* (1981, Cambridge, 1989); Keith Wrightson, *English Society, 1580–1680* (London, 1982); J.A. Sharpe, *Early Modern England:*

A Social History, 1550–1760 (London, 1987); Paul Langford, *A Polite and Commercial People: England, 1727–1783* (Oxford, 1989); Douglas Hay and Nicholas Rogers, *Eighteenth-Century English Society: Shuttles and Swords* (Oxford, 1997); Frank O'Gorman, *The Long Eighteenth Century: British Political and Social History, 1688–1832* (London, 1997); Kerby A. Miller, *Emigrants and Exiles: Ireland and the Irish Exodus to North America* (Oxford, 1985); Bernard Bailyn, *Voyagers to the West: Emigration from Britain to America on the Eve of the Revolution* (London, 1986); A. Roger Ekirch, *Bound for America: The Transportation of British Convicts to the Colonies, 1718–1775* (Oxford, 1987); Ida Altman and James Horn, eds, *'To Make America': European Emigration in the Early Modern Period* (Berkeley, 1991); Robert J. Steinberg, *The Invention of Free Labor: The Employment Relation in English and American Law and Culture, 1350–1850* (Chapel Hill, 1991); Ian Adams and Meredyth Somerville, *Cargoes of Despair and Hope: Scottish Emigration to North America, 1603–1803* (Edinburgh, 1993); Nicholas Canny, ed., *Europeans on the Move: Studies on European Migration, 1500–1800* (Oxford, 1994); David Dobson, *Scottish Emigration to Colonial America, 1607–1785* (Athens, GA, 1994); Marilyn C. Baseler, *'Asylum for Mankind': America, 1607–1800* (Ithaca, 1998); Alison Games, *Migration and the Origins of the English Atlantic World* (Cambridge, MA, 1999); Marianne S. Wokeck, *Trade in Strangers: The Beginnings of Mass Migration to North America* (University Park, PA, 1999); Allan Kulikoff, *From British Peasants to Colonial American Farmers* (Chapel Hill, 2000); Ian D. Whyte, *Migration and Society in Britain, 1550–1830* (London, 2000); James Horn and Philip D. Morgan, 'Settlers and Slaves: European and African Migrations to Early Modern British America', in Carole Shammas and Elizabeth Mancke, eds, *The Creation of the British Atlantic World* (Baltimore, forthcoming).

For introductions to the slave trade and slavery, see Peter Kolchin, *American Slavery, 1619–1877* (London, 1993); Kenneth Morgan, *Slavery, Atlantic Trade and the British Economy, 1600–1800* (Cambridge, 2000); *Slavery and Servitude in North America, 1607–1800* (Edinburgh, 2000); and for a reference work on the black experience of empire see Philip D. Morgan and Sean Hawkins, eds, *Black Experience and the Empire (Oxford History of the British Empire Companion)* (Oxford, 2004). For more detail see K.G. Davies, *The Royal African Company* (London, 1957); David Brion Davis, *The Problem of Slavery in Western Culture* (Ithaca, 1966); *The Problem of Slavery in the Age of Revolution* (1975, Oxford, 1999); Winthrop D. Jordan, *White Over Black: American Attitudes Toward the Negro, 1550–1812* (Chapel Hill, 1968); Philip D. Curtin, *The Atlantic Slave Trade: A Census* (Madison, WI, 1969); Roger Anstey, *The Atlantic Slave Trade and British Abolition, 1760–1810* (London, 1975); Sidney W. Mintz and Richard Price, *The Birth of African-American Culture: An Anthropological Perspective* (1976, Boston, 1992); Ira Berlin and Philip D. Morgan, eds, *The Slaves' Economy: Independent Production by Slaves in the Americas* (London, 1991); *Cultivation and Culture: Labor and the Shaping of Slave Life in the Americas* (Charlottesville, 1993); Barbara L. Solow, ed., *Slavery and the Rise of the Atlantic System* (Cambridge, 1991); Michael Mullin, *Africa in America: Slave Acculturation and Resistance in the American South and the British Caribbean, 1736–1831* (Urbana, IL, 1992); John Thornton, *Africa and Africans in the Making of the Atlantic World, 1400–1680* (Cambridge, 1992); James Walvin, *Black Ivory: A History of British Slavery* (London, 1993); Alden T. Vaughan, *Roots of American Racism: Essays on the Colonial Experience* (Oxford, 1995); Theodore W. Allen, *The Invention of the White Race: The Origin of Racial Oppression in Anglo-America* (London, 1997); Hugh Thomas, *The Slave Trade: The History of the Atlantic Slave Trade, 1440–1870* (London, 1997); Betty Wood, *The Origins of American Slavery: Freedom and Bondage in the English Colonies* (New York, 1997); Ira Berlin, *Many Thousands Gone: The First Two Centuries of Slavery in North America* (Cambridge, MA, 1998); Robin Blackburn, *The Making of New World Slavery: From the Baroque to the Modern, 1492–1800* (London, 1998); Sylvia R. Frey and Betty Wood, *Come Shouting to Zion: African American Protestantism in the American South and British Caribbean to 1830* (Chapel Hill, 1998); David Eltis, *The Rise of African Slavery in the Americas* (Cambridge, 2000). Ira Berlin's *Generations of Captivity: A History of African-American Slaves* (Cambridge, MA, 2003) takes the story to the end of slavery in the United States in 1865.

Chapter 3 The Chesapeake

Collections of essays on colonial Chesapeake economy, society and culture include Aubrey C. Land, Lois Green Carr and Edward C. Papenfuse, eds, *Law, Society, and Politics in Early Maryland* (Baltimore, 1977); Thad W. Tate and David L. Ammerman, eds, *The Chesapeake in the Seventeenth Century: Essays on Anglo-American Society* (New York, 1979); and Lois Green Carr, Philip D. Morgan and Jean B. Russo, eds, *Colonial Chesapeake Society* (Chapel Hill, 1988). The principal authority on early settlement is James Horn, *Adapting to a New World: English Society in the Seventeenth-Century Chesapeake* (Chapel Hill, 1994). Monographs covering Virginia and Maryland throughout their colonial periods include Edmund S. Morgan, *American Slavery, American Freedom: The Ordeal of Colonial Virginia* (New York, 1975); Aubrey C. Land, *Colonial Maryland: A History* (New York, 1981); Warren M. Billings, John E. Selby and Thad W. Tate, *Colonial Virginia: A History* (White Plains, NY, 1986); Allan Kulikoff, *Tobacco and Slaves: The Development of Southern Cultures in the Chesapeake* (Chapel Hill, 1986).

More specialized studies include John W. Reps, *Tidewater Towns: City Planning in Colonial Virginia and Maryland* (Charlottesville, 1972); Lois Green Carr and David W. Jordan, *Maryland's Revolution of Government, 1689–1692* (Ithaca, 1974); Paul G.E. Clemens, *The Atlantic Economy and Colonial Maryland's Eastern Shore: From Tobacco to Grain* (Ithaca, 1980); Rhys Isaac, *The Transformation of Virginia, 1740–1790* (Chapel Hill, 1982); Gloria L. Main, *Tobacco Colony: Life in Early Maryland, 1650–1720* (Princeton, 1982); Darrett B. Rutman and Anita H. Rutman, *A Place in Time: Middlesex County, Virginia, 1650–1750* (New York, 1984); T.H. Breen, *Tobacco Culture: The Mentality of the Great Tidewater Planters on the Eve of Revolution* (Princeton, 1985); David W. Jordan, *Foundations of Representative Government in Maryland, 1632–1715* (Cambridge, 1988); Jon Kukla, *Political Institutions in Virginia, 1619–1660* (New York, 1989); James R. Perry, *The Formation of a Society on Virginia's Eastern Shore, 1615–1655* (Chapel Hill, 1990); Lois Green Carr, Russell R. Menard and Lorena S. Walsh, *Robert Cole's World: Agriculture and Society in Early Maryland* (Chapel Hill, 1991); Albert H. Tillson, Jr., *Gentry and Common Folk: Political Culture on a Virginia Frontier, 1740–1789* (Lexington, KY, 1991); Kathleen M. Brown, *Good Wives, Nasty Wenches, and Anxious Patriarchs: Gender, Race, and Power in Colonial Virginia* (Chapel Hill, 1996); Trevor Burnard, *Creole Gentlemen: The Maryland Elite, 1691–1776* (London, 2002); April Lee Hatfield, *Atlantic Virginia: Intercolonial Relations in the Seventeenth Century* (Philadelphia, 2004).

Many of the aforementioned works address Amerindians, African-Americans, race and slavery, but the following focus principally on those subjects: Gerald W. Mullin, *Flight and Rebellion: Slave Resistance in Eighteenth-Century Virginia* (Oxford, 1972); T.H. Breen and Stephen Innes, *'Myne Owne Ground': Race and Freedom on Virginia's Eastern Shore, 1640–1676* (Oxford, 1980); Mechal Sobel, *The World They Made Together: Black and White Values in Eighteenth-Century Virginia* (Princeton, 1987); Helen C. Rountree, *The Powhatan Indians of Virginia: Their Traditional Culture* (Norman, OK, 1989); J. Douglas Deal, *Race and Class in Colonial Virginia: Indians, Englishmen, and Africans on the Eastern Shore during the Seventeenth Century* (New York, 1993); Frederic W. Gleach, *Powhatan's World and Colonial Virginia: A Conflict of Cultures* (Lincoln, IN, 1997); Helen C. Rountree and Thomas E. Davidson, *Eastern Shore Indians of Virginia and Maryland* (Charlottesville, 1997); James Sidbury, *Ploughshares into Swords: Race, Rebellion, and Identity in Gabriel's Virginia, 1730–1810* (Cambridge, 1997); Lorena S. Walsh, *From Calabar to Carter's Grove: The History of a Virginia Slave Community* (Charlottesville, 1997); Philip D. Morgan, *Slave Counterpoint: Black Culture in the Eighteenth-Century Chesapeake and Lowcountry* (Chapel Hill, 1998); Anthony S. Parent, Jr., *Foul Means: The Formation of a Slave Society in Virginia, 1660–1740* (Chapel Hill, 2003).

Chapter 4 The West Indies

Broad and inclusive Caribbean histories include Eric Williams, *Capitalism and Slavery* (1944, Chapel Hill, 1994); Richard S. Dunn, *Sugar and Slaves: The Rise of the Planter Class in the English West Indies, 1624–1713* (Chapel Hill, 1972); Richard B. Sheridan, *Sugar and Slavery: An Economic History of the British West Indies, 1623–1775* (Barbados, 1974); Franklin W. Knight, *The Caribbean: The Genesis of a Fragmented Nationalism* (1978, Oxford, 1990); David Watts, *The West Indies: Patterns of Development, Culture and Environmental Change since 1492* (Cambridge, 1987); J.H. Parry, Philip Sherlock and Anthony Maingot, *A Short History of the West Indies* (London, 1989); Roderick A. McDonald, ed., *West Indies Accounts: Essays on the History of the British Caribbean and the Atlantic Economy in Honor of Richard Sheridan* (Mona, Jamaica, 1996).

   Scholarship specializing in conflict among different European and Amerindian groups in the Caribbean includes Carl Bridenbaugh and Roberta Bridenbaugh, *No Peace beyond the Line: The English in the Caribbean, 1634–1690* (Oxford, 1972); Kenneth R. Andrews, *The Spanish Caribbean: Trade and Plunder, 1530–1630* (New Haven, 1978); *Ships, Money and Politics: Seafaring and Naval Enterprises in the Reign of Charles I* (Cambridge, 1991); Clinton V. Black, *Pirates of the West Indies* (Cambridge, 1989); Philip B. Boucher, *Cannibal Encounters: Europeans and Island Caribs, 1492–1763* (Baltimore, 1992).

   Particular islands and particular aspects of Caribbean history, including slavery, are treated in Michael Craton, *A History of the Bahamas* (London, 1962); *Searching for the Invisible Man: Slaves and Plantation Life in Jamaica* (Cambridge, MA, 1978); *Testing the Chains: Resistance to Slavery in the British Caribbean* (Ithaca, 1982); Richard S. Dunn, 'The Downfall of the Bermuda Company: A Restoration Farce', *William and Mary Quarterly*, 3rd Ser., XX (1963), pp. 487–512; Clinton V. Black, *The Story of Jamaica* (London, 1965); Michael Craton and James Walvin, *A Jamaican Plantation: The History of Worthy Park, 1670–1970* (London, 1970); Jerome S. Handler and Frederick W. Lange with Robert V. Riordon, *Plantation Slavery in Barbados: An Archaeological and Historical Investigation* (Cambridge, MA, 1978); David Barry Gaspar, *Bondmen and Rebels: A Study of Master-Slave Relations in Antigua with Implications for Colonial British America* (Baltimore, 1984); Hilary McD. Beckles, *Black Rebellion in Barbados: The Struggle Against Slavery, 1622–1838* (Bridgetown, Barbados, 1984); *White Servitude and Black Slavery in Barbados, 1627–1715* (Knoxville, 1989); *A History of Barbados: From Amerindian Settlement to Nation State* (Cambridge, 1990); Gary A. Puckrein, *Little England: Plantation Society and Anglo-Barbadian Politics, 1627–1700* (New York, 1984); Richard B. Sheridan, *Doctors and Slaves: A Medical and Demographic History of Slavery in the British West Indies,*

1680–1834 (Cambridge, 1985); Mavis C. Campbell, *The Maroons of Jamaica, 1655–1796: A History of Resistance, Collaboration, and Betrayal* (Granby, MA, 1988); Douglas Hall, *In Miserable Slavery: Thomas Thistlewood in Jamaica, 1750–86* (London, 1989); Karen Ordahl Kupperman, *Providence Island, 1630–1641: The Other Puritan Colony* (Cambridge, 1993); Roderick A. McDonald, *The Economy and Material Culture of Slaves: Goods and Chattels on the Sugar Plantations of Jamaica and Louisiana* (Baton Rouge, 1993); Arthur L. Stinchcombe, *Sugar Island Slavery in the Age of the Enlightenment* (Princeton, 1995); B.W. Higman, *Montpelier, Jamaica: A Plantation Community in Slavery and Freedom, 1739–1912* (Mona, Jamaica, 1998); Virginia Bernhard, *Slaves and Slaveholders in Bermuda, 1616–1782* (Columbia, MO, 1999); Larry Gragg, *Englishmen Transplanted: The English Colonization of Barbados, 1627–1660* (Oxford, 2003); Trevor Burnard, *Mastery, Tyranny, and Desire: Thomas Thistlewood and His Slaves in the Anglo-Jamaican World* (Chapel Hill, 2004).

Chapter 5 New England

Studies of New England puritanism include Perry Miller, *The New England Mind: The Seventeenth Century* (New York, 1939); *The New England Mind: From Colony to Province* (Cambridge, MA, 1953); Edmund S. Morgan, *Visible Saints: The History of a Puritan Idea* (Ithaca, 1963); T.H. Breen, *The Character of the Good Ruler: Puritan Political Ideas in New England, 1630–1730* (New Haven, 1970); Sacvan Bercovitch, *The American Jeremiad* (Madison, WI, 1978); Harry S. Stout, *The New England Soul: Preaching and Religious Culture in Colonial New England* (New York, 1986); David D. Hall, *Worlds of Wonder, Days of Judgment: Popular Religious Belief in Early New England* (Cambridge, MA, 1989); Stephen Foster, *The Long Argument: English Puritanism and the Shaping of New England Culture, 1570–1700* (Chapel Hill, 1991); Cedric B. Cowing, *The Saving Remnant: Religion and the Settling of New England* (Urbana, IL, 1995); Mark A. Peterson, *The Price of Redemption: The Spiritual Economy of Puritan New England* (Stanford, 1997); James F. Cooper, Jr., *Tenacious of Their Liberties: The Congregationalists in Colonial Massachusetts* (Oxford, 1999). The gruesomely fascinating subject of witchcraft has received abundant attention from historians, including Paul Boyer and Stephen Nissenbaum, *Salem Possessed: The Social Origins of Witchcraft* (Cambridge, MA, 1974); John Putnam Demos, *Entertaining Satan: Witchcraft and the Culture of Early New England* (New York, 1982); Carol F. Karlsen, *The Devil in the Shape of a Woman: Witchcraft in Colonial New England* (New York, 1987); Richard Godbeer, *The Devil's Dominion: Magic and Religion in Early New England* (Cambridge, 1992); Peter Charles Hoffer, *The Salem Witchcraft Trials: A*

Legal History (Lawrence, KS, 1998); Mary Beth Norton, *In the Devil's Snare: The Salem Witchcraft Crisis of 1692* (New York, 2002).

There are many studies of migration to and cultural transplantation in New England, including David Grayson Allen, *In English Ways: The Movement of Societies and the Transferal of English Local Law and Custom to Massachusetts Bay in the Seventeenth Century* (Chapel Hill, 1981); David Cressy, *Coming Over: Migration and Communication between England and New England in the Seventeenth Century* (New York, 1987); Virginia DeJohn Anderson, *New England's Generation: The Great Migration and the Formation of Society and Culture in the Seventeenth Century* (New York, 1991); Roger Thompson, *Mobility and Migration: East Anglian Founders of New England, 1629–1640* (Amherst, 1994). On New England Amerindians and Euro-Amerindian relations, see Neal Salisbury, *Manitou and Providence: Indians, Europeans, and the Making of New England, 1500–1643* (New York, 1982); William Cronon, *Changes in the Land: Indians, Colonists, and the Ecology of New England* (New York, 1983); Patrick M. Malone, *The Skulking Way of War: Technology and Tactics among the New England Indians* (Baltimore, 1993); John Demos, *The Unredeemed Captive: A Family Story from Early America* (New York, 1994); Daniel R. Mandell, *Behind the Frontier: Indians in Eighteenth-Century Massachusetts* (Lincoln, NB, 1996); James D. Drake, *King Philip's War: Civil War in New England* (Amherst, 1999).

For life in various parts of New England, see George D. Langdon, *Pilgrim Colony: A History of New Plymouth, 1620–1691* (New Haven, 1966); John Demos, *A Little Commonwealth: Family Life in Plymouth Colony* (Oxford, 1970); Sydney V. James, *Colonial Rhode Island: A History* (New York, 1975); Robert J. Taylor, *Colonial Connecticut: A History* (Millwood, NY, 1979); Benjamin W. Labaree, *Colonial Massachusetts: A History* (Millwood, NY, 1980); Jackson Turner Main, *Society and Economy in Colonial Connecticut* (Princeton, 1985); Eugene Aubrey Stratton, *Plymouth Colony: Its History and People, 1620–1691* (Salt Lake City, 1986); H. Roger King, *Cape Cod and Plymouth Colony in the Seventeenth Century* (Lanham, MD, 1994); Gloria L. Main, *Peoples of a Spacious Land: Families and Cultures in Colonial New England* (Cambridge, MA, 2001). Town studies have been another staple of New England historiography and examples include Sumner Chilton Powell, *Puritan Village: The Formation of a New England Town* (Middletown, CT, 1963); Darrett B. Rutman, *Winthrop's Boston: Portrait of a Puritan Town, 1630–1649* (Chapel Hill, 1965); Kenneth A. Lockridge, *A New England Town, The First Hundred Years: Dedham Massachusetts, 1636–1736* (New York, 1970); Philip J. Greven, *Four Generations: Population, Land, and Family in Colonial Andover, Massachusetts* (Ithaca, 1970); Michael Zuckerman, *Peaceable Kingdoms: New England Towns in the Eighteenth Century* (New York, 1970); Roger Thompson, *Divided We Stand: Watertown, Massachusetts, 1630–1680* (Amherst, 2001).

Some of the above works deal with economic, social and political conditions in New England, but those below focus on these issues and change over time: Bernard Bailyn, *The New England Merchants in the Seventeenth Century* (Cambridge, MA, 1955); Richard L. Bushman, *From Puritan to Yankee: Character and the Social Order in Connecticut, 1690–1765* (Cambridge, MA, 1967); *King and People in Provincial Massachusetts* (Chapel Hill, 1985); Richard R. Johnson, *Adjustment to Empire: The New England Colonies, 1675–1715* (New Brunswick, NJ, 1981); Laurel Thatcher Ulrich, *Good Wives: Image and Reality in the Lives of Women in Northern New England, 1650–1750* (New York, 1982); Stephen Innes, *Labor in a New Land: Economy and Society in Seventeenth-Century Springfield* (Princeton, 1983); *Creating the Commonwealth: The Economic Culture of Puritan New England* (New York, 1995); Christine Leigh Heyrman, *Commerce and Culture: The Maritime Communities of Colonial Massachusetts, 1690–1750* (New York, 1984); Bruce C. Daniels, *The Fragmentation of New England: Comparative Perspectives on Economic, Political, and Social Divisions in the Eighteenth Century* (Westport, CT, 1988); John Frederick Martin, *Profits in the Wilderness: Entrepreneurship and the Founding of New England Towns in the Seventeenth Century* (Chapel Hill, 1991); Winifred Barr Rothenberg, *From Market Places to a Market Society: The Transformation of Rural Massachusetts, 1750–1850* (Chicago, 1992); Daniel Vickers, *Farmers and Fishermen: Two Centuries of Work in Essex County, Massachusetts, 1630–1850* (Chapel Hill, 1994); Margaret Ellen Newell, *From Dependency to Independence: Economic Revolution in Colonial New England* (Ithaca, 1998); Phyllis Whitman Hunter, *Purchasing Identity in the Atlantic World: Massachusetts Merchants, 1670–1780* (Ithaca, 2001).

Chapter 6 The Middle Colonies, the Lower South and the West

On the Middle Colonies in general, see Randall H. Balmer, *A Perfect Babel of Confusion: Dutch Religion and English Culture in the Middle Colonies* (New York, 1989). For New York, see Patricia U. Bonomi, *A Factious People: Politics and Society in Colonial New York* (New York, 1971); Michael Kammen, *Colonial New York: A History* (New York, 1975); Thomas J. Archdeacon, *New York City, 1664–1710: Conquest and Change* (Ithaca, 1976); Robert C. Ritchie, *The Duke's Province: A Study of New York Politics and Society, 1664–1691* (Chapel Hill, 1977); Sung Bok Kim, *Landlord and Tenant in Colonial New York: Manorial Society, 1664–1775* (Chapel Hill, 1978); Donna Merwick, *Possessing Albany, 1630–1710: The Dutch and the English Experiences* (New York, 1990); Joyce D.

Goodfriend, *Before the Melting Pot: Society and Culture in Colonial New York City, 1664–1730* (Princeton, 1992); Allan Tully, *Forming American Politics: Ideals, Interests, and Institutions in Colonial New York and Pennsylvania* (Baltimore, 1994); Cathy Matson, *Merchants and Empire: Trading in Colonial New York* (Baltimore, 1998); Simon Middleton, *Privileges and Profits: Tradesmen in Colonial New York City, 1624–1750* (Philadelphia, forthcoming). And for New Jersey: John E. Pomfret, *Colonial New Jersey: A History* (New York, 1973); Ned C. Landsman, *Scotland and its First American Colony* (Princeton, 1985); Brendan McConville, *These Daring Disturbers of the Public Peace: The Struggle for Property and Power in Early New Jersey* (Ithaca, 1999). Pennsylvania and Delaware: Frederick B. Tolles, *Meeting House and Counting House: The Quaker Merchants of Colonial Philadelphia* (Chapel Hill, 1948); Gary B. Nash, *Quakers and Politics: Pennsylvania, 1681–1726* (Princeton, 1968); James T. Lemon, *The Best Poor Man's Country: A Geographical Study of Early Southeastern Pennsylvania* (Baltimore, 1972); Joseph E. Illick, *Colonial Pennsylvania: A History* (New York, 1976); John A. Munroe, *Colonial Delaware: A History* (Millwood, NY, 1978); Allan Tully, *William Penn's Legacy: Politics and Social Structure in Provincial Pennsylvania, 1726–1755* (Baltimore, 1978); Jean R. Soderland, *Quakers and Slavery: A Divided Spirit* (Princeton, 1985); Thomas M. Doerflinger, *A Vigorous Spirit of Enterprise: Merchants and Economic Development in Revolutionary Philadelphia* (Chapel Hill, 1986); Sharon V. Salinger, *'To Serve Well and Faithfully': Labour and Indentured Servants in Pennsylvania, 1682–1800* (Cambridge, 1987); Sally Schwartz, *'A Mixed Multitude': The Struggle for Toleration in Colonial Pennsylvania* (New York, 1987); Mary M. Schweitzer, *Custom and Contract: Household, Government, and the Economy in Colonial Pennsylvania* (New York, 1987); Barry Levy, *Quakers and the American Family: British Settlement in the Delaware Valley* (New York, 1990); Billy G. Smith, *The 'Lower Sort': Philadelphia's Laboring People, 1750–1800* (Ithaca, 1990); William M. Offut, Jr., *Of Good Laws and Good Men: Law and Society in the Delaware Valley, 1680–1710* (Urbana, IL, 1995); Peter Thompson, *Rum Punch and Revolution: Taverngoing and Public Life in Eighteenth-Century Philadelphia* (Philadelphia, 1999).

On the Carolinas and Georgia: William S. Powell, *Colonial North Carolina: A History* (New York, 1973); Kenneth Coleman, *Colonial Georgia: A History* (New York, 1976); Harold E. Davis, *The Fledgling Province: Social and Cultural Life in Colonial Georgia, 1733–1776* (Chapel Hill, 1976); A. Roger Ekirch, *Poor Carolina: Politics and Society in Colonial North Carolina, 1729–1776* (Chapel Hill, 1981); Jon Butler, *The Huguenots in America: A Refugee People in a New World Society* (Cambridge, MA, 1983); Robert M. Weir, *Colonial South Carolina: A History* (New York, 1983); Peter A. Coclanis, *The Shadow of a Dream:*

Economic Life and Death in the South Carolina Low Country, 1670–1920 (New York, 1989); James H. Merrell, *The Indians' New World: Catawbas and their Neighbors from European Contact through the Era of Removal* (Chapel Hill, 1989); Richard Waterhouse, *A New World Gentry: The Making of a Merchant and Planter Class in South Carolina, 1670–1770* (New York, 1989); Joyce E. Chaplin, *An Anxious Pursuit: Agricultural Innovation and Modernity in the Lower South, 1730–1815* (Chapel Hill, 1993); Tom Hatley, *The Dividing Paths: Cherokees and South Carolinians through the Era of Revolution* (Oxford, 1993); Rebecca Starr, *A School for Politics: Commercial Lobbying and Political Culture in Early South Carolina* (Baltimore, 1998); Marjoleine Kars, *Breaking Loose Together: The Regulator Rebellion in Pre-Revolutionary North Carolina* (Chapel Hill, 2002).

On slavery in the region, see Peter H. Wood, *Black Majority: Negroes in Colonial South Carolina from 1670 through the Stono Rebellion* (New York, 1974); Betty Wood, *Slavery in Colonial Georgia, 1730–1775* (Athens, GA, 1984); Daniel H. Usner, Jr., *Indians, Settlers, and Slaves in a Frontier Exchange Economy: The Lower Mississippi Valley before 1783* (Chapel Hill, 1992); Philip D. Morgan, *Slave Counterpoint: Black Culture in the Eighteenth-Century Chesapeake and Lowcountry* (Chapel Hill, 1998); Robert Olwell, *Masters, Slaves, and Subjects: The Culture of Power in the South Carolina Low Country, 1740–1790* (Ithaca, 1998).

On Florida and the west see J.M. Sosin, *Whitehall and the Wilderness: The Middle West in British Colonial Policy, 1760–1775* (Lincoln, NB, 1961); Robert V. Mitchell, *Commercialism and Frontier: Perspectives on the Early Shenandoah Valley* (Charlottesville, 1977); Richard R. Beeman, *The Evolution of the Southern Backcountry: The Case of Lunenburg County, Virginia, 1746–1832* (Philadelphia, 1984); John Mack Faragher, *Daniel Boone: The Life and Legend of an American Pioneer* (New York, 1992); Stephen Aron, *How the West Was Lost: The Transformation of Kentucke from Daniel Boone to Henry Clay* (Baltimore, 1996); Eric Hinderaker, *Elusive Empires: Constructing Colonialism in the Ohio Valley, 1673–1800* (Cambridge, 1997); George Lloyd Johnson, *The Frontier in the Colonial South: South Carolina Backcountry, 1736–1800* (Westport, CT, 1997); Elizabeth A. Perkins, *Border Life: Experience and Memory in the Revolutionary Ohio Valley* (Chapel Hill, 1998); Jane G. Landers, ed., *Colonial Plantations and Economy in Florida* (Gainesville, 2000); James F. Brooks, *Captives and Cousins: Slavery, Kinship, and Community in the Southwest Borderlands* (Chapel Hill, 2002); Paul E. Hoffman, *Florida's Frontiers* (Bloomington, IN, 2002); Warren R. Hofstra, *The Planting of New Virginia: Settlement and Landscape in the Shenandoah Valley* (Baltimore, 2004).

Chapter 7 The politics of empire, 1607–1763

On demographic, economic, social and cultural development in the colonies, see James F. Shepherd and Gary M. Walton, *Shipping, Maritime Trade, and the Economic Development of Colonial North America* (Cambridge, 1972); *The Economic Rise of Early America* (Cambridge, 1979); Robert V. Wells, *Population of the British Colonies in America before 1776: A Survey of Census Data* (Princeton, 1975); Alice Hanson Jones, *The Wealth of a Nation to Be: The American Colonies on the Eve of the Revolution* (New York, 1980); Edwin J. Perkins, *The Economy of Colonial America* (1980, New York, 1988); John J. McCusker and Russell R. Menard, *The Economy of British America, 1607–1789: Needs and Opportunities for Study* (1985, Chapel Hill, 1991); Jack P. Greene, *Pursuits of Happiness: The Social Development of Early Modern British Colonies and the Formation of American Culture* (Chapel Hill, 1988); Carole Shammas, *The Pre-Industrial Consumer in England and America* (Oxford, 1990); David S. Shields, *Civil Tongues and Polite Letters in British America* (Chapel Hill, 1997); Richard L. Bushman, *The Refinement of America: Persons, Houses, Cities* (New York, 1992); Marc Egnal, *New World Economies: The Growth of the Thirteen Colonies and Early Canada* (Oxford, 1998); Michal J. Rozbicki, *The Complete Colonial Gentleman: Cultural Legitimacy in Plantation America* (Charlottesville, 1998); C. Dallett Hemphill, *Bowing to Necessities: A History of Manners in America, 1620–1860* (Oxford, 1999).

On theory and practice in British and American colonial and imperial economy and politics, see Jack P. Greene, *The Quest for Power: The Lower Houses of Assembly in the Southern Royal Colonies, 1689–1776* (Chapel Hill, 1963); *Peripheries and Center: Constitutional Development in the Extended Polities of the British Empire and the United States, 1607–1788* (New York, 1986); *Negotiated Authorities: Essays in Colonial Political and Constitutional History* (Charlottesville, 1994); J.R. Pole, *Political Representation in England and the Origins of the American Republic* (Stanford, 1966); *The Gift of Government: Political Responsibility from the English Restoration to American Independence* (Athens, GA, 1983); T.C. Barrow, *Trade and Empire: The British Customs Service in Colonial America, 1660–1775* (Cambridge, MA, 1967); Bernard Bailyn, *The Origins of American Politics* (New York, 1968); Ian K. Steele, *Politics of Colonial Policy: The Board of Trade in Colonial Administration, 1696–1720* (New York, 1968); *The English Atlantic, 1675–1740: An Exploration of Communication and Community* (Oxford, 1986); Michael Kammen, *Deputyes and Libertys: The Origins of Representative Government in Colonial America* (New York, 1969); *Empire and Interest: The American Colonies and the Politics of Mercantilism* (Philadelphia, 1970); James A. Henretta, *'Salutary Neglect': Colonial Administration under the Duke of Newcastle* (Princeton, 1972); Stephen Saunders Webb, *The Governors General: The English Army and the Definition of Empire, 1569–1681* (Chapel Hill, 1979); *1676: The End of American Independence* (New York, 1984); Jacob M. Price, *Capital and Credit in British Overseas Trade* (Cambridge, MA, 1980); J.M. Sosin, *English America and Imperial Inconstancy: The Rise of Provincial Autonomy, 1696–1715* (Lincoln, NB, 1985); John Brewer, *The Sinews of Power: War, Money, and the English State, 1688–1783* (London, 1989); Richard D. Brown, *Knowledge is Power: The Diffusion of Information in Early America, 1700–1865* (Oxford, 1989); Robert M. Bliss, *Revolution and Empire: English Politics and the American Colonies in the Seventeenth Century* (Manchester, 1990); Alison Gilbert Olson, *Making the Empire Work: London and American Interest Groups, 1690–1790* (Cambridge, MA, 1992); Robert M. Calhoon, *Dominion and Liberty: Ideology in the Anglo-American World, 1660–1801* (Arlington Heights, IL, 1994); Nancy E. Koehn, *The Power of Commerce: Economy and Governance in the First British Empire* (Ithaca, 1994); Kathleen Wilson, *The Sense of the People: Politics, Culture and Imperialism in England, 1715–1785* (Cambridge, 1995); H.V. Bowen, *Elites, Enterprise and the Making of the British Overseas Empire, 1688–1775* (London, 1996); Michael J. Braddick, *The Nerves of State: Taxation and the Financing of the English State, 1558–1714* (Manchester, 1996); Steven C.A. Pincus, *Protestantism and Patriotism: Ideologies and the Making of English Foreign Policy, 1650–1668* (Cambridge, 1996); Eliga H. Gould, *The Persistence of Empire: British Political Culture in the Age of the American Revolution* (Chapel Hill, 2000); Gillian Brown, *The Consent of the Governed: The Lockean Legacy in Early American Culture* (Cambridge, MA, 2001); Bruce Lenman, *England's Colonial Wars, 1500–1688: Conflicts, Empire, and National Identity* (Harlow, 2001); *Britain's Colonial Wars, 1688–1783* (Harlow, 2001).

On Britain, America, the Glorious Revolution and parliament, see Geoffrey Holmes, ed., *Britain after the Glorious Revolution, 1689–1715* (New York, 1969); David S. Lovejoy, *The Glorious Revolution in America* (New York, 1972); J.G.A. Pocock, ed., *Three British Revolutions: 1641, 1688, 1776* (Princeton, 1980); J.M. Sosin, *English America and the Restoration Monarchy of Charles II: Transatlantic Politics, Commerce, and Kinship* (Lincoln, NB, 1981); *English America and the Revolution of 1688: Royal Administration and the Structure of Provincial Government* (Lincoln, NB, 1982); Robert Beddard, ed., *The Revolutions of 1688* (Oxford, 1991); Linda Colley, *Britons: Forging the Nation, 1707–1837* (New Haven, 1992); Stephen Saunders Webb, *Lord Churchill's Coup: The Anglo-American Empire and the Glorious Revolution Reconsidered* (New York, 1995); Mark Kishlansky, *A Monarchy Transformed: Britain, 1603–1714* (London, 1996); W.A. Speck, *James II* (London, 2002).

On Anglo-French-Amerindian rivalries and the French and Indian War and its consequences, see Alan Rogers, *Empire and Liberty: American Resistance to British Authority, 1755–1763* (Berkeley, 1973); Richard Middleton, *The Bells of Victory: The Pitt-Newcastle Ministry and the Conduct of the Seven Years' War, 1757–1762* (Cambridge, 1985); Francis Jennings, *Empire of Fortune: Crowns, Colonies, and Tribes in the Seven Years War in America* (New York, 1988); Richard White, *The Middle Ground: Indians, Empires, and Republics in the Great Lakes Region, 1650–1815* (Cambridge, 1991); Gregory E. Dowd, *A Spirited Resistance: The North American Indian Struggle for Unity, 1745–1815* (Baltimore, 1992); Michael N. McConnell, *A Country Between: The Upper Ohio Valley and Its Peoples, 1724–1774* (Lincoln, NB, 1992); Daniel K. Richter, *The Ordeal of the Longhouse: The Peoples of the Iroquois League in the Era of European Colonization* (Chapel Hill, 1992); Fred Anderson, *Crucible of War: The Seven Years' War and the Fate of Empire in British North America, 1754–1766* (New York, 2000); William R. Nester, *The Great Frontier War: Britain, France, and the Imperial Struggle for North America, 1607–1755* (Westport, CT, 2000); John Oliphant, *Peace and War on the Anglo-Cherokee Frontier, 1756–63* (Baton Rouge, 2001); Stephen Brumwell, *Redcoats: The British Soldier and War in the Americas, 1755–1763* (Cambridge, 2002); Gregory Evans Dowd, *War under Heaven: Pontiac, the Indian Nations, and the British Empire* (Baltimore, 2002); Jane T. Merritt, *At the Crossroads: Indians and Empires on a Mid-Atlantic Frontier, 1700–1763* (Chapel Hill, 2003).

Chapter 8 The American Revolution, 1764–1783

For a reference work on the Revolution, see Jack P. Greene and J.R. Pole, eds, *A Companion to the American Revolution* (Oxford, 2000). General histories and broad interpretations include Lawrence Henry Gipson, *The Coming of the Revolution, 1763–1775* (New York, 1954); Edmund S. Morgan, *The Birth of the Republic, 1763–89* (1956, Chicago, 1977); Merrill Jensen, *The Founding of a Nation: A History of the American Revolution, 1763–1776* (New York, 1968); Peter D.G. Thomas, *British Politics and the Stamp Act Crisis: The First Phase of the American Revolution, 1763–1767*; *The Townshend Duties Crisis: The Second Phase of the American Revolution, 1767–1773*; *Tea Party to Independence: The Third Phase of the American Revolution, 1773–1776* (Oxford, 1975, 1987, 1991); Robert Middlekauf, *The Glorious Cause: The American Revolution, 1763–1789* (Oxford, 1982); Robert W. Tucker and David C. Hendrickson, *The Fall of the First British Empire: Origins of the War of American Independence* (Baltimore, 1982); Marc Egnal, *A Mighty Empire: The Origins of the American Revolution* (Ithaca, 1988); Theodore Draper, *A Struggle for Power: The American Revolution* (New York, 1996); Francis D. Cogliano, *Revolutionary America: A Political History, 1763–1815*

(London, 2000); John Ferling, *A Leap in the Dark: The Struggle to Create the American Republic* (Oxford, 2003).

Analyses of particular events during the revolution include Edmund S. Morgan and Helen M. Morgan, *The Stamp Act Crisis: Prologue to Revolution* (Chapel Hill, 1953); Benjamin W. Labaree, *The Boston Tea Party* (Oxford, 1964); John Shy, *Towards Lexington: The Role of the British Army in the Coming of the American Revolution* (Princeton, 1965); Hiller Zobel, *The Boston Massacre* (New York, 1970); David Ammerman, *In the Common Cause: American Response to the Coercive Acts of 1774* (Charlottesville, 1974); John L. Bullion, *A Great and Necessary Measure: George Grenville and the Genesis of the Stamp Act, 1763–1765* (Columbia, MO, 1983); Jerrilyn Greene Marston, *King and Congress: The Transfer of Political Legitimacy, 1774–1776* (Princeton, 1987); David Hackett Fischer, *Paul Revere's Ride* (Oxford, 1994). On the Declaration of Independence, see Carl L. Becker, *The Declaration of Independence: A Study in the History of Political Ideas* (1922, New York, 1970); Garry Wills, *Inventing America: Jefferson's Declaration of Independence* (New York, 1978); Jay Fliegelman, *Declaring Independence: Jefferson, Natural Language and the Culture of Performance* (Stanford, 1993); Scott Douglas Gerber, *To Secure These Rights: The Declaration of Independence and Constitutional Interpretation* (New York, 1996); Pauline Maier, *American Scripture: How America Declared Independence from Britain* (New York, 1997); Allen Jayne, *Jefferson's Declaration of Independence: Origins, Philosophy, and Theology* (Lexington, KY, 1998). Works on leading figures in the Revolution, and a recent renaissance of scholarship on the Founding Fathers include Bernard Bailyn, *The Ordeal of Thomas Hutchinson* (Cambridge, MA, 1974); Eric Foner, *Tom Paine and Revolutionary America* (Oxford, 1976); Jack Fruchtman, Jr., *Thomas Paine: Apostle of Freedom* (New York, 1994); John Keane, *Tom Paine: A Political Life* (London, 1995); H.W. Brands, *The First American: The Life and Times of Benjamin Franklin* (New York, 2000); Joseph J. Ellis, *Founding Brothers: The Revolutionary Generation* (New York, 2000); John K. Alexander, *Samuel Adams: America's Revolutionary Politician* (Lanham, MD, 2002); Edmund S. Morgan, *Benjamin Franklin* (New Haven, 2002); Bernard Bailyn, *To Begin the World Anew: The Genius and Ambiguities of the American Founders* (New York, 2003); Gore Vidal, *Inventing a Nation: Washington, Adams, Jefferson* (New Haven, 2003).

Works on British and American ideologies and actions include William H. Nelson, *The American Tory* (Oxford, 1961); Bernard Bailyn, *The Ideological Origins of the American Revolution* (1967, Cambridge, MA, 1992); Wallace Brown, *The Good Americans: The Loyalists in the American Revolution* (New York, 1969); Mary Beth Norton, *The British-Americans: The Loyalist Exile in England, 1774–1789* (Boston, 1972); Robert M. Calhoon, *The Loyalists in Revolutionary America, 1760–1781*

(New York, 1973); J.G.A. Pocock, *The Machiavellian Moment: Florentine Political Thought and the Atlantic Republican Tradition* (Princeton, 1975); John Brewer, *Party Ideology and Popular Politics at the Accession of George III* (Cambridge, 1976); Colin Bonwick, *English Radicals and the American Revolution* (Chapel Hill, 1977); H.T. Dickinson, *Liberty and Property: Political Ideology in Eighteenth-Century Britain* (New York, 1978); Quentin Skinner, *The Foundations of Modern Political Thought* (2 vols, Cambridge, 1978); *Liberty before Liberalism* (Cambridge, 1997); Morton White, *The Philosophy of the American Revolution* (Oxford, 1978); Robert A. Becker, *Revolution, Reform, and the Politics of American Taxation, 1763–1783* (Baton Rouge, 1980); Ian R. Christie, *Wars and Revolutions: Britain, 1760–1815* (London, 1982); John Patrick Diggins, *The Lost Soul of American Politics: Virtue, Self-Interest, and the Foundations of Liberalism* (New York, 1985); Michael Kammen, *Spheres of Liberty: Changing Perceptions of Liberty in American Culture* (Madison, WI, 1986); John Phillip Reid, *The Concept of Liberty in the Age of the American Revolution* (Chicago, 1988); *The Concept of Representation in the Age of the American Revolution* (Chicago, 1989); *Constitutional History of the American Revolution: The Authority of the Law* (Madison, WI, 2003); Jack P. Greene, *Understanding the American Revolution: Issues and Actors* (Charlottesville, 1989); Steven M. Dworetz, *The Unvarnished Doctrine: Locke, Liberalism and the American Revolution* (Durham, NC, 1990); Isaac Kramnick, *Republicanism and Bourgeois Radicalism: Political Ideology and Late Eighteenth-Century England and America* (Ithaca, 1990); H.M. Scott, *British Foreign Policy in the Age of the American Revolution* (Oxford, 1990); Joyce Appleby, *Liberalism and Republicanism in the Historical Imagination* (Cambridge, MA, 1992); Paul A. Rahe, *Republics Ancient and Modern: Classical Republicanism and the American Revolution* (Chapel Hill, 1992); John E. Crowley, *The Privileges of Independence: Neomercantilism and the American Revolution* (Baltimore, 1993); Gordon S. Wood, *The Radicalism of the American Revolution* (New York, 1993); J.C.D. Clark, *The Language of Liberty, 1660–1832: Political Discourse and Social Dynamics in the Anglo-American World* (Cambridge, 1994); Michael P. Zuckert, *Natural Rights and the New Republicanism* (Princeton, 1994); Jerome Huyler, *Locke in America: The Moral Philosophy of the Founding Era* (Lawrence, KS, 1995); H.T. Dickinson, ed., *Britain and the American Revolution* (London, 1998); Stephen Conway, *The British Isles and the War of American Independence* (Oxford, 2000); Eliga H. Gould, *The Persistence of Empire: British Political Culture in the Age of the American Revolution* (Chapel Hill, 2000); Lee Ward, *The Politics of Liberty in England and Revolutionary America* (Cambridge, 2004).

On the War of Independence, see Don Higginbotham, *The War of American Independence: Military Attitudes, Policies, and Practice,*

1763–1789 (New York, 1971); *War and Society in Revolutionary America: The Wider Dimensions of Conflict* (Columbia, SC, 1988); Robert A. Gross, *The Minutemen and Their World* (New York, 1976); Charles Royster, *A Revolutionary People at War: The Continental Army and American Character, 1775–1783* (1979, Chapel Hill, 1996); Wayne E. Carp, *To Starve the Army at Pleasure: Continental Army Administration and American Political Culture, 1775–1783* (Chapel Hill, 1984); John Ferling, ed., *The World Turned Upside Down: The American Victory in the War of Independence* (Westport, CT, 1988); John Shy, *A People Numerous and Armed: Reflections on the Military Struggle for American Independence* (revised edn, Ann Arbor, 1990); Colin G. Calloway, *The American Revolution in Indian Country: Crisis and Diversity in Native American Communities* (Cambridge, 1995); Stephen Conway, *The War of American Independence* (London, 1995); Mark V. Kwasny, *Washington's Partisan War, 1775–1783* (Kent, OH, 1996); Patrick Neimeyer, *America Goes to War: A Social History of the Continental Army* (New York, 1996); Richard M. Ketchum, *Saratoga: Turning Point of America's Revolutionary War* (New York, 1997).

Chapter 9 Afterword: The United States and the new British Empire

There is a huge literature on radical ideas and social change in revolutionary America. For classic statements see Carl L. Becker, *The History of Political Parties in the Province of New York, 1760–1776* (Madison, WI, 1909) and J. Franklin Jameson, *The American Revolution Considered as a Social Movement* (Princeton, 1926). The best and most widely read modern treatments include Pauline Maier, *From Resistance to Revolution: Colonial Radicals and the Development of American Opposition to Britain* (New York, 1972); *The Old Revolutionaries: Political Lives in the Age of Samuel Adams* (New York, 1980); Ronald Hoffman, *A Spirit of Dissension: Economics, Politics, and the Revolution in Maryland* (Baltimore, 1973); Duncan J. McLeod, *Slavery, Race, and the American Revolution* (Oxford, 1974); Richard Alan Ryerson, *The Revolution Is Now Begun: The Radical Committees of Philadelphia, 1765–1776* (Philadelphia, 1978); Linda K. Kerber, *Women of the Republic: Intellect and Ideology in Revolutionary America* (Chapel Hill, 1980); Mary Beth Norton, *Liberty's Daughters: The Revolutionary Experience of American Women, 1750–1800* (1980, Ithaca, 1996); *Founding Mothers and Fathers: Gendered Power and the Forming of American Society* (New York, 1997); Edward Countryman, *A People in Revolution: The American Revolution and Political Society in New York, 1760–1790* (Baltimore, 1981); *The American Revolution* (Harmondsworth, 1985); Gary B. Nash, *The Urban Crucible: Social Change, Political Consciousness, and the Origins of the American Revolution* (Cambridge,

MA, 1986); *Race and Revolution* (Madison, WI, 1990); Steven Rosswurm, *Arms, Country and Class: The Philadelphia Militia and the 'Lower Sort' during the American Revolution* (New Brunswick, NJ, 1989); Sylvia R. Frey, *Water from the Rock: Black Resistance in a Revolutionary Age* (Princeton, 1991); Carol Berkin, *First Generations: Women in Colonial America* (New York, 1996); Joan R. Gunderson, *To Be Useful to the World: Women in Revolutionary America, 1740–1790* (New York, 1996); Jesse Lemisch, *Jack Tarr vs. John Bull: The Role of New York's Seamen in Precipitating the Revolution* (New York, 1997); Woody Holton, *Forced Founders: Indians, Debtors, Slaves, and the Making of the Revolution in Virginia* (Chapel Hill, 1999); Harry M. Ward, *The War for Independence and the Transformation of American Society* (London, 1999); Marcus Rediker and Peter Linebaugh, *The Many Headed Hydra: Sailors, Slaves, Commoners, and the Hidden History of the Revolutionary Atlantic* (Boston, 2000); Michael A. McDonnell, *Popular Mobilization and Political Culture in Revolutionary Virginia* (Chapel Hill, forthcoming). For essay collections exhibiting the breadth and depth of this scholarship see Alfred F. Young, ed., *The American Revolution: Explorations in the History of American Radicalism* (Dekalb, IL, 1976); *Beyond the American Revolution: Explorations in the History of American Radicalism* (Dekalb, IL, 1993); Ronald Hoffman and Peter J. Albert, eds, *The Transforming Hand of Revolution: Reconsidering the American Revolution as a Social Movement* (Charlottesville, 1996). The subject is ably and handily summed up in Ray Raphael, *A People's History of the American Revolution: How Common People Shaped the Fight for Independence* (New York, 2001).

Scholarship on constitution making between 1776 and 1791 includes Gordon S. Wood, *The Creation of the American Republic, 1776–1787* (Chapel Hill, 1969); J. Paul Selsam, *The Pennsylvania Constitution of 1776: A Study in Revolutionary Democracy* (New York, 1971); Ronald M. Peters, Jr., *The Massachusetts Constitution of 1780: A Social Compact* (Amherst, 1978); Jack N. Rakove, *The Beginnings of National Politics: An Interpretive History of the Continental Congress* (Baltimore, 1979); Willi Paul Adams, *The First American Constitutions: Republican Ideology and the Making of the State Constitutions in the Revolutionary Era* (Chapel Hill, 1980); Donald S. Lutz, *Popular Consent and Popular Control: Whig Political Theory in the Early State Constitutions* (Baton Rouge, 1980); *The Origins of American Constitutionalism* (Baton Rouge, 1988); Robert J. Dinkin, *Voting in Revolutionary America: A Study of Elections in the Original Thirteen States, 1776–1789* (Westport, CT, 1982); Peter S. Onuf, *The Origins of the Federal Republic: Jurisdictional Controversies in the United States* (Philadelphia, 1983); Forrest McDonald, *Novus Ordo Seculorum: The Intellectual Origins of the Constitution* (Lawrence, KS, 1985); Jack P. Greene, *Peripheries and Center: Constitutional Development in the Extended Polities of the*

British Empire and the United States, 1607–1788 (New York, 1986); Leonard W. Levy, *Constitutional Opinions: Aspects of the Bill of Rights* (Oxford, 1986); *Original Intent and the Framers' Constitution* (New York, 1988); Edmund S. Morgan, *Inventing the People: The Rise of Popular Sovereignty in England and America* (New York, 1988); George Anastaplo, *The Constitution of 1787: A Commentary* (Baltimore, 1989); Samuel H. Beer, *To Make a Nation: The Rediscovery of American Federalism* (Cambridge, MA, 1993); Roger H. Brown, *Redeeming the Republic: Federalists, Taxation, and the Origins of the Constitution* (Baltimore, 1993); Michael P. Zuckert, *Natural Rights and the New Republicanism* (Princeton, 1994); Lance Banning, *The Sacred Fire of Liberty: James Madison and the Founding of the Federal Republic* (Ithaca, 1995); Christopher M. Duncan, *The Anti-Federalists and Early American Political Thought* (Dekalb, IL, 1995); Stuart Leibiger, *Founding Friendship: George Washington, James Madison, and the Creation of the American Republic* (Charlottesville, 1999); Gary Rosen, *American Compact: James Madison and the Problem of Founding* (Lawrence, KS, 1999); James H. Read, *Power versus Liberty: Madison, Hamilton, Wilson, and Jefferson* (Charlottesville, 2000); Leonard L. Richards, *Shays's Rebellion: The American Revolution's Final Battle* (Philadelphia, 2002); David J. Seimers, *Ratifying the Republic: Antifederalists and Federalists in Constitutional Time* (Stanford, 2002).

For the reordering of the British Empire as a whole, see Vincent T. Harlow, *The Founding of the Second British Empire, 1763–1793*, Volume I: *Discovery and Revolution*, Volume II: *New Continents and Changing Values* (London, 1952, 1964); Richard Koebner, *Empire* (Cambridge, 1961); Ralph Davis, *The Industrial Revolution and British Overseas Trade* (Leicester, 1979); Peggy K. Liss, *Atlantic Empires: The Network of Trade and Revolution, 1713–1826* (Baltimore, 1983); C.A. Bayly, *Imperial Meridian: The British Empire and the World, 1780–1830* (London, 1989); P.J. Cain and A.G. Hopkins, *British Imperialism: Innovation and Expansion, 1688–1775* (London, 1993); Eliga H. Gould, *The Persistence of Empire: British Political Culture in the Age of the American Revolution* (Chapel Hill, 2000). See also P.J. Marshall's Presidential Address series for the Royal Historical Society: 'Britain and the World in the Eighteenth Century: I, Reshaping the Empire', 'II, Britons and Americans', 'III, Britain and India', 'IV, The Turning Outwards of Britain', *Royal Historical Society Transactions*, Sixth Series, VIII (1998), pp. 1–18; IX (1999), pp. 1–16; X (2000), pp. 1–16; XI (2001), pp. 1–16.

For specific parts of the empire, starting with the West Indies, see D.J. Murray, *The West Indies and the Development of Colonial Government, 1801–1834* (Oxford, 1965); Edward Braithwaite, *The Development of Creole Society in Jamaica, 1770–1820* (Oxford, 1971); Seymour Drescher, *Econocide: British Slavery in the Era of Abolition* (Pittsburgh, 1977);

Selwyn H.H. Carrington, *The British West Indies during the American Revolution* (Dordecht, 1988); J.R. Ward, *British West Indian Slavery, 1750–1834: The Process of Amelioration* (Oxford, 1988); Andrew Jackson O'Shaughnessy, *An Empire Divided: The American Revolution and the British Caribbean* (Philadelphia, 2000). Continuing with Canada: E.E. Rich, *The Fur Trade and the Northwest to 1857* (Toronto, 1968); Robin W. Winks, *The Blacks in Canada: A History* (New Haven, 1971); C. Grant Head, *Eighteenth-Century Newfoundland: A Geographer's Perspective* (Toronto, 1976); James W. St G. Walker, *The Black Loyalists: The Search for a Promised Land in Nova Scotia and Sierra Leone, 1783–1870* (New York, 1976); Fernand Ouellet, *Lower Canada, 1791–1840: Social Change and Nationalism* (Toronto, 1980); Ann Gorman Condon, *The Envy of the American States: The Loyalist Dream for New Brunswick* (Frederickton, New Brunswick, 1984); Neil MacKinnon, *This Unfriendly Soil: The Loyalist Experience in Nova Scotia, 1783–1791* (Kingston and Montreal, 1986); Philip Lawson, *The Imperial Challenge: Quebec and Britain in the Age of the American Revolution* (Montreal and Kingston, 1989); J.M. Bumsted, *The Peoples of Canada: A Pre-Confederation History* (Oxford, 1992); Julian Gwyn, *Excessive Expectations: Maritime Commerce and the Economic Development of Nova Scotia, 1740–1870* (Montreal, 1998); Geoffrey Plank, *An Unsettled Conquest: The British Campaign against the People of Acadia* (Philadelphia, 2001).

Outside the Americas, beginning with Ireland, see R.B. McDowell, *Ireland in the Age of Imperialism and Revolution, 1760–1800* (Oxford, 1979); T.W. Moody and W.E. Vaughan, *A New History of Ireland* Volume IV: *Eighteenth-Century Ireland, 1690–1801* (Oxford, 1985); David Dickson, *New Foundations: Ireland, 1660–1800* (Dublin, 1987); Nicholas P. Canny, *Kingdom and Colony: Ireland in the Atlantic World, 1560–1800* (Baltimore, 1988); Thomas Bartlett, *The Fall and Rise of the Irish Nation: The Catholic Question* (Dublin, 1992). On India, see P.J. Marshall, *Problems of Empire: Britain and India, 1757–1813* (London, 1968); *Trade and Conquest: Studies in the Rise of British Dominance in India* (Aldershot, 1993); K.N. Chaudhuri, *The Trading World of Asia and the English East India Company, 1660–1760* (Cambridge, 1978); Ian Bruce Watson, *Foundation for Empire: English Private Trade in India, 1659–1760* (Delhi, 1980); Muzzafar Alam, *The Crisis of Empire in Mughal North India, Awadh and the Punjab, 1707–48* (Delhi, 1986); Colin G. Calloway, *Crown and Columet: British-Indian Relations, 1783–1815* (Norman, OK, 1987); Ashin das Gupta and M.N. Pearson, eds, *India and the Indian Ocean, 1500–1800* (Calcutta, 1987); H.V. Bowen, *Revenue and Reform: The Indian Problem in British Politics, 1757–1773* (Cambridge, 1991); Philip Lawson, *The East India Company: A History* (London, 1993). On Australasia, see David MacKay, *In the Wake of Cook: Exploration, Science and Empire, 1780–1801* (London, 1985); Bernard

Smith, *European Vision and the South Pacific* (New Haven, 1985); *Imagining the Pacific: In the Wake of the Cook Voyages* (New Haven, 1992); Robert Hughes, *The Fatal Shore: A History of the Transportation of Convicts to Australia, 1787–1868* (London, 1987); Glyndwr Williams and Alan Frost, eds, *Terra Australis to Australia* (1988, Oxford, 1989).

Index